Tourism Marketing

Devashish Das Gupta
Associate Professor
Indian Institute of Management Lucknow

Pearson

ISBN 978-81-317-3182-6

Published by Pearson India Education Services Pvt. Ltd, CIN: U72200TN2005PTC057128

Head Office: 1st Floor, Berger Tower, Plot No. C-001A/2, Sector 16B, Noida – 201 301,Uttar Pradesh, India.

Registered Office: Featherlite, 'The Address' 5th Floor, Survey No 203/10B, 200 Ft MMRD Road, Zamin Pallavaram, Chennai - 600044
Website: in.pearson.com; Email:companysecretary.india@pearson.com

Digitally printed in India by Trinity Academy for Corporate Training Ltd, New Delhi in the year of 2025.

Contents

About the Author

Professor Devashish Das Gupta is a faculty of Marketing at the Indian Institute of Management Lucknow. He has a Ph.D. in Business Administration and a masters in Business Management, besides a PG diploma in Marketing and Sales Management. Professor Das Gupta has more than 15 years of industrial and academic experience. He was initially working with a multinational corporation, where he got exposed to retail network development and product marketing in retail.

He is an active trainer and consultant in marketing innovations and retail strategies, besides tourist destination branding and vision development for developing a tourist destination. His research areas include shopping behaviour, innovations in contemporary marketing and tourism marketing practices.

Preface

Tourism, as an industry has been a big economic contributor to many economies for many decades. The most important is the fact that this is, perhaps, the only industry which does not get affected by WTO and which, if handled judiciously, has the least environmental concerns. One regularly hears claims that tourism supports many jobs in an area or that a festival or special event generated *x* million dollars in sales or income. 'Multiplier effects' are often cited to capture secondary effects of tourism spending and presents a wide range of sectors in a community that may benefit from tourism. Economic benefits and costs of tourism reach virtually everyone in the region in one way or another.

In tourism, the greatest role is played by the destination. Whether it is the Taj Mahal at Agra in India or the Great Wall of China, it is the destination which is the final influence on the decision to visit a place. Thus, the greatest challenge for tourism marketing is always from a destination perspective. The need to address this requirement was felt while looking at the way marketing was being done, especially in India. This urge became stronger when my international exchange students came back from their visits to various European and American countries and shared their experiences as a tourist. Hearing all the ideal marketing practices from the West and comparing with Indian practices finally pushed me to plan for this venture.

There are few titles available on the topic of tourism marketing, but none have a focus like this book. It endeavours to give the reader a field experience while reading. The following are the four main features of the book:

1. Destination perspective
2. International research
3. Complete marketing structure (does not deviate into any related areas)
4. Real-life examples from India and abroad as well as live experiences of tourists.

Finally, this book focuses on unsung tourist destinations in India. This makes it very useful not only for graduate students but also for industry practitioners. However, such a project is not possible without the support of many people. It is so because tourism does not follow the principles of product or service purchase behaviour. It is unique in all respects, which needs to be considered while executing a project like this. This book, therefore, contains various tourist experiences as well as short surveys.

This book took around four years of research and development to reach the present stage with multiple rounds of revision. This has resulted in multiple live case studies and live tourist experiences, both good and bad, which have been documented for the benefit of the reader. In few chapters, surveys have been conducted, and results discussed.

The book structure has been designed in such a way that a student logically flows down the theory in a sequence which brings the advanced, more complex as well contemporary issues towards the later stage of the book. Therefore, market environment, consumer behaviour, and customer satisfaction are discussed in the beginning. This is followed by technical marketing issues like service marketing, marketing mix, tourism life cycle, and differentiation and positioning. In the next phase, the book discusses tourism product development and packaging, destination branding, and the information and communication technology issues. Finally, summing up, is a chapter on planning, implementation, and control. Before closing, a chapter on contemporary avenues on tourism deals with the innovations in this dynamic field.

To make this book interesting to read, some features have been added.

1. Each chapter has a photograph of a prominent tourist destination along with its brief on chapter opener page only and reference for finding more information on the same.
   The following international monuments have been included:
   - Angkor Wat (Cambodia)
   - Big Ben, London (United Kingdom)
   - Cristo Redentor, Rio de Janerio (Brazil)
   - Coliseum, Rome (Italy)
   - Eiffel Tower, Paris (France)
   - Pyramids & Sphinx, Giza (Egypt)
   - Great Wall of China (China)
   - Leaning Tower of Pisa (Italy)
   - Machu Picchu (Peru)
   - Nelson's Column, Trafalgar Square (London)
   - St. Basil's Cathedral, Moscow (Russia)
   - Statue of Liberty, New York (USA)
   - Stonehenge, Wiltshire (UK)
   - Sydney Opera House (Australia)
2. In-depth academic research and marketing structure forms the basis of this book.
3. Real-life tourist experiences have been recorded and converted into short caselets for discussion as well as for knowledge assimilation. (IIM Lucknow and students of other institutes have shared their experiences.)
4. A glossary of terminologies and tourist destinations have been provided.
5. Each chapter is followed by a summary and discussion questions.
6. This book has been designed in a way that it can help the graduate students as well as Ph.D. scholars and at the same time, industry practitioners.
7. Each chapter ends with a detailed account of an unsung tourist destination in India.
8. In most of the chapters, the theories and models discussed have been applied to real-life destinations and a detailed discussion is given for the benefit of the reader.

A separate instructor's teaching aid has been created. It includes fill in the blanks, short answer questions, and detailed answer questions. Besides this, chapter slides for each chapter have been provided for facilitating the instructor.

The best way to utilize this book is to compare the existing practices with the ones given in the book. A comparison gives a better exposure as well as understanding of the text. A better way can be to maintain a log book. Be it an industry practitioner or researcher or a graduate student, it pays to capture the experiences as a tourist in a log book or diary.

However, the journey of an academic does not finish here. Research for the next edition has already been started. Any suggestions to improve the contents are welcome.

Devashish Das Gupta

Acknowledgements

It would not be physically possible to thank each of the people who have played a role in the form of ideas, concepts and life experiences that form the contents of this book as well as approvals and permissions. However it goes without saying that I am deeply indebted to all of them.

I am very grateful to Philip Kotler, S.C. Johnson, Distinguished Professor of International Marketing, Kellogg School of Management, Northwestern University; Arch Woodside, Professor of Marketing, Boston College; Liping A. Cai, Professor, Director of the Purdue Tourism and Hospitality Research Center, Purdue University; and Dr. Russell Arthur Smith, Interim Dean, Cornell-Nanyang Institute of Hospitality Management, Nanyang Technological University Nanyang Business School Singapore for painstakingly going through the text and giving their endorsements.

I would like to thank Shri Manas Bhattacharya, Economic Advisor, Ministry of Tourism, Government of India and Shri Avnish Awasthi, Director General, Uttar Pradesh Tourism, for their valuable inputs and encouragement.

This work could not have been completed but for the ungrudging efforts put in by 70 bright and energetic souls, who collectively constitute the Section E Class of 2010, IIM Lucknow who have devoted their time and energy to this book. Their creative ideas and relentless efforts kept pouring in through a hectic academic term, especially live experiences as a tourist and unsung tourist destinations which actually enhance the value of this book. Further amongst the students a special word of thanks to the core team of Rahul Sanghvi, Sachin Gupta, Amit Sharma, Aseem Sen Gupta, Vipin Nair, Mamatha, Sagar Tyagi, Pranav Sethi, Naveen, and Sagar Jain who with their enthusiasm and dedication never let me feel low even during testing times.

This book is based on planning and research for the last four years. Volumes of research papers were collected and studied. All major titles in this field were studied to develop a better table of contents. In this task, my research assistant Ruchi Maheshwari has sincerely been a great help. My other two research assistants, Harshit and Utkarsh, too deserve acknowledgement for their sincere and consistent contribution in preparing the teaching aids for this book.

This book could not have taken its final shape without Professor Krishna Kumar (Ex Director IIM Kozikhode) encouraging me to give my interest in tourism an opportunity to bloom by organizing conference on tourism. I am grateful for his motivation and words of wisdom.

I am really thankful to Professor Archana Shukla and Professor R Srinivasan (IIM Bangalore) for giving their moral support and guidance. My interactions with them at all times have been an enriching experience.

I would also like to thank Indiastat.com for kindly consenting for usage of tourism data given on their Web site in the book. This data will be very useful for the readers.

I wish to thank all the people who have helped in improving the quality of the text. Special thanks are due to Praveen Tiwari and Gaurav Jain of Pearson Education, who have particularly worked hard to improve the quality of this book.

Any project as large as this cannot be completed without the infrastructural support and positive environment. I feel deeply indebted to my institute, IIM Lucknow, for providing world class infrastructure along with dedicated staff and officers who have helped me in achieving this mission.

Finally, any work of this magnitude cannot be accomplished without the blessings of Almighty and best wishes of my parents and well wishers. I thank my parents and well wishers who have prayed for the success of this project. I am also grateful to my wife Mohua and my daughter Rimjhim who have stood by me in motivating me to finish this project on time.

Devashish Das Gupta

CHAPTER 1

Tourism Market Environment Scanning

ABOUT THE DESTINATION

One of the most popular and recognizable tourist spots with over 243 million visitors from 1889 to 2008, the Eiffel Tower was built for the centenary commemoration of the French Revolution of 1789 by Gustave Eiffel.

OBJECTIVES

- To appreciate the significance of market environment scanning in tourism
- To understand the macro- and micro-environment constituents
- To understand how to apply a specific tool to analyse the market environment both in case of national and international destinations

INTRODUCTION TO TOURISM MARKETING

Tourism emerged as the largest global industry of the 20th century and is projected to grow even faster in the 21st century. For India, since the opening up of the economy in 1991, the government has advanced several incentives to promote infrastructure growth in the tourism sector. India has significant potential for becoming a major global tourist destination. The travel and tourism industry is the second highest foreign-exchange earner for India, and the government has given export-house status to organizations in this industry. The industry is waking up to the potential of domestic tourism as well, with an estimated 4.7 billion domestic trips in 2001. Tourism spending within India in 2001 was US$ 22 billion.

In India, the travel and tourism industry has a predominant government presence. Generally each state has a chain of hotels operated by state tourism corporation. These tourism corporations also operate package tours. At the central government level, Indian Tourism Development Corporation (ITDC) runs at a national level. However a process of divestment in these state run tourism corporations is already into the process. Amongst the top source countries for foreign tourist arrivals in India, US is the leader with 15.4% Americans coming to India. UK is at number two with 14.67 % and Bangladesh at number three with 10.06 %. Regarding foreign exchange earnings from tourism, years 2003, 2004 and 2005 has been excellent in earnings. In 2003 there was an increase by 43.8 % followed by 38.2 % in 2004 and 21.4 % in 2005. In terms of country wise tourism receipts, US with 11.66 %, Spain with 6.35 %, France with 5.89 %, Italy with 4.84 %, China with 4.32 % and Germany with 4.24 % are the top contributors in 2008. Beside this UK, Australia, Turkey form the top ten countries for tourism receipts with a total of 48.55% share in total international receipts.

Indians have also become major globe trotters with an estimated 1,08,67,999 Indian nationals going abroad in 2008. Since 2004, this figure has been growing at an average of 15% per annum. (courtsey: *www.Indiastats.com*)

India has immense possibilities of growth in the tourism sector with its vast cultural and religious heritage, and varied natural attractions, but so far the country has only found a comparatively small role in the world tourism scene. From this standpoint, India should have been a tourism haven as the country is blessed with destinations and products catering to the tastes and preferences of tourists and travellers of all ages and economic backgrounds. There is no doubt that tourism, frequently referred to as the world's largest industry, is big business and is one of the major social and economic phenomena of modern times.

Tourism is primarily a services-based industry – the principal products provided by tourism businesses are experiences and hospitality. These are intangible products and more difficult to market than tangible products such as cars. The intangible nature of services makes quality control difficult but crucial. It also makes it more difficult for potential customers to evaluate and compare service offerings. But as long as the inherent sense of curiosity and adventure dwells in the hearts of human beings, the desire to travel and experience new things under different environments will grow. In addition, instead of the product moving to the customer, the customer must travel to the product, that is, the area and/or the community.

The last few years have seen considerable growth in India's tourism and hospitality sector. Driven by a surge in business traveller arrivals and a soaring interest in India as a tourist destination, it is becoming one of the most preferred tourist destination across the world. In 2008, an estimated 5.37 million tourist came to India which is 0.58% of world tourist arrivals. India is probably the only country that offers various categories of tourism, these include history tourism, adventure tourism, medical tourism (ayurveda and other forms of Indian medications), spiritual tourism and beach tourism (India has the longest coastline along the east). Thus, there is a need for establishing a strong business relationship between the ministry of tourism and the tourism industry.

In the following sections, we shall try to cover the major aspects of tourism-marketing principles that include strategy, micro-environment, prevailing market environment, tourism potential in India, and planning, implementation, and control aspects and take up a case study on tourism marketing.

THE SIGNIFICANCE OF MARKET ENVIRONMENT

For any marketer, it is necessary to understand the market environment first. A good understanding of this enables to formulate entry strategies and establish oneself well amidst strong competition. In tourism this competition is fiercer, since the competition is amongst destinations of various states as well as countries. Market environment scanning necessitates a thorough analysis of the market, using the right tools to enable a strong strategy for entry and early growth, and it goes a long way in determining how successful the new player will be.

The market environment consists of the macro-environment and the micro-environment, also known as broad and task environments, respectively, which are discussed in the next section. To succeed in any market, marketers must pay close attention to the trends and developments in these environments and make timely adjustments to their marketing strategies. Within these environments, marketers apply the marketing mix – the set of marketing tools used to achieve marketing objectives in the target market.

Market Environment

Market environment refers to all the constituent forces which exist in the environment and influence the customer decision making. It can be divided into two parts, macro-environment and micro-environment.

Macro-Environment. The *macro-environment* refers to all forces which influence the industry from a macro context. It consists of six components: demographic environment, economic environment, natural environment, technological environment, political-legal environment and social-cultural environment. These environments contain forces that can have a major impact on the actors in the task environment, which is why smart marketers track environmental trends and changes closely.

Demographic Environment: An important variable in the demographic environment will be existing classifications of age and their impact. For instance, India has got a relatively younger population than many other nations. This makes it a potential customer for education and related markets. Thus, countries, for example, Australia and New Zealand, look forward to Indian youth for joining their academic programmes. In tourism, this piece of data gives a fair amount of idea regarding the attraction power of destinations in the country for a specific demographic group.

Economic Environment: The *economic environment* refers to the purchasing power of potential customers and the ways in which people spend their money. Tourists spend mainly on travelling, staying and shopping. The economic environment data regarding a specific customer segment can throw much light on the spending pattern as well as affordability of the tourists coming from a specific country or a continent.

Natural Environment: The natural environment includes the natural resources that are used by companies as inputs and affect their marketing activities. Destinations like sea beaches, lagoons, deserts, coral reefs form a part of the natural environment. In tourism, one sub-classification can be created within the natural environment: heritage environment and modern man-made environment. India is amongst the few Asian countries to have heritage monuments in abundance. Countries which do not have this privilege have created multiple man-made modern tourist destinations. Any country having heritage monuments or natural destinations is always at an advantageous position to attract tourists in larger numbers.

Technological Environment: Today in the era of e-marketing, this environment is perhaps the most dynamic and effective sphere of a country's tourism macro-environment. This environment includes all the technological interventions which make a tourist more comfortable and efficient in decision making as well as further processing of his decision. It includes online ticket booking, payment gateways as well as exploring various tourism opportunities. With the advancement in travel now, nearly all the tourist destinations of the world can be reached within 36 hours. Any incidence of events detrimental to tourist interests is communicated at a lightning speed. Nations or states which have been able to harness themselves with the latest in technology are better off in reaping the benefits in terms of better destination, brand image and tourism revenue.

Political Environment: The political environment includes all laws and legislations that influence the tourism industry and government agencies and groups that influence or limit the scope of tourism and tourists. For instance, Rossebuurd is a legally authorized red light district of Amsterdam (Netherlands). However these types of activity will never be legally accepted in the country like India. Similarly Casinos are legally not allowed in many countries.

Socio-cultural Environment: This environment consists of institutions and basic values and beliefs of people; this helps in focusing of marketing campaigns to reflect the values of a target audience. This has got two dimensions. First, cultural aspects of the people reside at the tourist destination. At times, the culture and customs of the people become a major tourist attraction. For example, in India Deepawali in Northern India, Holi celebrations in Mathura, Kite flying festival during Uttarayan (Makar Sankranti) in Gujarat, Durga Puja in West Bengal, Ganesh Utsav in Mumbai, Dussehra in Mysore, State of Karnataka are some occasions which are directly connected to the culture of the people residing in the tourist destinations. Second, here is the culture of the people in target segments. For instance, Non-Asians would feel more enchanted to watch cultural festivals in India than their Asian counterparts.

Micro-Environment. The *micro-environment* refers to forces that are close to the tourist destination and affect its ability to serve its guests. This includes the immediate actors involved in communicating with the guests: bringing them to the destination, making them stay and visit the destination as well as taking them back. It encompasses travel organizations, hotels, restaurants, souvenir retailers and destination staff besides tourists themselves. Service suppliers such as marketing-research agencies, advertising agencies, Web site designers, and banking, insurance, transportation and telecommunications companies are included in the supplier group.

The government aspect of the micro-environment refers to the internal environment of the destination. To remain competitive, a destination must consider its biggest competitors, while considering its own size and position in the tourism market. The final aspect of the micro-environment is public, which is any group that has an interest in or impact on the destination's ability to meet its goals. Studies have established the fact that in any tourist destination the onus ultimately lies in the attitude of the local public towards tourists and tourism as an industry for the success of any tourist destination.

CONSTITUENTS OF TOURISM MARKET ENVIRONMENT

Tourism Micro-Environment — Porter's Five Forces Model

Michael Porter's five forces analysis is a framework for industry analysis and business-strategy development. It uses concepts developed in industrial organization (IO) economics to derive five forces that determine the competitive intensity and, therefore, attractiveness of a sector/market. Attractiveness in this context refers to the overall sector profitability. An "unattractive industry" is one where the combination of forces acts to drive down the overall profitability. A very unattractive industry would be one approaching "pure competition."

For the tourism sector in India, the following would be important:

- **New entrants:** New avenues of tourism such as development of new tourism sites
- **Threat of substitutes:** Creation of other sources of relaxation within the native city of the traveller
- **Buyers:** The consumer, that is, the tourist, who is the source of income for the tourism industry
- **Suppliers:** The various states/countries promoting their tourism destinations
- **Rivalry between existing competitors:** Competition to attract tourists by established tourist places

Tourism Macro-Environment — PEST Analysis

For scanning the tourism-market environment in India, the PEST (Political, Economic, Social and Technological) analysis is done. These are explained below.

- **Political:** Political stability, law-and-order situation and absence of terrorist activities in the place where tourism needs to be promoted
- **Economic:** Purchasing power of the tourist, also taking into account the foreign-exchange rate
- **Social:** Availability of facilities such as proper medical facilities, open culture and education of people
- **Technological:** E-connectivity of the tourist place and presence of good mobile network

The PEST analysis describes a framework of macro-environmental factors used in the environmental scanning component of strategic management. It is very important to understand the environment of the tourism sector in India before beginning the marketing process. In fact, environmental analysis should be continuous and feed all aspects of planning. Demographics, cultural factors and natural environment also need to be taken care of while studying the macro-environment factors.

MARKET ENVIRONMENT SCANNING OF SELECTED TOURISM DESTINATIONS

In this section, I have taken a few examples of Indian tourist destinations, Jaipur, Shimla and Hampi, to understand the market environment scanning.

Jaipur

Overview of Jaipur Tourism. Jaipur, popularly known as the Pink City, makes up one of the three points in the Golden Triangle of Indian tourism, the other two being Delhi and Agra. It is also the gateway to Rajasthan. A visit to the city gives a glimpse of the entire Rajasthan experience: forts, palaces, pink sandstone monuments and museums. Built in AD 1727 by the famous astronomer king Maharaja Sawai Jai Singh II, this fascinating city takes the visitor to an epoch of royalty and tradition. It took almost six years to complete the city of Jaipur, which was, interestingly, the country's first modern city to be designed in a grid form, over two centuries ago. The bustling bazaars of Jaipur, famous for Rajasthani jewellery, fabric and shoes, possess a timeless quality and are surely a treasure trove for shoppers.

Today, Jaipur is fast emerging as a commercial hub for handicraft exports, jewellery and semi-precious stones, besides witnessing a rapid growth in the hospitality sector. There is practically no off-season for tourists – although winters are preferred for visiting here.

Famous Attractions

Hawa Mahal: The famous Hawa Mahal, or the Palace of Winds, is the pride of Jaipur. Built in 1799 by Sawai Pratap Singh, this pink sandstone palace resembles a honeycomb structure. It was exclusively designed for the queens, who could watch the proceedings on the road and the colourful bazaars below through the intricately latticed windows. The five-storey pyramid-shaped structure Hawa Mahal has 953 perforated windows, or jharokhas, which keep the palace cool. The top three storeys are just of single-room thickness, while the base has two courtyards. The Hawa Mahal offers some great views of the city and its surroundings.

Hawa Mahal

City Palace: The City Palace spread over a large area is a beautiful blend of Rajputana and Mughal architecture with spacious courtyards, manicured gardens and temples. The palace houses the Diwan-e-Aam, Diwan-e-Khas, Chandra Mahal, Mubarak Mahal, Mukut Mahal, Maharani's palace, Shri Govind Dev Temple and City Palace Museum.

Jantar Mantar: The Jantar Mantar is an observatory built by Sawai Jai Singh II and has 16 astronomical instruments. These geometric devices built of local stone and marble were used for measuring time, predicting eclipses and determining celestial altitudes. The famous devices include Ram Yantra to determine the altitude of the sun, Rashivalaya Yantra to draw up horoscopes and the 23 metre high Samrat Yantra to forecast crop prospects.

Jal Mahal

Jal Mahal: The Jal Mahal, or Water Palace, is situated on the Man Sagar Lake, which gets filled up during the monsoons and creates a romantic sight. Inspired by the Lake Palace in Udaipur, the Jal Mahal built in the 18th century was used mainly for royal duck-shooting parties. The first four floors of the building are under water; only the top floor is visible outside. The Water Palace can be best viewed from the Nahargarh Fort.

Government Central Museum, or Albert Hall: It is a multi-layered museum designed by Sir Samuel Jacob. Located in Ramni was Gardens, the oldest museum of Jaipur displays portraits of royalty, metal wares, glazed pottery, jewellery, sculpture, and fine Mughal and Rajput miniature paintings. One of the world's largest Persian garden carpets is the pride of the museum and can be seen in the Durbar Hall on request.

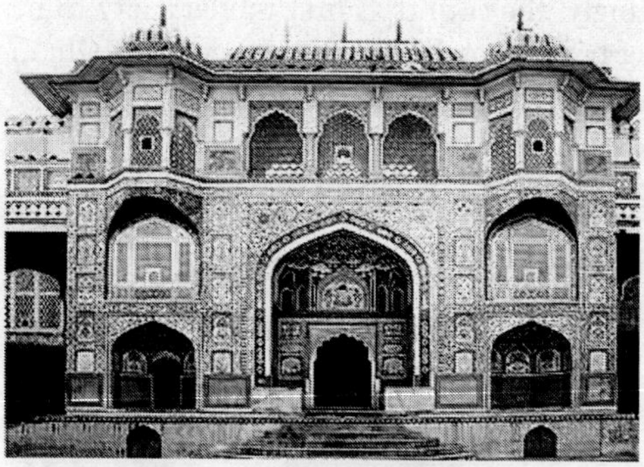

Amer Fort

Amer Fort: The Amer Fort, with the Maota Lake in the foreground, is built in white marble and red sandstone. The gigantic fort is perched high on the hills and protected by the Jaigarh Fort. The colossal fort was founded in 1952 by Man Singh I, but completed by Jai Singh I. The palace lies inside the massive Amer Fort complex with gateways, gardens, halls, stairways, pillared pavilions and temples. Intricate carvings on the walls and ceilings, delicate paintings of hunting scenes and detailed mirror work are some fascinating highlights of the Amer Fort. The Sheesh Mahal inside in the fort is a stunning sight with thousands of mirror pieces adorning the walls and ceilings. Other noteworthy marvels in the complex are the Diwan-e-Khas, the Jai Mandir, the Sukh Niwas, the Shila Mata Temple and Kali Temple, and the well laid-out garden Kesar Kyari.

Nahargarh Fort: The Nahargarh Fort, also called the Tiger Fort, was the first fort built by the kings of Jaipur. Perched high on the Aravali range, the fort offers a superb view of the city and the Man Sagar Lake. The most notable structure inside the fort is the Madhavendra Bhawan, which is laid out in a maze of terraces and courtyards. It has nine identical suites for the king's nine queens. The walls and pillars of the bhawan exhibit a unique form of *arayish*, or a form of plasterwork, which is handpolished with agate to produce a marble finish.

Elephant Festival

Fairs and Festivals of Jaipur

Elephant Festival: The Elephant Festival is one of the most popular festivals of Jaipur. It has its own charm and is celebrated every year in March on the occasion of Holi, the festival of colours. Elephants become the major attraction of this festival in their classy attires.

Gangaur Festival: It is a significant festival of Jaipur, meant only for the women. Gangaur Festival is widely acclaimed and celebrated throughout the state of Rajasthan. The word Gangaur is derived from two words: *Gan* and *Gauri*, which are synonyms of Siva and his consort Parvati, respectively.

Kite Festival: The Kite Festival is a popular festival of Jaipur. Kite flying is enjoyed by people of all age groups. However, 14 January, the day of Makar Sankranti, marks the official day for flying kites in Jaipur. People make the most out of the festival by flying kites for the whole day.

Kite Festival

Porter's Five Forces Analysis of Jaipur

Customers: The following are the key customers (tourists) which can be listed out of the analysis:

- Holidaying is the most common purpose of the visit to Jaipur.
- Hotels are the most used means of accommodation by tourists, while there are a few takers for guest houses.
- Holidaying in Jaipur is done generally in the company of one's family and relatives. Visiting with friends is also an option. Therefore, group travel is more preferred in this region.
- Tourist traffic is concentrated on a few places such as Amer Fort, Hawa Mahal, Albert Hall and City Palace. A large portion of Jaipur is yet to be explored.
- Tourists usually relate a rich shopping experience in the city. However, the city is also ranked very expensive by a large number of tourists.

Competition: The following are the key competitions which can be listed out of the analysis:

- Jaipur faces various levels of competition in the tourism industry. Within Rajasthan itself, there is competition from other destinations such as Udaipur, Jaisalmer and Mount Abu.
- Jaipur also faces competition at a higher level from other tourist spots such as Goa, Kerala, Himachal Pradesh (Shimla), Uttar Pradesh (Agra) and Uttaranchal (Haridwar) in India.
- To counteract these various levels of competition, Jaipur tourism must find ways to differentiate itself from others with its unique offerings, and position itself uniquely in the minds of the people. For this, it must build a unique selling proposition (USP). To match international competition, it must first benchmark itself with them.

Suppliers: The following are the key suppliers which can be listed out of the analysis:

- Suppliers in the tourism industry indicate service providers such as airline industry, railways, travel agents, locals, hotel industry and government.
- Services, unlike products, have different characteristics such as intangibility, inseparability, variability and perishability. To manage these, the use of the three Ps comprising physical evidence, people and place will come in handy.

Substitutes: The substitutes to Jaipur tourism are any other options that a person would consider on a holiday like mountain trekking and adventure sports, religious gatherings, Internet and television surfing, video games and strolls in parks. These substitutes, although not directly affecting tourism, can still be a deterrent to it. Instead of travelling to far-off places for a holiday, one may find easy entertainment in various alternate sources.

New Entrants: The concept of an annual holiday is yet to catch up in India. Potential tourists must, therefore, be sought after and persuaded to visit the tourist spots. Each state in India is now beginning to realize the potential of tourism and is uniquely positioning itself, as shown in the following examples:

- Temples in Tamil Nadu
- Wildlife in Assam
- Ayurveda in Kerala

PEST Analysis of Jaipur

Political Factors: The following are the key political factors which can be listed out of the analysis:

- The political arena has a huge influence on the regulation of businesses. It includes government regulations and legal issues under which businesses should operate
- Excellent law-and-order situation in the state
- Stable state government (issues like the Gujjar demand for reservation and the war against terror have had an effect on the political stability of the government)
- The state government has launched *Paryatan Rozgar Yojana* with active participation of Panchayati Raj Institutions (PRI) to promote rural employment and rural tourism
- Exemption of 50 per cent of stamp duty to new hotel units in urban areas and 100 per cent in rural areas
- Simplification of land-conversion rules for establishment of tourism units

Economic Factors: The following are the key economic factors which can be listed out of the analysis:

- Economic factors affect the purchasing power of potential customers and also affect the individual company's offerings
- Financial assistance to SMEs by banks has boosted the tourism industry in and around Jaipur
- Increasing disposable income of the population within Jaipur and across India

Socio-cultural Factors: The following are the key socio-cultural factors which can be listed out of the analysis:

- Good hospitality
- Increasing level of literacy in the state
- Availability of different cuisines
- Sound infrastructure and a vast pool of skilled talent
- Good connectivity to the country's capital through roads, railways and airways
- Latest trends of home entertainment and more awareness about diet and health issues

Technological Factors: The following are the key technological factors which can be listed out of the analysis:

- The rapid development of technology is affecting the tourism industry in Jaipur significantly
- Internet booking for tickets and holidays
- Web site to enquire about accommodation and other related issues
- Good connectivity through mobile phones even in remote locations

Shimla

Overview of Shimla Tourism. Shimla, once the summer capital of the British Raj in India, is now the capital of the Indian state of Himachal Pradesh. It is located in the Himalayas, and its elevation at 2,000 metres (6,500 feet) above sea level makes its climate enjoyable and temperate compared to the plains of northern India. During the scorching summers of India, tourists flock here to escape the hot plains, and during winters they come here to see the snowfall. Shimla had lived a glorious history during the British Raj, when many British soldiers and civilians would stay here for months and control the affairs of their vast Indian empire. The long association with them has left behind a heritage of many monuments, and the place has the stamp of its colonial past. It is well known for its Victorian architecture, which is reflected in certain areas of the Mall and Ridge. It is also a famous destination for honeymoon.

There are quite a few theories regarding the origin of the word Shimla. Locals insist that the name originates from Shyamali Devi, a reincarnation of the fearsome goddess Kali.

Sitting majestically above the searing plains, the town was designated by the British as the summer capital of India in the 19th century. The higher levels of the town reflect this British connection, comprising mostly buildings in the Victorian style, while the lower slopes are replete with Indian bazaars and restaurants. Traffic is banned from the historic central area (known as the Mall), which means that the atmosphere is calm and the air is pristine.

Cart Road runs south of the Mall and is connected to it via lifts. The Ridge, north of the Mall, is a good place to view the seven majestic hills of Shimla. Further along the same road is Lakkar Bazaar, which a good place to buy wooden crafts and articles.

Famous Attractions. In and around Shimla, you will find many heritage sites and places associated with its colonial past, as well as many spots that present the beauty of the Himalayas in their glorious splendour. Some of the major points of attraction are:

The Mall: The Mall is the main shopping centre of Shimla. It also has many restaurants, clubs, banks, bars, post offices and tourist offices. The Gaiety Theatre is also situated here. Mall is the main meeting place for everyone. Not only tourists but city locals can be found walking on the mall road. The Ridge and the Scandal Point are the two main meeting points at the mall.

Christ Church: Situated on the Ridge, the Christ Church is the second oldest church in northern India. It has a majestic appearance, and inside there are stained-glass windows that represent faith, hope, charity, fortitude, patience and humility.

Christ Church

Jakhu Hill: About 2 km from Shimla, at a height of 8,000 feet, the Jakhu Hill is the highest peak and offers a beautiful view of the town and snow-covered Himalayas. At the top of the hill is an old temple of Hanuman, which is also the home of countless playful monkeys waiting to be fed by the visitors.

Shimla State Museum: The museum, which was opened in 1974, has tried to project hill-out and the cultural wealth of the state. There is a collection of miniature *pahari* paintings, sculptures, bronzes, and woodcarvings, and also costumes, textiles, and jewellery of the region.

Summer Hill: Situated at a distance of 5 km from the Ridge is the lovely township of the Summer Hill at a height of 6,500 feet, on the Shimla-Kalka railway line. Mahatma Gandhi used to live in these quiet surroundings during his visits to Shimla. The Himachal Pradesh University is also situated here.

Summer Hill

Mashobra

Mashobra: Approximately 13 km away from Shimla, Mashobra has several excellent picnic spots. Mashobra is the site of the annual Sipi fair in June. The nearest rest house is at Craignano, which is 3 km from Mashobra and a beautiful holiday resort.

Tara Devi: About 11 km from the Shimla bus stand, Tara Devi has a temple dedicated to the goddess of stars on top of the hill. Here, there is a military dairy town as well as the headquarters of Bharat Scouts and Guides. At a height of 6,070 feet, Tara Devi is an ideal place for people wanting peace and some rest.

Sankat Mochan: A popular Hanuman temple is located here. We get an excellent view of Shimla from the temple. It can be reached by car or on foot.

Junga: Junga is a *tehsil* in the picturesque district of Shimla. Located at a distance of 26 km from Shimla, this place is known for a palace and a museum of the erstwhile Junga princely state, for its scenic beauty and for the numerous easy-to-hard treks it offers. Junga is surrounded by green hills with snow-capped mountains, and has a forest cover of kail, deodar, pine, cedar, oak, rhododendro, cheel, ban and other trees. It has a couple of resorts designed for maximum staying comfort, with all facilities and luxuries, but the essence has been to touch the natural space as little as possible. Easy accessibility and many other attractions make Junga a popular eco-adventure destination.

Kufri

Kufri: About 16 km from Shimla and at a height of 8,600 feet, Kufri is the capital of winter sports. During winter, visitors have the facility for skiing as the skiing season is at its best during January and February. Equipment for skiing is available from Himachal Pradesh Tourism Development Corporation (HPTDC) winter-sports club at Kufri. Apart from skiing, Kufri is a lovely picnic spot with a beautiful view of the hills around and the snowy peaks. There is also a zoo that delights children.

Naldehra: Nearly 22 km from Shimla and surrounded by beautiful deodar trees, Naldehra has a well-kept nine-hole golf course. It is a lovely and popular picnic spot. The annual Sipi fair in June is held in Naldehra.

Tatapani: Here, you can find the sulphur springs that are found near the Tatapani mandir (holy temple).

Chail: Chail is a little mountainous heaven 45 km from Shimla. It was the summer capital of the Maharaja of Patiala before Independence. The forests near Chail have many species of birds and deer. Chail is known for its cricket pitch, which is the highest cricket ground in the world.

Arki: About 40 km away from Shimla, Arki is a town and a nagar panchayat in Solan district of the state of Himachal Pradesh. The town is notable for its fort built in the late 18th century, when Arki was the capital of the erstwhile hill state of Baghal. The Arki fort is a converted hotel now.

Porter's Five Forces Analysis of Shimla

Customers: Visitors make their choices according to the time of the year; so, the number of visitors varies according to seasons. A great number of tourists visit Shimla in the summers as it is one of the most sought-after hill stations in the north; in winters, very few people visit the place to enjoy the snowfall. This makes the tourist's bargaining power high in the winters as compared to the summer season. A major reason for the high number of tourists in summers is that the season coincides with the school vacations of children.

Competition: Although there are many hill stations in North India, there is as yet a lot of scope for other tourist spots to join the competition. Various states are trying to promote their places to the tourists. States and other private players are also coming up with various man-made places and parks to join the party.

Suppliers

- **Hotels:** Depends on the number of hotels and how affordable they are to each class of tourists
- **Restaurants:** Again, depends on the number of restaurants and their variety, quality and prices
- **Trains:** Number of trains available and their fare
- **Road transport:** Number of buses, their timings and fares, and quality of roads
- **Travel agencies:** Number of agencies, their services, offers and price sensitivity
- **Government:** Tax policies, road charges and their support to the tourism industry

Substitutes: There are various hill stations in the northern region of the country, which come to the mind of tourists. The list includes Kullu, Manali, Nainital, Gulmarg and Mussoorie. Many of these places do not have good connectivity as compared to Shimla, though each has its own distinct features to lure the tourists.

New Entrants: In the short run, there is no perceived threat of new entrants in the industry. The reasons are:

- It is not easy to establish a new destination as it requires a great amount of money and time to create one.
- Even if the destination is already there, it needs a very good promotion strategy to catch tourists' attention.
- On the other side, malls, holiday resorts and villas are coming up in a big way to grab people's attention — a fact that will hearten the established destinations.

Hence, in the short run, Shimla as a tourist destination might face some issues because of people's tastes and choices, and a number of other potential tourist places. Additionally, the overall tourism industry in India might face tough times in the future if it fails to consider all these factors.

In the long run, the picture might change for the following reasons:

- Various states are promoting their places in a grand way. They are reaching out via television and print media to attract the customer.
- Various states are looking to grab market share so that they can establish themselves as a brand, and then, they will expect to launch their other small destinations to leverage the advantage.
- Currently, tourism is one of the fastest growing industries in India. More and more people can now afford to tour once or twice in a year. It is, therefore, necessary to come up with new destinations and tourist agencies to serve the needs of customers, and provide better facilities to grab the market properly. Also, current destinations need to provide new opportunities and better

connectivity to be competitive, and at the same time, leverage the market conditions to the maximum. This is also critical to securing the region as a profitable sourcing base.

PEST Analysis of Shimla

Political Factors: The following are the key political factors which can be listed out of the analysis:

- In India, Himachal Pradesh is one of the states where government is quite stable; so, there are no problems as such for tourists.
- The government gets a big chunk of income from tourism; so, it tries to promote tourism in the best possible manner.
- Road taxes and government policies are quite tourist friendly.

Economic Factors: The following are the key economic factors which can be listed out of the analysis:

- With the Indian economy on an upsurge for the last few years, people in the country are able to spend more and more on outings and family tours. Especially in North India, people plan to visit one or the other hill station in summers, and Shimla is not too far from major hubs in the northern region. Chandigarh (115 km) is the nearest large city. Delhi (365 km) is another point from where you may take a bus or a taxi via Chandigarh to reach Shimla. The journey would take about 6–8 hours, depending on traffic and weather.
- Hotels, restaurants and travel rates are affordable in Shimla. It has many hotels and guesthouses, and you are sure to find one matching your choice and within your budget. Shimla has several restaurants offering ethnic Indian food (vegetarian as well as non-vegetarian), and also other cuisines such as continental, Chinese and Thai. There are all kinds of restaurants depending on your affordability.

Socio-cultural Factors: The following are the key socio-cultural factors which can be listed out of the analysis:

- Indian society has been fundamentally different from other societies, and the impact of this can be seen on the preferences and choices of the people. People in India have always been quite a penny-savvy lot; they constantly look for better alternatives.
- Among recent trends, it is seen that urban people in India want to visit places that are not too far and exciting at the same time. In many instances, budget is given the last consideration.
- In the urban areas, people do not plan their holiday much in advance. Most of them have their own vehicles. Whenever they have a two-day holiday, they visit a place that is not too far.

Technological Factors: The following are the key technological factors which can be listed out of the analysis:

- Transportation to Shimla is a real issue for tourists. The nearest broad-gauge head is at Kalka – a four-hour journey from Delhi. After that, one has to take the mountain train from Kalka to Shimla. This railway track has recently been granted the status of a UNESCO World Heritage Site. The view is stunning, with the line passing through an amazing 103 tunnels. Nevertheless, there are not enough facilities of transportation to reach Shimla even today.
- In this information technology era, every tourist destination is made accessible through the Internet. Be it hotel bookings, train bookings or information about places, all can be accessed bya single click. In this department, Shimla lags behind compared to other popular tourist spots.
- Although Shimla is known for its scenic beauty, it would make the place a more competitive tourist destination if there were an amusement park or a man-made trekking course, which can be set up in the outskirts of the city.

Hampi

"If dreams were made out of stone, it would be Hampi."

Ugranarasimha at Hampi

Overview of Hampi Tourism. Listed as a World Heritage Site, Hampi, also known as the city of ruins, is one of the most captivating historical sites of South India. It is a city of nearly 500 monuments, each with a story behind it, reflecting a fascinating history reaching the pinnacle of glory and then stumbling to a decline of utter neglect. The name Hampi originated from the word Pampa, the ancient name of Tungabhadra river that flows through the city. There are other names that it goes by – Vijayanagara, named after the ruling kingdom, and Virupakshapura, named after the deity Shiva.

Hampi, in ruins today, once boasted riches known far beyond the shores of India. The 14th-century ruins lie scattered across an area of about 26 sq. km, amidst giant boulders and vegetation. Protected by the Tungabhadra in the north and rocky granite ridges on the other three sides, the ruins silently narrate the story of grandeur and splendour. The splendid remains of palaces and gateways of the ruined city tell a tale of man's infinite talent and power of creativity, together with his capacity for senseless destruction.

King's Balance

Famous Attractions. The temples of this city are noted for their large dimensions, florid ornamentation, bold and delicate carvings, magnificent pavilions, stately pillars, and a great wealth of iconographic and traditional depictions, which include subjects from the *Ramayana* and *Mahabharata*. Other temples in the surroundings are the Krishna temple, Pattabhirama temple, Hazara Ramachandra temple, Chandrasekhara temple and Jaina temple.

King's Balance: This nearly 5 metre tall balance is located near the Vittala temple, also called Tula Bhara or Tula Purushadana. The king used to weigh himself in gold, gems, silver and precious stones, which were then distributed to the priests.

Queen's Bath

Queen's Bath: This two-storey monument consists of a swimming pool that is 50 feet long and 6 feet deep, arched corridors, projecting balconies, and lotus-shaped fountains that once sprouted perfumed water.

Lotus Mahal: Shaped like a lotus flower when viewed from the top, this two-storey structure has beautiful archways set in geometric regularity. It was an air-cooled summer palace of the queen.

Elephant Stable

Vittala Temple

Elephant Stable: This huge stable, a beautiful example of the Hindu-Muslim style of architecture, housed about 11 elephants in separate compartments.

Mahanavami Dibba: This is the elevated place from which the royalty viewed Hampi with pomp, colour and revelry during the Mahanadu festival. The platform has beautiful carvings.

Vittala Temple: As the epicentre of Hampi's attractions, the Vittala temple is the most extravagant architectural showpiece of Hampi. Vittala, after whom the temple is known, is a form of Lord Vishnu. The highlight of the Vittala temple is its impressive pillared halls and the stone chariot.

Virupaksha Temple: It is the oldest and the principal temple in Hampi. It is believed that this temple has been functioning uninterruptedly ever since its inception in the 7th century AD, which makes it one of the oldest functioning temples in India.

Monolith Structures: Two famous monolith structures are Ugranarasimha and Ganapathi, which are noted for their massiveness and grace.

Virupaksha Temple

Porter's Five Forces Analysis of Hampi

Customers: The following are the key customers (tourists) which can be listed out of the analysis:

- Hampi, being a world heritage site, is visited by people from all over the world.
- Hotels and guesthouses are the most used means of accommodation by tourists. The nearest hotel is 5 km from Hampi.
- Generally, October to March is the best time to visit.
- One can travel from Bangalore to Hospet, to Kamalpur and then to Hampi; there are lots of Karnataka Tourism signboards and the place is very easy to reach.
- Hampi can be reached by rail, road or air. The nearest rail point is Hospet, from where one travels another 12 km by road to reach Hampi. There are regular bus services from Bangalore to Hospet. The nearest airport is Bellary (75 km); another nearby airport is in Belgaum.
- Karnataka Tourism has various packages for visitors.
- Hampi is a coveted destination for backpackers, history buffs and photographers.
- Hampi is a relatively small place, but it is very famous on the backpackers' circuit for its slow pace, ancient ruins and amazing

scenery. The fact that the traffic is limited to a small number of rickshaws (and even these are restricted to the main street) adds to the tranquillity. Boulder make up most of the surrounding area; their size and strength demand a peaceful air through the palm-strewn town. There are also plenty of temples and ancient centres to see, many of which are accessible only by bicycle or the most determined of walks.

- The only place for shopping is the Hampi Bazaar, where your bargaining skills will be tested to their limit.
- Sightseeing is pretty much the only activity in Hampi. One can also take a coracle ride on the river, which is pretty enjoyable.
- Bangalore being a prominent IT hub, people from all over the country visit Hampi, which is 353 km from Bangalore.
- The Vijayanagar Festival organized by the government of Karnataka in December recreates the grandeur of the bygone era.

Ganapathi at Hampi

Competition: The following are the key competitions which can be listed out of the analysis:

- Hampi faces various levels of competition in the tourism industry. Within Karnataka there are other historical places such as Belur, Halebeedu and Mysore. There are many waterfalls and hill stations such as Coorg and Ranganathittu Bird Sanctuary in Karnataka, and these are frequented by local tourists.
- Within South India, there is competition from other historical places in Tamil Nadu, which also has a huge share of temples and other historical monuments.
- Hampi also faces competition at a higher level from other tourist spots such as Agra, Goa and Rajasthan in India.
- To counteract these various levels of competition, Karnataka has succeeded in promoting Hampi as a major tourist attraction through various campaigns and special packages to cater to all kinds of customers.

Suppliers: The following are the key suppliers which can be listed out of the analysis:

- Suppliers in the tourism industry indicate all the service providers including airline industry, railways, travel agents, locals, hotel industry and government.
- KSRTC (state-owned bus-transport service) buses ply regularly from Hospet.
- Hospet is the nearest railway station (13 km) and is linked by rail to Bangalore, Bijapur, Hubliand Guntakal. Tickets can be booked online.
- There are plenty of travel agents (many of them online) who provide packages to Hampi, apart from government packages.
- There are state-owned guesthouses and hotels, as well as private hotels with good facilities.
- Hampi is a ruin and away from habitation. As such, local people do not play a major role.

Substitutes: The substitutes to Hampi tourism are other options that a person might prefer on a holiday: Internet surfing; television watching; visiting malls, water parks, or resorts; and so on. These substitutes, while not directly affecting tourism, can still be a deterrent. Instead of travelling to far-off places for a holiday, one can find easy entertainment from these sources.

New Entrants: The following are the key new entrants which can be listed out of the analysis:

- Each state in India is now beginning to realize the potential of tourism and attempting to uniquely position its chief attractions, for example temples in Tamil Nadu, wildlife in Assam and ayurveda in Kerala.

- Also, there are indirect threats from other entertainment sources such as theme parks, shopping malls and the Internet.

PEST Analysis of Hampi

Political Factors: Karnataka has always been a safe tourist destination. The government is politically stable and has been promoting tourism for a long time.

Economic Factors: The following are the key economic factors which can be listed out of the analysis:

- Hampi's economy is fuelled largely by agriculture and mining at present. The area is rich in iron ore and manganese. In addition, with its status as a World Heritage Site, tourism is another chief contributor to the economy.
- The tourist to Hampi can be a local or from other states or countries. There are transportation and accommodation facilities to cater to each of the above. Also, as part of the Incredible India campaign, there are special packages such as the Golden Chariot, named after the Stone Chariot in Hampi availed usually by foreign tourists.

Socio-cultural Factors: The following are the key socio-cultural factors which can be listed out of the analysis:

- The local language is Kannada, but guides and hotel staff can speak English and Hindi as well.
- Many of the present roads in Hampi are not original roads. There was a very good network of ring, radial and linear roads during the Vijayanagara period. The present asphalted roads do not merge with the monuments and stand out conspicuously. Heavy vehicular traffic in the prime archaeological zone of the site is causing serious damage to important archaeological remains. The site does not have any terminal and parking facilities.
- The entire Virupapura Gadda is characterized by illegal resorts, hotels and lodging activities.The construction of a controversial suspension bridge near Talarighat has endangered the entire site. The bridge stands on a major and extremely sensitive natural setting of the site – in the heart of the core protected area. It leads to heavy vehicular traffic and may affect the site environmentally. Besides this, it is very close to the ancient Anegundi gate and fort wall.

Technological Factors: There are plenty of Internet cafés in Hampi. Travel arrangements can be made online, including hotel bookings and reservations.

International Tourist Destination: Singapore

It will be interesting to see how the Porter's model applies to international destinations. In this respect we have discussed Singapore here.

Overview of Singapore Tourism. Situated on the southernmost tip of the Malaysian peninsula, Singapore is one of the only four remaining city-states in the world. A country that achieved independence half-a-century ago, Singapore offers a rich and diverse mix in its people, culture and cuisine – 3a mix that is the only homogeneity spread over the 700-odd square kilometres of its area. This mix mirrors its colonial history and Chinese, Malay, Indian and Arab ethnicities in an environmentally friendly way that maintains natural- and heritage-conservation programmes.

Famous Attractions of Singapore Tourism. It is perhaps this mix that makes Singapore such an attractive tourist destination. The government recognizes tourism as one of the major contributors to the country's economy, and, as such, makes every attempt to welcome visitors to the smallest country in Southeast Asia.

The Orchard Road district, dominated by hotels and multi-storey shopping centres, is considered the main attraction of Singapore tourism. A prime tourist attraction is the Singapore Zoo, which has adopted the concept of "open zoo." It allows people to explore Asian, African and American habitats at night without any visible barriers between the guests and the wild animals. The Jurong Bird Park is a zoological garden centred on birds, and is dedicated towards exposing the public to as much species and varieties of birds from around the world as possible, including a flock of about 1000 flamingos. The tourist island of Sentosa attracts more than 5 million visitors a year, and consists of about 20–30 different landmarks.

Some shopping belts in Singapore apart from the Orchard Road are situated in Marina Bay, Bugis Street, Chinatown, Geylang Serai, Kampong Gelam and Arab Street, Little India, North Bridge Road, Riverside, Shenton Way and Raffles Place, and the Suburbs.

To further encourage shopping in Singapore, the Singapore Tourism Board (STB) organizes the annual Great Singapore Sale where shoppers enjoy great discounts and bargains at participating outlets. The STB also introduced "Late Night Shopping" in 2007. Initiatives like these enable Singapore to receive millions of tourists every year and make it an exciting and fun-filled experience.

Porter's Five Forces Analysis of Singapore

Customers: The following are the key customers (tourists) which can be listed out of the analysis:

- Singapore is home to over 7,000 multinational companies and acts as a hub for business tours and meetings.
- Located at a geographical vantage point, Singapore attracts global businesses and is seamlessly connected to almost every part of the world.
- As English is one of its numerous official languages, it is generally easier for tourists to understand when speaking to the local population of the country.
- Indonesia, China, Philippines and Malaysia remain its most prominent sources of tourists owing to its rich cultural diversity.
- Tourists enjoy their stay in this city, which is rich in contrast and colour but with a harmonious blend of cultures, cuisines, arts and architecture.
- Singapore seeks to be the business hub of Southeast Asia and has an expansive shopping precinct located in the Orchard Road district. Singapore took top spot as the most affordable shopping destination for tourists in Asia Pacific, according to the results from a comparative study by Euromonitor International on retail pricing in eight leading shopping destinations in the Asia Pacific region.
- Singapore is fast positioning itself as a medical-tourism hub – about 200,000 foreigners seek medical care in the country each year, and Singapore medical services aim to serve 1 million foreign patients annually by 2012 and generate US$ 3 billion in revenue.
- Regional demand for travel will continue to be dominated by short trips by the Singaporean traveller to take advantage of cheap shopping. This trend seems to be supported by the growing popularity of low-cost carriers, which are being given access to the local market.

Competition: Singapore has been voted as the "best business city" by Asian readers of the *Time* magazine for five consecutive years. Yet, it faces close competition from other destinations like Hong Kong and Macau.

It also faces competition at a higher level from other tourist spots like Malaysia, Goa, Tokyo and Shanghai.

In order to maintain its competitive advantage, the tourism industry in Singapore should stress on the following issues:

- Positioning Singapore as a destination for the next 10 years to ensure tourism remains a sustainable engine of economic growth for Singapore
- Improving Singapore's position as a tourism hub in the face of developments in the aviation industry
- Developing Singapore as a strong "events" destination
- Developing Singapore as a choice "business travel" destination

Suppliers: The following are the key suppliers which can be listed out of the analysis:

- STB offices initiated a series of business travel, meetings, incentive travel, conventions and exhibitions (BTMICE) road shows, and established strategic partnership between STB, Sentosa, Star Cruises and Suntec Singapore to market Singapore as a BTMICE destination.
- STB has tie-ups with several cruises internationally to tap new markets and customer segments. ROYAL Caribbean International (RCI) is the latest cruise operator to tie up with the STB on a series of marketing initiatives under the recently launched Singapore Fly-Cruise Development Fund.
- An efficient public-transportation network of taxis, buses and the modern mass rapid transit (MRT) rail system ensures that getting from point A to point B is hassle-free and extremely affordable.
- To attract more tourists, the government decided to legalize gambling and to allow two casino resorts (euphemistically called Integrated Resorts) to be developed at Marina South and Sentosa.

Substitutes: The following are the key substitutes which can be listed out of the analysis:

- With the growth of globalization and the availability of the state-of-the-art technology, business tours are being replaced by video conferencing
- Virtual Web sites on the Internet

New Entrants: Each country is vying for more tourists in the age of rapidly increasing disposable incomes. Countries within the region like Malaysia, India, and China, and in the Middle East like UAE and Kuwait are aggressively promoting tourism, as represented by these slogans:

- India — Incredible India
- Malaysia — Truly Asia
- Taiwan — Touch your heart

PEST Analysis of Singapore

Political Factors: The following are the key political factors which can be listed out of the analysis:

- Very stable political environment and good control on immigration. The government is very lenient about tourist visa as they promote it as an excellent tourist spot

- Malaysia was found in 1963. Malay, Sabah, Sarawak and Singapore became one nation and established itself as a good shopping and tourist destination across the world
- Singapore is a parliamentary democracy representing different constituencies that have good representation of all classes and religions
- The government is very liberal in terms of spending and policies regarding tourism, which makes the place congenial, to enjoy the shopping experience and to attract tourists from all across the globe.

Economic Factors: The following are the key economic factors which can be listed out of the analysis:

- Singapore enjoys very low inflation and unemployment because of its stable government and financial stability.
- Experts are very hopeful about growth in the economy, and the same has been justified through the GDP growth rate since 2000.
- Hotels, restaurants and travel rates are not deterrents in Singapore. There is a plethora of hotels and restaurants. People of each class and various preferences can easily locate a guesthouse within their budget. As Singapore is a multi-ethnic city, it is easy to find food according to one's tastes. There are several restaurants offering ethnic Indian foods (vegetarian as well as non-vegetarian), continental foods, Chinese Foods or western foods.

Socio-cultural Factors: The following are the key socio-cultural factors which can be listed out of the analysis:

- All classes and religions are present in good numbers, whether it's Chinese, Indian, and Malaysian, or Hindu, Muslim, Buddhist, and Christian.
- Although many languages are spoken, English is the main language and is spoken and understood by most of the residents and local people.
- Although the country is recognized as highly literate and advanced, there is a low rate of education among women.

Technological Factors: The following are the key technological factors which can be listed out of the analysis:

- The air network of the country is exceptionally good, whether it is national or international. The country's airlines are renowned for their hospitality and comfort.
- As the country is highly advanced in technology, a variety of TV and radio stations are available for people to enjoy their leisure time and receive information.
- Country connectivity through the Internet is worth mentioning as numerous Internet service providers (ISPs) are available in all parts of the country. Ticket bookings and other Internet bookings are available at one's fingertips.
- Another major advantage for foreign visitors is that the country has a good number of airports with the latest facilities. Intra-city transportation is also very good.
- Singapore's government lays high emphasis on the tourism industry as it accounts for a good amount of the GDP. They have created a good information base on the Internet and other media. They also aggressively promote tourism by various means of communication throughout the world.

Unsung Tourist Destination: Meerut (Uttar Pradesh)

Overview of Meerut Tourism

Situated 67 km north of Delhi, Meerut is one of the largest cities in western Uttar Pradesh. It is believed to have been founded by Maya, the father of Mandodari (Ravana's wife). Its ancient name was Mayarastra.

The city has always been a centre of varied activities throughout the course of history. Archaeological excavations carried out at Alamgirpur village near Meerut threw up remains from the Harappan culture. An ancient well and painted Grey Wares stumbled upon the diggings date back to the Mauryan period. Hastinapur in Meerut is believed to be the capital of the Kauravas and the Pandavas. Also, the fact that a pillar was erected here by the emperor Ashoka in the 3rd century BC and the discovery of some Buddhist remains within the city leave little room for doubt that this city has been an important place in ancient times.

Today, the city is mainly known for the uprising of the 1857 Indian Mutiny that occurred here.

How to Reach Meerut

Meerut can be reached:

- **By air:** There is no direct air connection. Nearest airports are Pantnagar (62 km) and New Delhi (67 km).
- **By rail:** Trains on the Delhi-Dehradun route connect Meerut.
- **By road:** Well-developed network of buses connects Meerut to all the important places for local transport taxis, cycle rickshaws and auto-rickshaws are easily available.

Famous Attractions

Augarhnath Mandir: In the cantonment, there is a Lord Shiva temple called Augarhnath Mandir. It is said the "shiv linga" present in this temple emerged on its own – a miracle that has been attracting the followers of Lord Shiva ever since its inception. According to local priests, the great Maratha rulers used to worship here and seek blessings before proceeding with their victory processions.

During the British rule, it was a favourite place for the army. That time, the Indian army was called Kali Paltan (black army). Since the temple is located close to the army barrack, it is also known by the name Kali Paltan mandir. Its close proximity to the Indian army camps offered a safe haven for freedom fighters, who visited and stayed here for their secret meetings with the officers of Kali Paltan. On 10 May, 1857, Indian soldiers took an oath to win freedom at this temple, and the Sepoy Mutiny started from Meerut.

Dargah of Shah Pir: Situated near the Shah Pir Gate, the Mughal mausoleum, this red stone construction was built in 1620 by Noor Jehan. It was built to commemorate the death of an esteemed pir (seer) and is an excellent Mughal architectural piece of work.

St John's Church: Established in 1819 in Meerut Cantonment, this church was completed in 1822. It was dedicated to the people by Bishop Wilson on behalf of the East India Company. The church has a seating capacity of about 15,000. During the 1857 uprising, this church was the scene of heavy fighting between the rebels and the British forces. The church also has the distinction of being the oldest church in North India.

Sardhana (UNESCO World Heritage Site): About 19 km north-west of Meerut lies the fascinating town of Sardhana with a romantic and historically significant past. In the late 18th century, the French adventurer Walter Reinhardt came to India and soon became popular as Samru. He received Sardhana from Najaf Khan of Delhi. After his death in 1778, his formidable widow Begum Samru, who converted to the Roman Catholic faith, succeeded him and built the church.

Sardhana Church

Unsung Tourist Destination: *(Continued)*

In an aisle of the church, there is a monument to the begum (executed by Tadolini of Rome, the famous sculptor) which is a fine piece of sculpture (the crowning figure being that of the begum). It was brought to Sardhana in 1848 and set up in her memory by her adopted son David Sombre, whose mortal remains are buried at its foot.

Hastinapur: Hastinapur is one of the most respected shrines of the Jain religion. According to the Jain tradition, it is one of the earliest Indian cities – like Ayodhya and Kashi – and came into existence during the time of Rishabhadeva (the first tirthankara), whose grandson, Somaprabha, was the first ruler of the place. It is also said to be the birthplace of three Jain tirthankaras, Shantinatha, Kunthnnath and Arahanatha; their footprints can be seen on a small hill nearby. There are also some very important temples and stoops (pillars), which have been founded by different acharyas (teachers) of the Jain religion in different times, and include Digamber Jain Bada Mandir and Shwetamber temple. Every year, thousands of Jain pilgrims visit the place.

Even the *Mahabharata* gives an account of the early history of the place. In *Mahabharata*, the founder of the place is generally believed to be King Hastin, fifth in descent from Bharata. In fact, there are enough evidences towards a probable historic association. One of these is:

Draupadi-ki-Rasoi (Draupadi's Kitchen): Draupadi-ki-Rasoi in Meerut is believed to be the site of Draupadi's kitchen and is situated on the banks of the Burhganga. In the history of *Mahabharata*, it is narrated that when the Pandav brothers along with Draupadi were on exile at the Hastinapur forest, Lord Krishna came to visit them. Draupadi was left with just one grain of rice, which she offered to Lord Krishna with devotion and a lot of affection to appease his hunger. Lord Krishna readily accepted the grain of rice. Later, he bestowed His blessings upon her and appeased the hunger of thousands of Duruvasa's disciples when they came to her as guests. This is the history of Draupadi-ki-Rasôi in Meerut.

Suraj Kund Temple: The Suraj Kund temple in Meerut was built by a rich businessman Lawar Jahawar Lal, in 1714. This is filled up by water from Ganga Canal. There are several temples around the Suraj Kund. One of them is the well-known Baba Manohar Nath temple. It is said that it was built during the period of Shah Jahan.

Chandi Devi Temple: This temple is very near to the Suraj Kund. The Nauchandi mela is organized every year one week after the Holi festival, either in March-end or first week of April. This is a very famous mela. Lakhs of people visit this mela every year.

Bale Miyan ki Dargah: The dargah of Bale Miyan is very near to Chandi Devi Mandir. Ursis organized every year on this mazar during the Nauchandi mela. It was built by Kutubuddin Aibakin in 1194.

Jain Temple at Hastinapur

Bale Miyan ki Dargah

Unsung Tourist Destination: *(Continued)*

Jama Masjid: Jama Masjid, which is near the kotwali, was built by Hasan Mahdi, the minister of Mahmood of Ghazni, in 1019. The reconstruction of this mosque was done during the period of the Mughal ruler Humayun.

Best Time to Visit

Meerut is extremely hot during summer with temperature varying between 30° to 43°C. The best time to visit Meerut is between October to March when the temperature drops between 25° to 5°C.

Accommodation

One can easily find a place to stay in Meerut. There are around three two-star hotels and one three-star hotel in Meerut along with ample number of budget hotels.

Tourist Experience

This relates to one of the author's tourist experiences back in 2003. Along with his family, the author got a chance to visit Bihar. The trip involved visiting Jain pilgrimage places like Shikharji, Kundalpur, Pawapur and Champapur, followed by Bodhgaya, Rajgir, Vaishali, and ruins of the world-famous ancient university of Nalanda, to unearth the magnificent history of India.

During the trip, the author encountered with some good as well as bad experiences. Some of them are as follows:

Good Experiences

Bihar is a much-sought-after tourist destination, especially because of the rich variety of natural, historical and religious values it has to offer. Undoubtedly, it can be rated as one of the most tempting travel destinations in India for both domestic and international tourists. Visiting all the above-mentioned places and getting to know the past has been one of the most satisfying experiences. The place never fails to amaze us with its beauty, cultural diversity and majestic past. The place truly has the potential to make us fall in love with it at the very first sight. So, visiting the place in itself was a great experience. The temples and various tourist places are very well maintained, which contributes positively towards the entire experience.

Bad Experiences

If all the tourist destinations are well connected by road network, the place holds a lot of potential to enhance tourism in the state. However, the fact is that the roads to these pilgrimage centres are in a bad shape. Many a times, they had to take circuitous routes from one location to the other. So,

Jain Jalmandir in Pawapur

Lack of Basic Infrastructure in the State

Tourist Experience *(Continued)*

by the time they reached the destination, they were totally exhausted. Besides this, in all the places they were let down by tourist guides, overcharging shopkeepers and beggars.

All through the trip, keeping in view the great potential of tourism in Bihar, the author felt that the creation of basic infrastructure for tourism development is imperative. Important components for infrastructural development include arranging accommodation for increased number of tourists, building of highways on tourist circuits, international-level airports with total aviation backup and facilities, local transport, rail routes linking tourist spots with full amenities and facilities, vital telecommunication links, continuous electricity supply with elaborate arrangements and other essential amenities. Also, religious circuits for the Buddhist, Jain, Hindu, Sikh and Islam religions need to be developed with special work plans to promote religious tourism, making the religious circuits attractive with suitable tour packages and facilities. With road transport being the nerve line of tourism, the construction of roads and their proper maintenance, and the availability of vehicles for tourists should be given due priority.

SUMMARY

- Tourism is one of the most profitable industries in India. The chief reasons include economic growth resulting in increase in domestic tourism and the tourism ministry taking several initiatives such as the Incredible India campaign.
- The market environment refers to all the forces outside marketing that affect marketing management's ability to build and maintain successful relationships with target customers. The marketing environment can be divided into the task environment (micro-environment) and the broad environment (macro-environment).
- The micro-environment includes the immediate factors involved in producing, distributing and promoting the offering, including the company, suppliers, distributors, dealers and target customers. Porter's five forces model is used to analyse the micro-environment of the tourism market.
- Porter's five forces analysis of the tourism industry takes these factors into account: New entrants who are new avenues of tourism, such as development of new tourism sites; creation of other sources of relaxation within the native city of a foreign traveller can threaten as substitutes; buyers are tourists, who are the source of income for the tourism industry; suppliers are the various states promoting their tourism destinations; and competition involves attracting tourists by established tourist places.
- The macro-environment refers to all forces that are outside the immediate circle and affect the micro-environment. It consists of six components: demographic environment, economic environment, natural environment, technological environment, political-legal environment, and social-cultural environment. Tourism macro-environment is analysed using the PEST analysis.
- The PEST analysis of the tourism industry includes: Political factors like political stability, law-and-order situation and absence of terrorist activities in the place where tourism needs to be promoted; economic factors including purchasing power of the tourist and foreign-exchange rate; social factors are availability of facilities such as proper medical facilities and open culture; technological factors refer to e-connectivity of the tourist place and presence of good mobile network, among other aspects.

FIELD EXERCISES

1. For a destination you have visited, sum up your good and bad experiences.
2. Visit one of the UNESCO heritage sites and analyse its tourism market environment.

REFERENCES

Kotler, Philip, Kevin Lane Keller (2003), *Marketing Management*, New Jersey, USA: Pearson Publication.

Morrison, Alastrair M. (2009), *Hospitality and Travel Marketing*, USA: Thomson Learning Publication.

Web Sites

http://www.jaipur.org.uk/

http://www.indianholiday.com/tourism-in-india/tourism-in-jaipur.html

http://www.hill-stations-india.com/north-india-hillstations/

http://www.meerut.nic.in

http://www.meerutdistrict.com

http://www.hobotraveler.com/138hampi.shtml

http://www.bellary.nic.in/HMP/REPORT%20PDFs/CHAPTER-9.pdf

http://hampionline.com/

http://www.visitsingapore.com/publish/stbportal/en/

home.html

http://findarticles.com/p/articles/mi_m1NDC

CHAPTER 2

Tourist Consumer Behaviour

ABOUT THE DESTINATION

Big Ben, the Great Bell in the Clock Tower of the Palace of Westminster, is one of London's best-known landmarks. London is also known for its ubiquitous red double-decker buses, black cabs and red telephone boxes.

OBJECTIVES

- To understand and appreciate the consumer behaviour of tourists
- To understand the customer activity cycle
- To interpret the information search and decision-making process for tourists
- To appreciate the various motivators and deterrents for tourist behaviour

INTRODUCTION

In this chapter, various tourist typologies, tourist characteristics, tourist decision-making processes, motivators, deterrents and so on have been discussed.

Tourists, while visiting a specific destination, never behave the way they would in their native place. There are many reasons for the same. Tourists always would like to live a different life in the tourist destination. Depending on their background and nationality, the behavioural traits may differ a bit. While undertaking a journey to an unknown destination, they would always lean back on information, in the form of books, reviews, blogs, Web sites and word of mouth, available in the public domain.

In technological parlance, the tourism industry can be categorized as a service industry, dealing primarily with intangibles like the experience of the tourists. A significant point of difference between the purchase behaviour for tangible products and that for tourist products has been observed. Tangible products can be assessed prior to purchase, whereas it is difficult to develop and construct models of the decision-making process that relate to the purchase of tourism products.

Recently, academicians have paid attention to the changing patterns of tourism as an embodiment of broader societal changes and the shift towards post-modernism. It is said that leisure-related activities have become increasingly commoditized, reflecting a global "culture of consumption." In the leisure and travel industry, a focal point has been the growing emphasis on the creation and marketing of tourist experiences through place commoditization. These landscapes include amusement and theme parks, casinos,

spectacle events such as the Olympics and festival marketplaces. Destinations are being marketed to kindle desire among the tourists. The aim is to motivate them to visit the destination and enjoy the experience, which will help them to advocate for the same to other prospective tourists. The commoditization of experience as an intangible element of capitalistic accumulation has brought the emergence of symbolic or cultural capital. Cultural capital broadly involves the consumption and collection of touristic experiences to demonstrate social tastes, lifestyle choices and arid socio-economic status. Under the logic of this post-modern culture of consumption, the constant search for novelty and alternative experiences is emphasized, as the consumer becomes more discerning and sophisticated. Consequently, in the tourism industry, a premium has been increasingly placed on providing the "post-tourist" with a never-ending range of novel tourist experiences.

Needs of a Tourist

The importance of customer satisfaction/dissatisfaction derives from its purported impact on repeat-purchase behaviour and brand loyalty. An effective customer-satisfaction system provides management with early warning signals, which enable the prevention of loss of market share. Although defensive strategies (those that seek to retain existing customers) are vital to marketing managers; offensive strategies (those aiming to gain new customers and variety seekers) are also very important as they determine the long-term growth and profitability of a company. Understanding the buying behaviour of first-time buyers is essential for a firm's marketing strategy since first-time buyers are the potential repeat purchasers and may become loyal to a brand. Post-purchase rationalization is a common phenomenon, wherein people invest a lot of time, money or effort in something to convince themselves that it must have been worth it.

Many decisions are made emotionally and, so, are often rationalized retrospectively in an attempt to justify the choice. This rationalization is based on the principle of commitment and the psychological desire to stay consistent to that commitment.

Classification and Needs of a Tourist. There are three kinds of tourists – inbound, domestic and outbound. Inbound tourists are those that visit India from foreign countries. During the year 2007, the number of inbound (foreign) tourist arrivals was estimated at about 5 million, which represents a growth of about 12% as compared to the corresponding figures for the previous year (Ministry of Tourism Annual Report 2007–08). Domestic tourists are the Indian residents who are vacationing during summer, winter or during other holidays, utilizing leave travel concession (LTC) or are self-financed. The number of domestic tourist visits was estimated at 462 million in 2006, showing a growth of 17.8% as compared to the year 2005 (Ministry of Tourism Annual Report 2007–08). Outbound tourists are the resident Indians who opt to visit foreign countries. In this chapter, we focus only on inbound and domestic tourists.

The number of inbound tourists peaks during October to March and reduces by half during April to September. There has been an increase in domestic as well as outbound tourists, which is a healthy trend, as the WTO data show that countries whose residents spend more on tourism (whether domestic or outbound) have also received more inbound tourists. The reason for this could be partially attributed to the familiarity with Indian people and customs that foreigners gain from Indian tourists visiting their countries. After their trips abroad, the experience of these outbound tourists, if captured, can help plan, improve and promote better tourism facilities in India. In a way, it conveys that with more experience one has of foreign lands, more and more people get interested in you if you are interested in knowing them.

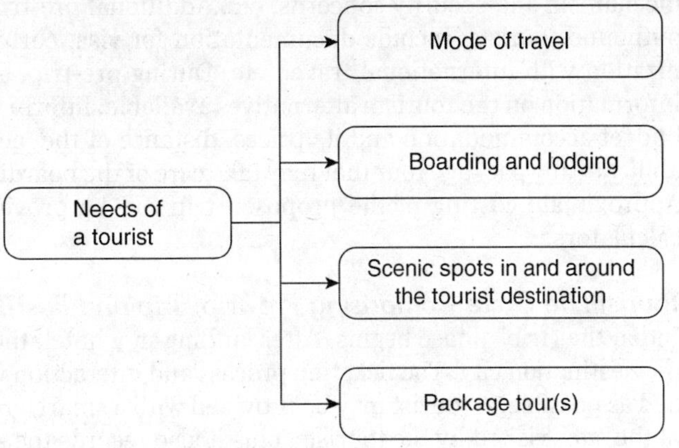

A tourist needs to know the best mode of travel (road, rail, air or sea) to a destination. Suitable boarding and lodging are the next items on his/her agenda. There were 1,437 hotels with 84,327 rooms on the approved list of the Ministry of Tourism up to December 2007. Thereafter, information on attractive tourist spots available in and around the destination holds his/her attention and then any package tours that provide the best value for money (or at least increase the perceived usefulness in the eyes of a prospective tourist).

Tourist Life Cycle

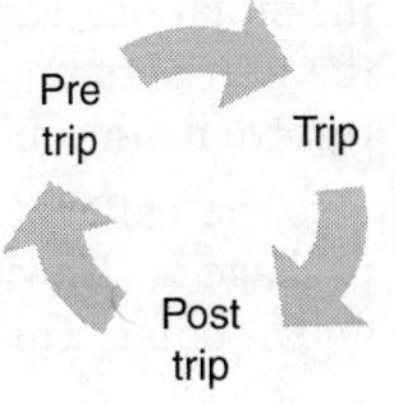

A tourist life cycle can be classified into three phases — pre-trip, trip and post-trip. Pre-trip (or planning) is the phase during which a potential tourist is considering tourism travel. In this planning phase, tourism intermediaries (travel agents, tour operators, hotels, airlines, etc.) play a vital part in forming the opinion of a potential tourist.

There are some similar pre-trip requirements for the three kinds of tourists (inbound, domestic and outbound). These include information about the destination, boarding/ lodging, mode of travel and package tour(s), advance payment

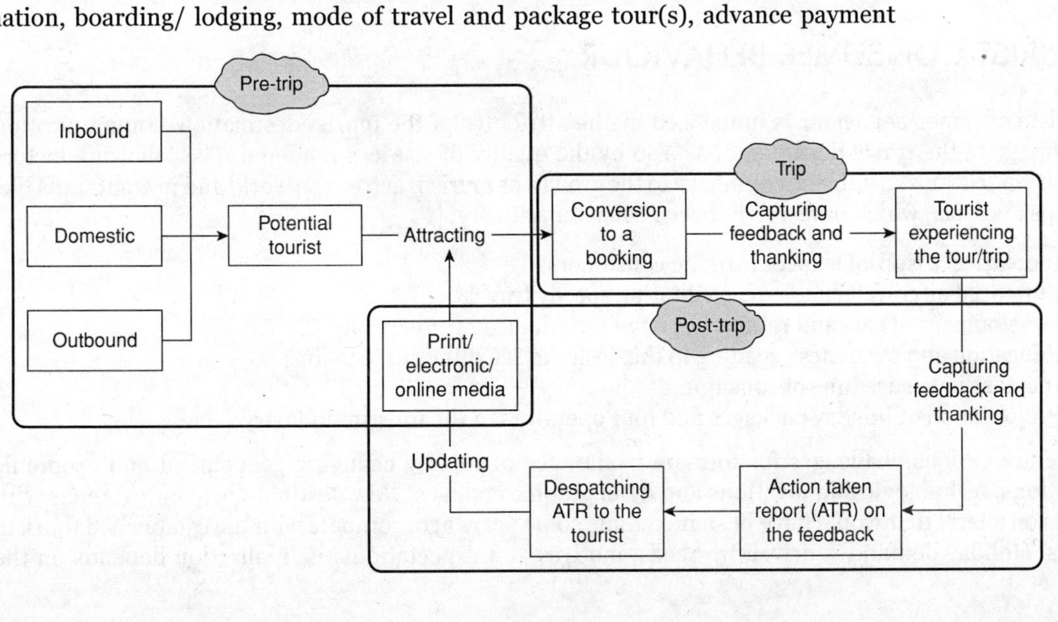

mechanism and security concerns, etc. Additional pre-trip requirements, specifically for inbound and outbound tourists, include documentation for visa, currency conversion issues, local travel synchronization with international travel, etc. During pre-trip, a potential tourist seeks reliable and current information on the tourism alternatives available: information about mode of travel, budget trip prices, budget accommodation and its prices, distance of the accommodations from the tourist spots, availability of any package tour that may take care of the boarding/lodging with additional local sight seeing. Approximate costing of the proposed trip can be provided to potential tourists using some online calculators.

Tourist Life Cycle Comprising Pre-Trip, Trip and Post-Trip. Once a potential tourist decides to visit India, the "trip" phase begins. After landing in a hotel, the tourist would begin visiting various sites in the destination city. The ticketing process and interaction with local populace should be made as simplified as possible. A tourist may be provided with a smart/credit/debit card that would have all the details of the sites visited by the tourists, plus it also records the sequence of the visit plu it contains all details about the tourist. A tourist needs to be made aware of the common rules of the land while eating in restaurants and general civic sensibility.

During the last 48–72 hours of the trip, again hand-holding is needed. Checking out of hotels and reaching airports need to be a pleasurable experience. Taking feedback of the trip is also important. Feedback forms need to be carefully designed so that each aspect of the trip can be carefully captured. Providing feedback should not become a chore for the tourist but it should be captured at every possible point while the tourist is in his/her trip.

Post-trip link with a tourist is very important for many reasons. Once the tourist leaves for his/her home country, after a few days, a feedback can be asked for seeking constructive suggestions to improve the situation. The customer should be provided an ATR on the feedback provided by the customer. If the tourist is upset or angry over some issue, someone should sympathetically look into it and try to resolve it amicably.

Thereafter, the tourist should be kept informed (through emails, etc.) constantly about any new package deals, with schemes like discounts for repeat customers. This will make the tourist feel wanted and at home. This would increase the word-of-mouth-impacted tourists.

TOURIST CONSUMER BEHAVIOUR

Tourist consumer behaviour is influenced by the attributes of the tourist destination, communication and image of the travel destination, as also by the quality of services rendered. The following factors have been recognized as being conducive to the growth of tourism across the world and in continents like Europe and Asia, which have a rich tourist consumer history:

- Increase in disposable income of the consumers
- Enhanced aircraft technology, facilitating speedy travel
- Development of cars and railroads, giving an enhanced connectivity
- Education and awareness, leading to the desire to see different locations
- Increase in leisure time of consumers
- Proliferation of holiday packages and tour operators in the tourism industry

There are various challenges for tourism in the face of rapidly changing geopolitical and economic situations, technological innovations and demographic changes. New destinations, new products with prices on a level that would have been incredible some years ago, compete with the established tourism offers. Holiday demand is driven by needs, motives and expectations; its realization depends on the

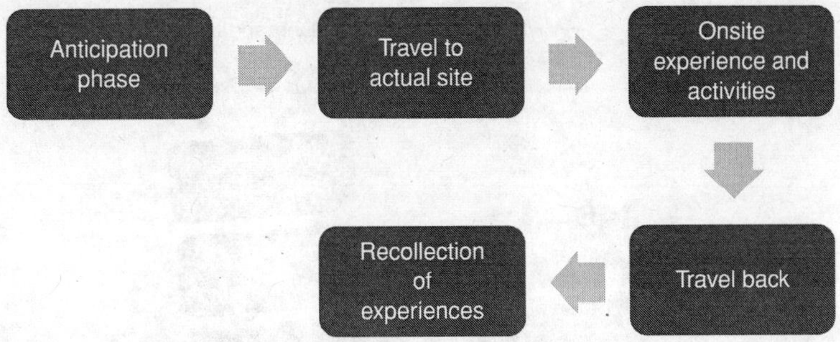

Fig. 2.1: The Five-Phase Experience Model

individual economic situation and the freedom to travel. Let us try to recapitulate the changing trends in the tourism sector:

- External factors like freedom, time, money and physical fitness directly affect the ability to travel.
- Consumer behaviour depends on external factors and is driven by internal factors (e.g., motives and abilities).
- Tourist demand is heterogeneous in nature and may be influenced by seemingly irrational factors, e.g., fashion and trends. It depends on images, perceptions, and attitudes and the availability of time and money. Tourists have various needs, desires and motivations, both of a "push" and "pull" nature.

A five-phase outdoor-recreation experience model has been proposed to delineate vacation experiences and the decisions involved in the process (Fig. 2.1). The five-stage travel model involves modelling decision processes of travellers from a macro-perspective and has the following stages: anticipation phase, travel to actual site, onsite experiences and activities, travel back, and recollection of experiences.

Another school of thought delineate tourists' decision-making process based on the realization that tourist behaviour is a rational decision activity. In other words, a potential traveller assesses the costs and benefits of his/her actions before committing to a purchase. This model asserts that tourism services have unique characteristics that differentiate them from other products (e.g., intangibility, involve risks). Tourism firms affect tourist behaviour, and the consumer, in turn, affects how firms make marketing-related decisions.

ANALYSING TOURIST CHARACTERISTICS

The ability to determine the proper target audience and their travel needs is crucial to a successful and efficient marketing campaign. After identifying the preferences of the target segment, the tour operator can successfully position the marketing strategy to enhance the attractiveness of a tourism destination. This can be done by psychological, objective or subjective means. The need to create and deliver purpose-adapted products has acquired more significance in the face of increased competitive market conditions.

Segmentation is the division of a market into distinct subsets of consumers who require specific products or services. To be of strategic value, the segments must be measurable, accessible, substantial and sufficiently different. Such segmentations assist marketers in properly identifying lucrative target groups and facilitating more cost-effective marketing through the design, promotion and correct positioning of purpose-designed products aimed at satisfying the identified needs of those groups. Segmentation is done on the basis of demographic, psychographic, geographic and behavioural factors.

Market segmentation is, thus, the process through which people (tourism providers and consumers) with similar needs are grouped together, so that a tourism business/organization can use greater

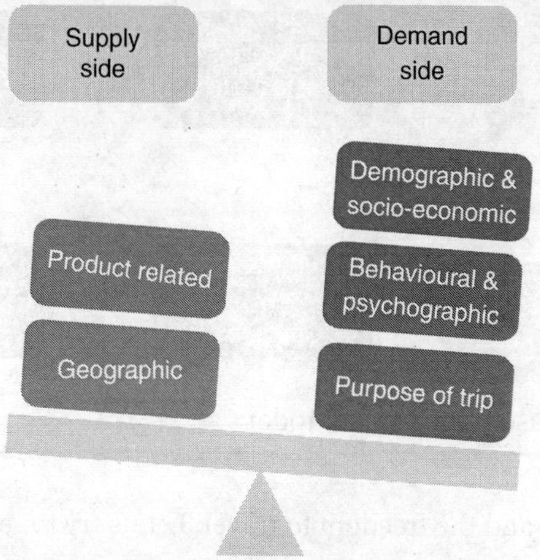

Fig. 2.2: Supply and Demand Side Influences

precision in serving and communicating with these groups (marketing). Market segmentation can be approached from two broad directions: supply side and demand side (Fig. 2.2). There has been an ongoing debate about "product push" versus "market pull." The former is designing a product, packaging it and hoping that there is a market for it; the latter attempts to find a niche market, identify the needs and wants of individuals within that market and design a product to meet those needs. Market segmentation can be product related or demand based.

Product-Related Segmentation

Product-related segmentation involves grouping similar products. The various categories under product-related segmentation are:

- **Accommodation**
- **Adventure operators/organizers:** Ranging from family adventures and motorcycle tours to hunting and bird watching
- **Attractions:** Ranging from museums and theme parks to sports clubs and festivals
- **Transportation and services:** Ranging from train and van tours to restaurants and gas stations
- **Seasons:** Varying across fall and winter
- **Nature of visit:** Business travel, leisure travel, pilgrimage, international sports events, travellers for arts and architecture, travellers for mountain sports, travellers to wildlife camps and bird sanctuaries, beach strollers, interest groups, etc.

Demand-Based Segmentation

Demand-related segmentation involves classification on the basis of demographics and behavioural patterns of tourists.

Life-Cycle Segments

- Youth market (age 18–35, with no children under 20 living at home)
- Family market (with children under 20 living at home)

- mature market (age 36–65)
- Seniors market (age over 65)

Traveller Profile

- Duration of trip/stay
- Destination

Socio-Economic Classification (SEC)

- Upper class
- Middle class
- Lower class

Demographics of Households

- Household make-up
- Age profiles
- Occupation profiles
- Income
- Lifestyle and life-stage profiles
- Race/ethnicity and
- Education level

TOURIST DECISION-MAKING PROCESS

The decision-research process attempts to understand the mechanism of decision making at the conscious and unconscious levels of thoughts. Researchers involved in the decision-making study are faced with the difficult task of measuring and understanding a process that is unobservable, and for which consumers are mostly only partially aware.

Buyer-decision behaviour forms the basis of marketing strategies. A comprehensive understanding of the decision-making process goes a long way in providing valuable inputs for the development of effective marketing strategies.

Behavioural Sequence Model

Alternative-decision participants' role and the specifics of the decision process can most easily be identified by constructing a behavioural sequence model (BSM) (Fig. 2.3). BSM uses a grid format to identify the decision of the target audience. The horizontal information enumerates the WHAT of the decision, specifically the major decision stages preceding, including and following the purchase. The vertical information, on the other hand, enumerates the data inputs relating to the following factors:

- WHO – the decision participants and decision roles
- WHERE – the locations of decision stages
- WHEN – the time and timing of each stage
- HOW – a capsule description of how each stage is accomplished

Information Search

Tourist information-search strategies determine the types and amounts of information sources, tourists refer to, in order to respond to internal and external contingencies in vacation planning.

	Need Arousal	Information Search about Destination	Travel Logistics	Purchase/ Consump-tion	Post-Purchase
WHO (Roles)	Initiator: family members; Influences: colleagues, friends and relatives; User: all travellers	Family members search data from secondary data sources and travel agents	Family members and travel agents	Family members	The travellers and the prospective travellers in the arena of influence are affected by the post-purchase behaviour
WHERE (Location)	Travel portals, media advertisements, travel books	Internet	Planning stage; homeland/ destination	Destination	Homeland
WHEN (Timings)	Prior to the preferred season/ holidays	Prior to the preferred season/ holidays	Prior to the preferred season/ holidays	Holiday season	Post-holiday
HOW (Description)	Evaluation of intrinsic needs: For a retreat, health/wellness, family commitment	Surf the travel portals and consult travel magazines	Travel-agent services	Classify destinations on the basis of preference and economic viability	By word of mouth, blogs

Fig. 2.3: Behavioural Sequence Model

Initially, the information-search process occurs internally, with tourists relying on their personal experience and relevant knowledge. However, when this internal search fails to provide sufficient information, tourists actively conduct an external information search. One key determinant of the type of search conducted is believed to be tourists' prior product knowledge. Consumers implicitly or explicitly determine the perceived costs and benefits associated with different external search strategies, and trade these factors off to make a final information strategy selection.

The key potential benefits considered by tourists are the ability of external search information to reduce uncertainty and perceived risk and to increase the likelihood of travel satisfaction. The associated costs, which vary with individual circumstances, include time, financial costs and effort expended. The proposed inverse relationship between traded costs and benefits, therefore, suggests that in the presence of low-perceived search cost, such as that potentially offered by the Internet, tourists are likely to extend their search behaviour, and vice versa (Fig. 2.4).

The growing significance of the Internet has made it an important information resource for tourists. The different decision styles orientate their search, either on price, destination, accommodation or activities, and are highly predefined or recommendation-oriented. The detail of information requested also varies among different segments of tourists.

Recommendations are also an important type of information considered by tourists during the decision-making process. Some researches have pointed out that rather than simply consulting others for opinions and recommendations, consumers (read "tourists") often relinquish control of all or part

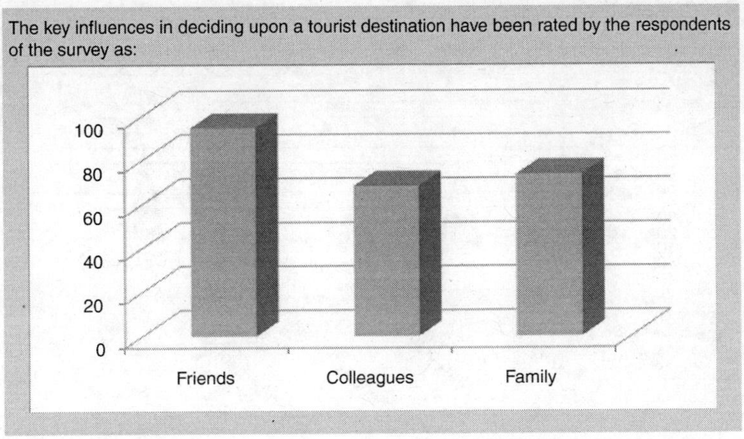

Fig. 2.4: Key Influences

of the decision-making process to external experts, agents or surrogates. Travel agents represent a key influence in the tourism marketing industry. In addition to helping travellers in booking tickets and vouchers, travel agents influence tourism planning decisions and outcomes.

Information-Search Process. The information-search process involves the evaluation of alternatives, purchase decision, consumption and post-purchase behaviour. The relatedness of numerous factors on both the information-search processes conducted and the overall destination-purchase process is depicted in Figs. 2.5 and 2.6.

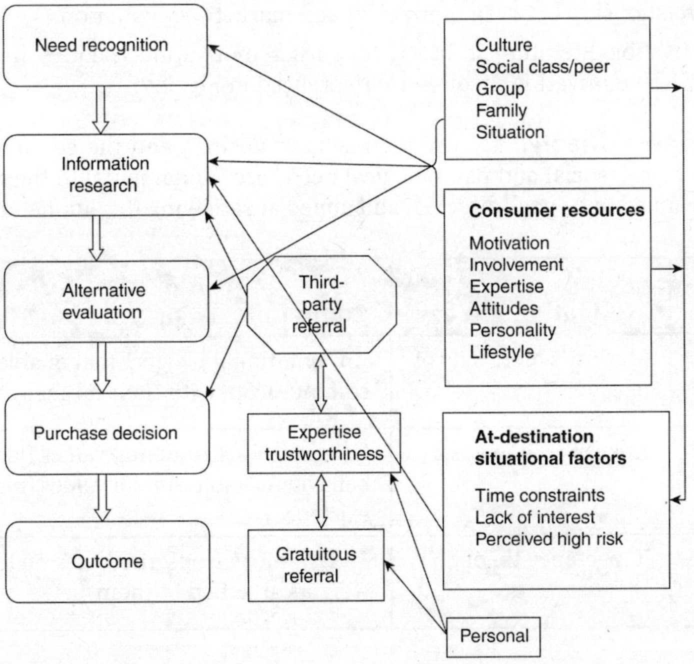

Fig. 2.5: Information Search Model

A group interacting with the tourists in India had interesting results to share in this regard. A summary of the most significant information sources is depicted here.

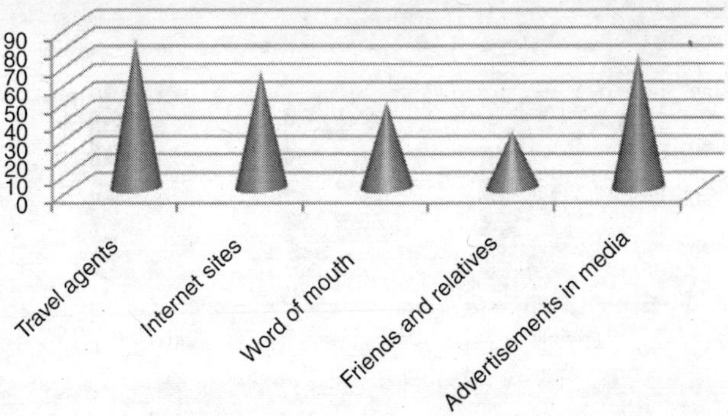

Fig. 2.6: Information Sources for Tourists

MOTIVATORS AND DETERRENTS FOR TOURIST CONSUMERS

Motivators

Motivation is considered a critical variable in the tourist decision-making process. Measures of motivation are often used as one of the segmentation bases for tourists and other consumer markets, thereby indicating a strong relationship between motivation and market segmentation.

The tourist-motivation literature is based on earlier motivation theories from other consumer behaviour literature. The motivation theories are referenced in Fig. 2.7.

Need-Based (Maslow's Theory). Satisfying needs or desires, and the equilibrium that is sought from meeting the physical, social and psychological needs are fundamental to the motivation theories. Pleasure travel is assumed to be goal-directed, and aimed at satisfying the "unmet needs."

Basis of Segmentation	Motivation Theory	Comments
Need-based	Maslow's hierarchy of needs	An "emotional trigger" that enables marketers to communicate with their target audiences
Values-based	Rokeach value theory	Consists of instrumental values (ideal modes of behaviour) and terminal values (ideal end-states of existence)
Valence of attributes	Expectancy theory	Judges the various attributes on the basis of relative weights attached to them

Fig. 2.7: Motivators

Maslow's theory is often subjected to hierarchy-related criticism, as there is no way to measure precisely how satisfied one need is before the next higher need becomes operative.

Yet, Maslow's need hierarchy has been called an "emotional trigger" that enables marketers to communicate with their target audiences on a personal level–one that goes beyond product benefits.

Values-Based (Rokeach Theory). The Rokeach Value Survey (1968) consists of 18 instrumental values (ideal modes of behaviour) and 18 terminal values (ideal end states of existence). The values approach is extremely helpful in developing advertising messages for appealing to the intrinsic motivations of the target customers.

The various criteria are:

- Attribute-based (e.g., using attributes or features of a destination or tourism service)
- Psychology-based (e.g., grouping customers on the basis of the importance they attach to a combination of sensory, rational and emotional benefits expected from the product or service)
- A very significant issue encountered in benefit-segmentation research is the timing of the collection of benefit-statement ratings from the tourists. Whereas some inputs are sought prior to visitor's departure, other inputs are sought after the benefits have been realized (that is, after the trip is completed or based on the past trip)

Work Motivation (Expectancy Theory). This has been suggested by Witt and Wright (1992). The various factors are:

- Emotional aspects of a tourist's motivation–the needs that instigate the desire to travel in the first place
- Cognitive aspect–the decision making involved in choosing what to do on holiday and, if so, where
- Attractiveness (valence) of holiday attributes, relative preference of different holidays, influencing factors of knowledge of holiday-destination characteristics, limiting factors such as cost, preferences of others and expectations

All of these are further influenced by a variety of sources including brochures, guidebooks and experience of other people, and also by the individual's own experience of previous holidays of the same or a similar type; hence, the feedback loops are built into the model. All of these also result in a theoretical choice of holiday which acknowledges the importance of both push and pull factors (Fig. 2.8).

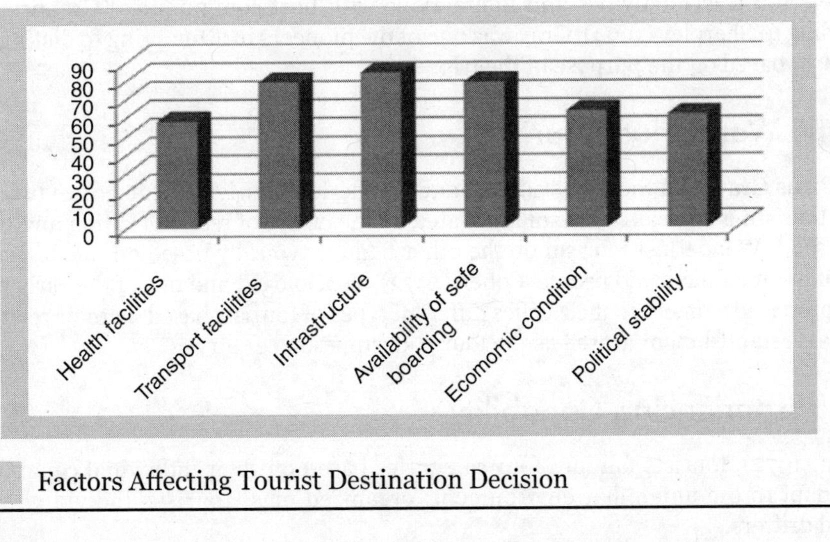

Fig. 2.8: Factors Affecting Tourist Destination Decision

A survey conducted brought to light the significant deterring factors for tourists visiting India. The results are summarized here.

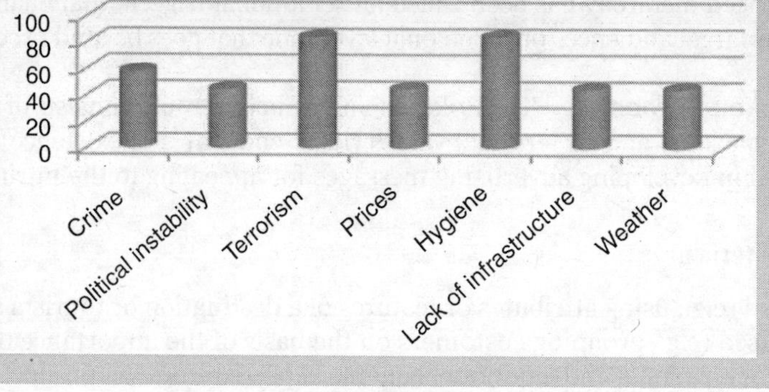

Fig. 2.9: Deterrents for Tourists' Destination Decision

Deterrents

The sensitivity of tourists to a multitude of factors acts as a deterrent to a robust tourism environment. Although the factors are very specific to the geographical, cultural and psychological factors, the most frequently observed deterrents are: adverse climatic conditions, political instability, language barriers, terrorism, unfavourable health and hygiene conditions, difficulty in getting visa for international tourists, and lack of infrastructure, transport network, adequate connectivity in terms of telecommunication, and appropriate and safe boarding facilities(Fig. 2.9).

TOURISM CONSUMER BEHAVIOUR — TYPOLOGIES

Typologies of tourism roles have been defined in various ways (Cohen 1979). Some of the typologies of tourists focus on tourist behaviour, remaining others take a more psychological approach (Sharpley, 1994). The behavioural typology approach underlines distinctive patterns of tourist behaviour with regard to preferred travel activities and interactions with host communities (Graburn, 1977; Smith, 1977). According to Sharpley (1994), Gray was one of the pioneers in attempting to distinguish different types of tourism based on the purpose of the trip.

Sunlust and Wanderlust Tourism

In the early 1970s Gray used the terms sunlust and wanderlust tourism to categorize two types of tourism. Sunlust tourism is basically tourism motivated by the desire of rest, relaxation and the three S's — sun, sea and sand. Wanderlust tourism on the other hand is typically based on the desire to travel and experience different cultures and people. Cohen (1972), a sociologist and one of the early researchers on this subject, proposed a theory that classifies different types of tourists based on their relationship to the tourist business establishment as well as the tourist destination country.

Individual-Experiencing Capability

As per Cohen (1972), tourists fall into four categories based on their individual capabilities to experience and adapt to the unfamiliar environment: organized mass tourists, individual mass tourists, explorers and drifters.

- Organized mass tourists prefer to stay in familiar environment as far as possible. Thus, well-organized and well-planned packaged tours are their top priority.
- Individual mass tourists are similar to organized mass tourists except the fact that a small percentage of personal freedom or decision making is maintained by this category of tourists.
- Explorers do not tread the beaten path as far as possible. Another important aspect of explorers is that they associate with the people of the visited destination, at the same time a percentage of basic routine based on their comfort level is maintained.
- Drifters are complete wanderers and do not stress on familiarity at all. Such tourists intend to venture away from their accustomed ways of life as far as possible, so that they can immerse completely in the culture of the host destination.

Smith (1977) suggested typology of tourism based on tourist behaviour. His classification included ethnic, cultural, historic, environmental and recreational tourists. Ethnic tourism includes visiting one's native place and experiencing customs and shopping for local products. Cultural tourism is based on people's thirst for vanishing lifestyles like folklore performances, handmade crafts and homespun fabrics. Historic tourism aims to venture most into monuments and ruins that represent the past glories. Environmental tourism primarily is geographic in nature. Such tourists enjoy indigenous food and culture as well as customs. Recreational tourism attracts tourists interested more into relaxations in the company of nature.

Shopping and Tourism

Earlier sun, sea and sand were the three S's of tourism. However, of late shopping has become the most important S of tourism. Shopping as a tourist activity has prospered in various tourism markets. Although surveys on travel motivations have rarely indicated the intention to shop as a primary motive, shopping has emerged as the most universal element in tourist experiences (Jansen-Verbeke, 1991; Kent, Shock & Snow, 1983). According to the Tourism Works for America 1998 Report (Travel Industry Association of America, 1998), shopping was ranked among the most popular leisure activities among US resident travelers as overseas travelers to the US.

Tourists not only enjoy spending considerable time on shopping, they are spending approximately one third of their total tourism expenditures on shopping (Gratton & Taylor, 1987; Littrell, Baizerman, Kean, Gahring, Niemeyer, Reilly & Stout, 1994). Regarding the consumer products most sought after by tourists, textile crafts and apparel items constitute a substantial portion (Anderon, 1993; Littrell, 1996). Each tourist has an attitude towards acquiring different possessions.

Possessions as per different researches are a major contributor to and reflection of one's identity (Belk, 1988, Csikszentmihalyi & Rochberg-Halton, 1981). Possessions may also serve as a means of storing the memories and feeling from one's past experiences (Belk, 1988). Tourists are influenced by their past travel experiences regarding shopping experiences for crafts. Tourists may purchase crafts directly from artisans among local communities while travelling, or they can shop from the craft shops (Kein & Littrell, 1992)

Unsung Tourist Destination: Ganapatipule

Ganapatipule is a small village, known for its serene, sedate and clean beach. Located on the western coast of India, with sparkling blue waters, endless stretches of golden sand and swaying palms, the pristine land of Ganapatipule is one of Maharashtra's virgin beaches. Enclosed in the greenery of this land lies the 4,000 years old Swayambhu Ganapati temple, from which the place derives its name. (Swayambhu means "self-made"; this is a temple of the self-originated idol Ganapati.) This temple is flooded with thousands of devotees and tourists every year. Thus, the village got its name Ganapatipule: Ganapati, the lord of the "ganas," or army, and "pule," which means "sand dunes."

Unsung Tourist Destination: *(Continued)*

Swayambhu Temple

Attractions at Ganapatipule

The land is endowed with various tourist attractions. Situated a kilometre away from Ganapatipule is Malgund village, the birthplace of the famous Marathi poet Keshavsoot. The main attraction at Malgund is the renovated house of the poet; it now serves as a students' hostel. Another attraction is the the Keshavsoot Smarak, constructed by the Marathi Literature Society in memory of this great poet.

The ancient Swayambhu temple is very unique because of the fact that the deity faces the west (to guard the western gates according to local legends), unlike other deities in Indian temples who face the east. This temple is situated at the base of a hill, and all the pilgrims walk around the hill as a mark of respect. The Jaigad Fort, which is located around 35 km from Ganapatipule, is on a cliff just at the entrance of the Sangameshwar River. It has a beautiful beach and offers a breathtaking view of the sea.

South of Ganapatipule lies Ratnagiri, the birthplace of freedom fighter Bal Gangadhar Tilak. Velneshwar, situated about 170 km from Ratnagiri, is an ideal destination for water sports as the beach is free of rocks.

How to Reach Ganapatipule

Ganapatipule relies on the airport and railway facilities at Ratnagiri, about 50 km away from Ganapatipule. The land is well connected by frequently available bus services. Tourists can also drive down to Ganapatipule from Mumbai, Pune, Kolhapur or Belgaum.

- **By rail:** There is no railway station at Ganapatipule. One has to get down either at the Ratnagiri station or at Karbude. All the express and local trains stop at Ratnagiri. Karbude is a small village and only passenger trains stop there.
- **By road:** While moving towards Ratnagiri, on Mumbai Goa National Highway No. 17 (NH 17), after Sangameshwar is a small village called Nivali. From Nivali, one has to take a right turn for Ganapatipule (32 km). Alternatively, one can continue on NH 17 till Hathkhamba (Nivali-Hathkhamba: 4 km), and then take a right turn to go to Ganapatipule.

Accommodation and Food

Tourists can stay at the Maharashtra Tourism Development Corporation (MTDC) resort situated on the beach. There are also a number of economy hotels available. Konkani houses are the most sought-after lodging. They are mostly privately owned and come at a premium. Vegetarian food is easily available. Since Ganapatipule is a pilgrim centre, a tourist has to venture to the outskirts for non-vegetarian food.

Shopping

Ganapatipule offers a wide range of fruits produced using horticulture and a variety of local preparations. The specialities include ambapoli and phanspoli – thin pancakes made of dried and crushed mango and jackfruit. Ganapatipule is also famous for its crop of mangoes, especially during the summers.

Best Time to Visit

The climate in Ganapatipule is typically coastal with warm and humid atmosphere. The summer is hot with maximum temperature touching 38°C. Rainfall is quite frequent. Though winter is the touristy time to get to most of the beaches in India, Ganapatipule can be spectacular during and just after the monsoons.

Tourist Experience — Trip to Vaishno Devi and Varanasi

Experiences: Good and Bad as Tourist

Many students from European countries come to India on student-exchange programmes. IIM Lucknow is one destination that has become very popular among them. During their stay, these students visit various tourist locations in India. One thing that has impressed them the most is the warm nature and hospitality of Indians. Here, we narrate some of the delightful experiences that these students had while travelling in India.

Trip to Vaishno Devi—Celebrating Diwali, the Festival of Lights

Nuria and Isabel, both from Spain, were studying at IIM Lucknow on the exchange programme and visited Vaishno Devi during their term break. In their words, "It was a memorable experience." For them, visiting the Vaishno Devi temple after walking for hours and finally going through the tunnel was a very novel experience. But the best moment of their trip was celebrating Diwali, on their way to Jammu, with their driver's family. They were overwhelmed by the gesture and hospitality of the driver. Celebrating Diwali is one thing that has been entrenched in their memories forever. This experience of theirs epitomizes Incredible India – Diwali celebration by Europeans in the house of a Muslim Indian.

"Older than history, older than tradition, older even than legend. And looks twice as old as all of them put together." – Mark Twain

Trip to Varanasi

The exchange students of IIM Lucknow set out on a journey to visit the ancient religious city of Varanasi. While the tradition and history of this ancient city beckoned them, there were some unpleasant experiences as well. The city and its religious embodiment are really captivating; a boat ride in the calm waters is one of the precious memories Nuria and her friends have ofthe place. However, the swarm of humanity on thestreets did not seem to be very accommodative tothem. They were charged exorbitant rates duringshopping. As said by Vivian, "The rickshaw pullers and the locals were not very warm, instead they treated us with suspicion." So, what could have been a great journey left some bitter memoriesbecause of improper hospitality.

SUMMARY

- The behaviour sequence model uses a grid format to identify the target audience's decision. The horizontal information enumerates the WHAT of the decision, specifically the major decision stages preceding, including and following purchase. The vertical information, on the other hand, enumerates the data inputs relating to the following factors: WHO – the decision participants and decision roles, WHERE – the locations of decision stages, WHEN – the time and timing of each stage and HOW – a capsule description of how each stage is accomplished.
- Motivation is considered a critical variable in the tourist decision-making process. Measures of motivation are often used as one of the segmentation bases for tourist and other consumer markets, thereby indicating a strong relationship between motivation and market segmentation. The motivation theories considered for detailed analysis are: need based, values based and valence of attributes based.
- The sensitivity of tourists to certain factors acts as a deterrent to robust tourism environment. Although the factors are very specific to the geography, culture and the psychological factors, the most frequently observed deterrents are: adverse climatic conditions, political instability, language barriers, terrorism, unfavourable health and hygiene conditions, difficulty in getting visa for international tourists and lack of infrastructure, transport network, adequate connectivity in terms of telecommunication, and appropriate and safe boarding facilities.
- Tourist consumer behaviour can be classified on the basis of different variables.
- The three S's of tourism are sun, sea and sand. Of late shopping has become the fourth but the most importants.
- As per Cohen (1972) tourists fall into four categories based on their individual capabilities to experience and adapt to the unfamiliar environment: organized mass tourists, individual mass tourists, explorers and drifters.
- Tourists not only enjoy spending considerable time on shopping, they are spending approximately one third of their total tourism expenditures on shopping.

FIELD EXERCISES

1. Make a plan of destinations visit with your family members and try to analyse their decision-making process.
2. Make a report after analysing the various factors affecting the consumer behaviour of foreign tourists visiting India.

REFERENCES

Anderson, L.F. (1993), Lowa Women as Tourists and Consumers of Souvenirs. Unpublished doctoral dissertation, Lowa State University, Ames

Field, Arthur M. (1999), "The College Student Market Segment: A Comparative Study of Travel Behaviors of International and Domestic Students at a Southeastern University," *Journal of Travel Research*, Vol. 37, No. 4, pp. 375–381.

Belk, R.W. (1998), "Possessions and the Extended Self," *Journal of Consumer Research*, Vol. 15, pp. 139–168.

Bigné, J.E., Sanchez, M.I., Sanchez, J. (2001), "Tourism Image, Evaluation Variables and After Purchase Behavior: Inter-relationship", *Tourism Management*, Vol. 22, pp. 607–616.

Cohen, E. (1972), "Toward a Sociology of International Tourism," *Social Research*, Vol. 39, pp. 164–182

Cohen, E. (1979), "A Phenomenology of Tourist Experiences, Sociology," Vol. 13, pp. 179–201.

Csikszentmihalyi, M. and E. Rochberg-Halton, (1981), *The Meaning of Things: Domestic Symbols and the Self*, Cambridge: Cambridge University Press.

Ioannides, Dimitri and Keith Debbage (1997), "Post-Fordism and Flexibility: The Travel Industry Polyglot," *Tourism Management*, Vol.18, No. 4, pp. 229–241.

Gamble, Paul, Chalder Melanie and Stone Merlin (2001), "Customer Knowledge Management in the Travel Industry," *Journal of Vacation Marketing*, Vol. 7, No.1, pp. 83–91

Gnoth, J. (1997), "Tourism Motivation and Expectation Formation," *Annals of Tourism Research*, Vol. 24, No. 2, pp. 283–304.

Goldsmith, Ronald E. and Litvin Stephen W. (1999), "Heavy Users of Travel Agents: A Segmentation Analysis of Vacation Travelers," *Journal of Travel Research*, Vol. 38, No. 2, pp. 127–133.

Graburn, N.H.H. (1977), "Tourism: The Sacred Journey," in V. Smith (ed.), *Hosts and Guests: The Anthropology of Tourism*, pp. 17–31, Philadelphia: University of Pennsylvania Press.

Gratton, C. and P. Taylor, (1987 March), "Leisure and Shopping," *Leisure Management*, pp. 29–30.

Jansen-Verbeke, M. (1991), "Leisure Shopping: A Magic Concept for the Tourism Industry?" *Tourism Management*, Vol.12, No.2, pp. 9–14

Kay Pandora (2003), Consumer Motivation in a Tourism Context: Continuing the Work of Maslow, Rokeach, Vroom, Deci, Haley and Other, ANZMAC 2003 Conference Proceedings, Adelaide, 1–3 December 2003, pp. 600–614.

Kent, W.E., Shock, P.J. and Snow, R.E. (1983), "Shopping: Tourism's Unsung hero (in)," *Journal of Travel Research*, Vol.38, pp 153–162.

Leferink Jude (2008) Information Search Strategies Conducted by Overseas Tourists Visiting New Zealand, *Otago Marketing Review*, Issue 1.

Littrel, M.A. (1996), Shopping Experiences and Marketing of Culture to Tourists, Paper presented at the Conference on Tourism and Culture: Toward the 21st Century Northumberland, United Kingdom.

Littrel, M.A., S. Baizermn, R. Kean, S. Gahring, S. Niemeyer, R. Reilly, and J. Stout, (1994), "Souvenirs and Tourism Styles," *Journal of Travel Research*, Vol.33, No.1, pp. 3–11.

Market Segmentation in Tourism (Discussion Paper, December 2002), Vision Link Consulting, Web: www.taskbc.bc.ca/documents/SegmentationDiscussionPaper_000.pdf.

Rossiter, R.J. and L. Percy (1996), *Advertising Communication and Promotion Management*, McGraw Hill-International Editions.

Sharpley, R. (1994), *Tourism, Tourists and Society*, Society House, England: ELM.

Sirakaya, E. and A. Woodside (2005), "Building and Testing Theories of Decision Making by Travelers," *Tourism Management*, Vol.26, No. 6, pp. 815–832.

Smith, V.L. (1977), "Introduction," In V. Smith (ed.), *Hosts and Guests: The Anthropology of Tourism*, pp.1–14, Philadelphia: University of Pennsylvania Press.

Swarbrooke, John and Horner Susan (2006), *Consumer Behaviour in Tourism* (Second Edition), Butterworth-Heinemann.

Travel Industry Association of America (1998a). Record year for Travel and Tourism Industry, Web: http://www.tia.org/press/122298twfar.stm.

Travel Industry Association of America (1998b).Tourism Works for America 1998 Report: Industry Highlight, Web: http://www.tia.org/pubs/twfar98.stm.

Leaning Tower of Pisa

CHAPTER 3

Customer Value, Loyalty and Satisfaction

ABOUT THE DESTINATION

The freestanding bell tower of the cathedral of Pisa, a physicist's delight, began leaning soon after the onset of construction due to a poorly laid foundation and loose substrate that has allowed the foundation to shift direction.

OBJECTIVES

- To identify the parameters that govern customer-perceived value in terms of benefits and cost
- To analyse the factors critical in providing customer value proposition in tourism and offer solution to those
- To provide an exhaustive study on customer relationship management in tourism
- To develop marketing strategies to attract and retain customers
- To present an unsung tourist destination and narrate real-life tourist experiences

INTRODUCTION

Tourism is all about experiences and taking back memories. Each tourist destination aspires to make tourists so satisfied and happy that not only do they decide to come back again but also motivate others to visit that destination.

Creating loyal tourists is at the heart of every tourism destination. The term "tourist loyalty" is used to describe the behaviour of repeat tourists and those who give good ratings, reviews or testimonials. Some tourists do a great service to a particular company by offering favourable word-of-mouth publicity regarding a product, telling friends and family, thus adding them to the number of loyal tourists. However, a tourist's loyalty includes much more. It is a process, a programme or a group of programmes geared towards keeping clients happy, so that they provide more business.

Customer-perceived value (CPV) is the difference between a prospective customer's evaluation of all the benefits and costs of an offering, and the perceived alternatives.

Customer satisfaction is directly related to the performance of products and services supplied by a specific company in terms of customer expectation. In today's competitive market place where different brands are competing for share in the market, customer satisfaction is one of the key differentiators. It is also a key result area of business strategy.

Let us explore how these three concepts fit in with tourism. As we move along in this chapter, we will look at the three aspects of customer value, loyalty and satisfaction from the perspective of tourism. We will see how they differ for tourism as compared to products and other services.

CUSTOMER-PERCEIVED VALUE

The perceived value is presented by Zeithaml (1988) as "the consumer's overall assessment of the utility of a product based on what is received and what is given." Most researches view costs in terms of a monetary price to be paid. However, other costs such as time, cognitive activity and behavioural effort should be included when considering what customers have to give up in order to get something.

There are several popular theoretical frameworks for customer value.

The Value Hierarchy Model

This model was given by Woodruff and Gardial (1996). This model suggests that

1. Customer value must be seen as different depending on whether a product or a service is valued for contributing to a means-to-an-end value, or if the value is based on the pure possession of the product or the service.
2. Customer value is a trade-off between positive and negative consequences of using a product or a service.
3. Customer value is highly dependent on the "use" situation.

The value hierarchy model provides levels. At attribute level, which is the lowest level, customers are concerned with defining the product in terms of its attributes. At consequence level, customers define what the product can do for them. At the top of the hierarchy, desired end states are customers' core values, purposes and goals. These desired end states are served by the product or the service.

This model presents a utilitarian view on customer value and the businesses providing products or services with attributes that are believed to satisfy needs and wants of a customer.

The Typology of Consumer Value

The typology of the consumer value model was given by Holbrook in 1999. This typology includes the means-to-an-end perspective but also takes into account the intrinsic value of the consumption of a product or a service in itself. As such, it offers a more holistic view of perceived customer value.

The eight different types of value presented in the typology are:

1. Efficiency
2. Excellence
3. Status
4. Esteem
5. Play
6. Aesthetics
7. Ethics
8. Spirituality

Sheth, Newman and Gross Model

This model identifies the value dimensions and categorizes them in order to distinguish between the functional dimensions and the socio-psychological dimensions.

The model suggests that four value categories (as defined in the following) are discrete and provides an appropriate interpretation of people's views. The four value categories are functional, emotional, social and epistonic values.

1. **Functional value:** It is defined as the perceived utility acquired from an alternative's capacity for functional, utilitarian or physical performance. The attributes include the quality of the tour, the price of the tour, the tour vehicle and sightseeing in the natural environment.

2. **Emotional value:** It is defined as the ability of the product or the service to arouse feelings or affective states. Feelings such as being happy and feeling good are included.
3. **Social value:** It is defined as the perceived utility acquired from an alternative's association with one or more specific social groups.
4. **Epistemic value:** It is defined as the perceived utility acquired when the product arouses curiosity, provides novelty and/or satisfies a desire for knowledge. The novelty has been shown to be a major satisfaction component for many tourists.

CPV, as already stated, is the difference between prospective customers' evaluation of all the benefits and costs of an offering, and the perceived alternatives. It is dependent on what they get and give for the offering.

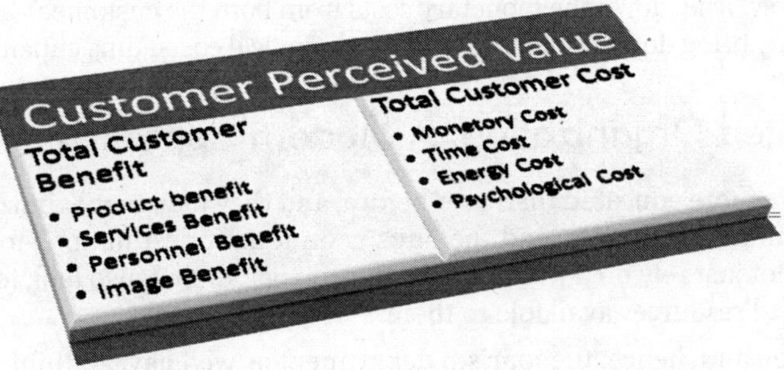

Source: Modified from *Marketing Management* by Kotler, Keller, Koshy and Jha.

Customer Benefit

Customer benefit is the perceived monetary value of the bundle of economic, psychological and functional benefits that a customer expects from a given market offering because of the products, services, personnel and images involved. This is an area where any tourism board should look to maximize.

Given India's poor infrastructure, the product benefit offers a lot of scope for improvement. Many such initiatives are being undertaken at state levels by state governments, though there needs to be a more comprehensive effort at the national level for the same.

India has a good image as far as the services industry goes, and, hence, one should try and leverage the same into the tourism industry and maximize the benefits that can be drawn out of this.

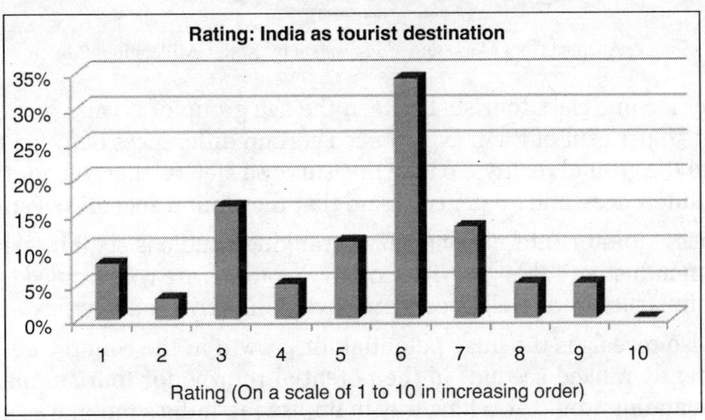

Source: Author's survey.

An attempt to collect people's perception of the tourism environment in India was done by asking a survey group to rate India on an increasing rating scale of 1 to 10. The result showed that the majority rated India at a 6, a value just above the average standard.

Customer Cost

It is the perceived bundle of costs that customers expect to incur in evaluating, obtaining, using and disposing of the given market offerings including monetary, time, energy and psychological costs. The tourism board should look to offer a complete end-to-end package to ensure that all costs are minimized. The survey results clearly show a demand for such packages, since the results point to a majority of respondents falling in the "less than INR 50,000 for a one-week trip" category.

This would effectively bring down the monetary costs from both the customer's and the industry's end. It would also significantly bring down the energy and psychological costs, thus enhancing the value greatly.

Customer-Oriented Organization: A Modern Approach

Customers (tourists) are more educated than ever before, and they look to maximize value. Increasingly, they are now making informed choices, and the onus is on tourist destinations to maximize values for them. The tourists do not just rely on a word-of-mouth propaganda but also look for information within the bounds of the limited resources available to them.

A tourist destination and, hence, the tourism department as well have to think and act differently to be able to position themselves the best they can to derive and generate the maximum value for a tourist. As in the modern customer-oriented chart, the tourism industry, too, has to place the customer at the top of the pyramid.

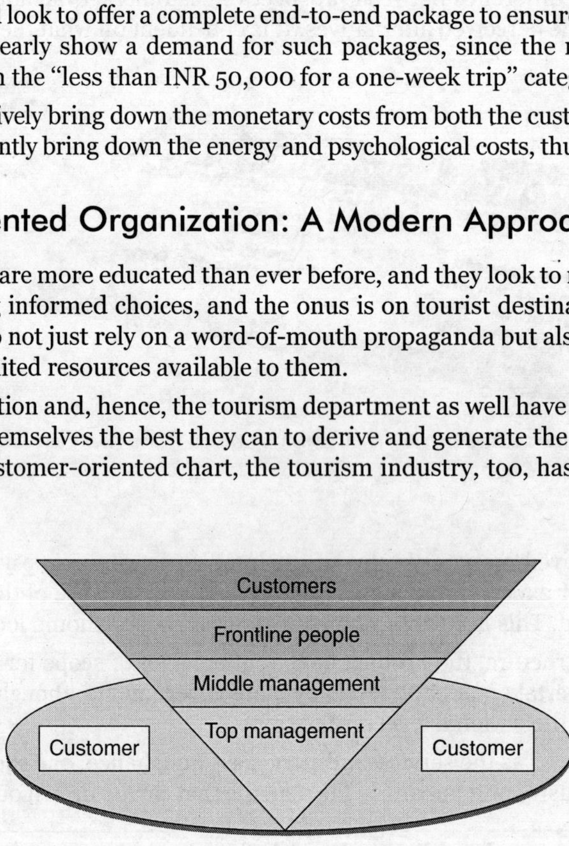

Source: Adapted from *Marketing Management* by Kotler, Millennium Edition.

A survey of upper income class tourists between the age group of 20 and 30 years was conducted, and it was found that 59 per cent of them experienced certain differences between the factual information about a place and the ground reality. To take this survey a step further, the tourists were asked how they reacted to such differences, and 78 per cent said that they found such discoveries interesting.

As per the Business Monitor International (BMI) rankings, India is sixth in Asia in the new ratings on CPV in the tourism industry (Table 3.1). The country's ratings are constrained by a relatively poorly developed tourism infrastructure as well as concerns over long-term country risk.

What the table also reveals is the huge potential for growth in the country. India is ranked higher than Singapore (currently ranked second) in the potential returns for tourism market. Right strategy and effective implementation would go a long way in improving India's ranking as a tourist destination. During the course of the rest of the chapter and the book, we try and explore various options available to do the same.

Table 3.1 Asian Tourist Destination Rankings

	Potential Returns				
Country	Tourism Market	Country Structure	Limits	Tourism Rating	Regional Ranking
Hong Kong	73	58	67.8	72	1
Singapore	67	57	63.1	69	2
Malaysia	67	61	64.8	67	3
Thailand	77	69	*73.8*	61	4
China	63	80	*69.0*	59	5
India	**70**	**68**	***69.3***	**57**	**6=**
Indonesia	60	65	*61.9*	57	6=
Vietnam	47	70	*54.7*	57	6=
Sri Lanka	27	67	*40.9*	44	9

Source: BMI—Scores out of 100.

CUSTOMER VALUE PROPOSITION

The essence of customers' real value proposition lies in the customers' resulting experience. But what is a resulting experience? It includes one or a series of related physical or mental events that happen in the life of the customer. The customers can perceive this experience as superior, inferior or equal to some earlier experience, and this will determine the value they perceive of it.

When asked about what must be included in one's holiday tourism plan, most people assigned higher importance to safety compared to the beauty and significance of the places.

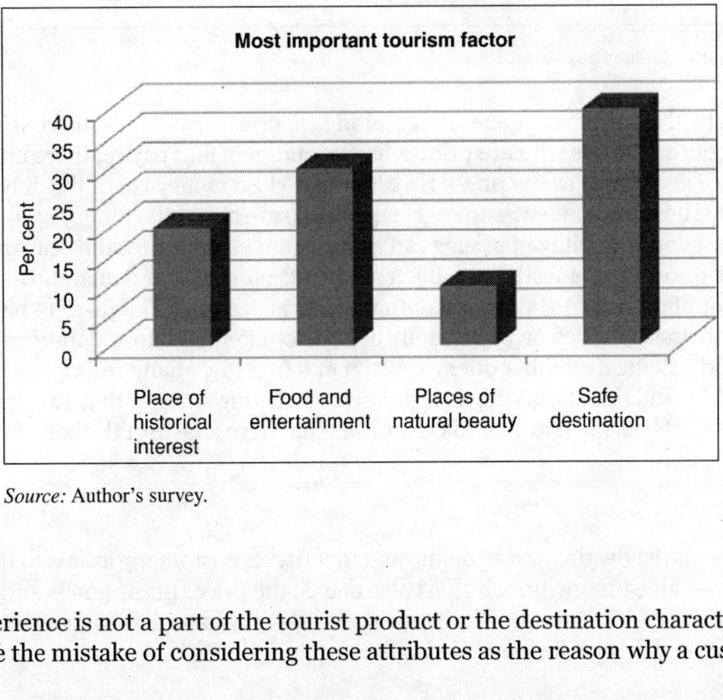

Source: Author's survey.

Problems

The resulting experience is not a part of the tourist product or the destination characteristics. Organizations usually make the mistake of considering these attributes as the reason why a customer should buy their products.

These customer experiences can be either directly observable or invisible. An experience about tangible changes is measurable. However the same cannot be claimed about intangible aspects. What about the emotional joy and the mental pleasure the customer obtains out of your service? These are all not directly observable. The resulting experiences can be rational or otherwise. The value of experiences may be driven by the emotions. Tourists coming to the same destination again show an emotional attachment and may prefer this destination to a better experiential destination. In doing so, they are not being irrational. They just have a different priority to determine their pleasure. Similarly, the customer value of tourists may come from different stages of their experiences. Most pleasures can come from the first step of their experiences, and this may be followed by incremental pleasures coming from each subsequent stage of improvement. For example, getting aboard a luxury liner thrills a traveller the most. The beauty of the liner, the treatment from the crew and the fun and amusement aboard are noticed later, but have their share of enriching the total customer experience and, hence, the end value that the customer attaches to this experience of travelling on a liner.

The survey asked respondents why they would want to revisit a particular destination. The replies were attributed to a number of factors.

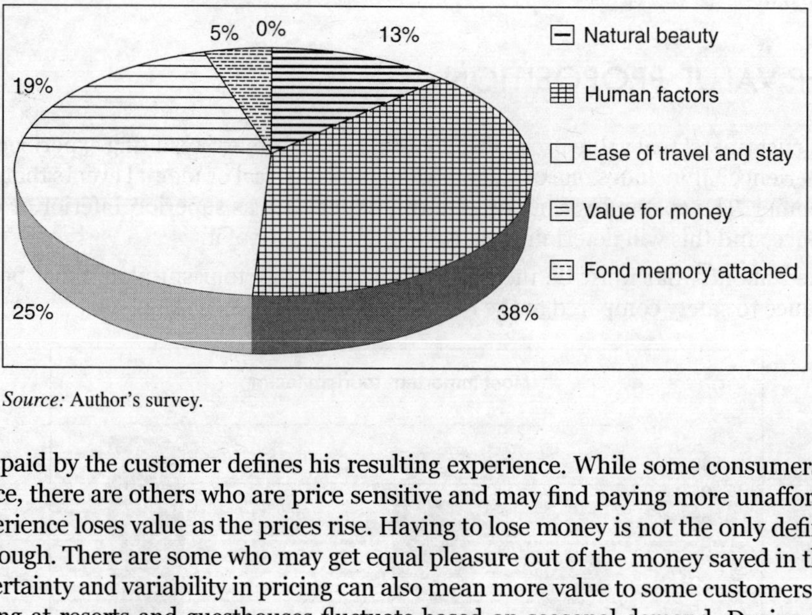

Source: Author's survey.

The price paid by the customer defines his resulting experience. While some consumers prefer better product to price, there are others who are price sensitive and may find paying more unaffordable. For the latter, the experience loses value as the prices rise. Having to lose money is not the only defining factor for a customer, though. There are some who may get equal pleasure out of the money saved in the experience. Reducing uncertainty and variability in pricing can also mean more value to some customers. For example, prices of staying at resorts and guesthouses fluctuate based on seasonal demand. During the peak periods tourists may not find place to stay in hill stations/resorts despite willingness to pay high tariffs. Club Mahindra, among others, identified an opportunity here. They attempted to add more permanent members to their club of resorts. Being a member offers a customer a free stay at any resort, any time of the year, all at a fixed membership. And this starts with an aggressive marketing strategy that attempts to send potential customers to their resorts during non-peak days and let them have a taste of the benefits offered.

Solutions

It is important for a tourist destination to define and identify its customers as it is to them that the destination will deliver its value proposition. It must also decide the prices of the goods and services it will sell to those customers. The prices, along with the service or the product quality, determine the end experience of the customer and, hence, his perceived value.

A destination's business is the only means of delivering the value proposition. There is a one-to-one correspondence between the business and the value proposition delivered. Multiple destinations of a country cannot be said to have a single value proposition. Each business must deliver its own value proposition. To deliver a value proposition means to let a customer feel, or be aware of, the experience in that proposition. This consists of two functions – "providing" and "communicating."

Providing refers to the case where the customer buys products or services and actually perceives the benefits and the prices associated with the proposition. Communicating means that the customer is told that the proposition will have those experiences.

Every organization that sells something automatically delivers a de facto value proposition. When the business is planning or developing a new product, without actually selling anything, there is no proposition being offered. But as soon as there is something offered to sell, the value proposition comes along. Now, a superior value proposition that can be actually delivered can always win more customers.

The solution to delivering a value proposition involves identifying answers to the following questions:

- Who are my customers?
- What is being bought and how is it consumed?
- What are the alternatives available to my customers? Are there offerings available if I do not sell to them? Am I offering them the best alternative?
- What are the resultant experiences for them out of purchasing our services, especially when I am not the best alternative available to them?

CUSTOMER LOYALTY

As the tourism industry is reaching the maturity stage, the industry has turned its attention to building long-term relationships with its customers. Many authors have noted a recent shift in marketing philosophy, from a focus on single transactions to long-term customer–provider relationships. In a survey conducted on hundred people, including students and working professionals mostly between the age of 20 years and 30 years, it was seen that 56 per cent of them travelled more than once a year and around 25 per cent travelled once a year.

Customer loyalty is a crucial aim in relationship marketing, as it gets translated into consistent and devoted relationship with providers (Day 1969; Jacoby and Kyner 1973).

Attitude based framework has emerged as the only theoretical explanation for development of loyalty amongst researchers (Dick and Basu 1994; Oliver 1999; Pritchard, et al., 1999). This framework prescribes that customers develop positive, effective attachment and beliefs about a provider and experience increasing intentions to purchase preferentially from that provider. Patronizing behaviour towards the provider is, therefore, the result of attitude development.

It was not very surprising that most of them loved to go back to the same places again and again. This must be a manifestation of the loyalty, the people had come to develop for the places.

CUSTOMER SATISFACTION

Customer satisfaction is one of the most frequently examined topics in tourism because it plays an important role in the survival and future of any tourism product or service. It also significantly influences the choice of destination, the consumption of products and services and the decision to return to the same tourism destination.

Satisfaction is defined as a person's feelings of pleasure and disappointment that result from comparing a product's perceived performance to his or her expectations; it is a function of tourist perception.

The expectation disconfirmation model (Oliver 1980) suggests that consumers have prior expectations from a product before actually purchasing. After product consumption they have a positive disconfirmation if the actual performance is better than their expectations. This further suggests that consumers are highly satisfied and there is a high likelyhood of repeat purchase, however if actual performance is not up to expectations they are likely to have a negative disconfirmation. This indicates a dissatisfied consumer. Such consumers are likely to look for other product alternatives.

Consumer satisfaction has also been examined by Equity Theory of Oliver & Swang 1989. As per their research consumer satisfaction is the result of the relationship between the costs and the rewards/benefits which a consumer anticipates. Costs are associated with price, time and effort in making the purchase. If the rewards exceed the cost anticipation, consumers are likely to be satisfied (Heskett et al. 1997). Thus if travellers perceive that their travel experience value exceeds the costs incurred, they are likely to evaluate their travel experience as a likely one.

The norm theory (Latour and Peat 1979) is almost identical to the expectation-disconfirmation model approach. In norm theory, norms serve as reference points for evaluating the product. Satisfaction occurs in the event of confirmation of those norms. Comparing travellers' previous images of the destination (norms/reference points) and what they actually see, feel and achieve at the destination decides their level of satisfaction.

The cognitive-affective model of tourist satisfaction attempts to provide an examination of the role of image during this process. According to the more recent studies, a cognitive-affective approach is used in this model. This new and more complex view is useful in building a broad, theoretical perspective of consumer psychology in tourism. A combination of qualitative research and quantitative research is used in this model. Overall, the results provide a strong support for the following results: one, image has a significant role in the process of tourist satisfaction; two, expectations (assimilation effect) explain satisfaction to a greater extent than disconfirmation (contrast effect); three, cognitions contribute to the formation of emotions and, four, satisfaction is influenced by emotions during the stay.

The industry distinguishes various groups according to their purpose for travel and their place of origin – international, domestic, intrastate, interstate, etc.

Overall Satisfaction with Travel and Tourism Services Model

A survey was conducted to study tourist satisfaction in the relevant Indian scenario as per overall satisfaction measurement model. It reports that tourist satisfaction is the result of the relationship between tourists' expectations about the destination based on their previous images of the destination (norms/reference points), and their evaluation of the outcome of their experience at the destination area. Consumers develop these norms or reference points on the basis of not only their previous experiences with a product, but also their experiences with similar products. It also suggests that leisure satisfaction is determined by the perceived gap between the preferred and the actual leisure experiences as well as the perceptions of barriers (both internal and external) that prevent a consumer from achieving the desired experience. Tourists are likely to compare their experiences at a travel destination with other alternative destinations or places they have visited in the past. They are likely to use past experiences to form a norm (a reference point) to evaluate their experiences at the new destination and to determine whether their new experience was a satisfactory one.

The survey indicated that the most desired factors for comfort are sightseeing and food. The other prominent factors are travel and safety.

The survey also indicated that at least 67 per cent of the tourists had unpleasant experiences while touring in India. The survey attempted to identify the causes of discomfort. It was revealed that travel- and lodging-related problems were the major reasons for spoiling the touring experiences in India.

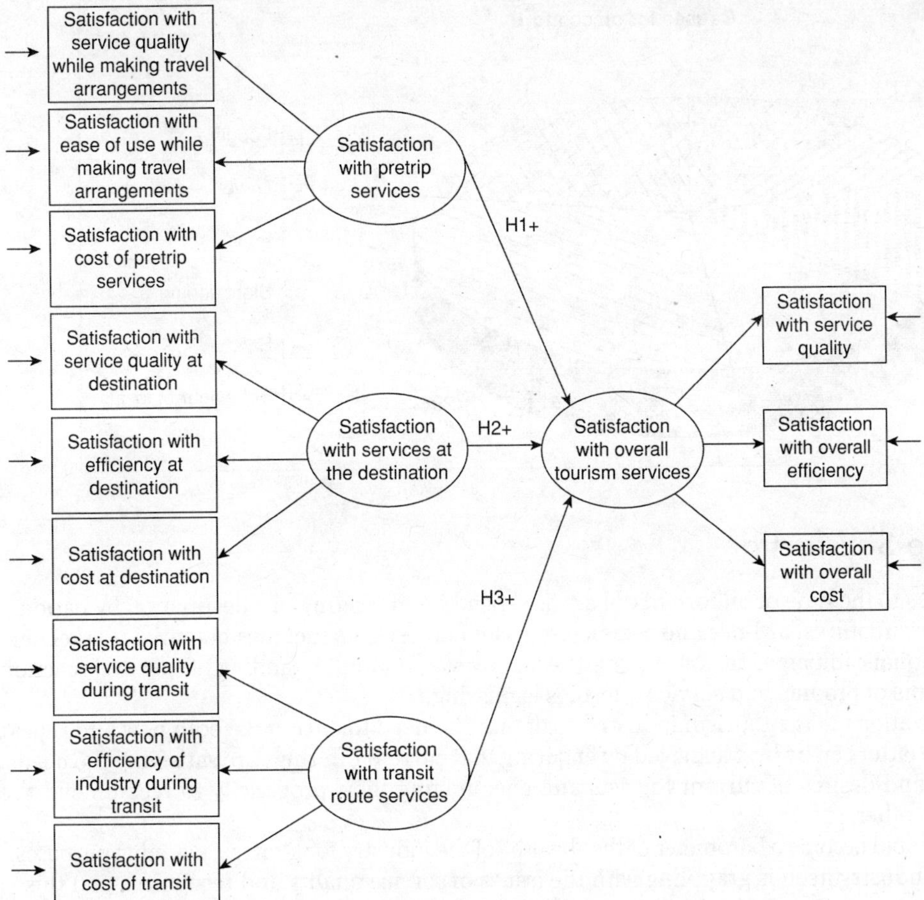

Source: A multifaceted analysis of tourism satisfaction – Janet D. Neal and Dogan Gursoy.

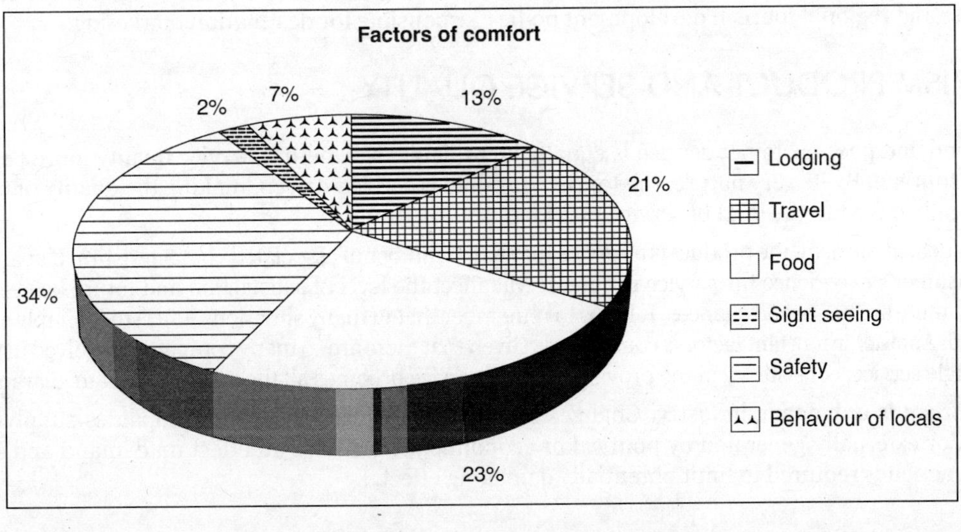

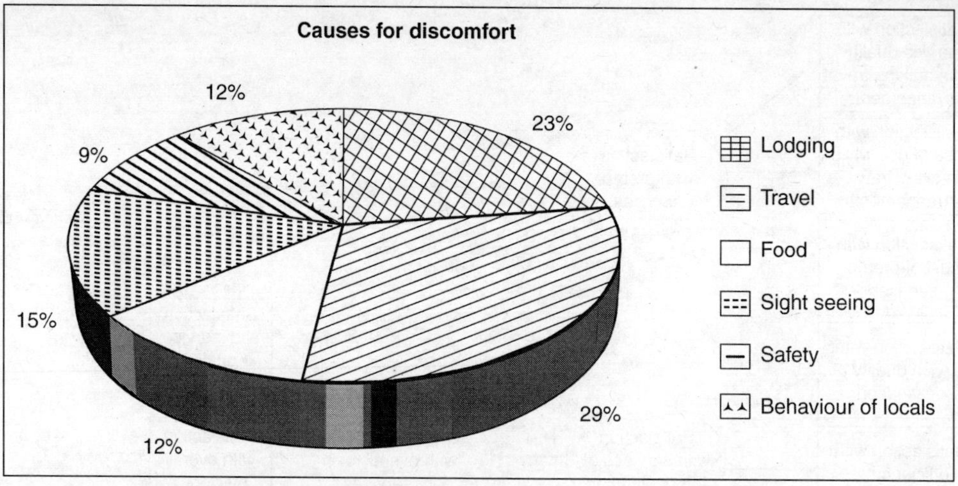

Why Measure Satisfaction?

- Huge expenses to the tune of billions of dollars are spend on marketing of a destination by national and state tourism offices, airlines and regional tourism bodies. This includes potential market surveys, promotional campaigns in source countries. However, an understanding of tourists' reaction pattern in terms of product and service offerings is missing.
- Bigger organizations in the tourism industry recognize the need to encourage both new and repeat business. The latter can be best achieved by ensuring that current offerings are satisfying the needs, expectations and desires of current tourists and encouraging their propensity to recommend the destination to others.
- The measure could become a barometer of the "health" of the industry for strategic planning purposes.
- The tourism industry itself is grappling with the issues of service quality and recognizes that this is the key to long-term success. Monitoring tourists' satisfaction at the more global level would provide a valuable framework for this.
- Government agencies are now recognizing the value of assessing the success of their programmes in terms of outcomes rather than inputs. In the case of tourism, this is particularly relevant to national, state and regional tourism development bodies responsible for destination marketing.

TOURISM PRODUCT AND SERVICE QUALITY

Both good and poor customer service is equally identifiable. Nowhere is service quality more pertinent than in tourism. By its very nature, the tourism product is service-driven, making the quality of product intrinsically linked to the level of service provided.

As such, in tourism, the product is a service that has a number of associated characteristics. If at any stage in a consumer's experience the service is poor, it will affect the level of satisfaction and future behaviour. In tourism, there are no second chances. It helps to remember that in many situations, tourism is simply a means to an end. Another important factor is consistency. Given that there are so many companies involved in providing a single service, consistency in the provision of that service becomes all the more difficult to guarantee.

Tourism is a dynamic industry. Changes either internally generated by companies supplying the product or externally generated by political or economic factors have an effect on demand and supply. Prompt action is required to limit potentially damaging effect.

The quality of service provided throughout the experience can differentiate one company from the next. In tourism, both technical and personal aspects are important. Personal service virtually pervades every situation in tourism, making its importance undisputed. Technical service, too, plays a vital role.

CUSTOMER RELATIONSHIP MANAGEMENT: THE TOURISM PERSPECTIVE

CRM stands for customer relationship management. It is a process or methodology used to learn more about customer's needs and behaviours. There are many technological components to CRM. The more useful way to think about CRM is as a process that will help bring together lots of pieces of information about tourists, holiday destinations, holiday packages, marketing effectiveness, responsiveness and tourism trends.

The CRM objectives increase business opportunities by:

- Improving the process of communication with regular tourists
- Providing the right deal or package to tourists
- Providing the right holiday package through the right channel to the tourists
- Providing the right holiday package during the correct season to the tourists. By doing the above, the CRM provider receives the following benefits:
- Increased customer retention and loyalty: If tourists are provided with proper service at a tourist location, then they are surely going to become loyal to that location and spread its name to others.
- Higher customer profitability: If unique or customized services are provided to the customers, then a greater amount of profit can be extracted from time to time, while at the same time providing them with value for the money they are spending.
- Creation of value for the customer: If value can be created for tourists by providing them with a unique experience then their loyalty can be won which will in turn translate into an increase in revenue for that tourist location.

There are many different types of tourists as well as many different reasons for tourism. The different types of tourist are as follows:

- International
- Interstate
- Intrastate

The different purposes of travel are:

- Corporate: Business, sales trip, overseas meeting
- Leisure: Holiday, visit friends or relatives, honeymoon
- Educational: Study excursion, student exchange
- Religious: Pilgrimage

The CRM techniques should be different and customized for each type of tourist as well as purpose of travel.

The application of CRM in the tourism industry can be achieved by various means that are explained below:

- Developing a tourist database for all major tourist locations. Keeping tourists informed of upcoming events at that particular tourist location
- Providing pre- and post-tour services such as booking facilities and feedback surveys
- Tourism Web sites where tourists can get information on the locations of their choice.

ATTRACTING AND RETAINING CUSTOMERS

There can be many reasons for a tourist to shift to another location during the next available holidaying opportunity. Here is an attempt to classify these.

Type	Description
Price	Defecting to a lower-price alternative location
Offering	Defection to a superior or more interesting tourist location
Service	Defection to a similar location due to poor service
Sector	Tourists who stop touring resort to other means of relaxation
Others	Whims and fancies of the tourists: There are those who prefer to tour a different location every time

While the "others" cannot be controlled, the rest of the reasons for defections can be controlled and avoided. In the following subsection, we attempt to bring forward a few ways to prevent the loss of tourist customers.

Differentiating Services: An Approach

Differentiating services and thereby providing a unique tourism experience to tourists is probably the most effective way of retaining them. Differentiated service gives a service provider a very effective tool to combat many other kinds of shortcomings. It is an effective way of turning an inherent weakness into a unique feature and an everlasting experience, as in the case of adventure tourism.

In the tourism industry, there are two ways of differentiating services and providing a unique experience to the tourists:

- Differentiation based on tourists' preferences
- Differentiation based on nature of service provided

Differentiation Based on Tourists' Preferences. Given unique characteristics and complex nature of the tourism industry, there are many different demands for tourist services. On the basis of these demands, travel companies offer varying combinations that travellers can choose from in terms of destination, accommodation, types of transport, services and activities and have thus created a wide range of differentiated products. Over a span of time and experience, different types of tourist experiences have been developed to include

- Domestic and international travel
- Sun-and-sea holiday – chosen area being in a coastal area with good weather
- Cultural tourism – focused on arts, events, museums, visits to historical and archaeological sites
- Sports tourism – motivation is to participate in or to attend a sports event
- Health tourism – aim is to undergo some type of health treatment, ranging from spas to surgeries
- Rural tourism – entails the use of resources in the rural area to enhance the general welfare of the community and the visitor
- Leisure and business travel

Differentiation Based on Nature of Service Provided. This type of differentiation is based on multiple factors. Once a service product is decided upon by consumers as per the differentiation discussed in the previous section, travel companies offer varying service levels within each tourism product. Within a product, varying service levels are offered based on customers' buying power, preferences and motivation for travel, destination positioning, etc. For example, within leisure travel, a tourism company may offer two different services – one for family visits with a greater focus on a particular set of locations and another for honeymoon packages, with a focus on luxury suites in resorts. Also, service differentiation can be on pre- and post-travel service. Depending again on customers' preferences, varying service levels can be packaged as parts of products before and after the tours. For instance, pre-tour service differentiation could include taking care of all visa requirements of an individual, helping potential tourists in applying for passports, detailing a customized itinerary for tourists and giving them a virtual tour of a choice of hotels/rooms.

Advertisement: Impact on Customer Value

Advertising provides an important channel for communicating the benefits of the destination to customers. For most people, when it comes to choosing a destination to visit for vacations, it is very similar to selecting a product. Painting a tourist destination in a positive light, so that it becomes more attractive to potential tourists and is transformed into a popular tourist destination, is the main purpose of advertising in tourism. Therefore, advertising plays an important role in decision-making. Being able to identify with the theme of the advertisement helps create a recall value and, therefore, enhances the loyalty aspect for old customers and creates an expected value for new customers.

Today, a tourist destination is looked at more as a product than ever before. The "product" must be branded and must create a reputation and perception in the mind of the consumer i.e., a tourist which is unique, appealing and consistent.

Case Study: Advertising and Web Sites—Medium for Communicating Value

A popular advertising campaign communicates the benefits and projects a positive perceived value for the customer. In India, Kerala – "God's own country" and Goa – "God's own holiday destination" – have been popular campaigns used to promote and demonstrate the customer benefits associated with the location. Advertising did the trick for these two tourist destinations.

A View from Kerala

Kerala was a relatively unknown destination, as most tourist circles focused on North India, especially Agra and Rajasthan. After the early 1980s, Kerala Tourism Development Corporation, the government agency that oversees tourism prospects of the state, laid the foundation for the growth of the tourism industry. Through upland marketing strategy, within a few decades, Kerala's image got transformed as one of the top holiday destinations in India. The tagline "Kerala – God's Own Country," originally coined by Dr Vipin Gopal, who created the first Web page on Kerala, has been widely used in Kerala's tourism promotions and soon became synonymous with the state.

Marketing is, indeed, alive and well in the world of tourism. In fact, it is on the upswing, and more and more states in India are leveraging advertising to attract tourists. Relevant Web sites are created and promoted. The Web sites provide easy access and, hence, a convenient medium for getting information on the attributes and features of the offerings.

Good Travel Experience: Manali

Manali is a hill station in Himachal Pradesh, India, and is located 40 km north of Kullu, near the northern end of the Kullu Valley of the Himalayas. The place derived its name from Manavalaya, which literally means the "home of Manu," the Indian mythological character who saved the world from the Great Flood. Spectacular views of snow-capped peaks, wooded slopes and grassy meadows carpeted with wild flowers make Manali the perfect retreat for a family holiday

A Snapshot from the Rohtang Pass

Panoramic View of Manali

Manali is a charmingly beautiful place with the majestic mountain ranges of Himalayas flanking it from the north, river Beas cutting across the town, green valleys with meadows and flower beds on hillsides and the sweet scent of clear, thin mountain air. The experience is enriched by visits to ancient temples, villages and handicraft and shawl-weaving centres. It is an excellent place for a holiday and a favourite resort for trekkers to Lahaul, Spiti, Kinnaur, Leh and Zanskar regions in Kashmir valley. As its magical charms captivate your soul, you ebulliently agree that it has rightly been christened as the "Valley of the Gods."

Places Around

Rohtang Pass: It is a high mountain pass that connects the Kullu Valley with the Lahaul and Spiti valleys of Himachal Pradesh. Situated at an altitude of 13,050 feet above sea level and 51 km from Manali, it is the highest point on the Manali-Keylong road and provides a wide panoramic view of mountains rising far above clouds, which is truly breathtaking. Close by is a small lake called Dassaur Lake. Beas Kund, the source of river Beas, is also nearby. In winters, the Rohtang Pass is closed. Typical tours to Rohtang Pass cover visit to Nehru Kund, Solang valley, Kothi, Gulaba camp, Rahla Fall, Rani Nala and Rohtang Pass. The other sightseeing spot is Solang valley. At Solang valley, adventure activities on ski and snow scooters are conducted in winters. In April, May and June, adventure activities like paragliding, hot-air balloon rides, rappelling, rock climbing and river rafting are conducted in and around Manali.

Hadimba Temple: It is a four-tiered, pagoda-like wooden temple, which stands in a clearing amid tall

Hadimba Temple

Good Travel Experience: *(Continued)*

and stately deodar trees. The temple is built around a natural cave, enshrining the footprints of the goddess Hadimba.

Vashist Kund: Around 3 km from Manali, across the Beas River, is Vashist, a small village with natural sulphur springs and a pair of old stone temples.

Vashist Kund in Manali

Tibetan Monastery: This colourful Buddhist temple is famous for its carpet weaving and Tibetan handicrafts. To help preserve ancient Tibetan art, articles of handicraft are also kept for sale to outsiders.

Manikaran: Situated 85 km from Manali and 45 km from Kullu, in the Parvati valley, is the holy pilgrimage place of Manikaran. It is known for its hot-water springs that gush out from below the rocks at temperature of 88°C to 94°C and also possess healing properties. Here, icy cold waters of the Parvati River coexist with hot-water springs.

Solang Valley: Solang valley, the venue for the annual skiing courses, is 13 km outside Manali.

Tibetan Monastery of Manali

How to Reach Manali

By Road

Manali-Shimla: 290 km (13 hrs)

Manali-Parwanoo: 160 km (8–9 hrs)

Manali-Chandigarh: 300 km (7–8 hrs)

Manali-Delhi: 585 km (12–13 hrs)

Manali-Dharamshala: 256 km (7–8 hrs)

Nearest Railhead

Chandigarh: 300 km

Nearest Airport

Bhuntar: 50 km

Unsung Tourist Destination: Tarkarli (Maharashtra)

Tarkarli can be referred to as an undiscovered paradise on earth. Undiscovered because many people do not yet know about this lovely holiday destination – even those who live in Mumbai, Maharashtra.

Where Is Tarkarli Located?

A perfect weekend getaway, Tarkarli is situated in Maharashtra — about 6–7 km south of Malvan and approximately 40–45 km from Mumbai. Falling on the coast of Maharashtra, Tarkarli is bestowed with loads of natural beauty and is a wonderful confluence of greenery and awe-inspiring beaches.

Tarkarli Beach

Tarkarli Beach

Ask any traveller/tourist what they liked best about Tarkarli, and they are bound to mention the Tarkarli beach – a long and narrow stretch with sparkling blue water and lined by trees. Possessing a serene and hypnotic beauty, this is a perfect place to spend some quite moments with oneself and the wonders of nature.

There is a lot you can do while in Tarkarli – enjoy the beauty of nature, go on a boat ride, rest, relax, and unwind at the Tarkarli beach, or visit Sindhudurg and Padmagarh forts of Maharashtra, located Tarkarli Beach close to Tarkarli.

Tarkarli Creek

North of Tarkarli, about 6–7 kilometres away is the Tarkarli Creek, an estuary that is a must-visit place while you are holidaying in Tarkarli. A boat ride through the Tarkarli creek is a romantic experience that must not be missed! The beauty of the clean water and the greenery around will leave you spellbound.

Tarkarli Creek

How to Reach Tarkarli

- **By air:** There is no direct air connection with Tarkarli. The nearest airport is at Mumbai.
- **By rail:** The nearest railway station is Kudal from where state transport buses are available.
- **By road:** State transport buses – Mumbai-Malvan-Tarkarli.

Best Time to Visit

The best time to visit Tarkarli is between October to March. The temperature varies between 22° to 40°C during summer and during winter it drops to 12° to 33°C.

Accommodation

Tourists can stay at MTDC Holiday Resort Tarkarli and Siddhivinayak Beach Resort. Few of the new sea view resorts have come up during the recent years.

SUMMARY

- The CPV is the difference between a prospective customer's evaluation of all benefits and costs of an offering, and the perceived alternatives. There is a one-to-one correspondence between business and the value proposition delivered.
- Customer benefit is the perceived monetary value of the bundle of the economic, psychological and functional benefits that a customer expects from a given market offering because of products, services, personnel and images involved. Customer cost is the perceived bundle of costs that the customer expects to incur in evaluating, obtaining, using and disposing of the given market offering including monetary, time, energy and psychological costs.
- The customer value may come from different stages of his experience. Most pleasures can come from the first step of his experience, and this may be followed by incremental pleasures coming from each subsequent stage of improvement.
- The tourism industry consists of a number of sectors including the travel, hospitality and visitor services sector. By its very nature, the tourism product is service-driven, making the quality of product intrinsically linked to the level of service provided. The quality of service provided throughout the experience can differentiate one company from the next.
- CRM is a process that will help bring together lots of pieces of information about tourists, holiday destinations, holiday packages, marketing effectiveness, responsiveness and tourism trends.
- In the tourism industry, there are two types of service differentiation—based on tourists' preferences and on nature of service provided. Once the service product is decided by a consumer as per the differentiation, travel companies offer varying service levels within each tourism product.
- The advertising word today is growing exponentially. The main purpose is transforming a destination into a popular tourist destination. The destination is looked at more as a product and must create a "reputation and perception" in the mind of a consumer.

FIELD EXERCISES

1. Try to develop a customer relationship management technique for Indian tourism industry by focussing on foreign tourists.
2. Make 3 groups of five members each, visit your city as a tourist and summarize your group experiences. Finally discuss the factors for satisfaction and dissatisfaction.

REFERENCES

Heskett J.L., W.E. Sasser Jr and L.A. Schlesinger (1997), *The Service Profit Chain. How Leading Companies Link Profit and Growth to Loyalty, Satisfaction, and Value*, The Free Press, New York, NY.

Holbrook, M. (1999), "Introduction to Consumer Value," in Holbrook, M. (Eds), *Consumer Value: A Framework for Analysis and Research*, Routledge, New York, NY, pp. 1–28

Janet D. Neal and Dogan Gursoy (2008), "A Multifaceted Analysis of Tourism Satisfaction," *Journal of Travel Research*, Vol. 47, No. 1, 53–62

LaTour, S. A., and N.C. Peat (1979) "Conceptual and Methodological Issues in Consumer Satisfaction Research," *Advances in Consumer Research*, Vol. 6, pp. 431–437

Oliver, R.L. (1980), "A Cognitive Model of the Antecedents and Consequences of Satisfaction Decisions (Eds)," *Journal of Marketing Research*, No. 17, pp. 460–469

Oliver R.L. and J.E. Swan (1989), "Consumer Perceptions of Interpersonal Equity and Satisfaction in Transactions: A Field Survey Approach," *Journal of Marketing*, Vol. 53, No. 2, pp. 21–35

V.A. Zeithaml (1988), "Consumer Perceptions of Price, Quality, and Value: A Means-End Model and Synthesis of Evidence," *Journal of Marketing*, Vol. 52, pp. 2–22

Woodruff, R.B. & and S.F. Gardial, (1996). *Know Your Customer: New Approaches to Understanding Customer Value and Satisfaction*, Cambridge, MA, Blackwell Publishers

Web Sites

http://store.businessmonitor.com/products/list_all/industries/iq/tourism/

CHAPTER 4

Services Marketing Issues in Tourism

ABOUT THE DESTINATION

Cristo Redentor (Portuguese: "Christ the Redeemer") is one of the most recognized images of Brazil. The soapstone statue was sculpted in France by Paul Landowski and then its pieces were transported to Brazil and assembled.

OBJECTIVES

- To understand tourism as a service
- To understand how and which service industries are related to tourism
- To understand the special characteristics of tourism services
- To sensitize about the marketing issues in tourism services
- To understand Parasuraman's gap model and how it applies to tourism services

INTRODUCTION

Building a sound customer value proposition and enhancing customer loyalty and satisfaction are essential for the tourism industry to thrive. The various issues faced by the customers visiting India have been identified with respect to these three parameters in the preceding chapter. Apart from these, a robust CRM system is also necessary to ensure excellence in service delivery in the tourism industry. The backbone of the tourism industry is the quality of the services that a tourist experiences at various points during his/her visit. Therefore, organized marketing of the services related to the tourism industry assumes prominence. At the same time, it is necessary to address the issues that one may possibly face while marketing services in tourism.

Services marketing is based on services and values. Instead of marketing physical goods, as in the traditional sense of marketing, services marketing concentrates on intangibles such as after-sales service, ambience in a monument, safe and comfortable journey, or even a simple massage.

The intangible nature of services poses a critical problem for the marketer and makes them less responsive to the traditional marketing techniques. For a service, the customers do not know what they are getting until they do not get it. Satisfaction, hence, is mute, and dissatisfaction dwells only on the absence of services. Charles Revson explained services marketing in perhaps the best words when he said this for the business of Revlon Inc.: "In the factory we make cosmetics. In the store we sell hope."

Innovations in information technology have, in the recent decades, attached a lot of significance to services. Customers today demand better quality of services in each and every transaction. Information technology not only created entirely new business avenues but also engendered highly flexible, innovative and market demand-oriented firms.

Today, services are associated with almost all sectors. In the tourism sector, firms offering services strive hard to create and deliver on an elaborate customer value proposition. An entire meta market ranging from activities such as online ticket booking to airways and hotels has developed around the tourism industry. This meta market itself spans various industries. Firms in most of these industries face high competition due to various reasons, and they have to continuously innovate in order to retain customers. Moreover, in such a competitive atmosphere, a firm not only has to deliver superior quality of services but also has to present it to the customers in an appealing way. In the light of this, design and delivery of appropriate marketing strategies for the service offerings can often differentiate one firm from another. The organizations have to carefully gain a clear insight of the tourists' needs and deploy the right services marketing strategy.

This chapter focuses on the various services provided in the tourism industry and the possible marketing strategies that can be employed for sales promotion. An analysis of gaps using Parasuraman's service quality model and possible means of addressing these gaps have been presented for the marketing strategies adopted for each of the services.

TOURISM AS A SERVICE

Tourism has always been a major social phenomenon in any society. It is motivated by the natural urge of every human being for new experience, adventure, education, knowledge and entertainment. In order to understand cultures and values of each other, as well as to cater to several other social, religious and business interests, many tourist and infrastructure facilities have been developed. This, along with the progress of proper transportation network globally, especially of airways and waterways, has encouraged people to venture out to foreign lands. It has facilitated trade and commerce between the different regions of a country and between the different countries. As a result, over the years, it has acquired the status of a service industry.

Tourism, being one of the largest industries, plays a key role in achieving the socio-economic goals of the development plans of a nation. It is an important service-oriented sector, which has made rapid strides globally in terms of gross revenue and foreign-exchange earnings. It is a composite of service providers, both public and private, and includes travel agents and tour operators; air, rail and sea transportation operators; guides; and owners of hotels, guesthouses, inns, restaurants and shops. They are involved in meeting the diverse interests and requirements of domestic and international tourists. The tourism industry provides incentives to foster the quality of environment, generates more employment opportunities – particularly in remote and backward areas and develops necessary infrastructure facilities like roads, telecom and medical services in the economy.

Tourists, in general, can be divided into the following:

- Domestic tourists
- Foreign tourists

Considering the population of a country like India, even if a minor percentage of the population contributes towards domestic tourism, the amount of revenue generated out of it is going to be enormous. Also, the current trend of many public and private organizations offering tourist packages for their workers has contributed greatly to the increase in domestic tourism. The number of foreign tourists in any country can be increased by promoting unexploited tourist destinations. Also, the contribution of globalization in terms of increased business travels is on the rise.

Service Industries Related to Tourism

The service sectors related to tourism include airlines, hotels, transport (local), tourist guides, security/police, basic sanitation and other amenities at the tourist places. The following are service industries related to tourism:

Airlines Industry. The airlines industry is one of the significant contributors to tourism, especially in developing countries. Previously, developing countries used tourism as a means to generate essential foreign currency and to generate employment. But due to the emergence of low-cost airlines, which offers better connectivity within the country, the developing countries are slowly entering into the tourism market. Further, the liberalization of the airlines sector and the minimization of constraints from the government side have been seen as an opportunity for airlines to enter the tourism market. The airlines sector is one of the important industries by which any country can get into the tourism market. For any country, airlines serves as the first gateway for tourism. So, improving the services offered will directly have an impact on the tourists' turnover.

Hospitality Industry. Hospitality is the act or practice of being hospitable, that is, the reception and entertainment of guests, visitors or strangers, with liberality and goodwill. Hospitality frequently refers to the hospitality-industry jobs for hotels, restaurants, casinos, catering, resorts, clubs and any other service position that deals with tourists. Hotels are among the most visible and important aspects of a country's infrastructure. The hotel industry is closely linked to the tourism industry. A number of factors like promotion of tourism and rapid industrial progress have given a boost to hotel management. The recent liberalization of trade and the opening up of the economy will further lead to revolutionary growth in this sector.

The hospitality industry caters to both accommodation and food needs. The hospitality sector, propelled by the tourism and business travel boom, is growing considerably fast. The requirement for hotels and the competitive quality of their services open up great opportunities in this sector. With the growth of the hotel industry, propelled by foreign and domestic tourism and business travel, the demand for well-trained quality personnel has also grown impressively. So, training the personnel so that they better serve the tourists is one of the challenges that any tourism-projecting country has. Today, the rise in the corporate activity – leading to a greater number of business trips – and more

Box 1: A "Live" Example of Hotel Marketing

Publicity of your hotel can be a big drain on the budget. Ginger hotels in Mumbai could not use the normal tactics to advertise, so they came up with an innovative way to showcase their rooms. They built a mock-up of their room in Mumbai near the Mahim Causeway, and put an 18-year-old as a live customer inside it. The mock-up lasted for 10 days with the "customer" sitting inside it for 13 hours every day.

Industry critics call it ambient advertising and say that it is a new concept that will grow in the future. Now that there are highways and flyovers; these new creative ideas will show through the clutter. The advertising is unusual, but the client is happy. According to Indian hotels, the end user (that is, the consumer) will be satisfied, too.

The mock-up of the low-cost hotel room from Indian hotels is attracting some curiosity from onlookers, too. They feel if the actual hotel is as good as what is promised, they will not mind a few nights at Ginger. "If the quality is good, we do not mind paying," says one passer-by.

pronounced aspiration to travel on holiday have made the hotel industry very competitive. The tourist's food need is also an important aspect to be considered by a country entering the tourism market. Serving tourists from various locations and adhering to their tastes involve having quality cooks and serving personnel.

Scope for Improvement in Existing Tourist Services

Local Transport/Tourist Guides. The local transportation within the tourist spots should be well connected. Also, the tourists who are not part of the tourist packages should be made to utilize the government or government-authorized facilities so that they are charged the right amount of money and are not cheated. The tour operators should provide competent tourist guides to bus operators because they are the representatives with whom the tourists are going to interact mostly. They should portray a positive image of the country among the tourists.

Basic Amenities in Tourist Locations. The tourist locations should be maintained properly so that they remain clean. This can be done by a team that takes care of the maintenance of monuments and surroundings, and protects these from misuse. The basic amenities of food and toilets should be available, and also maintained continuously. The food should be of the needed quality level, and the revenue generated through the food outlets/paid toilets should be reinvested only for renovation.

Security. The concerns of personal security and also the security of the belongings can be taken care of by the tour operators. They should constantly monitor the foreign tourists, so that they do not end up in troubles because of local people. Proper guidelines should be given regarding the shops they should purchase from, the point of contact in case they get lost, etc. These might seem to be small issues, but if not addressed rightly, they can portray the country in a darker light.

Role of Marketing in Tourism Services

Firms in the tourism industry, just like those in any other services industry, extensively employ different types of services marketing strategies in order to stay ahead of competition. Among the key services they need to market are airlines and hospitality. The strategies vary from one firm to another, and depend on the customer segment that the firm is targeting. It does not matter what the marketing strategy of the firm is; it has to necessarily account for the following aspects of a tourism-service offering: intangibility, inseparability, variability and perishability. These are all described as follows:

Intangibility. Unlike physical products, services cannot be verified by any of the human senses. However, consumers often infer the quality of the service from place, people, equipment, price, communication and material associated with the service. This has a crucial bearing on the perceived value of service for a customer. In case of tourism, a customer would have a different perception about the quality of services, for example, a room or food offered in a five-star luxury hotel as compared to an economy hotel, owing to the various factors listed above. This indicates that a hotel, depending on its value proposition, may target the appropriate segment of the market by leveraging the factors listed above. Likewise, a holiday agency that intends to cater to the middle class may aptly choose the intangible aspects associated with its service, so that it attracts most of the middle-class populace.

Inseparability. A unique aspect of services is that unlike physical goods, they have to be produced and consumed simultaneously. In tourism, the tourist and the service providers interact continuously, right from the tourist's arrival in the country till the completion of the entire tourism process. The service providers in such cases can continuously gauge the level of satisfaction of the tourists.

Variability. Services vary from one place to another, and from one time to another. It is extremely difficult to maintain the same standard of service delivery. The service delivery standard also depends on the person who delivers it. For example, the type of hotels found in a tourist destination known for its beaches is different from the type of hotels found in a hill station. Each type of hotel has its own value proposition and intends to offer a different type of service to the tourists, and hence, the quality of service would invariably vary. However, the hotels in each case have to ensure that they necessarily meet the consumer expectations as often as possible. Likewise, the services offered by different travel agents and holiday planners would vary immensely. The level of service quality will, nevertheless, depend largely on the segmentation, targeting and positioning strategies of the firms. For example, a holiday-planning agency intending to cater to the requirements of the upper-middle class will have to ensure that the services offered by it match the prices charged.

Perishability. Unlike products, services cannot be stored. This implies that during the peak season as well as during unfavourable seasons, a potential mismatch may occur between the demand for tourism services and the supply, which is often the case with most hotels in hill stations during summers. To rein in huge variances in demand and supply of tourism services, firms may adopt either demand-side strategies or supply-side strategies, or a combination of both. Some of these strategies have been listed in Table 4.1.

Channels of Marketing in Tourism Services

Firms in the tourism industry, just like those in any other service-oriented industry, have an entire gamut of marketing channels to choose from. The exact choice of any one channel or a combination of channels depends solely on the market-penetration objectives of the firm and the resources at its disposal. The available channels vary from ads, brochures and Web sites, to extensive advertising campaigns targeted at specific segments of the population.

Over the last decade, Web sites have grown to be a key source of information for almost all tourists across the world. The ease with which accurate information can be gathered using the Internet makes it the most sought-after medium by tourists. Therefore, by means of the Internet, firms can communicate with a large number of potential tourists at the same time. The Internet, however, is dominated by service providers of different types. In such a scenario, it becomes unavoidable for a firm to have a robust differentiating strategy to boost its visibility in the market. Not only should the firm choose the right place to communicate on the Internet, it should also choose the appropriate pricing strategy and product offerings while promising the best service quality.

Table 4.1 Demand-Side and Supply-Side Strategies for Tackling Seasonal Variances

Demand-Side Strategies	Supply-Side Strategies
Differential pricing to shift demand from peak season to off season, by charging tourists more in peak season	Hire part-time employees to meet peak-season demand to serve more tourists
Install reservation systems to better manage demand levels. In tourism, this can be done by hiring other small hotels for facilitating increasing tourist numbers rather than missing the huge customer base	Plan facilities for future expansion to increase supply. This can be done by estimating tourists for a long term and constructing those facilities beforehand

An example of such strategies may be found in the tourism-promotion initiatives of Indian Railway Catering and Tourism Corporation (IRCTC). IRCTC hosts a Web site (http://www.irctc.co.in) for booking railway tickets in India. However, this is only one of the services offered by IRCTC. Its key initiative is to promote tourism in India by providing ample information to potential tourists. It hosts detailed descriptions of most tourist destinations in India. Moreover, it provides a list of budget hotels at various tourist places. It also provides tourists with facilities such as pick-up and drop, hotel booking, tour planners, tour guides, package tours and telephonic bookings. In short, it is a one-stop solutions provider for almost all the needs of a tourist in India.

SERVICE QUALITY IN TOURISM

Tourism Services Marketing Strategies

A product can be an idea, a good or a service. Since tourism is primarily a service-based industry, the principal products provided by recreation/tourism businesses are recreational experiences and hospitality. These intangible products are more difficult to market than tangible products such as automobiles. The intangible nature of services makes quality control difficult but crucial. It also makes it more difficult for potential customers to evaluate and compare service offerings. In addition, instead of moving the product to the customer, the customer must travel to the product – area/community. Travel is a significant portion of the time and money spent in association with recreational and tourism experiences, and is a major factor in decisions of people on whether or not to visit your business or community.

As an industry, tourism has many components comprising the overall travel experience. Along with transportation, it includes aspects like accommodation, food and beverage services, shops, entertainment, aesthetics and special events. It is rare for one business to provide the entire range of activities or facilities that tourists need or desire. This adds to the difficulty of maintaining and controlling the quality of the experience. To overcome this hurdle, tourism-related businesses, agencies and organizations need to work together to package and promote tourism opportunities in their areas, and align their efforts to ensure consistency in product quality.

What makes tourism marketing all the more difficult? The principal products that recreation and tourism businesses provide are recreational experiences and hospitality. The factors that create a quality recreational experience often differ among people. A quality experience for one tourist might include an uncrowded, natural location, while for another it might be a crowded place and a chance to socialize. Many tourism businesses and communities fail to recognize their role in improving travel to and from their areas. They focus, instead, on servicing the customer once they arrive at the site/community. This is important because a bad experience in getting to or leaving a site can adversely affect a person's overall travel experience. Most of the times, this is not in the hands of the tourist operators and other service providers.

Some people may not want to pay much for a service or may prefer to go to a place that is less crowded. This encourages off-season and non-peak-period sales. All the above-mentioned factors should be taken into account before deciding a marketing strategy for a particular place.

Issues in Tourism Marketing

The quality of a service is an essential factor that determines the service provider's ability to attract more customers. Unlike the quality of goods, which may be measured objectively by such indicators as durability and number of defects, service quality is an elusive construct that is difficult to measure. Mackay and Crompton (1990) defined service quality as "the relationship between what customers desire from a service and what they perceive that they receive." Additionally, service quality is also a

Box 2: Attracting Tourists or Adding Infrastructure?

A perpetual dilemma of the service industry in the tourism sector is whether to cater to the current fleet of tourists or invest in adding infrastructure to meet future demands. An interesting example of this was played out in Kashmir.

Former Jammu & Kashmir Chief Minister Farooq Abdullah came under the radar of the environmentalists soon after he authorized a new golf course in Srinagar, with regard to the forests that had to be cleared and the claims that INR 250 million spent on the 250-acre course could be used to improve the state's infrastructure.

Hoteliers, on the other hand, were glad that the course had come up and said that this would help bring the upper segments of tourists to the state. They felt that this course was the only thing in Kashmir that was "21st century," and in fact, the golf course helped Srinagar play host to the Hero Honda India Golf Tournament, which saw much higher attendance than anticipated – to the delight of hoteliers.

way of thinking about how to satisfy customers so that they hold positive attitudes towards the service they have received.

The quality of the service plays an important role in the process of delivery and, thus, is the standard used to assess the effectiveness of a particular leisure-service agency, including the tourism-service sector. Service quality is an intangible, but crucial area of interest to travel service providers.

Quality is gaining in importance in areas of modern life. In tourism, too, guests look for products which are of top-quality, services which are value-for-money. The further reasons for systematic quality management in tourism are widely documented: growing competition, lack of willingness to provide a service, growing loss of individuality through standardization of products, adverse price-performance ratio and so on. Quality in tourism is an extremely complex phenomenon. The parameters involved in judging the quality of a tour are shown in Fig. 4.1.

From a guest's point of view, tourism services are always the product of a whole package of individual services. Like a chain, these services are all linked: advance information from a tourist centre, the train journey to the destination, stay in vacation hotel, eating in a restaurant, mountain-railway excursions, and lastly, the trip back home. Each individual service leaves its mark on, and influences, the holiday experience.

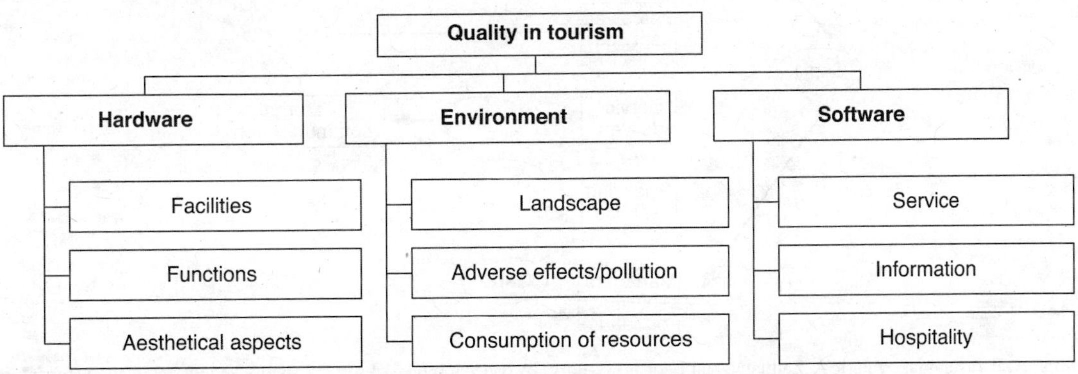

Source: Based on Felizitas Romeiss-Stracke: Service-Qualität im Tourismus, Munich 1995.

Fig. 4.1: Parameters Involved in Judging the Quality of a Tour

Also, at the level of the individual hotel, a guest experiences the whole service package as a chain in which one service is linked to the next: information, arrival, check-in, moving into the room, eating in the restaurant and checkout. These service chains, which are specific to guests, provide an aid for systematic checking of a hotel's services and processes, showing where practical quality improvements can be made and suggesting the introduction of appropriate measures.

Providing services and direct contact with guests are exacting tasks because each guest has his/her specific expectations, needs and opinions. No matter how tactful the staff may be, the odd mistake or misunderstanding is virtually unavoidable.

Such occurrences are described as critical incidents. These are defects of varying degrees in a service chain, which result in failure to satisfy guest expectations, thereby triggering dissatisfaction.

Parasuraman's Service Quality Model

Parasuraman's service quality model highlights the following gaps in service quality (Fig. 4.2).

Gap Between Consumer Expectations and Management Perceptions (Gap 1): In service industries, where the consumer is directly involved in the process, this gap plays a crucial role. Sometimes, the customer might want something and the management could be focusing on something else. The customer might be interested in low-cost hotel rooms while expecting good hygiene, whereas the management might be cutting costs by compromising on the hygiene. This is one of the important factors creating dissatisfaction among the travellers.

Gap Between Management Perceptions and Service-quality Specifications (Gap 2): Sometimes, even if the management is able to identify the customer's wants, it is not in a position

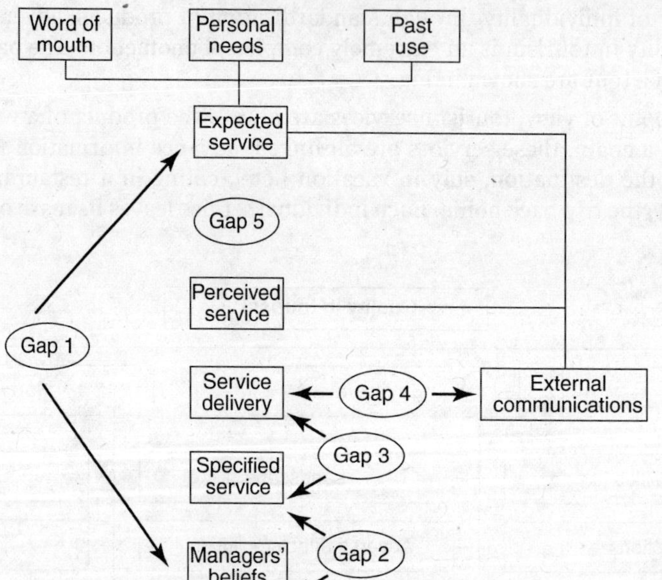

Source: A. Parasuraman, Valarie A. Zeithami, and Leonard L. Bary, "A concept model of service quality and its implications for future," *Journal of Marketing* (Fall 1985).

Fig. 4.2: Parasuraman's Service Quality Model

to provide the same due to cost constraints or other limiting factors. For example, a professional tourist operator is more interested in the number of trips he can do in a month than the level of satisfaction of people in each trip.

Gap Between Service-quality Specifications and Service Delivery (Gap 3): The quality of service depends on the capability of the person who is serving. For example, people expect a certain standard from the tourist guide, hotel receptionist or stewardess in the flight. If a person is not fit enough for the job, the tourist will be dissatisfied.

Gap Between Service Delivery and External Communications (Gap 4): This gap is highly prevalent in the Indian scenario. The hotels will advertise high-end facilities, a great range of services and competitive costs. But when the tourist actually visits the hotel, the reality is nowhere close to what is advertised; in fact, there will be some hidden costs associated with the service. A tourist might not be able to know these things beforehand, and these issues will come to light only when he actually avails the service.

Gap Between Perceived Services and Expected Services (Gap 5): This gap occurs when the consumer misperceives the service quality. For instance, if a hotel advertises low price as its unique feature, the customer might think that the service provided by the hotel will not be good. Sometimes, the service might be really good, but the consumer might have a preconceived expectation, which if not met will lead to dissatisfaction. This happens when the tourist is not well informed about what to expect or when the company sends wrong communication to the target customers.

In order to improve the service quality, the above-mentioned gaps should be identified and suitable measures taken to increase customer satisfaction. Some of the gaps can be identified only by the consumer and, hence, effective feedback should be taken and properly analysed to find these gaps.

The following case of "tourism in Goa" studies Goa as tourist destination, and various service activities which contributes in making Goa a successful destination.

Case Study: Tourism in Goa

Tourism plays an important role in the economy of Goa. It generates 13.7 per cent of the state's net domestic product, 7 per cent of employment and 7 per cent of tax revenues. Goa capitalizes on its unique cultural and historical heritage while promoting tourism. The main attractions that Goa as a region affords the tourist are sun-filled beaches, good food, and hotels and resorts.

Over the years, the percentage of international tourists coming to Goa has been increasing constantly. The international tourists are of two types – backpackers and charter tourists. Backpackers prefer to mingle with the local communities and roam on their own, whereas charter tourists stay in starred hotels and enjoy the lazy beaches. Hence, these two types of tourists need different services targeted at them, which needs to be taken into account.

As for the domestic tourists, they come mostly to experience the different cultures that are prevalent in Goa – a sense of freedom and an unconventional dressing style. The domestic tourists typically tend to spend lesser per capita than their international counterparts. Hence, the services geared towards the domestic tourists should be low-cost models.

Considering the food-service industry, it needs to be recognized that food and beverages comprise the largest component of the expenditure of domestic tourists (40 per cent), and the second largest component of the expenditure – accommodation being the largest – of the international tourist (20.5 per cent). Increasing the amount of local food used in the tourism industry is a way of increasing backward linkages from tourism and involving the local community, and, therefore, moving towards a more diversified and

Case Study: *(Continued)*

sustainable development. Yet, policymakers have not focused on strengthening the economic linkages between tourism and the food sector. The hotel food-supply chain has not been studied in Goa; local surplus production from agriculture and fishing could be potentially integrated into this chain as an additional means to generate local income. However, a careful balance must be struck between producing for tourists' requirements and ensuring food supply at reasonable prices to the locals. This issue of the food-service industry is delicate and can be solved only by involving all interested parties in the decision-making process.

For the transport industry, it has been observed that even though air and sea travel do not pose issues to the sustainability of the ecosystem, the alignment of the Konkan Railway is causing environmental impact. The gigantic embankments, several kilometres long, supporting the rail lines along the lowlands of Goa have led to substantial alterations in physical, chemical, biological and geomorphological setups. Blocking, diminuting or increasing the tidal flow has resulted in a major redistribution of sediments, giving rise to erosion/deposition with conspicuous changes in shorelines or near-shore realms. This is causing major problems for the tourism industry, which deals with maintaining the sustainability of its trade routes.

The hospitality industry in Goa has been growing in leaps and bounds, although this excessive growth itself has led to quite a few problems. Previously, local beach shacks provided a cheap and natural way of accommodation. Now, the growing number of these shacks in an unorganized manner is causing cramped shacks with no facilities of toilets and bathrooms. The tourists are almost exclusively accommodated along the 150 km stretch of the coastline, while little effort has been made to adhere to the regional plans of creating other types of tourism besides beach tourism.

Box 3: Tourist Experiences

A survey was carried out to understand the tourist experiences and the problems that tourists usually face. Among the problems faced by tourists, a high number of respondents said that the crowding of tourist destinations is leading to degradation in their experience. Poor roads, rains and sub-standard food quality were mentioned across all the tourist destinations. Also, it was found that there was, in general, a lack of coordination between the tourist agent and the actual hotels, resulting in different accommodations being given from the ones promised earlier. This could also be a deliberate attempt on the part of tour agents to promote their services while keeping costs down. While travelling, people were concerned about the quality of state-owned tourist buses. Poor roads were also blamed. In some places there was no direct transport route and a major time was lost while switching transport modes. In the hospitality sector, the usual complaints were about the non-functioning geysers, TVs, heaters, air conditioners and phones. The food quality served in the hotels was not appealing. Also, regional differences between the preparations of food were a major concern. All in all, the tourism experience of any tourist was not perfect. Each tourist had an experience that was felt lacking in some respect or the other. While it could be said that the responses received were only of the experiences that people remembered due to their negative nature, it can still be reasonably concluded that to make average Indian tourists happy about their overall experience, all the segments of the tourism industry must be improved.

INTERNATIONAL DESTINATION: SEATTLE, WASHINGTON

Space Needle

Space Needle is the symbolic icon of Seattle, Washington. A significant amount of tourists either send or bring home a postcard with this looming tower on centrestage. Space Needle was constructed for the 1962 World's Fair; during that fair, an estimated 2.3 million people paid homage to this beautiful sight. It was designated as a historical landmark in 1999, and no one can go to Seattle without either a trip to Space Needle, or a view of it. It might be a problem if you want to use the public transport on a weekend as it is available only thrice on weekends.

Space Needle, Seattle, Washington

The Pike Public Market

Most people who have walked through the grounds of the Pike Public Market know all about Rachel. Rachel is the bronze pig, which is the mascot of the Pike Public Market. Opened in 1907, the Pike Public Market is the largest market of its kind in America.

It would suffice to say that Pike is the most travelled area for any tourist in Seattle. However, it is highly difficult for someone suffering from dust allergy to travel through the market. One should make sure the availability of hygienic food in the market before consuming it.

Pike Public Market, Seattle, Washington

Underground Touring

Has anyone watched the History Channel and been privy to the programmes showing the underground cities? Underground touring in Seattle is a walk through the old downtown area of Seattle. What an experience! But not for anyone who wears high heels, or is not in reasonably good shape. You will walk up about six flights of stairs throughout your journey. It gets difficult to travel during the rains, and since Seattle is a place known for rains throughout the year, the tour can be enjoyed only during the summers.

Underground Touring, Seattle, Washington

Seattle Tulip Festival, Seattle, Washington

Seattle Tulip Festival

If you know anything about flowers and flower shows, you should know that the Seattle tulip festival is one of the coolest places to see fields and fields of gorgeous tulips and other flowers. If you have been in Seattle for more than a couple of hours, you also know that the weather can change pretty quickly, going from cloudy to sunny, and then back to cloudy, all in what seems like 10 minutes. When you check out the tulip festival, you will want to have a room to rest for a while, some boots to avoid sloshing through the mud, and some more.

Unsung Tourist Destination: Srivardhan – Harihareshwar (Maharashtra)

Srivardhan, a small town located around 230 km south of Mumbai, provides an excellent weekend get away from the fast-paced life of the city. Srivardhan is famous for its vast serene beach, and its proximity to the town of Harihareshwar, which houses an ancient temple of Lord Harihareshwar. Apart from this, Srivardhan is also famous for another ancient temple of Lord Shiva. It is also the place where the peshwas (prime ministers) of Maharashtra originally resided. The Peshwa Smarak, which is a memorial for the peshwas of Maharashtra, may also be of interest to tourists. Moreover, the Bankot fort at Bagmandala is around 4 km away.

Ancient Lord Shiva Temple in Srivardhan

How to Reach Srivardhan

Srivardhan is around 230 km from Mumbai, and is accessible by road. It is around eight hours' drive from Mumbai. The nearest railway station is Mangaon, which is about 65 km from Srivardhan.

Accommodation

There are a few good resorts in and around Harihareshwar. One of the better ones is owned by Maharashtra Tourism Development Corporation (MTDC), which is quite close to the Harihareshwar temple. However, it is advisable to make the bookings in advance since the resort is almost always occupied. The MTDC resort is surrounded by hills on two sides and the sea face in front. It also has a number of small huts for accommodation. Besides, the villagers also offer their homes (most of which are directly sea facing and provide a scenic view) as temporary accommodations.

Unsung Tourist Destination: *(Continued)*

Places to See Around

Harihareshwar is quite close to Srivardhan and houses an ancient temple dedicated to Lord Harihareshwar. One may also visit the ancient temples dedicated to Lord Shiva in Srivardhan. However, the clinching experience remains the calm and serene beach of Srivardhan.

Srivardhan Beach

Best Time to Visit

The best time to visit Srivardhan is undoubtedly during the summers, when the climate in Mumbai is simply too hot to handle. Srivardhan not only affords an easy escape from the rising temperatures and humidity levels of Mumbai, but also provides a much-needed break for those who have been working constantly under stressful conditions. Moreover, due to significantly lesser tourist volumes, Srivardhan also provides a lot of solitude and time to ponder over a lot of things by "detaching oneself from the world." Nonetheless, one may also visit Srivardhan during the monsoon in order to appreciate the rich fauna and flora of the region. The temperature drops to around 10°c during the winters, creating an ideal location for a bonfire and camping.

SUMMARY

- Tourism market is growing at a rapid pace due to the globalization and liberalization of airline and other tourism-related industries.
- Earlier, tourism was seen as a means to earn foreign income. Now, a transformation is happening in appreciating tourism as a new market for countries to enter. Countries are more focused on promoting tourism in order to compete in the tourism market as a whole.
- Competence comes through better tourism services, which can be achieved only by the elimination of certain core services marketing issues.
- Issues in tourism which have been identified have to be looked at and resolved by the countries in order to make the most of the growth in the sector. All that is needed is a transformation of the tourism industry from a means of secondary income generator to a key revenue generator in services.

FIELD EXERCISES

1. Contact five people who recently have been to a destination and try to assess the service quality based on their experiences.
2. Choose any well-known destination and assess its services marketing strategies.

REFERENCES

Kotler, Philip, Margaret H. Cunningham, Ronald E. Turner (2000), *Marketing Management*, Millennium Edition, Pearson Education Canada.

Parasuraman, A., Valarie A. Zeithami and Leonard L. Bary (1985) "A Concept Model of Service Quality and its Implications for Future," *Journal of Marketing*, Vol. 49, pp. 41–50.

St. Basil's Cathedral

CHAPTER 5

Marketing Mix and C's of Marketing in Tourism

ABOUT THE DESTINATION

Church constructed on Red Square in Moscow by Tsar Ivan IV 'The Terrible', as a votive offering for his military victories. Its distinctive and colourful onion-shaped domes continue to attract tourists to Moscow.

OBJECTIVES

- To understand the concept of marketing mix
- To understand the customer's evaluation of 4 P's in the form of 4 C's
- To know how each constituent of the marketing mix applies to tourism marketing
- To understand how each constituent of the 4 C's actually applies to the practical tourism context

INTRODUCTION

A marketer always looks forward to persuade and impress the potential tourists to visit the destination. For this a marketer can use a range of tools and techniques, which are discussed in this chapter. However, the multi-billion dollar question arises that whether tourists are buying the thoughts presented to them or not. This chapter thus delves into the marketing mix, which consists of the tool set in the hands of the marketer and includes the 4 P's (product, price, place and promotion). Thereon, it discusses the customer perspective denoted by the 4 C's (customer solution, cost, convenience and communication).

HOW TOURISM MARKETING IS DIFFERENT

A product can be an idea, a good or a service. Since tourism is primarily a service-based industry, the principal products provided by recreation/tourism (R/T) businesses are recreational experiences and hospitality. These are intangible products and more difficult to market than tangible products like FMCG products, apparels and automobiles. The intangible nature of services makes quality control difficult, but crucial. It also makes it more difficult for potential customers to evaluate and compare service offerings. In addition, instead of moving the product to the customer, the customer must travel to the product (area/community). Travel is a significant portion of the time and money spent in association with recreational and tourism experiences, and is a major factor in customers' decisions. As an industry, tourism has many components comprising the overall travel experience. Along with transportation, it includes accommodation, food and beverage

services, shops, entertainment, aesthetics and special events. It is rare for a business to provide the variety of activities or facilities that tourists need or desire. This adds to the difficulty of maintaining and controlling the quality of the experience. To overcome this hurdle, tourism-related businesses, agencies and organizations need to work together to package and promote tourism opportunities in a particular area, and align efforts to ensure consistency in product quality.

Like any other service industry, tourism also has all the attributes of a generic service-marketing approach. Tourism itself is a complex phenomenon as there is an entire gamut of factors responsible for making a tourist experience worthwhile. Hence, it is important to realize that tourism marketing cannot happen in isolation.

Some of the basic factors that the tourism market needs to embrace and always consider while designing strategies to target customers are as follows:

- **Anticipation of market changes:** Consumer market changes dramatically, thereby making tourist destinations depend on a host of socio-economic factors. The growth and decline of a tourist

Case Study: Hong Kong — The Transformation

Hong Kong has emerged as one of the most favoured global tourist destinations with overall visitors close to 30 million in 2008 with an increase of 4.7 per cent from 2007. With total tourism expenditure crossing US$ 148.6 billion, this means serious business, too. This emergence can be attributed to conscious efforts by the Hong Kong Tourism Board towards working closely with authorities and trade to make Hong Kong an essential component of all multi-destination itineraries.

Apart from this, a tourist commission was set up in 1999 to promote Hong Kong as Asia's premier city that combines business with fun. A tourist development group has been set up to advise the government on tourism development from a strategic perspective. Hong Kong boasts of attractions ranging from the Hong Kong Museum of Art to Disneyland, catering to every taste. It strongly showcases its culture through various shows and festivals.

Hong Kong is being promoted through a worldwide "Live it, Love it" campaign, and celebrated a "Discover Hong Kong Year" to signify the opening of several new attractions. Apart from attractions, Hong Kong is well connected and boasts of one of the best airports in the world. Other tourist infrastructure like hotels and travel is also well developed to make one's stay at Hong Kong really a good experience. This combination of well-designed promotion and exciting tourist attractions backed by sound infrastructure seems to be the recipe that has brewed success for Hong Kong as a tourist destination.

destination is tightly linked to the economic growth of not only its own region but also the regions that command the maximum tourist traffic coming to it.

- **Highly competitive market:** For major tourist destinations, the tourist traffic and income generated from them are the highest source of revenue for the entire city or town. Hence, the market among major tourist destinations is highly competitive in nature.
- **Social and environment consideration:** Social factors play a critical role in determining the experience of customers at a tourist destination. The crime rate and community outlook towards tourists are important social factors that alter the face of a tourist destination. In addition, overexposure of destinations brings to the fore environment issues that lead to a long-term detrimental impact on the popularity of the destination.
- **Consumer power:** Finally, the most important factor to remember is the fact that consumers are final decision makers for the success of a destination. Therefore, the emphasis should be on providing a holistic experience to consumers by filling up the gaps seen in the customer experience. Based on these factors, tourism marketing can be defined as a managerial process of anticipating and satisfying wants of existing and potential visitors more effectively than a competitive supplier or destination. The management of exchange is driven by profit, community gain or both; either way, long-term success depends on satisfactory interactions between customers and suppliers. It also means securing environmental and social needs as well as consumer satisfaction.

MARKETING MIX

The marketing strategy should be viewed as a package of offerings designed to attract and serve the customer or the visitor. The tourism market consists of internal and external marketing.

Internal Marketing Mix

Internal marketing aims at building employee morale as well as setting quality standards to ensure that each and every employee plays a pivotal role in building the customer experience. The success of internal marketing depends on creating an atmosphere wherein employees desire to deliver good services to the customers. Internal marketing encompasses all stakeholders of the organization. It would include all the levels of management of the organization, the suppliers, the creditors/financers, the channel partners and all others involved in the working of the organization.

A number of factors such as customer relations, quality control and employee morale can be achieved by providing tangible benefits such as incentives during peak season and intangible morale boosters such as support from supervisors, regular trainings and an environment where quality is a natural practice rather than a forced exercise.

External Marketing Mix

The 4 P's. The external marketing mix includes product/service, price, place/location and promotion.

Product: It is the element to which all the other elements relate, but without which they would be inaccessible or have little meaning. "People do not buy products; they buy the expectation of benefits. It is the benefits that are the product" (Levitt 1969). A business product comprises whatever is being delivered to satisfy consumer needs. It is much more than goods or services and is what the customer buys to satisfy a want. The fact that a product exists is, therefore, only a part of the story. What is the product offered by Airtel and Vodafone? It is certainly much more than the services and the mobile handsets that they provide. It is a communication, a reassurance when one can call an elderly relative, happiness when one receives a call from someone they love, excitement when one hears good news and sadness when one hears bad tidings. Similarly, a hotel is much more than a place to sleep and eat. It could be a surrogate home for a company's director while away on business, a haven of refuge for a sales representative when stranded or even a prison for a tourist if caught up in a war zone. It may be a place to relax, work, entertain or be entertained, confer or just lie around in the sun. The first step in tourism marketing is to understand the wants of the customer.

Price: Price is the one element in the marketing mix which produces revenue. Most of the others involve cost, which may explain why marketing is less popular than it might be. Price is often determined by the cost, with a margin being added to yield a profit or return on the investment. Marketing, however, would recommend using price tactically to help achieve the goals of the business, varying the price according to the level of demand and the willingness of the market to pay the price. Marketing is about giving each product or business its own unique selling proposition, so that it is different from all competing products and can command a premium price. Price is also an indicator of perceived quality, particularly for the first-time buyer, and while it remains so, subsequent purchases are much more concerned with the judgement of value for money. When establishing prices, tourism businesses should give attention to pricing strategies that may encourage off-season/non-peak-period sales, longer stays, group business and sale of package plans (combination of room, meals and recreational facilities).

Place: A packet of tissues can be bought from almost anywhere, but the places where tourism can be bought are relatively few. Tourism is not very well packaged in the domestic market – it is much easier to buy an all-inclusive holiday abroad than to buy one in India. Tourism is different from many other products, in that we travel to the product, for example, to enjoy a weekend in Shimla, one must first travel to get there, whereas most of the other goods we buy, from cars to tomato sauce, travel to us, or at least to the nearest car dealer or shop. Tourism is a service, mainly intangible at the point of sales and often not to be inspected. Many service products like travel and tourism are "ideas" in the minds of prospective buyers. They cannot easily be measured, touched or evaluated at the point of sale prior to performance. In travel and tourism, the point of sale is, more often than not, remote from the product. The role of third-party product evaluation and reporting is vital here. A customer cannot hold an experience, and the familiar "wish you were here," written on postcards by holidaymakers. The role of holiday snaps is interesting as they are an attempt to capture the experience so that it can be shared and relived. In much the same way, third-party product evaluation and reporting is vital as part of promotion in the form of recommendations and testimonials.

Promotion: This P is the term many people confuse with marketing. Promotion is about telling people what is on offer. Promotion refers to all the methods and tools used to spread information about the product, and encourage consumers to buy it. Once a business is in operation, it is this part of marketing that the business will have to spend money on every year. Knowledge of the product and market is essential for keeping the promotion budget in line and producing results. It is not entirely separate from the product because what is said and how it is said influence how the product is seen. Promotion includes not only advertising but also direct mail, public relations, printed brochures, presence at trade shows and participation in joint marketing schemes. Promotion can be very expensive, and it is often difficult to decide whether or not it is successful.

The 4 C's. With market competition shifting from the product-oriented focus to a customer-oriented paradigm, some defects of the 4 P's framework emerge.

Under this condition, the 4 C's marketing-mix model is put forward by Robert Lauterborn, who suggests that the marketing strategies that involved product, price, place and promotion are passé. The C's developed by Robert Lauterborn are the customer decision points corresponding to the marketer tools. They are customer solution, cost to the user, convenience and communication.

Case Study: The 4 C's of Tourism

What makes a tourist destination more attractive? "Adherence to 4 C's," says Mr. Cherian Varghese, CMD of Corporation Bank. These C's are curiosity, courtesy, cleanliness and culture. He was addressing delegates at the national seminar on "Emerging trends in tourism sector" in Mangalore.

Mr. Varghese feels that it is essential to generate curiosity among people about a place to market it effectively. Branding a place helps in generating curiosity among the people. Kerala, which is better known as "God's Own Country" in the tourism circuit, is attracting a large number of tourists.

After generating curiosity among tourists, they should be welcomed with courtesy. However, he regretted that this is not the case in many tourist destinations.

Curiosity and courtesy can yield better results only if the destination is clean. Some of the destinations are filled with garbage and plastic waste, distracting the tourist from the spot. Clean tourist spots create a positive impact on the mind of the customers, and they would like to visit these places again.

The memories of the area last forever if a person is made to experience the culture of the area. The Yakshagana art form of coastal Karnataka could be effectively used in marketing the tourist potential of the area. Stating that he had a chance to witness a Yakshagana performance recently, Mr. Varghese said he was impressed by the art form.

- **Product (customer solution):** Customers look forward to solve their problems. Incidentally the solution is the product. In tourists the problem can be how to best utilize the vacation, or how to have a break from the monotony in life.
- **Price (cost to the user):** Cost to the user may far exceed the price of the product. A tourist destination may focus on the economy of the expenses at the destination. However, for a tourist the cost will include complete transport expenses to and from the destination, local transport along with all sundry expenses as well as shopping.
- **Place (logistics) (convenience):** Even if there are multiple logistics options for tourists they will always weigh them as per their convenience. Thus, even if the midnight flight is least priced it may just not be the convenient option for them. Convenience can again have multiple dimensions. It can be convenience in terms of logistics, language, culture and, the most basic, travel.
- **Promotion (communication):** Each destination undertakes an effort to promote itself in the most impressive manner. However, how it gets communicated is most important. A great Web site, along with lovely advertisements can all go waste with the media report of harassment or exploitation of tourists or even the spread of some health threats some hundreds of miles away from the destination.

The 4 C's reflects the customer perspective. This, in turn, gives valuable insights to the tourism marketer to fine tune the offering as well as the promotion along with the needs of the tourist. This model considers a marketing problem from the consumer's perspective.

INDIA AS A TOURIST DESTINATION

The Indian subcontinent is bounded by the majestic Himalayan ranges in the north and edged by a spectacular coastline surrounded by three seas – Arabian Sea in the west, Bay of Bengal in the east and Indian Ocean in the south. India is a vivid kaleidoscope of landscapes, magnificent historical sites and royal cities, golden beaches, misty mountain retreats, colourful people, rich cultures and festivities. The world's leading travel and tourism journal *Conde Nast Traveler* ranked India among the top four preferred holiday destinations in the world. There are a number of factors responsible for the growth of Indian tourism at the global level.

- India is a peaceful country without any political disturbance, with the exception of a few destinations where a tourist is required to get special permission from the local authority to enter those areas.
- The country has a federal structure with elected governments in states. There are 28 states and 7 union territories administered directly by the central government.
- There is a healthy competition among all the states to attract tourists from all over the world for speedy economic growth and employment generation.

Types of Indian Tourism

There are all types of tourism in India, projecting the country as the ultimate tourist spot. The reason why India has been doing well on this front is that it is a multi-lingual, multi-cultural and multi-religious country with tremendous geographical diversity, hospitality, uniqueness and charm. Different types of tourism in India are religious or pilgrimage, adventure, fun/leisure (coastal and beach), archaelogical, heritage, ecological (wildlife), cultural, ayurvedha and meditation and ecotourism tourisms that are explained as followed.

Religious or Pilgrimage Tourism. India is famous for its temples and for this reason, among the different kinds of tourism in the country, pilgrimage tourism is increasing most rapidly.

Narayan Sarovar, Sudamas Porbandar, Kabirvad Shuklatirth, Kayavarohan, Bhadrakali, Haridwar, Badrinath, Kedarnath, Varanasi, Gangotri and Yamunotri, Rishikesh, Shamlaji, Bodh Gaya and Ajmer are important pilgrimage destinations, which have kept alive the religious sentiments of the people and have inspired millions of pilgrims to visit from all over the world.

Adventure Tourism. As a kind of tourism, adventure tourism in India is endless because the country has a rich diversity in terms of climate and topography. The various kinds of adventure tourism in India are rock climbing, skiing, camel safari, paragliding, mountaineering, rafting in white water and trekking. The various places in India where tourists can go for adventure tourism are Badami, Kanheri Caves, Manori Rocks and Kabbal for rock climbing. The places for skiing are Manali, Shimla, Nainital and Mussoorie. The rivers for white-water rafting are Ganga, Alaknanda and Bhagirathi.

Fun/Leisure (Coastal and Beach) Tourism. Beaches in India provide the most perfect destination for sun, sand, sea and surf, which are too hard to resist for a beach lover or a water-sports enthusiast. In almost every part of the subcontinent, one can enjoy beach holidays. Some of the famous beaches of India are Anjuna, Bogmalo, Benaulim, Calangute, Chapora, Colva and Cavelossim.

Archaeological Tourism. There are a number of places of archaeological importance, and can be broadly classified into Stone Age, Indus Valley, Neolithic-Chalcolithic, Megalithic-Early Historic and Late Historic periods. Famous archaeological sites of the Stone Age abound in peninsular India, more prominently at Pallavaram in Tamil Nadu, Hunsgi in Karnataka, Kuliana in Orissa, Didwana in Rajasthan and Bhimbetka in Madhya Pradesh. The sites of Neolithic-Chalcolithic age include Inamgaon, Walki, Navdatoli, Ahar, Balathal, Gilund, Budhihal, Sangankalur, Maski, Brahmagiri, Utnur, Golbai, Pandu-Rajar-Dhibi, Chirand and Burzoham. Famous sites from the Buddhist phase are Sanchi, Saranath, Ajanta, Kaneheri, Amravati, Sanati and Lalitgiri. Sites from the Jainism phase are Khandagiri-Udayagiri and Mathura. Some Islamic archaeological sites are in Delhi, Agra, Lucknow, Hyderabad, northern Karnataka, Aurangabad and Bhopal.

Heritage Tourism. Heritage tourism in India has always been famous for its ancient cultural diversity, which attracts millions of tourists each year. India's rich heritage is amply reflected in various temples, palaces, monuments and forts that can be found everywhere in the country. The most popular heritage tourism destinations in India include Taj Mahal in Agra, Mandawa castle in Rajasthan, Mahabalipuram in Tamil Nadu, Madurai in Tamil Nadu and Lucknow in Uttar Pradesh. The most famous heritage sites in Delhi are Red Fort, Jama Masjid, Humayun's Tomb and Tughlaqabad Fort.

Ecological (Wildlife) Tourism. India has a rich forest cover that has some beautiful and exotic species of wildlife – some of which are even endangered and very rare. Among the famous wildlife tourism attractions are Bandhavgarh National Park, Corbett National Park, Pench National Park, Ranthambore National Park, Kanha National Park, Bandipur Wildlife Park, Gir Wildlife Park, Dudhwa Wildlife Park, Sariska Wildlife Sanctuary, Keoladeo Ghana National Park, Panna Wildlife Park, Sunderbans Wildlife Park and Bharatpur Bird Sanctuary.

Cultural Tourism. India is known for its rich cultural heritage and an element of mysticism, which is why tourists come to India to experience it themselves. One can see the influence of various cultures in dance, music, festivities, architecture, traditional customs, food and languages. This richness in culture goes a long way in projecting India as the ultimate cultural tourism destination. The various fairs and festivals to visit are the Pushkar Fair, Taj Mahotsav and Surajkund mela.

Ayurveda and Meditation Tourism. Ayurveda and meditation originated in India some 6,000 years ago and are a natural way of healing body, mind and soul. Today, ayurveda and meditation have become the first preference of every person all over the world not only because of their curing capacity, but also because they do not have any side effects, if taken under proper guidance. Tourists can visit both North and South India for meditation and ayurvedic treatment. North India's prestigious institutes of ayurveda and meditation are set amidst natural surroundings, giving visitors enough space to breathe in the natural atmosphere. Kerala in the South has innumerable ayurveda and meditation treatment centres.

Ecotourism. Ecotourism entails the sustainable preservation of a naturally endowed area or region while ensuring not to damage the ecological balance. Places such as Kerala and Lakshadweep, the Himalayan region, northeast India and Andaman and Nicobar Islands are among the destinations in India where tourists can participate in ecotourism-related activities. The major national parks in India for ecotourism are Corbett National Park in Uttarakhand, Bandhavgarh National Park and Kanha National Park in Madhya Pradesh, Gir National Park and Sanctuary in Gujarat and Ranthambore National Park in Rajasthan.

Tourist Experience: Medical Tourism

Early this year, Rosemarie Lyntzberger — who is in the tourism business — encountered a leg ailment that curtailed her active life. She made extensive enquiries with the Turkish hospitals. She wanted to know what exactly was wrong with her leg, what are the corrective procedures available, what are the latest advances in the field, what is the success rate and how long will it take her to bounce back to her active life. Unfortunately, she could not find a satisfactory answer to her queries. Around this time, she happened to read *Stern*, a popular German magazine, which had a special feature on India. It featured India's advancement in the medical field. After corresponding with Wockhardt Hospital through mails and satisfied with the replies that she would have to undergo special hip-resurfacing surgery, she landed in Mumbai. Rosemarie during her visit to Wockhardt Hospital, Mumbai, where she is undergoing post-surgery physiotherapy, told southasia.de that her entire medical experience in India was wonderful. Dr. Kaushal Malhan of Wockhardt, who performed the surgery, told southasia.de that the cost of the operation in India is only around Euro 5,000, whereas it would cost a patient somewhere around Euro 35,000 in the United States or Europe.

Lyntzberger is highly impressed by the dedication of the medical team, which was headed by Dr Malhan, and the medical standards at the Wockhardt Hospital. She would recommend other patients like her in Europe and elsewhere to come to India for such surgeries. She would be more than happy to be the "goodwill" ambassador for India.

The 4 P's of Indian Tourism

Product. In the context of tourism destination, the product is said to include the destination's attractions, its environment, facilities and services, accessibility and price, as perceived and paid by the consumer.

Price. Tourism has been identified as an important avenue for employment, income generation and foreign-exchange earnings, and at the same time, it has a multiplier effect on the economy. The expenditure of the tourist circulates at all the three levels of the economy, namely, national, regional and local.

This means that if the tourist expenditure circulates locally and the leakages are low, a significant improvement can be made in the income and living standards of the people of the region or locality. However, a developed region can often divert the benefits towards itself at the cost of the underdeveloped neighbouring regions. Such situations have been experienced in international as well as domestic tourism.

Further, intense competition exists within a country between different regions, destinations or leisure spots and among the various suppliers of services. As tourism is becoming an established economic activity, marketing strategies concentrate on increasing the volume of tourists. This, at times, creates a host of unforeseen consequences. Thus, it is necessary that the objectives of tourism development in relation to a region, city or (a rural area) leisure spot be clearly stated. In fact, the developmental role of marketing has to be kept in mind while marketing regions, cities or leisure spots (rural area). This developmental role is to be further strengthened by socially responsible marketing.

Destination marketing in the international markets includes a variety of aspects ranging from information gathering to planning and image building.

Pricing decisions are becoming more critical than ever due to increasing complexity of the markets. The various factors that influence the price of tourism product are

- Organizational marketing policy and objectives
- High price elasticity of demand in segments such as leisure, recreation and vacation travel markets

- Relationship between pricing and customer perception, and perceived quality and status of products and services
- Degree of competition
- Seasonal demand that leads to peak and low-season periods, which require demand-management pricing to cope with short-run capacity problems
- High vulnerability to demand changes due to volatility of the external macroeconomic environment and currency exchange-rate fluctuation
- Extent to which tourism is considered to be a luxury or a necessity and the number of trips taken in a year

A number of options exist when it comes to determining the pricing strategy to be adopted. Key approaches followed are

- **Cost plus pricing:** Involves a fixed percentage markup on fixed and variable costs
- **Marginal pricing:** The high fixed cost and low variable cost of operating airlines, hotels and visitors' attractions often serve as a rationale for the adoption of marginal-pricing technique and yield-management strategies
- **Differential pricing based on demand:** Different market segments will pay different prices for a similar bundle of core benefits
- **Price skimming:** When market innovators are being targeted, price skimming is frequently adopted as a strategic imperative. Initially, the highest possible price is set for a niche segment, and, when saturation price is achieved, the price is reduced to accommodate the next segment of the market
- **Penetration pricing:** A frequent strategy when imitation is a key objective. In the absence of unique product features, a low initial price can be used to encourage people who show little brand loyalty to switch service supplies
- **Price bundling:** A typical approach adopted in tour operations sector wherein a holiday package includes a bundle of products, and a consolidated price is charged to the customer

Case Study: Lakshadweep — Untapped Potential

With its clean and untouched beaches, lush green canopy and corals, Lakshadweep looks like an ecotourist's dream come true. The place also provides facilities for scuba diving and other adventure sports. One would guess that such a place should have a thriving tourism industry, but statistics reveal a sad picture, with just 3,259 Indian and 539 foreign visitors in 2002. The inadequate exploitation of the potential of this place can be attributed to the same factors that had led to the successful emergence of Hong Kong as a tourist destination. There has hardly been any planned marketing effort to promote Lakshadweep, and most of the tourists are not even aware of its existence. Connectivity has improved only recently with a single flight operating between Cochin and Lakshadweep. Ship as a mode of transport is available, but it takes 14–20 hours. Also, the place lacks infrastructure to support a bigger influx of tourists. Lakshadweep was showcased in Discovery Channel's *Lonely Planet* show as one of the best places to connect with the nature. Still, it has not realized its potential because of a lack of efforts towards developing it.

- **Tactical pricing:** It includes a multitude of techniques such as periodic price reductions, early-booking discounts and group discounts to secure high volume and loyalty packages
- **Business-to-business pricing:** Here, tour operators purchase blocks of seats on aircraft and blocks of rooms in hotels in advance

Place. It is defined as routes of exchange through which a tourist accesses, books, confirms and pays for a tourism product. Tourism is special because no ownership exists and no actual product is being distributed. The tourist relies on distribution channels that fulfil the following functions:

- Present a wide range of travel opportunities to customers
- Provide information on crucial aspects at the pre-purchase stage such as price, availability and other dimensions
- Offer feedback to the supplier of tourism products which would not otherwise be feasible from distant markets

The most common forms of intermediaries in tourism industry are the tour operator and the travel agent. They bring together essential components of a holiday and make holiday products available through various outlets of distribution. In tourism, two main strategic choices exist. One is to adopt an intensive, selective or exclusive distribution strategy regarding outlet types and numbers, while another is to adopt a push or pull strategy.

The push or pull strategy is fundamental to all tourism-related organizations. A push strategy focuses on distribution outlets, urging them to sell to a tourist, while a pull strategy is directed at generating tourism demands, which is then addressed by the appropriate distribution outlets. A traditional push channel of distribution involves a service principal aggressively promoting its service to intermediaries by means of personal selling, trade advertising and use of trade incentives. The onus is then on the intermediary to push the service through the system to the final consumer, generating a balance between "maximizing the customer's benefit" and "maximizing the incentives offered to intermediary by the service principal." For a pull strategy, the intermediary's role is reduced to one of dispensing pre-sold branded services.

Promotion. The role played by promotion is instrumental to the growth of modern mass tourism. Promotion has often been misinterpreted and restricted in meaning. Marketing communications is a more generic term for communicating with producers, intermediaries and consumers.

Marketing communications can also be either push or pull in nature. The pull elements refer to instances of business-to-consumer marketing where close attention needs to be paid to patterns of buying behaviour, demonstrated by selected target markets and the marketing communication messages to which they are likely to be most responsive. In "push," the focus is more frequently on business-to-business (B2B) marketing situations, where suppliers are using the array of communication methods at their disposal to push the product through necessary channels of distribution to reach the desired targeted markets.

All aspects of communication need to be consistent with the overriding marketing objectives and be set with a realistic and achievable budget in mind. Objectives of communication include the following:

- Increasing awareness, interest, desire or action in the target audience
- Strengthening or changing destination image or positioning
- Generating prospects and new business opportunities
- Shifting buyer-behaviour patterns according to seasonality
- Developing word-of-mouth recommendation to increase referred business

The tourism marketers use the following techniques to convey the desired message and induce a response from target markets.

- **Public relations:** A planned and sustained effort to establish and maintain goodwill and mutual understanding between an organization, its products and its public. Media relations, crisis

Case Study: From Cricket to Olympics

For the ICC Cricket World Cup West Indies 2007, nearly 3 million people visited that island – 1.68 million stopover passengers and 1.33 million cruise passengers. While a lot of people went there for the cricket, many of them also used the opportunity to tour the place for the party of their lifetime. The Caribbean expected the event to have a knock-on effect on its tourism industry for years to come.

For the Olympics too, more than 400,000 tourists visited Beijing in 2008. Many hotels and travel agencies in Beijing turned their focus to September and October in hopes of developing a tourism market that the Olympics helped kick-start for the traditional autumn travel season. Ctrip.com, China's leading online travel-service provider, had launched a brand-new English Web site to attract more overseas travellers and stepped up its associations with various hotels in anticipation of a travel boom. Many tourists were getting increasingly interested in knowing the human side of Beijing, like finding out how locals' lives had been affected by the Olympics and what the traditional lifestyle of Beijing was like. To promote tourism before, during and after the Olympic Games, local travel authorities had rented airtime from CNN and BBC for Beijing TV shows, featuring the full spectrum of Beijing. The TV shows, directed by prominent Chinese filmmakers, were divided into four chapters, namely, scenery, culture, cuisine and shopping. The Beijing Olympic Economy Research Association estimated that by 2010 Beijing would receive between 5 million and 5.3 million overseas tourists, creating more than 5 billion U.S. dollars for China's economy.

management, product placement and sponsorship and attendance at exhibitions and travel fairs are public relations activities common to tourism

- **Advertising:** It acts as a highly effective, long-term image-building tool that legitimizes the brand and can be very economical
- **Sales promotion:** These are temporary, short-term incentives designed to stimulate action in the target audience
- **Direct marketing and database marketing:** Here, the organization promotes and deals directly in relation to the customer
- **Personal selling:** Verbal communication between prospective purchasers and salespersons for the purpose of making a sale

The complexity of the tourism industry, the fast pace of change, the rapid growth in volume of more experiences, demanding and sophisticated customers and growing role of information and communications technology underline the necessity of strategic marketing planning and the evaluation and exploitation of future trends for any tourism organization that wishes to compete in today's dynamic market environment.

The 4 C's of Tourism Marketing

Customer Solution. Customers receive thousands of offers on daily basis, trying to persuade them to buy one product or another. Then, what is it that actually makes them purchase something, parting with their hard-earned money? The answer lies with this C of marketing, that is, customer solution. It is only when the product solves a perceived customer problem or satisfies a desire that it will be bought. It can be further linked to the perceived utility or value of the product, which according to a simple economic theory, should be more than the cost of the product in order to make the customer buy the product. That is why most successful products that command a premium are those that are able to otter real value to the customer, either real or perceived. For instance, Nokia mobile phones provide real value in terms of reliable mobility solutions, while most of the value coming with a Mercedes car is perceived. The same theory applies to tourist destinations, too, when they are being marketed as products. The basic question that a tourist destination has to clarify while marketing is what is the customer problem that it is trying to solve or what is its customer value proposition. This value proposition, in turn, can be derived from the unique capabilities of the destination – for example, Rishikesh trying to promote itself as a destination for rafting. Yet, it will be meaningless to present a value without understanding what customers want – it is similar to designing a product without even analysing what features customers would want in it. Here are a few needs that the customer usually expects to be fulfilled at a tourist destination, and a destination can promote itself as meeting one or many of them. Although a few items in this list are generic enough to be applied anywhere, they are mostly pertinent to Indian customers. They are religious tourism or pilgrimage, leisure/fun/relaxation, adventure, medical and bussiness tourism.

- **Religious tourism or pilgrimage:** India presents a milieu of people from numerous cultures and faiths and has innumerable places of religious importance. The number of people visiting some of the most important destinations such as Tirupati in Andhra Pradesh or Varanasi in Uttar Pradesh runs into millions, which shows how important religion is to people.
- **Leisure/fun/relaxation:** This is one universal need that most of the tourist destinations are associated with. The importance of this need has been enhanced even further in recent times by an increasingly hectic lifestyle, which has led to higher levels of stress. This need can be addressed in an even better way by packaging various de-stressing features like serene environments, close-to-nature living conditions and spas offering ayurvedic massage. Kerala can easily be recognized as one such destination that offers all this.
- **Adventure:** The need of adventure sports is increasing at an appreciable rate all over the world. In India too, this need is building up among the burgeoning youth workers with higher disposable income.
- **Medical:** Travelling for the sake of treatment is common in India, especially with good health facilities concentrated only in a few places. Though a traditional Indian would usually not associate this kind of travel with tourism, the new trend is emerging. It is further strengthened by the influx of foreign tourists, who have started considering India as a place offering high-quality medical facilities at low cost and also excellent opportunity for tourism and sightseeing.
- **Business tourism:** With an onslaught of software and BPO companies, the traditional image of the Indian employee who worked "9 to 5" is fast changing into that of a fun-loving person, who loves to work hard, but parties harder. Companies have also started seeing fun activities as opportunities to create bond among the employees and, thus, promote teamwork and reduce attrition. This has created the need for tourist destinations that can be booked by corporate companies for a number of employees at once. Money is usually not a problem, but these customers need high levels of service and also assurance of safety of their employees. Also, since employee time is at a premium, there is a need for destinations located closer to business centres.

Cost. India has been a highly price-sensitive market. The economic growth has definitely increased income levels and spending power, giving rise to a new class of Indian consumers, who have the ability and the desire to spend for premium products. The tourist destinations, while providing enough avenues for such tourists, should not leave out middle-class customers. This becomes especially important for destinations like religious places, which people from all classes would want to visit. Another problem is measuring the cost of a tourist destination, as it is not just one single product but constitutes various components. Broadly, the spending components can be characterized into transportation, study and actual tourist activity:

- **Transportation:** How much does it cost to reach the destination? This will largely depend on the personal choice of the visitor, as multiple modes of transport are usually available to reach a particular destination.

- **Stay:** This will depend on the cost of living in the area. For example, this component will be much higher in a metro like Mumbai as compared to a tier II city like Agra.
- **Actual tourist activity:** In case the destination is famous for some particular activity or site, for example, rafting or safari, the cost of actually carrying out that activity – like hiring of equipment, ticket costs, etc., should be taken into account. For example, if somebody is going to Bandhavgarh, the cost of hiring a vehicle or an elephant and a guide to see the jungle and the tigers will be a major component of cost.

Convenience. This C addresses the question related to the user-friendly nature of the tourist destination. The obvious issue that comes first to the mind is the availability of transport. Just think of the untapped beauty of the northeastern region of India, and one would realize how big a detriment this can be in developing a tourist destination. Another important factor in today's era of the emerging global threat of terrorism is the safety of the tourists. If a destination is marked as unsafe, no matter how attractive it is, it is bound to see a steep fall in number of visitors. Kashmir, which was the favourite tourist destination in the 1980s, owing to its beauty that had earned it the status of "heaven on earth," hardly finds any tourist today. Safety is also linked to general law-and-order situation in the region. Even a few untoward incidents publicized in media can get a destination branded as unsafe and drive away tourists. There are a few more factors such as local travel options, places of stay and cuisines/quality of food as listed below.

- **Local travel options:** Good travel facilities enable the quick movement of tourists within the destination, so that they can visit more places. This gives more value for both money and time to the tourists.
- **Places of stay:** Convenient places of stay like hotels and resorts are important for a tourist. Though the type of place one wants is a matter of personal choice, a place should ideally have hotels ranging from five stars to inexpensive dorm rooms in order to be able to cater to all types of customers. In case a destination is trying to project itself as belonging to a particular class – for example, of luxury type – it should then have places of stay to match the same. One can positively expect upper-class tourists to look for luxury resorts.
- **Cuisines/Quality of food:** Food is a factor that works both ways. To understand this, consider a north Indian tourist visiting a south Indian destination or vice versa. For some time, the person would enjoy the local food and welcome the change. Hence, it is important to have good-quality local cuisine available. But at the same time, a lot of tourists cannot digest the change and want the food

Mini-Europe is a park located in Bruparck at the foot of the Atomium in Brussels, Belgium. Mini-Europe has the reproductions of the most attractive monuments in the European Union on show, at a scale of 1:25. It offers one a journey across Europe by means of some 350 exquisitely made model buildings and sites, which are exact replicas of these architectural jewels of the European Union. All the monuments have been recreated, down to the smallest detail. Big Ben is 4 m high. With its height of 13 m, the Eiffel Tower projects above a three-storey building. One may marvel at many other working models, like the erupting Mount Vesuvius.

they are accustomed to. So, it is also critical to ensure availability of multiple cuisines serving people from various cultural backgrounds.

Communication. This is the final step in understanding the customer. One has to understand the point of view of target customers while communicating the value proposition of the destination and realize how they will interpret the message. It is also worth noting that tourists usually love to talk about the places they visit. So, word of mouth is an important medium, especially now when one can spread one's opinion with the click of a mouse. This further points out the need to recognize the channels of communication where visitors look for information and putting the message across by using these. There can also be hidden messages going in the form of souvenirs being taken back by the tourists.

What is the one product that does not need marketing?

Try this: What is the one product that might be lethal and yet sells like crazy? Still no clue?

Since this is a book on tourism, let us try to look for the tourism product (a tourist place) that fits the description.

The smart mind will scream the answer — a famous religious place. Add the element of danger to life, and it is set in Jammu & Kashmir.

Maa Vaishno Devi Temple, or Bhavan as it is called, is perched on the Trikuta Mountain at a height of 5,300 feet. It is considered as one of the holiest pilgrimages and is the most visited after Tirupati in southern India.

Maa Vaishno Devi is also called *mooh maangi muradein poori karne wali mata* — the goddess who fulfils every wish her devotees ask for. Millions of devotees brave the 13-km stretch from Katra (50 km from Jammu) to reach the holy cave, to fulfil their *mannat* — a vow to a deity. It is visited by the poorest of the poor and the richest of the rich, and they stand together united, while waiting for *mata ke darshan* — a glimpse of the goddess. Fervent shouts of *Jai Mata Di* are heard throughout, as all pilgrims wish each other with chants of devotion.

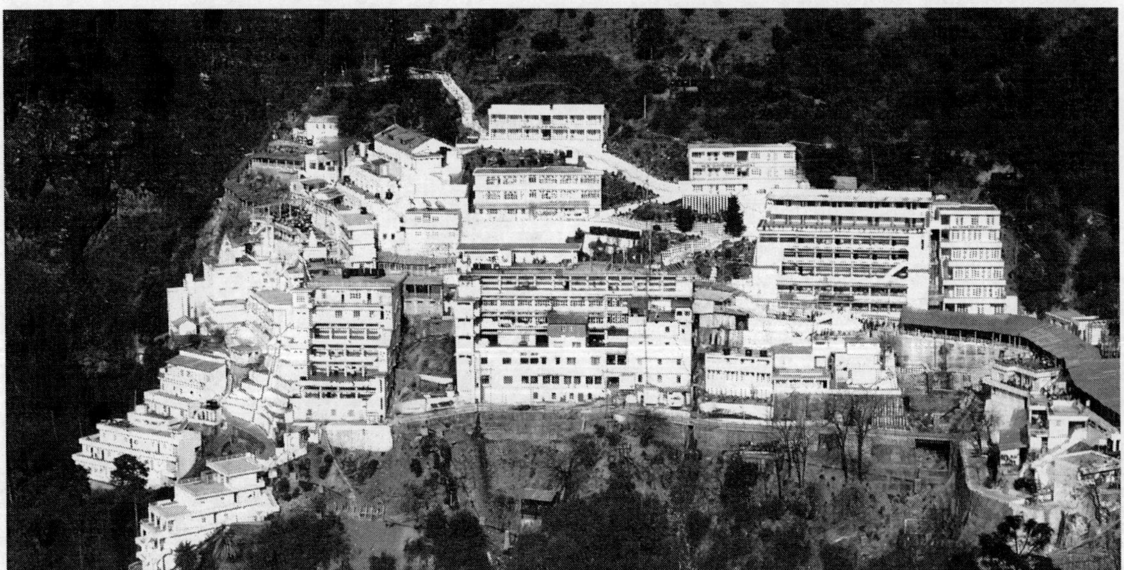

A View of Vaishno Devi Bhavan

Location: Jammu & Kashmir in North India

Altitude: 5,300 feet

Best Time to Visit: Throughout the year

Famous as: Pilgrimage centre of Hindus

Languages: Hindi, English

A unique angle of the visit to the shrine is that devotees believe that they can go there only if the goddess calls them, which is called *mata ka bulawa*. Devotees go through extreme physical strain and brave the entire arduous journey based only on the faith that they will make it since the goddess has summoned them.

The shrine is governed and handled by Shri Mata Vaishno Devi Shrine Board. It provides food, accommodation, travel and contingency services at affordable rates. They also arrange for online travel arrangements, souvenirs and online donations.

Truly, such a place is the dream product of any marketer — one that sells itself.

Tourist Experience: Trails Through the Desert

One fine October, I went on a tour of Rajasthan with my family. Our family is settled in South India, though our roots are in Rajasthan. We understand the language and identify with the culture very much, since we follow the same at home. So, when we disembarked the train at Jaisalmer and were greeted by the turbaned porters running towards us with a great smile and "Haanji Saah," we felt a sense of homecoming. We were quickly settled into a jeep with a very talkative guide who doubled as the chauffeur. As he took us to our accommodation, we saw why the city is called the "Golden "City." It is full of yellow sand-stone structures, especially the majestic Sonar Kella – The Golden Fort, which in the early morning reflects the sunlight and shines like the precious yellow metal. Our guide entertained us with his knowledge of 15 different languages, including Spanish, Italian, French, Bengali, Telugu and Tamil – entirely self-taught through listening to the tourists to the place.

We went for the desert safari to Sam Sand Dunes and enjoyed the very familiar-looking scene of sand dunes. A little Marwari lady, decked in her traditional chunnadi, came to us and performed a little ghummar jig and told us that all the Bollywood desert movies like *Lamhe* were shot at that very spot. As part of the package, we camped out in the desert, enjoyed ethnic Rajasthani food of *bajre ka khichda*, *kair-sangar*, *gatte ki sabji* and *daal-baati-churma*. After a professional *ghummar* performance, which soon turned into a dance floor, we slept on the soft sand like true sons of the soil. We did visit the *havelis* and museums that Jaisalmer is known for, but the sand-dune experience was truly unforgettable.

Unsung Tourist Destination: Ranikhet

Ranikhet is a little known tourist's paradise — a picturesque hill station with an old world charm. Queen's Meadow (as is its literal English translation) is situated at the foothills of the Himalayas in Uttarakhand. The biggest attraction of Ranikhet is that it is one of the very few places in the North that command the longest, uninterrupted view of the Himalayas. The best time to visit Ranikhet is April–June and September–November.

One can relax and play golf, enjoy the beauty of the coniferous forests and visit some ancient temples. The main feature about Ranikhet is its flora and fauna. The apple orchids and the wildlife nature walks are another incentive for anyone visiting the place. Visitors must visit the KRC Shawl and Tweed Factory to get a firsthand look at how weavers spin the beautiful shawls.

Woollens and handicrafts are the major shopping items. The more adventurous can descend on a whole lot of day excursions to

- Binsar Mahadev (14 km)
- Dwarahat (35 km)
- Sitlakhet (30 km)
- Almora (45 km)
- Kausani (75 km)
- Jim Corbett Park (90 km)

Golf Course at Ranikhet

Places to See Around

Cantt. Aashiyana Park – The Multifarious Environmental Zone: It contains a complete children's park, a herbal garden for those interested in herbal and medicinal plants, a lawn, colourful fountains and an awe-inspiring view of the Himalayan peaks.

Bhalu Dam: It is a beautiful artificial lake situated in the reserved forest, about three kilometres below Chaubattia.

Sunset points: These are the major attractions of Ranikhet, the prominent points being Machkhali from the hilltop near Woodvilla, Golf Ground (between Transit Camp and Ganiadeoli) and one on the road leading from Jhoola Devi to Bhargaon, a kilometre away from Jhoola Devi Temple.

Nanda Devi Mela: Nanda Devi Mela is a fair of great religious and cultural significance held at Nanda Devi Temple in September to commemorate the memory of goddesses Nanda and Sunanda.

Upat Kalika: A golf link about 6 km from the town on Almora Road, it is one of the best mountain golf links (nine holes) in the country and is surrounded by dense forests. Just a kilometre away from Upat is Kalika with its famous temple.

Chaubatia: Situated 10 km from Ranikhet, it is known for the botanical gardens and a government fruit research institute where one can see different varieties of exotic flowers and orchids. It also serves as a vantage point to view snow-clad Himalayan mountain peaks including Nanda Devi, Trishul, Nandaghunti and Nilkanth.

Jhoola Devi Temple: It is a famous temple of Goddess Durga with thousands of bells hanging in the temple premises. There is a tradition of hanging bells as an offering for fulfillment of one's wishes.

Unsung Tourist Destination: *(Continued)*

Majhkhali: On the Ranikhet-Almora road is a spot of entrancing, celestial beauty. Here is an awe-inspiring view of the majesty of snowy peaks. The Uttar Pradesh Government Agriculture Farm is situated here.

How to Reach Ranikhet

- **By train:** Nearest railway heads are Kathgodam (80 km) and Ramnagar (96 km).
- **By air:** Nearest airport is Pantnagar, 112 km away, but flights are not operational at present.
- **By road:** Ranikhet is well connected by roads to Almora (49 km), Delhi (386 km), Nainital (59 km) and Kathgodam (80 km). Private taxis and bus services are also available.

Accommodation

Ranikhet has a number of tourist resorts that are self-contained with all amenities and cater to travellers with various budgets ranging from economy to elite. A standard double-room rent can range from INR 500 to 1,500 per night, depending on the quality of room and the location of the resort. Resorts also offer family suites that can accommodate up to six people and come with a mini kitchen as well.

Best Time to Visit

Ranikhet has a cool climate all through the year. Summers (March to May) are very pleasant with a temperature range of 8°C to 22°C. Winters are chilly cold and have a temperature range of 3°C to 7°C. Snowfalls are common during winters. Monsoons during June to August receive average to heavy rainfall. Best period to visit here is all through the year; however tourist frequent to this place during summer season.

SUMMARY

- Like most other service industries, tourism is also an industry based on customer experience; hence, it is important to understand the rapidly changing socio-economic conditions that shape travel behaviour, as well as to realize the revenue it can generate for certain towns, cities and even countries.
- The major forms of tourism in India include religious, adventure, leisure, archaeological, heritage, ecological, cultural, ayurvedic and ecotourism. Each of these forms has a set of tourist destinations to provide people with the right and relevant experience.
- Price is becoming critical in branding of tourist destination and, hence, new pricing strategies such as marginal pricing, differential pricing and price bundling are being used in an effective manner.
- Various marketing communication channels such as public relations, advertising and word-of-mouth publicity play an important and crucial role in building the image of a particular destination.
- Tourism industry is now looking at building customer solutions by viewing the services at a particular destination from the customer's point of view and building solutions around the same.

FIELD EXERCISES

1. Identify the 4 C's and 4 P's for a tourist destination you have visited recently.
2. On the basis of type of tourism popular in a particular state, classify the states of India, for example, Kerala for ecotourism.

REFERENCES

Begde, Prasad (May 2008) "Opportunities and Challenges for Medical Tourism in India," *Conference on Tourism in India – Challenges Ahead*, 15–17 May 2008, IIMK.

Edgell, David E. (2002), "The Ten P's of Travel, Tourism and Travel Marketing," Best Practices for International Tourism Development for Rural Community

Etchner, Charlotte M. & Pushlaka Prasad (2003), "The Context of Third World Tourism Marketing" *Annals of Tourism Research*, Vol. 30, No. 3, pp. 660–682.

Fyall, A. & B. Garrod (2005), "Tourism Marketing : A collaborative approach," Channel View Publication

Lusch, R.F. & V.N. Lusch (1987), "Principles of Marketing," This Week, South Western Education Publishing Marketing in Tourism and Travel.

Mahoney, Edward M. and Gary R. Warnell (1987), "Tourism Marketing," Michigan State University Extension-Tourism Educational Materials.

Statue of Liberty

CHAPTER 6

Tourism Life Cycle

ABOUT THE DESTINATION

Officially titled 'Liberty Enlightening the World', it was presented to the USA by the people of France in 1886 to commemorate the centennial of American Independence and representing their friendship established during the American Revolution.

OBJECTIVES

- To identify the various theories that deal with tourism life cycle (TLC) and determining the different stages in TLC
- To assess the validity of Butler's theory with respect to some existing destinations
- To identify five tourist destinations in India and the life-cycle stages they are in and had been in
- To develop marketing strategies for promotion of these destinations as tourist hotspots
- To identify tourist life-cycle theories and relating real-life tourist experiences with the theories

INTRODUCTION

In the previous chapter, we studied 4 P's and 4 C's of marketing. In this chapter, we will try to apply these 4 C's and 4 P's of marketing to tourists and to the tourism industry as a whole, specifically with reference to the concept of life cycle. In case of marketing of products a theory which has been vogue for a long time is the theory of life cycle. This theory, as the reader will know in the following pages, treats the journey of a product or service as the journey of life of a human being. The only difference here is that the lifespan here is spent in a dynamic place known as the market. In case of tourism, the theory which deals with this issue is known as tourism area life cycle (TALC). Knowledge of this theory helps the marketer to analyse the destination and formulate marketing strategies accordingly.

Tourism areas, even though similar, are far more complex than a product. The tourism area life cycle concept is similar to the product life cycle (PLC) and is used to track the progress of the tourist region. It can provide vital cues about appropriate timely action intended to avoid decline, which may otherwise be predestined. Several tourist regions have gone into the decline stage due to lack of expert analysis and advice. This has caused unemployment in the region and, consequently, inflicted an adverse impact on the local economy of the region, further giving rise to social problems. This situation, while common, can be avoided by using the TALC model to provide timely marketing-intervention strategies over the life cycle of a region.

TALC also provides a focal point for both policymakers and tourists to ask pertinent questions — such as what leads a destination to change over time, how destinations and their markets change, which stage the current destination is in and, given the knowledge of the stage, what can be expected of the destination even before researching it. It, thus, provides a convenient mechanism for tourists to help them to shortlist the destination of their choice and for a policymaker to determine vital issues such as determining the amount of funding and how to utilize this funding for the selected tourism area.

Butler (1980) adapted the PLC model to the tourism industry and created the TALC concept. He established six stages under this model: exploration; involvement; development; consolidation; stagnation; decline and rejuvenation.

Stage 1: Exploration

During this stage, a small number of visitors arrive seeking unspoiled destinations. Tourism facilities hardly exist, and so the tourists share facilities with locals. Consequently, contact with the locals is likely to be high, but the economic return from tourism is insignificant.

Stage 2: Involvement

During this stage, the number of incoming tourists increases. This results in an increase in the number of professionally maintained facilities. However, it is generally observed that businesses mostly remain family based and the tourist-host relationship from the previous stage continues.

Stage 3: Development

Heavy advertising of tourism venues takes place during this stage. Characterized by externally (domestic or overseas) owned and controlled facilities, local ownership and control declines. In this stage, local attractions are marketed specifically. The landscape of the venue starts to change, particularly, in terms of new development and buildings.

Stage 4: Consolidation

The rate of increase in number of visitors declines during this stage. The industry responds to the decline in the growth rate through wide-ranging advertising campaigns and efforts to extend the tourism season and the market area. Facilities and infrastructure start to show signs of age.

Stage 5: Stagnation

This stage starts when peak visitor numbers have been reached and capacity levels exceeded for many variables, resulting in environmental, social and economic problems. The region is well known and well established but no longer fashionable. As a result, some venues diversify into serving as host to conventions and conferences in order to maintain visitor numbers.

During the final stage, the area will either decline or be rejuvenated.

Stage 6a: Decline

In this stage, there will be an inability to maintain market share. The venue would no longer be on the favourite lists of people, but might be used for day trips. Tourism-related structures would get converted to non-tourism uses such as retirement centres, apartments and offices, since the tourism destinations also attract permanent residents. In the end, the tourism sector there offers a low level of facilities or dies completely.

Stage 6b: Rejuvenation

This requires a complete change in the attractions on which the tourism region is based. Rejuvenation can be achieved, first, by using man-made attractions such as casinos and, second, by taking advantage

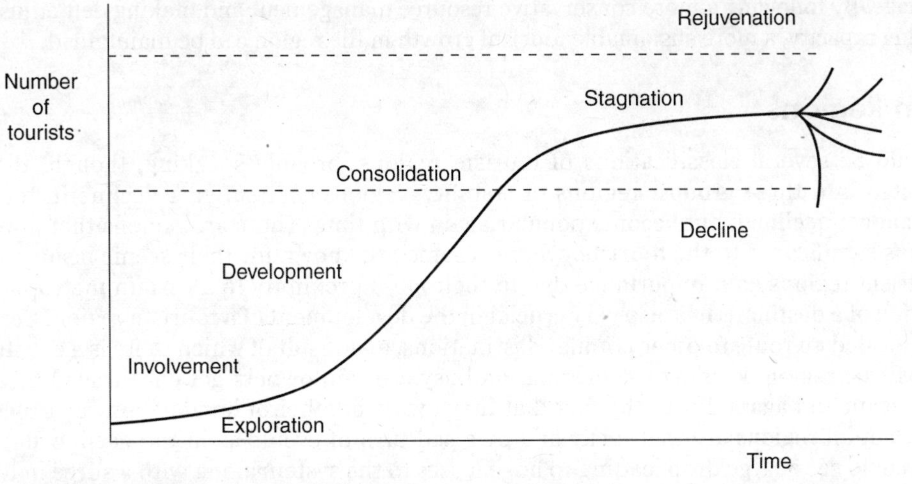

Fig. 6.1: Tourism Life Cycle

of previously untapped natural resources. Other special-interest groups could be catered to through activities such as cycling, mountain biking, diving and fishing (Fig. 6.1).

TOURISM AREA LIFE CYCLE THEORY

Life Cycle Theory: Origin and Use

Human life is divided into several stages from birth till death. Man takes transformation biologically from a child to an adolescent, then to a middle-aged man and finally to an old man gradually approaching his death. This biological transformation forms the genesis of the life-cycle theory too. This concept was developed by product researchers to explain the process of growth in product sale and profit levels. A typical life cycle consists of five stages namely design, introduction, growth, maturity and decline. Introductory stage of a PLC is important because the marketing strategy followed during this period sets the tone of market success for the product. Of course, different subsequent stages require different strategies depending on the PLC stage requirements. Different companies having varying leverage ratios tend to behave differently in terms of marketing strategies for their products. For example, companies having a high debt-to-equity ratio are found to follow more aggressive marketing strategies during each life-cycle stage of the product.

Implication of TALC Theory

Certain people in the society, particularly the local entrepreneurs, live under the impression that the growth potential for tourism is unlimited in a resort region. This notion is, however, grossly misplaced as every resort area has a limited lifespan. The fact of the matter is that there is a certain degree of structural unemployment and social as well as spatial adjustments, as the rapid growth stage of a resort area gives way to a more restrained tourism activity. This is bound to happen as the local financial investment eventually dries up leading to a decrease in construction developments.

Once local inhabitants start understanding and accepting the realities of the TLC, the process becomes smoother as appropriate decisions and actions can be taken by the inhabitants to avoid the decline stage. By following a more conservative resource management and making deft adjustments to the carrying capacity, a more sustainable tourism growth in the region can be maintained.

Tourism Regions

There could be several classifications of tourism regions, broadly speaking, though, they can be appropriated into three groups: regions of stability, regions that suffer a decline in tourism and regions that get declined, but become popular again with time. There are regions that have cultural or religious significance to the tourists, whereas some are known for their scenic beauty. Similarly, some tourism regions gain importance due to their close proximity to a certain metropolitan area. The location of a destination is also very crucial in the development of a tourism region. Certain locations are located en route to other popular destinations, as a result of which there is a constant traffic flow across the region, keeping the destination busy. Certain owners get encouraged to visit these locations again and again due to the fact that they own a number of holiday homes at these places. However, not all regions are that lucky and by a sad turn of events as in the decline stage, tourist numbers could see a large drop leading to huge losses to the system along with a surge in unemployment and mortgage foreclosures.

Tourism Regions of Long-Term Stability. Certain tourism regions never seem to lose their sheen. It is due to the fact that these regions have cultural and/or religious significance. Prominent examples could be that of Rome, Israel, Athens and Cairo. Rome was the heart of the Roman Empire and an important seat of cultural and religious beliefs. The city houses significant remains of the Roman civilization, which forms the core of the European culture. Apart from this, Rome houses the Vatican, the house of the pope, which could be considered the Mecca of Catholics. Israel, Athens and Cairo are other similar examples in their own right.

Tourism Regions That Have Declined. There are regions whose complete economy is based on tourism. If tourism as a business goes down, the economic base of the region could come under threat. Various authors have put forward their theories behind the declining number of tourists at such destinations; however, the comprehensive list put up by Cooper could be considered a genuine attempt at diagnosing the issues involved herein. The list was originally prepared for the "cold water resorts" of Europe and the United Kingdom; but most of the points are valid for any resort that is facing a decline. As per Cooper, the following factors were identified:

- Growth in low-status, low-spend visitors and day visitors
- Competition from holidays abroad
- Over dependence on long-holiday market
- Limited appeal to overseas visitors
- Highly seasonal destinations
- Outdated, poorly maintained accommodation and amenities
- Local opposition to tourism as resorts' residential roles increase
- Lack of professional, experienced staff
- Local government reorganization creating amalgams of resorts and diluting political power of resorts in larger authorities
- Demands for increased operational efficiency and entrepreneurial activity in local government
- Shortage of research data

Rejuvenated Tourism Regions. The word rejuvenated means that the region has returned back to its days of old glory as a thriving tourist destination or as a centre of economic activity. The only aberration could be the fact that the region would be now dominated by other groups of industries. In certain cases, the resort area, which faced decline in its primary product of tourism, tries to diversify into other areas of enterprise. Certain examples are New York, Bournemouth and Nice, all centres of tourism that declined. Los Angeles (LA) was a seaside resort town that was never able to complete its life cycle and reach the decline stage. During the Cold War, LA's economy diversified into aviation, electronic and shipbuilding industries, aptly supported by the military contracts. This diversification led to new employment opportunities, and cheap mortgages were made available by the Federal Housing Association. As a result, the population of LA rose from about 4 million in 1950 to nearly 7 million in 1980.

Validation of TLC Theory on Real Destinations

This model developed for the TLC generated more academic interest than any of the earlier works done in this area, conceivably because its simplicity makes it applicable to a wider set of destinations with much more relevance. There also have been criticisms of the theory from various quarters because its simplicity creates difficulty in drawing boundaries between the various stages.

Different researchers have tried to validate this model on actual tourist destinations, and the majority of results have reinforced the validity of this model. A summary of significant findings on some specific destinations is shown in the appendix at the end of this chapter.

Identifying Butler's Stages

This section performs a stage-by-stage analysis of the TALC theory, starting with the identification of the exploration stage. The main aim of this analysis is to investigate the degree of compliance for identifying TALC stages.

Testing for Exploration Stage. Theoretically, the exploration stage is characterized by the presence of a few adventurous tourists who are attracted to the area because of its unique and different natural and cultural attractions. There are little or no specific tourist facilities, and contact between visitors and locals is high compared to the latter stages of TALC.

Testing for Involvement Stage. It is characterized by an increase in visitor numbers and local involvement in the provision of services for them. Contact between visitors and locals is still high, and there is some advertising to attract tourists. A market area can be identified. A tourist season develops, and there is some organization in the travel arrangements made for tourists. Governments come under pressure to bear and provide tourist facilities such as airports, roads and harbours.

Testing for Development Stage. Butler's development stage is characterized by a well-defined tourist market area, which is partly the result of heavy advertising. At the same time, natural and cultural attractions are marketed specifically and supplemented with man-made attractions. Local involvement and control of development decline rapidly, and locally owned facilities (particularly accommodation) give way to large-scale facilities provided by external investors. Changes in the physical appearance of the region are noticeable and sometimes these changes are not accepted. Regional and national involvement in planning and provision of facilities occurs, and, again, this may or may not be necessarily accepted by local residents. The number of visitors exceeds locals in peak periods and imported labour is used.

Testing for Consolidation Stage. The first criterion for the consolidation stage is that the rate of increase in visitor numbers starts to decline. Total number of visitors exceeds local residents and a major part of the region's economy is tied to tourism. Marketing, advertising and promotion are far reaching, and efforts are made to extend the tourist season. Major tourism franchises and chains have a presence in the region, but there will not be many new additions during this stage. The large number of visitors and facilities provided for them are expected to arouse some opposition and discontent among residents. There is a well-defined recreational business district (RBD), and some older facilities are regarded as second rate and not desirable.

Testing for Stagnation Stage. According to Butler's model, during the stagnation stage tourist numbers do not rise further from the peak level. Nature of the visitors' changes. Capacity levels are reached resulting in environmental, social and economic problems. The resort has a well-established image, but is no longer fashionable, and there is a reliance on repeat visitation. There is an increase in conventions, and older property ownership turnover rates are high. New developments are still occurring but on the periphery of the original tourist area. Large numbers of imported attractions start to outnumber natural and cultural attractions, and local people consider visitors annoying.

Testing for Decline Stage. The decline stage is characterized by a declining market and an inability to compete with newer attractions. Holiday makers stay away, but the number of day trippers increase if the region is located close to a centre of population. Property turnover is high, and tourist facilities are converted to other uses. Hotels may become apartment blocks or retirement and convalescent homes. Local involvement and control increase as residents are able to buy back into the tourism industry at reduced prices.

Testing for Rejuvenation Stage. The rejuvenation stage is almost certainly not reached without a complete change in the attractions on which tourism in the region is based. Such a change is brought about by either introducing man-made attractions such as theme parks and casinos or making better use of previously untapped natural resources. Winter sports at Aviemore in Scotland are an example of the latter.

Tourist Life Cycle

Cohen's Theory. Cohen (1972) categorized tourists into character types. He identified four character types: drifter, explorer, individual mass tourist and organized mass tourist.

- **Drifter:** The tourists classified as the drifters venture farthest away from the beaten track and from their own culture. They are the travellers unwilling to be associated with the tourism industry. They have no schedule, tend to take work when they need money and live the way the host culture lives, sharing their shelter, food and habits. The hippy travellers of the late 1960s and the early 1970s can be included in this category. These people became associated with the so-called hippy trail from India and Nepal to Europe. Butler associated this type of tourist with the initial stages of the tourist area cycle of evolution.
- **Explorer:** The explorer tourists are similar to the drifters in that they arrange their own trips and they like to get off the beaten track as much as possible. This type of person, however, likes to stay in more comfortable accommodation and looks for more reliable and better transport than the drifter. They try to meet with locals as much as possible and try to learn their language and culture. In Butler's model, these people would come after the drifters, but are still in the initial stages.
- **Individual mass tourist:** The individual mass tourists do not arrange their own trips but use a tourist agency. They live in an "environmental bubble" of their home country and only venture outside this familiar territory occasionally. They differ from the organized mass tourist because they are not totally organized, do not travel in groups and the tour is not totally pre-planned. In Butler's

model, these people are in the development, consolidation and stagnation stages, but predominantly in the consolidation stages.

- **Organized mass tourist:** The organized mass tourists are the least adventurous of all; they always travel with groups of people from their own culture and stay within an environmental bubble of their culture and stay isolated from the local community. These tourists commute locally in hired air-conditioned buses and boats insulated from the outside environment. Accommodation is also in air-conditioned hotels that are micro-environments of their home country. They are met by people who speak their language and on all tours are provided with guides who speak their language. They are guided into shops that are familiar with their needs and wants and where the salespeople speak their language. The itinerary is all planned in advance, and an all-inclusive fare is paid in the country of origin. These are the tourists that Butler puts at the end of his cycle, particularly in the "stagnation" stage and to a lesser extent in the "consolidation" stage.

GENERAL MARKETING STRATEGIES

As tourism is a highly competitive industry, the traveller has a wide range of choices and looks for good value for money. The lack of quality infrastructure, uncompetitive rates, indifferent or poor product quality, difficulty in getting access to information on travel and tourist destinations and untrained service providers have an enormously negative effect on the competitiveness of the tourism product. For all these, it is necessary for tourism industry to formulate marketing strategies that include overall business objectives, an assessment of the market environment, a business/community profile-based market identification (segmentation) and the marketing objectives for each segment, the best combination of the 4 P's (product, price, place, promotion) for each segment, an implementation plan, a marketing budget and a method for evaluation and change.

Some of the strategies that tourism industry should adopt need to take care of the following:

- Tourists should have access to information regarding tour operators, tour agents and tour guides.
- There is a shortage of skilled manpower in the tourism industry. So, some attention should be given to this area.
- Tourism businesses should also view their services/products in generic terms. Thinking of products/services in this manner helps focus more attention on the experiences desired by customers and also on the facilities, programmes and services that produce those experiences.
- Tourism can retain existing customers, attract new customers, increase brand awareness, build business, reduce customers' perceived risk and gain the trust of customers through promotional campaigns. The marketers should promote their products by means of appropriate media (radio, television, print) aimed at specific markets. They need to develop and maintain Web sites specific to tourism.
- **Enhance local awareness of offerings:** The majority of tourists to India visit friends or relatives who live here. The local population has an important role to play in ensuring the success of the events, facilities and attractions that are promoted for tourists. Currently, there is a perception amongst stakeholders that residents lack awareness or have negative perceptions of what is available in the country. One aspect of the tourism marketing campaign should be aimed at enhancing local pride, appreciation and awareness of India's cultural offerings in order to ensure that residents participate in promoting Indian attributes to visitors.
- **Develop new partnerships and packages for tourism:** Increased understanding will kindle appreciation for and interest in collaborative activity that can benefit all parties involved. Partnerships should be encouraged between hoteliers, restaurateurs, retailers and cultural groups. New packages

such as museum tours coupled with meals at local establishments, theatre packages with accommodations/meals or a package of festival tickets are just some of the possibilities.

- **Conduct research specific to the tourism sector:** Research should include quantitative information such as attendance, origin of respondents, spending patterns and demographics, as well as qualitative information such as visitor satisfaction and accessibility and programme aspects. This results in assisting the development of presentations that can be made to non-tourism sectors. In addition, it results in informed decision making on operations, programme and capital funding, infrastructure improvements and tourism initiatives to grow.
- **Enhance funding for tourism development:** With the evolution of the tourism strategy, there is an opportunity to diversify and expand funding. Though it is not easy to determine how much new funding might be needed in the long term, majority of stakeholders feel strongly that infrastructure and tourism marketing require more stable and sustained funding in the future.

TOURIST DESTINATIONS IN INDIA

For tourism area life cycle study, five destinations have been chosen: the Taj Mahal, Fatehpur Sikri, Bada Imambara, Hampi and Valley of Flowers. The first section discusses the destination along with a brief background. In the subsequent section, stages of those destinations in TALC are discussed. Finally, possible marketing strategies for the destination at that stage of life cycle have been discussed.

Criteria for Selecting the Destinations

The criteria for selecting the destinations are

- Location
- Availability of relevant data
- Historical and cultural significance
- Popularity among domestic tourists
- Personal experience

The Taj Mahal. Taj Mahal is a mausoleum located in Agra. It was built by Mughal emperor Shah Jahan in memory of his wife, Mumtaz Mahal. The Taj Mahal is considered the finest example of Mughal architecture, a style that combines elements from Persian, Turkish, Indian and Islamic architectural styles. In 1983, the Taj Mahal became a UNESCO World Heritage Site and was cited as "the jewel of Muslim art in India and one of the universally admired masterpieces of the world's heritage."

Taj Mahal, Agra

Taj Mahal is built entirely out of white marble, which was brought from all over India and Central Asia. The entire Taj complex consists of five major constituents – namely Darwaza (the main gateway), Bageecha (the gardens), Masjid (the mosque), Naqqar Khana (the rest house) and Rauza (the main mausoleum). A shadowy burial crypt inside the Taj Mahal houses the tombs of Shah Jahan and his wife Mumtaz Mahal. Above these tombs is the main chamber that has the false tombs, typical of mausoleums of the Mughals. Perforated marble screens were used to transmit light into the central chamber.

Taj Mahal also appears in several listings of the seven wonders of the modern world, including the recently announced New Seven Wonders of the World, a recent poll with 100 million votes.

Fatehpur Sikri. Fatehpur Sikri is a ancient township in Agra district in the state of Uttar Pradesh. It was the political capital of the Mughal Empire under Akbar's reign, from 1571 until 1585, when it was supposedly abandoned due to lack of water. It is regarded as one of the finest works of architecture during Akbar's period and is an ode to Mughal architectural legacy. Its numerous palaces, halls and masjids testify to Akbar's creative and aesthetic impulses, which were very much typical of the Mughals. Some of the places to visit are Jama Masjid, Tomb of Sheikh Salim Chisti, Diwan-e-Khas, Diwan-e-Aam and Panch Mahal. It is also a World Heritage Site. Some contemporary Indian architects have cited it as an important source of inspiration. Be it an architect or a common man on the road, Fatehpur Sikri captures the imagination and wonder of all who visit and experience the grandeur of its buildings.

Fatehpur Sikri (Diwan-E-Khas)

Bada Imambara. The Bada Imambara is an important tourist attraction of Lucknow. It is neither a mosque nor a mausoleum but a huge building featuring interesting elements within it.

There are, in fact, three halls under the same roof. The Persian Hall is the central hall, simply astonishing in proportions. The China Hall is square at ground level, becomes octagonal at mid-height and 16 sided at the top. The India Hall has been fashioned like a watermelon. These are only minor structural variations. The roof, common to these halls, is flat and in one piece.

On the top terrace, approached through a narrow flight of steps, is an amazing set of passages designed to confuse the most alert minds, being a labyrinth of interconnected passages that seem to lead nowhere. This is called *bhul bhulaiya* (maze), which adds an element of wonder to the construction. There are about 1,000 narrow passages where the air is trapped for cross-ventilation. This labyrinth served the important purpose of supporting the thick walls of the Imambara, which, in turn, bore the brunt of the mammoth roof.

The construction of the halls and the use of vaults show a strong Islamic influence. The great Imambara was built at a time when a great famine raged through the state in 1784.

Hundreds of men and women thronged the city as utter destitutes. Even the rich and the noble were reduced to beg for food. Asaf-ud-daula, the then *nawab* of Awadh, hit upon a novel plan to help the poor. He decided to build the great Imambara and employed some 22,000 people to work day and night. One fourth of the quantum of work achieved during the day timing was demolished at night and payment made for the labour. Thus, there was enough work for everyone. The names of the nobles were called out

Bada Imambara

at night for payments to spare them the indignity of working with the masses. They would have jewels inserted into muskmelons before distribution among the poor.

The Stone Chariot, Hampi

Hampi. Hampi was the medieval capital of the Vijayanagara empire that ruled South India from 14th century AD to 16th century AD. It is situated in Karnataka state and is listed as a UNESCO World Heritage Site.

The ruins of Hampi lie scattered across an area of about 26 square km, amidst giant boulders and vegetation. The spectacular ruins are packed with giant temples, palaces, market streets, aquatic structures, fortifications and an abundance of ancient monuments. The important monuments dotting the landscape include the Vittala Temple complex with its 56 musical pillars; the iconic stone chariot, which is a shrine built in the form of a temple chariot; the Hampi Bazaar, a 35 yards wide and nearly 800 yards long street and Ugra Narasimha, a 6.7 metres tall monolith carved from a single boulder.

Hampi has mythological associations too, adding to its significance as a religious destination. According to local folklore, Hampi and its environs formed Kishkindha, the capital of the monkey king Sugreeva. Sugreeva was an ally of the Hindu god, Lord Rama, in the mythological epic *Ramayana*.

Valley of Flowers. The valley is bounded by peaks from all sides, and an area of 8,950 hectares here was declared as a national park in September 1982. It was only in July 2005 that the valley was added to the list of World Heritage Sites by UNESCO. The valley attains its significance because of the rich diversified flora it has in its bounds. The valley itself is located at a transition point of the Zanskar and Himalayan ranges and the eastern and western Himalayas. This has resulted in bringing together a rich diversified flora at one place. Several of the flower species found here are internationally endangered. There are also many endangered medicinal plants here.

A View from the Valley of Flowers

The snow on the Himalayas adds majesty to the mountains, and innumerable flowers add to its beauty. This famous spot is not very difficult to reach. When the sun shines hot on this field, thousands of flowers bloom. Tourists from all over the world come here. This valley was unknown till a British mountaineer Frank Smith first visited here.

In 1931, Smith wanted to scale a peak, called Comet, in Garhwal. While returning after successfully completing his mission, he took the western pass and lost his way and reached this valley after many difficulties.

All of a sudden, he came upon a sea of flowers that totally enchanted him. He put up a tent and stayed here for many days. During those days, he collected 260 different species of flowers and took back some seeds along with him. In 1937, he came back again to this valley and stayed here for a long time. Then he wrote a book called *The Valley of Flowers*. Soon after, this place became world famous.

Many small streams flow within this valley, adding to its overall beauty. The high mountain peaks surrounding this valley look like they are guarding it. The glaciers amongst these look very attractive.

The valley itself is covered with majestic peaks. The river Pushpawati flowing through it divides it into two sections.

IDENTIFICATION OF LIFE-CYCLE STAGES AND MARKETING STRATEGIES

In this section, we try to identify the life-cycle stage for a particular tourist destination based on various data points. On the basis of this stage, we also recommend specific marketing strategies to be used for developing these tourist destinations.

Taj Mahal

Life-Cycle Stage. Taj Mahal has been one of the few tourist destinations in the world symbolizing a timeless cultural attraction. Consequently, ever since its recognition as a tourist destination, it has attracted people in huge numbers. We found that the period from 1647 (the year in which the construction of Taj Mahal was completed) to 1947 (the year in which India attained Independence) had not been a period of high tourist involvement. Local population and the people from surrounding areas formed the bulk of the tourists during this period. Moreover, the existing statistical data meant that a suitable period for a detailed analysis of this monument could only be from 2001 onwards. Prior to that year, statistics were extremely limited.

Taj Mahal is a structure that has always remained in focus since its conception more than three centuries ago. Thus, the "exploration" stage is not applicable to this monument. Our research suggests that the period from 1947 to 1983 can be considered as "early involvement" phase for the monument. The number of tourists, both domestic and foreign, was not very high due to the limited accessibility of the monument and a lack of focus on tourism by policymakers in the pre-Independence era and then in the immediate post-Independent era as well. The monument was declared a UNESCO World Heritage Site in 1983. This marked a new chapter in the history of the monument, and, since then, there has been a gradual increase in the number of foreign tourists visiting it.

The year 1983, thus, also signalled the beginning of the "late involvement" stage for the monument. The increase in number of tourists exerted pressure on the government to provide infrastructural facilities for the development and projection of Taj Mahal as a tourist destination. Absence of a civilian airport forced the government to allow landing of flights at the Kheria airport which is a defence airport.

The late 1990s and the early 2000 period marked the "development" phase for Taj Mahal. There were concerted efforts by the authorities to promote Taj Mahal. The year 2004 was celebrated as the International Taj Year. It also marked 350 years of existence of Taj Mahal. The Uttar Pradesh ministry for tourism also started participating and promoting the monument at international platforms such as the International Tourism Meet held in Berlin in March 2004. Consequently, the number of foreign tourists visiting Taj Mahal showed a significant rise in 2004 and beyond as indicated in Figure 6.2.

The increase in the number of foreign tourists during this period can also be attributed to the combination of two factors – economic prosperity of India in the early 2000 and the proximity of Taj Mahal to the capital of the country. Thus, a large number of foreign tourists visiting the capital for business purposes also visited the monument.

Taj Mahal continues to be in the "development" stage. The following parameters further strengthen this conclusion:

- The revenue collected from foreign exchange earned from Taj Mahal and the expenditure incurred are presented in Figure 6.3.

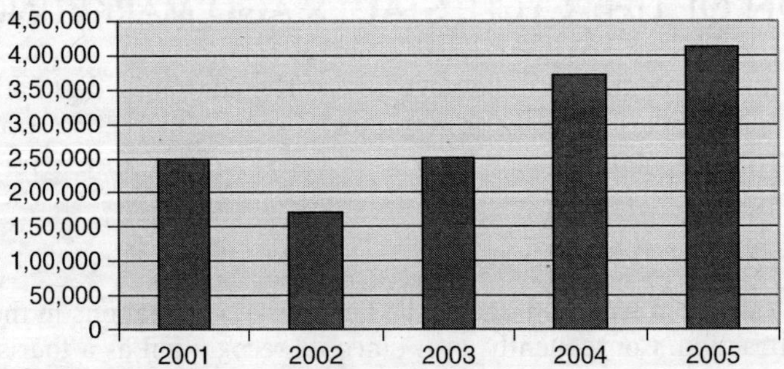

Source: www.indiastat.com

Fig. 6.2: Foreign Tourists Visiting Taj Mahal

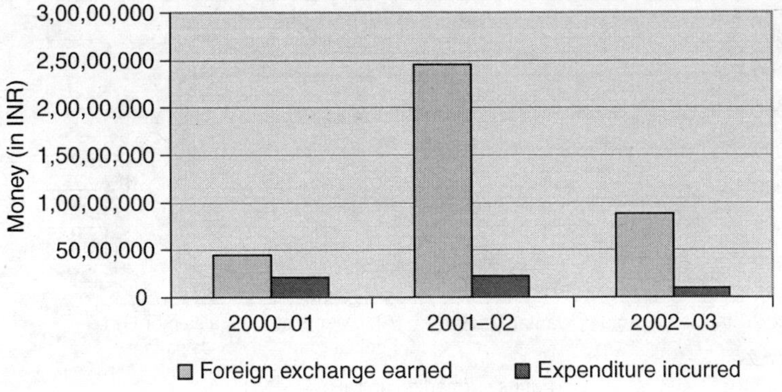

Source: www.indiastat.com

Fig. 6.3: Foreign Exchange

The revenue collected from foreign tourists is also an indication of the number of tourists visiting the monument. Moreover, the revenue earned has consistently exceeded the expenditure incurred on Taj Mahal.

- The number of domestic visitors to Taj Mahal from 2004 to 2006 is shown in Figure 6.4.

The monument continues to attract even the local populace within the country. As per the statistics above, the number of visitors rose – from 1,847,955 in 2004 to 2,048,120 in 2006.

- The funds earmarked for monuments under custody by the government of India (as in May 2007) are given in Figure 6.5.

Taj Mahal, with an estimated fund allocation of about INR 18.7 million, is the second highest in the given list. This shows that regarding the amount of expenditure incurred on the monument to market and advertise, it is among the highest in India.

- The allotment of fund by the Archaeological Survey of India (ASI) for the year 2007–2008 is shown in Figure 6.6.

Taj Mahal ranks in the top five heritage sites in terms of funds allocated by the ASI. Thus, Taj Mahal enjoys funding from both ASI and the Government of India.

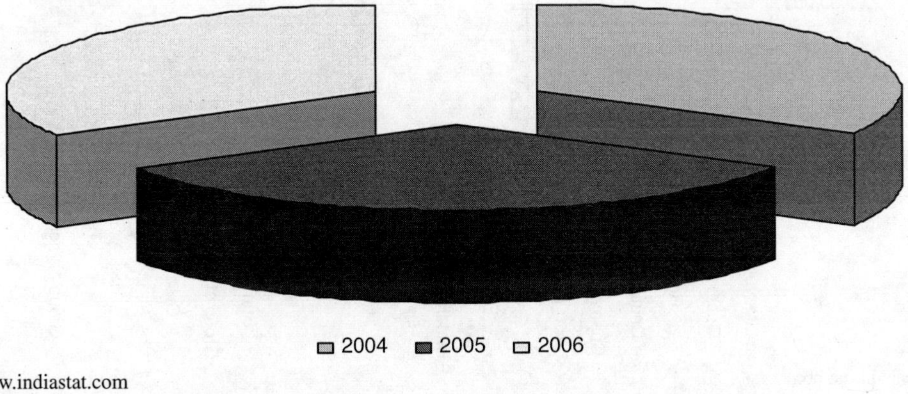

Source: www.indiastat.com

Fig. 6.4: Number of Domestic Visitors to Taj Mahal

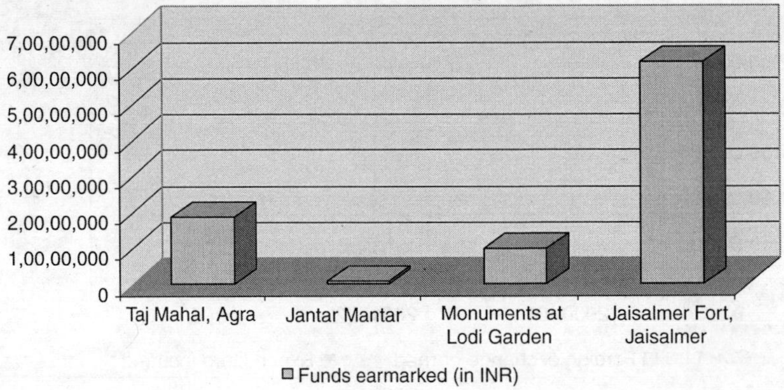

Source: www.indiastat.com

Fig. 6.5: Funds Earmarked

Marketing Strategies

Segmentation. Domestic tourists visiting the Taj Mahal can be segregated on the basis of the reasons for their visit which are as follows:

- LTC/summer and winter vacations
- Durga pooja holidays
- Religious trip to Mathura, Vrindavan and Varanasi (Agra comes in between)
- Visiting Delhi for some official/personal work

Foreign tourists, on the other hand, normally have the following reasons:

- Pleasure trip to India
- Business/conferences in India
- Trips by international students studying in India

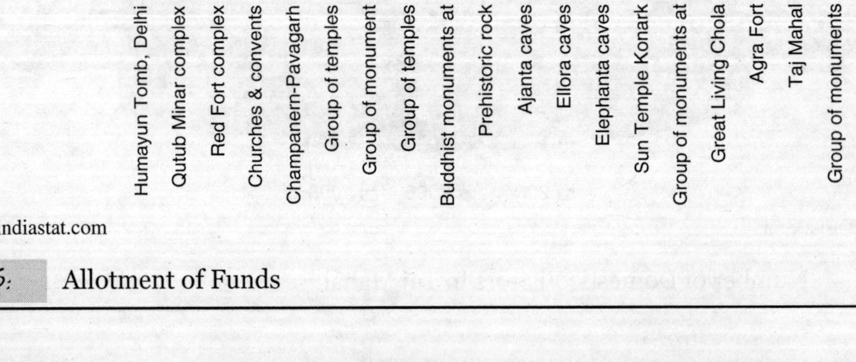

Source: www.indiastat.com

Fig. 6.6: Allotment of Funds

Targeting Specific Segments

Domestic Tourists: Due to the extreme climate in India during the summer months of April to June, most schools are closed for summer vacations. This time is utilized by domestic Indian tourists to visit places such as Taj Mahal. This is the time that needs to be utilized through special marketing strategies such as

- Providing free drinking water along with tickets
- Arrangement of umbrellas on a returnable basis
- Putting matting on the main monument floors to save the feet of tourists from scalding
- Special solar buses to ensure that tourists walk a minimum distance in the hot weather
- Expansion of green cover in the city with a special emphasis on areas within a 2 km radius of the monument, so that it helps in controlling the temperature naturally. For this, special tree-plantation campaigns should be launched and private participation encouraged.

Foreign Tourists: Since most foreign tourists visit the city during winters, no event is organized for tourists during the off-season. This can be compensated with a few events that will make the tourist's stay more enjoyable and memorable. Specific recommendations in this regard are

- Creation of small shopping-cum-cultural fests in April and May
- Small cultural events in April to June
- Special light-and-sound shows during that period on specific days across the monument (once a week)

Generic Strategies

The generic strategies are:

- Standardizing the services of tourist guides in terms of their qualification and the fee they charge. Guide services should be clubbed with tickets to prevent harassment of tourists by unqualified guides.
- Special alternate services – such as renting audio tapes with history of Taj Mahal – could be sold to tourists who cannot afford the services of guides.
- Viewing Taj Mahal in the night holds special significance for tourists. Thus, the monument should be opened for public viewing at nights. Special ticket packages can be devised to encourage only limited income groups of tourists visiting the monument. This practice was allowed by Supreme Court of India some time back but later discontinued by the authorities.
- A tourist visiting a historic monument is generally inclined towards history. For instance, the area around Taj Mahal could be developed to promote folk culture and activities.
- Special arrangements to promote visits by physically challenged people in terms of their movement within the monument need to be undertaken.

Fatehpur Sikri

Life-Cycle Stage. The number of tourists visiting Fatehpur Sikri — both foreign and domestic tourists — is quite large and has remained more or less constant over the years. The monument has an internal mystic quality about it, attracting tourists over the years. The remains of the Mughal Empire's aura and splendour can still be seen at the monument. Ticket price is also reflective of the kind of importance tourists attach to the place. A decent percentage of people visiting Agra make it a point to visit Fatehpur Sikri too. Keeping all these factors in mind, Fatehpur Sikri can be classified into the "consolidation" stage of life cycle. Although the number of tourists visiting the monument over the years has been high, there has been no significant growth over the years. There has also been a slight decrease in the number of tourists in a certain year, which gets picked up in the consequent years again. A brief discussion on the earlier life-cycle stages of Fatehpur Sikri would be prudent here.

- **Stage 1 – Exploration:** Akbar made Fatehpur Sikri the Mughal headquarters in the 16th century. Since its construction, Fatehpur Sikri has been visited by tourists due to the inherent beauty of its architectural splendour. The idea of exploration of Fatehpur Sikri, hence, does not form a part of its life cycle, as it was never one of those destinations that were visited by unobtrusive visitors, nor was it a destination that was unexplored hitherto and came into public news by the experiential evidences provided by the tourists. Since its early days, Fatehpur Sikri has been one monument that has been in the public eye.
- **Stage 2 and 3 – Involvement and Development:** It would be difficult to delineate the different life-cycle stages in the growth of Fatehpur Sikri as a tourist destination in terms of time division. However, it could be easily said that prior to India's Independence, Fatehpur Sikri was largely at the "involvement" stage. Due to the lack of proper infrastructural facilities in terms of transportation, the number of visitors was less during that period. The place was mostly visited by foreign tourists and people of Indian origin who could afford an expensive trip to Fatehpur Sikri.

Pir Muhammed Kawwal is a 73-year-old singer who lives in Fatehpur Sikri and still sings at one corner of the Darwaaza of Salim Chisti's *dargah*. In an interview with him in 2005, this is what he had to say: "In the British times, there were less travellers. Not many people came to see the Taj, or the Agra fort or Fatehpur Sikri, but since Hindustan and Pakistan separated, a lot of tourists come from all over the world. The time has changed now (*Ab daur badal gaya hai na*)."

The development stage of Fatehpur Sikri has taken shape mostly after Independence, when the number of Indian tourists increased tremendously over the years. With advances in travelling options and better boarding facilities, the site became more visited by domestic as well as international tourists. It was also the stage when heavy advertising of the site took place and externally owned and controlled facilities came into the picture. The number of tourists visiting Fatehpur Sikri increased manifold during this period (Fig. 6.7).

Marketing Strategies. The rate of increase in visitor numbers declines during this (consolidation) stage. The industry needs to respond to the decline in the growth rate with wide-ranging advertising campaigns and efforts to extend the tourism season and market area. The city's facilities and infrastructure might have started showing signs of age. There could be a need to work on the infrastructure needs of the site, if so required. The distance of Fatehpur Sikri from Agra is around 40 km, and it needs to be ensured by the government that the journey time to the place is convenient and short. Roads might need to be worked on and the commuting options improved. There can be an alternative strategy of ensuring that a large percentage of tourists (if not all) to Taj visit Fatehpur Sikri too. This is important keeping in mind the fact that Taj is such a huge puller of tourists that a centrally protected monument like Fatehpur Sikri should get maximum leverage out of its proximity to the Taj.

Travel operators should provide special incentives in the form of concessions to tourists for trips to Fatehpur Sikri. Price for the local tourists can be reduced to observe if that helps in increasing the number of domestic tourists visiting the site along with the associated revenue. If so, more research would be required on the entry pricing of the site.

There could be more cultural programmes conducted at Fatehpur Sikri to keep the interests of tourists alive. There could be better resorts and hotels constructed around Fatehpur Sikri to allow the tourists to stay at the location far from the hustle-bustle of the city and enjoy the serenity of the

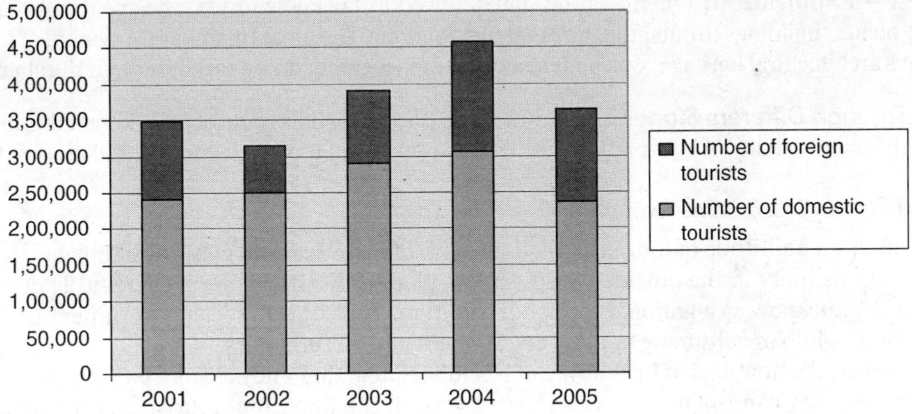

Source: www.indiastat.com

Fig. 6.7: Number of Tourists Visiting Fatehpur Sikri

countryside. This would allow the number of foreign tourists as well as tourists coming from various parts of India to grow.

Last but not the least, the government will have to shell out money in promoting the site in the best possible way. It could be either in the way of different promotional strategies or through advertising via different communication media. The word has to reach out stating that there exists a historical monument close to Taj which is such a cultural heritage that missing out on the opportunity of visiting the site would be a loss to the tourist community of India and world at large.

Bada Imambara

Life-Cycle Stage. Lucknow is an ancient city. It has been the hub of *nawabi* culture for centuries, and Bada Imambara epitomizes this spirit. The data that we found about the number of tourists visiting Lucknow and the number visiting Bada Imambara gave us some interesting insights into this issue (Table 6.1).

Here, we see that though the number of domestic tourists to Lucknow is increasing at a very fast rate in the last few years, the number of these same tourists to Bada Imambara has been steadily declining. This leads us to the conclusion that Bada Imambara is at a "declining" stage, while Lucknow as a tourist destination is at a "growth" stage, which provides an opportunity to Bada Imambara to use this to enter into a "rejuvenation" stage.

Table 6.1 Number of Tourists

Number of Tourists	1999	2000	2001	2002	2003
Lucknow	523,807	485,087	541,104	769,407	952,961
Bada Imambara	426,500	423,000	440,100	390,366	390,400

Source: www.indiastat.com

- **Stage 1 – Exploration:** When Asaf-ud-daula moved to Lucknow in 1777, he spent huge amount of money on new buildings to outshine the Mughal splendour. The great Imambara, a symbol of Lucknow's fabulous architectural heritage, was built at a time when a great famine raged through the state in 1784.

Evolution Through Different Stages. It is difficult to trace the whole route of evolution of this monument because of the unavailability of information through the years from its establishment until present times.

Marketing Strategies. Some marketing strategies are:

- Lucknow has a multitude of tourist attractions both of historical and cultural significance. But the problem is visibility to the outside world, so this place only attracts local tourists. There is a need to promote Lucknow as a national tourist destination. The Uttar Pradesh government can promote Lucknow as a hub of culture by holding conferences and cultural fairs.
- All the tourist destinations of Lucknow can be clubbed together and sold as a package by tour operators. Maybe, they can run a bus service that covers all the important tourist destinations and promote it as a one-stop avenue to discover Lucknow.
- Lucknow has a locational advantage as it is very near to Kanpur and Varanasi. These can be packaged as a combined tour package.
- Services at Bada Imambara can be improved, including the availability of food, toilets and helpful guides to explain the historical significance of the site.

Hampi

Evolution of Life-Cycle Stages for Hampi. It is important to peek into the history of Hampi to understand how it has transitioned through the different TALC stages.

Saint Vidyaranya established the seat of Vijayanagara (the city of victory) empire in AD 1336, with the help of his devotee disciples Hakka and Bukka. Over the next 200-plus years (AD 1336–AD 1565), four dynasties ruled Vijayanagara. Hampi, the seat of the famed Vijayanagara empire, was the capital of the largest empire in post-Mughal India, covering the states of Karnataka, Maharashtra and Andhra Pradesh. The empire reigned supreme under King Krishnadeva Raya (1509–1529) of the Tuluva dynasty.

During the 17th century, the destruction of Vijayanagara by marauding Deccan sultanates was sudden, shocking and absolute. They reduced the city to ruins amid scenes of savage massacre, and ransacked its palaces and temples for months. Hampi turned into a ghost city, and, over the centuries, this erstwhile metropolitan with more than half-a-million population turned into a jungle where wild animals roamed freely.

It was only during the colonial period that Hampi evoked curiosity among the western archaeologists. Robert Sewell's (1845–1925) seminal work, aptly titled *A Forgotten Empire: Vijayanagar*, was a major attempt to narrate the glory of the empire. In 1917, A. H. Longhurst's *Hampi Ruins Described and Illustrated* became the first travel guide for visitors to Hampi.

For nearly half a century after the archaeological discovery of Hampi, hardly anyone came to see the ruins. According to the account of a local, who runs a restaurant near Hampi village, strange foreigners (the hippies) suddenly began to appear in 1971. They lived in caves or local houses and integrated pretty well with the local population. These foreigners, leading a hermit-like existence with a minimalist set of requirements, characterized the "exploration" stage for Hampi over the next few years.

In 1986, Hampi shot into prominence as UNESCO conferred World Heritage status upon the "Group of Monuments at Hampi." From a nondescript hamlet, it quickly turned into an architectural wonder equal in splendour to Cambodia's Angkor Wat. The wave of interest grew over the years, both among domestic and international tourists. The hippie presence faded and they were replaced by a new breed of tourists, clutching their *Lonely Planet* guidebooks, travelling on a more focused schedule to explore the cultural, historical and religious significance of the place. This ushered in the "involvement" phase.

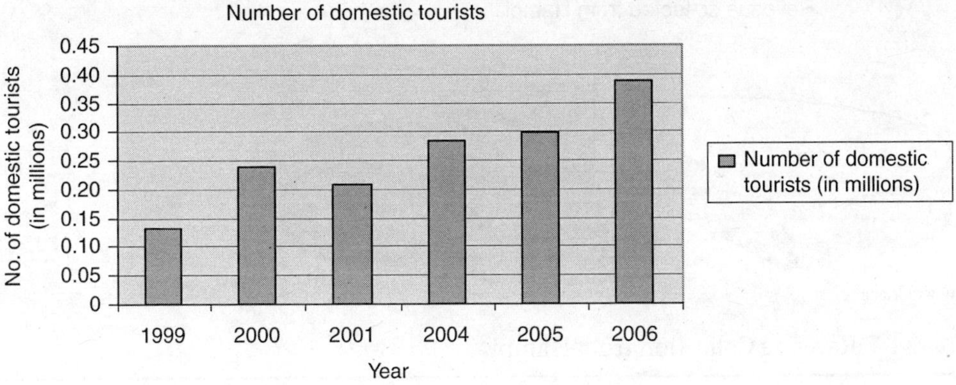

Source: www.indiastat.com

Fig. 6.8: Number of Domestic Tourists Visiting Hampi

In April 2002, Karnataka officially set up the Hampi World Heritage Area Management Authority (HWHAMA) with wide-ranging powers as well as a state-level advisory committee. The main objective was to preserve the monuments and attract more tourists. Additionally, the allocation of funds by the government for maintenance of the monuments has been consistently in excess of INR 1000 million since 2001. The result of these efforts has borne fruit, as can be seen from the statistics of tourists visiting Hampi.

From Figure 6.8, it is evident that the number of domestic tourists frequenting Hampi has been steadily growing over the years. From 0.132 million tourists visiting Hampi in 1999, the figure has tripled within 7 years to 0.387 million tourists.

Another interesting metric to look into is the number of foreign tourists who made Hampi their travel destination across the years.

On the basis of Figure 6.9, it is easily seen that the number of foreign tourists visiting Hampi has also increased over the years. Another useful indicator is the revenue collections at Hampi as shown in Figure 6.10.

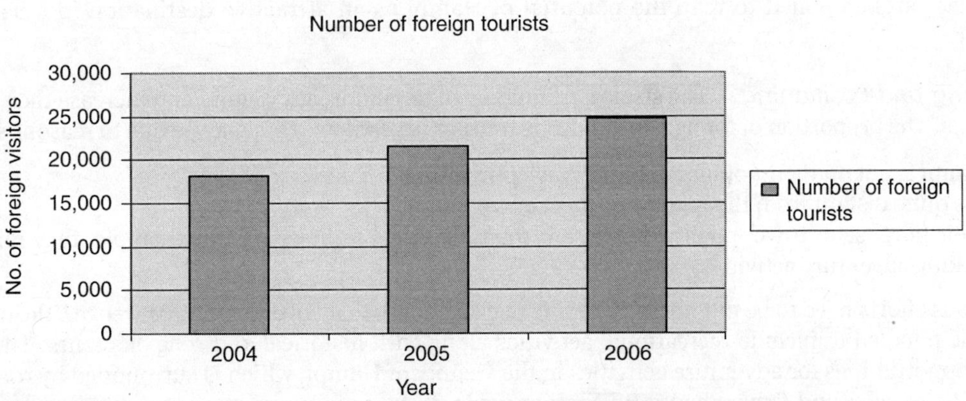

Source: www.indiastat.com

Fig. 6.9: Number of Foreign Tourists Visiting Hampi

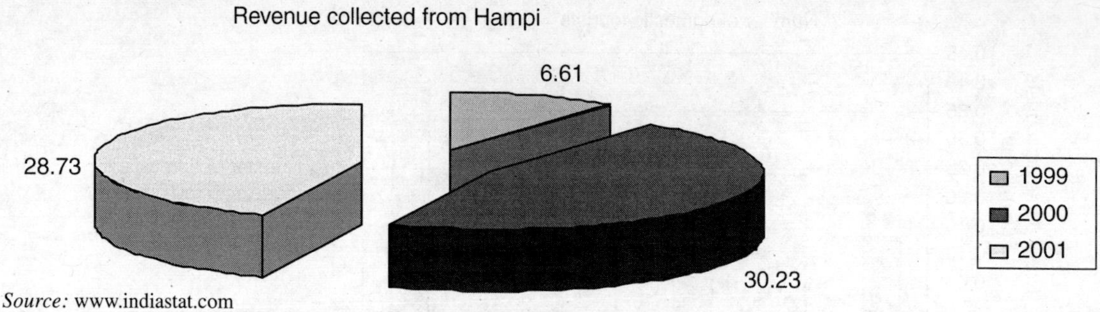

Source: www.indiastat.com

Fig. 6.10: Revenue Collection from Hampi

Based on the analysis of number of tourists arriving in Hampi and the corresponding revenue collections over the years, it can be deduced that Hampi has now reached the "development" phase. From a small dot on the tourism map, it has turned into a full-fledged attraction.

Strategies for Developing Hampi as a Tourist Place. Hampi's awe-striking landscape strewn with weather-beaten granite boulders, rolling hills and verdant valleys provide a perfect backdrop to the marvellous architectural ruins. However, the commercial potential of Hampi has remained largely untapped. As it is a UNESCO Heritage Site, the authorities have to do tightrope walking between conservationists' concerns and wide-scale development of the destination. Restrictions on constructing buildings above two storeys and refusal to grant permission to build bridges across Tungabhadra to allow free access of vehicles are some such measures.

Hampi was also afflicted by the ills of mass tourism, though to a smaller scale, in the 1990s. There were widespread instances of narcotic peddling by foreign tourists as well as a spate of burglaries. Only after the Archaeological Survey of India imposed round-the-clock security for the monuments and the local police mandated all foreign nationals to register with the police station, did the situation improve.

Considering the numbers of visitors per year and the rate of increase, the following marketing strategies can be applied to reap the potential of Hampi as an attractive destination in a balanced manner.

Targeting and Positioning. The strategy should be to target foreign visitors and increase their inflow to Hampi. The proportion of foreign-to-domestic tourists is very low. This may be due to reasons such as

- Hampi is not on their popular destinations' tourist map
- It is quite distant from the regular ports of entry
- Their purpose of travel might be different than historical sightseeing (for example, they might be seeking adventure activities)

Conscious efforts need to be put into developing package tours that cover Hampi. Moreover, the offering could be bundled to include recreational activities along with historical and religious tours. There are ample opportunities for adventure activities in the vicinity of Hampi, which is surrounded by rocky terrain on three sides and Tungabhadra River on one side.

Government Initiatives and Incentives. The government is showing the right intent in terms of actual and planned expenditure towards development of these historically significant ruins. This can be observed from the expenditure budget for Hampi's monuments in Table 6.2.

Table 6.2 Year-Wise Expenditure for Development of Historically Significant Ruins

Year	2004	2005	2006
Expenditure (in million)	13.3	17.8	16.6

Source: www.indiastat.com

In 2007–2008, the earmarked funds for development of Hampi had gone up to INR 19.4 million. Hence, the allocation is growing steadily over the years. This intent needs to be supplemented with promotions taken up by Karnataka tourism board to woo domestic as well as foreign tourists. In conjunction with these incentives, infrastructure development to provide faster access – such as increasing the number of trains from Bangalore or conveniently timing the trains – would help further. A unique initiative in this regard has been a super-luxury train called the Golden Chariot (based on the name of Hampi's famed stone chariot), covering the major tourist destinations of Karnataka including Hampi.

Golden Chariot Train

Promotions. Tour operators across the country need to be involved in the promotion offer. The spectacular nature of the ruins and the historical value are parameters that can be used for hard selling. The Web sites specifically dedicated to Hampi tourism (such as www.hampi.in and www.hampi-online.com) can carry promotional offers around the holiday seasons for domestic as well as foreign tourists.

Valley of Flowers

Life-Cycle Stage. Even about 70 years after its discovery, Valley of Flowers is a relatively unknown place among domestic tourists. Its popularity has been increasing, though, on account of word-of-mouth publicity by the trekkers who are beginning to frequent this place. A look at the data regarding the number of people visiting this place gives us a fair amount of idea about the reputation of this place (Table 6.3).

We saw no perceptible trend in the number of tourists coming to this place. The number seems to depend on what we call "good years" and "bad years" – that is, cycles of some years where the place becomes a kind of fad and people throng the place, interspersed with some years where the numbers sharply decline, with tourists preferring nearby destinations to that destination. There had been some

Table 6.3 Number of Domestic Tourists who Visited Valley of Flowers

Year	92–93	93–94	94–95	95–96	96–97	97–98	98–99	99–00	00–01	01–02	02–03	03–04
Number	3244	1857	1451	291	1113	1256	415	770	1081	1959	2277	3445

Source: www.indiastat.com

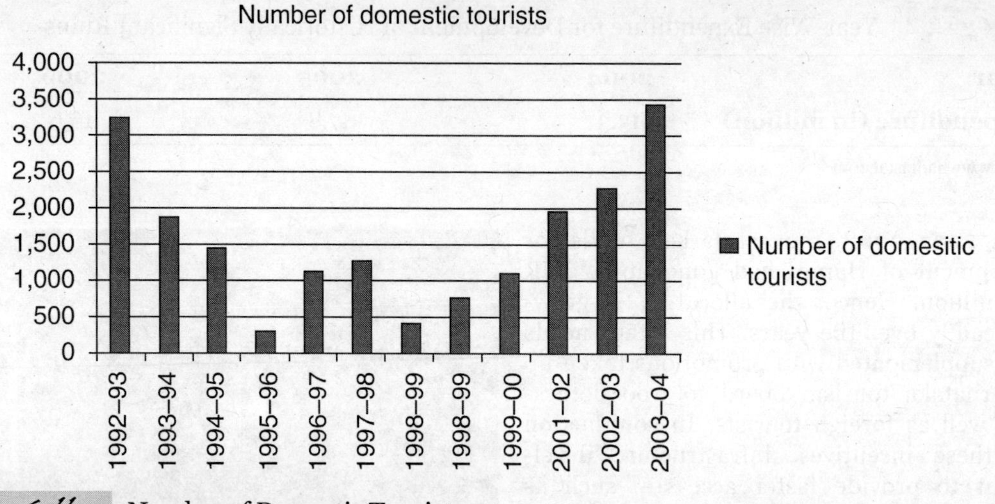

Fig. 6.11: Number of Domestic Tourists

increase in the number of tourists in the last few years, which can be attributed to Valley of Flowers coming into the radar of the growing trekker community in India, who seem to be driving up this number. From this, we can conclude that the Valley of Flowers is at an "involvement" stage. The number of tourists is growing, but there is a lot of scope for further growth and development (Fig. 6.11).

Life–Cycle Stage Analysis

- **Stage 1 – Exploration:** As related earlier, this valley was unknown until a British mountaineer Frank Smith first visited here. In 1931, Frank Smith wanted to scale a peak in Garhwal called Comet. While returning after successfully completing his mission, he took the western pass and lost his way and reached this valley after many difficulties. He put up a tent and stayed here for many days. In 1937, he came back again to this valley and stayed here for a long time. Then, he wrote a book called *The Valley of Flowers*. Soon after, this place became world famous. Nature lovers started visiting here.
- **Stage 2 – Involvement (present stage):** In 1982, this valley was named the Republic Park. Its area was fixed at 87.5 square km. After reading Frank Smith's book, many foreign tourists came here. One of them was an English woman called Margaret Lague, who came here in 1939. She was very fond of flowers. On the 4th of July, when she was trying to pick one of the rare flowers, she slipped from a rock and fell into a chasm below to her death. In her memory, the tombstone on her grave reads: "My eyes will forever drink in the beauty of the mountains which gave me strength and inspiration." The tourists who visit this valley never fail to visit her grave and pay homage.

Marketing Strategies. The following strategies can be used:

- Valley of Flowers should be promoted as a weekend getaway, suitable for the family. As of now, it only attracts trekkers and nature enthusiasts.
- Hemkund Sahib attracts a lot of religious tourists. Valley of Flowers being very close to this place can be promoted to tourists as an additional destination.
- In order to present tourism as an all-season as well as an all-purpose activity in the state of Uttarakhand, it is necessary to develop as well as promote adventure tourism, sports tourism and wildlife tourism, in addition to pilgrimage tourism.

Tourist Experience — Trek to Khatling Glacier

Details of the Route:

Ghuttu – Reeh (10 kms) – Gangi (10 kms) – Bhetbagi (17 kms) – Chawki (12 kms) – Khatling Glacier (6 kms)

Total Distance Covered: 110 km

Lying between Gangotri and Kedarnath, Khatling glacier lies on one of the most treacherous and arduous trek routes. But this route is also one of the most pristine and untamed. Nestled in the foothills of the mighty Himalayas, this trek route is quite beautiful and replete with excitement and adventure.

- **Day 1:** We reached Ghuttu, via Ghansyali and Rishikesh, at 3:30 in the afternoon. Going against the popular opinion, trek leaders decided to march on to Reeh on the same day, covering a distance of 10 km. But even at the time of nightfall, Reeh was nowhere to be seen. Amidst fears of wild animals nearby and losing the way, the team decided to camp on the route itself. Spending the night in a single tent with all the seven members in it was uncomfortable, but a memorable experience.
- **Day 2:** Waking up early in the morning, we realized that we had camped just a few metres away from Reeh. With renewed enthusiasm, we marched on. However, an almost vertical climb of 10 km on the way to Gangi exhausted the team thoroughly. The team had a meal of Maggi, cooked on a gas cylinder, which everyone agreed that was the best Maggi they ever had.
- **Day 3:** Taking along a guide, we walked on to the most treacherous and difficult part of the route. There were landslides all along the route and the going was extremely difficult, but the team persevered. When finally we reached Kharsali, joy was evident on every face. The twilight hours were spent around the campfire, cooking the dinner and enjoying Bakar.
- **Day 4:** It was another difficult day for the trekking. The route at times was almost vertical, and we faced a vertical landslide of about 500 metres. At the top of this, the entire team was hoping that they had never come here. Keeping our motivation high, we walked on nevertheless. We also noticed a spot where a recent incident of suicide had taken place. But since no one was interested to commit suicide, we walked on. It was christened "Baba suicide point." In the afternoon, we divided the team into two groups, one camping at Khatling and the other at Chawki. By evening, we were engulfed in a sea of fog. The scene looked unworldly and it gave us quite a chill, but it was a memorable experience.
- **Day 5 and day 6**: The team retraced the route and in the process covered 28 km on the final day. The total distance covered came out to be 102 km. By the time we reached Ghuttu, everyone was dead tired, but the sense of achievement was overwhelming. It was a memorable and wonderful experience for all. The return journey was spent debating on the reasons for the defeat of Germany in World War II.

- Local people should also be motivated and involved in the tourism process. It has been suggested that the people of the region should come forward and help in providing a safe and secure atmosphere for the tourists.

- There is an urgent need for ecotourism. Planned infrastructure and tourism development without disturbing the ecological balance of Uttarakhand is to be given the top priority.
- It has also been suggested that different independent tourism organizations like tour operators, hoteliers and restaurateurs should be involved in promoting tourism in Valley of Flowers. These organizations should make use of various promotional tools at different times.

SUMMARY

- Butler adapted the product life-cycle model to the tourism industry and created the concept of TALC. He established six stages under this model: exploration, involvement, development, consolidation, stagnation and decline/rejuvenation.
- Resort regions have a finite life span and there are chances that the region can decline given certain circumstances, a fact that may belie the wishes of the local population, particularly the developers of the region. The TALC concept contradicts the belief that there is an unlimited growth potential in tourism.
- Tourism regions can be classified broadly into three groups: regions of stability, regions that suffer a decline in terms of tourism and regions that have declined, but become popular again.
- Tourist life cycle: Cohen identified four character types among the tourists: drifter, explorer, individual mass tourist and organized mass tourist.
- The lack of quality infrastructure, uncompetitive rates, indifferent or poor product quality and difficulty in getting access to information on travel and tourist destinations lead to a negative effect on the tourism destination's competitiveness.
- Taj Mahal, Imambara, Fatehpur Sikri, Valley of Flowers and Hampi are destinations in India which are in different stages of the life cycle and have unique histories behind them. All have stood the test of time, and all are affected by the vagaries of the TLC.
- Various marketing strategies like targeting specific segments, introducing various promotional strategies and packages, releasing of funds by governments, improving the services provided in terms of better food and hygiene and motivation and involvement of the local populace should be adopted to enhance the lifespan of a tourist destination.

FIELD EXERCISES

1. Choose world's most popular tourist destination (on the basis of number of tourists) and identify which stage of TALC is applicable to it, also figure out the marketing strategies utilized.
2. Develop a marketing strategy for your city by identifying its stage with help of tourism area life cycle (TALC) concept.

REFERENCES

Aledo, A. & T. Mazón (2004), "Impact of Residential Tourism and the Destination Life Cycle Theory," Sustainable Tourism, First International Conference on Sustainable Tourism, WIT Press.

Baum, Tom (1998), "Taking the Exit Route: Extending the Tourism Area Life Cycle Model," *Current Issues in Tourism*, Vol. 1, No. 2, pp. 167–175.

Berry, Edward Norman (2001), "An application of Butler's (1980) Tourist Area Life Cycle Theory to the

Cairns Region, Australia 1876-1998," James Cook University of North Queensland. School of Tropical Environment Studies and Geography.

Butler, Richard W. (2006), "The Tourism Area Life Cycle," in Richard W. Butler (ed.) Applications & Modifi cations, Vol. 1, Channel View Publications.

Butler, R.W. (1980), "The Concept of a Tourist Area Cycle of Evolution: Implications for Management of Resources," *Canadian Geographer*, Vol. 24, No. 1, pp. 5–12.

Cooper, Chris (2002), "Sustainability and Tourism Visions," VII Congreso Internacional del CLAD sobre la Reforma del Estado y de la Administración Pública, Lisboa, Portugal, 8–11 Oct. 2002

Cooper, C.P. (1992), "The Life Cycle Concept and Strategic Planning for Coastal Resorts," *Built Environment*, Vol. 18, No. 1, pp. 57–66.

Das Gupta, Devashish Prof. (2008), "Marketing Interventions for Tourism Promotion Recommendations for the Top Tourist Destination of India," Conference on Tourism in India – Challenges Ahead, Indian Institute of Management, Kozhikode.

Knowles, Tim and Simon Curtis (1999), "The Market Viability of European Mass Tourist Destinations – A Post-Stagnation Life-Cycle Analysis," *International Journal of Tourism Research*, Vol. 1, pp. 87–96.

Web Sites

http://geographyfi eldwork.com/TourismLifeCycle.htm

http://www.unesco.org/courier/2000_07/uk/signe.htm

http://www.emeraldinsight.com

http://www.indiastat.com/

http://www.tajmahal.org.uk/

http://www.xe.com/

http://www.karnataka.com/tourism/hampi/

http://www.indiamike.com/india/agra-f61/an-interviewwith-pir-md-kawwal-of-fatehpur-sikri-t15876/

http://www.indiatourismstat.com/

APPENDIX

Author Date	Region	Aspect Tested/Method/ Special Emphasis	Results
Hovinen, 1981	Lancaster County	Butler's theory in total. Uses visitor numbers, otherwise a perceptual/historical approach	Substantially consistent with model. No sign of a decline in region
Oglethorpe, 1984	Malta	Uses visitor numbers, number of beds, hotels and percentage of foreign ownership. Emphasizes dependency on foreign tour operators	Accepts relevance of TALC and makes the point that dependency has led to rapid decline in the tourism industry
France, 1991	Barbados	Mainly a perceptional approach, but also uses visitor numbers, number of establishments, number of rooms, etc.	The island is split into different market segments that are at different stages in TALC. One area is in decline, another is still in the growth stages
Getz, 1992	Niagara Falls	Examines carrying capacity and planning aspects. Uses historical data, existing statistical data, interviews, field observations, maps, and questionnaires	"Exploration" and "involvement" stages correspond partly with Butler's model, but there are many points of divergence and no dating of stages is possible. Niagara Falls appears to be in a long "maturity" stage similar to Lancaster County

APPENDIX *(CONTINUED)*

Agarwal, 1997	Torbay region (Torquay, Paignton, and Brixham)	Tests the validity and applicability of TALC. Justifies this work by stating that the universal applicability of TALC is not yet proven	The application of TALC is reasonably consistent with Butler's (1980) model except for the post "stagnation" stage, which requires more research

Source: An Application of Butler's (1980) Tourist Area Life Cycle Theory to the Cairns Region, Australia 1876–1998, thesis submitted by Mr Edward Norman Berry.

CHAPTER 7

Coliseum, Rome

Tourism Market Segmentation and Targeting

ABOUT THE DESTINATION

The largest amphitheatre of the Roman Empire, built under the Flavian Dynasty, it could hold 50,000 spectators and was frequently used for gladiatorial battles and other public spectacles.

OBJECTIVES

- To understand the concepts of tourism market segmentation and targeting
- To understand the various bases for segmenting tourism market
- To understand the concept of positioning
- To be able to practically apply all concepts

INTRODUCTION

Whatever may be the stage of the life cycle of a tourist destination, it does attract a cross section of tourists. Any destination at any given point of time cannot be sought after by all potential tourists, be it domestic or international. Depending on the profile, lifestyle and aspirations tourists have different tastes and preferences. Based on specific variables, tourists can be divided into homogeneous groups or tourist segments. Segmentation gives the marketer valuable insights into different tourist groups. It helps in catering to the tourist needs better. Most importantly, while designing promotion campaigns, the communication strategy can be so designed to influence the decision making of the target segment positively.

Consumers of tourism-based packages and services have varied needs and wants. Like any other market, the tourism market can rarely be satisfied by a single offering. Market segmentation is based on the notion that different tourism destinations appeal to different types of tourists. Therefore, target market segments must be selected before tourism marketers can begin to entice these potential customers.

The following basic terms have been used in the chapter:

Market Segmentation: To identify and profile distinct groups of tourists who might have homogeneous characteristics or needs, and hence, prefer varied genres of tour packages. Market segments can be identified by examining demographic, psychographic and behavioural differences among buyers. The firm, then, decides which segments present the greatest opportunity – whose needs the firm can meet in a superior fashion.

SOTC Trade Fair Tours – The Smartest Way to Trade Fair

SOTC Trade Fair Tours specialize in organizing business-travel arrangements to trade fairs and exhibitions around the world. With access to especially negotiated room rates in hotels, coupled with the best available airfares from all the major and low-cost airlines, SOTC Trade Fair Tours are able to meet one's business-travel requirements. SOTC Trade Fair Tours work closely with the Indian representatives of all major trade fair companies, trade federations and trade fair promoters to provide all the information that one needs to make a visit a success. They provide senior management with the choice of luxury hotels and luxury cars. The trade fairs cover a wide range of industries like automobiles, semiconductors, IT and medical. This is a typical example of market segmentation, targeting and positioning (STP) in the tourism industry. One example of their trade-fair tour packages is Electronica, held from November 11, 2008, to November 14, 2008, in New Munich Centre, Germany. This tour package was specifically targeted at professionals from the electronics industry – semiconductors, passives, electromechanical components, solutions for system peripheries, servo-technology, printed circuit boards or EMS, etc.

Market Targeting: To select one or more market segments to cater to their needs. For each chosen target market, the firm develops a market offering. The offering is positioned in the minds of the target buyers as delivering some central benefit.

Market Positioning: To establish and communicate the package/programme's distinctive features to the target market. Positioning is a communications strategy that is the natural follow-through of market segmentation and target marketing.

How does segmentation and targeting help in tourism market? Let us take an example of the tourism market of North East India. It can be segmented on the basis of origin into domestic (Indian) and foreign tourists. The variables identified for principal factors for the tourist destination are infrastructure and external influence. Consumers in the two segments would differ in the importance they attach to these variables and also their perception of them. Foreign tourists look for higher levels of infrastructure and external influence at a tourist destination. Since the North East is largely underdeveloped in terms of infrastructure, there is a gap between the importance of the variable and the perception of its fulfilment. On the other hand, for Indian travellers the gap is minimal, and, thus, the domestic travellers may be the candidate segment for targeting.

Inadequate segmentation and clustering problems could cause a tourism destination to either miss a strategic marketing opportunity or not cash in on the rewards of a tactical campaign. Market segmentation has developed as a methodology to identify target segments, with the outcomes of the process used to help understand tourists' relationship with the destination.

MARKET SEGMENTATION, TARGETING AND POSITIONING (STP)

To satisfy the needs of the tourists more successfully and reach them in the most effective and efficient way, tourist operators should identify groups of tourists or potential tourists with homogeneous characteristics and behaviours, and try to adapt their service as much as possible to the unique needs and desires of the segment members. STP in tourism involves three steps: market segmentation, market targeting and market positioning.

- **Market segmentation:** Identify and profile distinct groups of tourists who might have homogeneous characteristics or needs, and hence, prefer varied genres of tour packages

- **Market targeting:** Select one or more market segments to cater to their needs
- **Market positioning:** Establish and communicate the package/programme's distinctive features to the target market

SEGMENTATION

Segment Identification

The first stage of market analysis consists of segment identification. The analyst has the option of segmenting the market using different sets of criteria, including personal characteristics of the consumer, benefits sought and behavioural measures of the consumer. Within these categories the options available are truly overwhelming, and in many cases different segmentation approaches will steer strategy along very different paths. Utilizing multiple segmentation approaches is recommended.

There is no recipe for choosing which variables to utilize when segmenting. The identification of segmentation variables is among the most creative parts of the segmentation process because it involves conceiving dimensions along which products and buyers differ, and carries important structural or value-chain implications. Operators can meet the tourists' needs better than their competitors or improve relative cost position by using new ways of segmenting.

Segmentation Techniques

Once segmentation variables have been selected and the data is collected, it is necessary to choose the statistical process by which the segments will be identified. The segmentation technique to be used depends largely on the type of data available (metric or non-metric variables) and the kind of dependence observed (dependence or interdependence). Among the most common segmentation techniques used are factor analysis, cluster analysis, discriminant analysis and multiple regressions. Among newer and increasingly utilized techniques are chi-squared automatic detection (CHAID), LOGIT and log linear modelling.

Traditionally, cluster analysis has been utilized, but its use has declined because of increased criticism of its empirical nature and the emergence of new methods. Newer systems and algorithms such as CHAID permit the use of chi-squared analysis, which does not force ordinal and nominal data into continuous variables, and permits not only the identification of segments, but also their ranking by profitability or some other measure of desirability. The segmentation process is complex and, thus, prone to error. Data integrity tests and validity assessments should be included along the process as well as in the final outcome review.

Once the clusters have been identified, they are described using other variables not included in forming the clusters. This descriptive process is intended to yield a full-bodied description of the market segments, which will be useful in the evaluation process, but most importantly in the marketing-mix creation stage.

Segment Evaluation

The second stage consists of evaluating the segments. The first element that needs to be defined is the criteria by which the segments will be evaluated. In a non-profit setting segment, desirability is not necessarily determined by profitability and market-share objectives. If a measure of profitability or desirability can be quantified, the markets can be ranked using tree analysis or gains charts. Approaches vary with some suggesting a quantitative evaluation of the resulting segments, while others highlight other strategies for evaluation. A way to approach market segment evaluation is through the examination of a market structure by constructing a spatial model where similarities and dissimilarities are mapped. This representation of the market is then used in conjunction with demand estimating and forecasting models to determine possible positioning alternatives for a product. This analysis can be enhanced by using a chi-squared tree analysis and correspondence analysis to generate compositional perceptual maps.

Other elements such as simplicity and potential adaptability of the segmentation structure across national boundaries should also be considered. According to Philip Kotler, the key factors to be considered are segment size, growth and structural attractiveness. Michael Porter proposed a similar approach, but also recommended studying the firm's (That is, operator's in the case of tourism marketing) resources and skills, as reflected in the value chain, and their suitability to target market alternatives. Aaker based his selection criteria on the SWOT analysis produced during the strategic marketing planning process. Berrigan and Finkbeiner proposed a somewhat similar process that includes market structure analysis, market opportunity analysis, resource capabilities analysis and competitive analysis.

Levels of Market Segmentation

Mass marketing, segment marketing and niche marketing are the three levels of market segmentation. These are discussed as follows:

Mass Marketing. The operators engage in serving a broad range of tourists and in mass promotion of one package for all the tourists. Mass marketing creates a large potential market, which leads to the lowest cost, which in turn can lead to lower prices or higher margins. But with the increasing splintering of the market, mass marketing gets more difficult. For example, a two-week South India tour package attracts people from different geographical locations, age groups, income levels, etc.

Segment Marketing. A market segment consists of a large identifiable group within a market with similar wants, purchasing power, geographical location, buying attitudes or buying habits.

Buyers from each segment are assumed to be quite similar in needs and wants. It is advisable to present a flexible market offering instead of a standard offering (one size fits all) to all members within the segment. A flexible market offering consists of two parts:

- **Naked solution:** Product and service elements valued by all segment members
- **Options:** Product and service elements valued by some segment members. Each option carries extra charge

Benefits of segment marketing are:

- The company can create more fine-tuned product or services offering, and price it appropriately for the target audience.
- Choice of distribution channel and communication channel becomes much easier.
- The company also may face fewer competitions in a particular segment.

Niche Marketing. A niche is a more narrowly defined group, typically, a small market whose needs are not well served. Marketers usually identify niches by dividing a segment into sub-segments or defining a group seeking a distinctive mix of benefits. Niches are fairly small and attract very few competitors. Large companies lose pieces of their market to nichers. Dalgic has labelled this confrontation as "guerrillas against gorillas." Niche marketing requires more decentralization and changes in the way normal business is done. Niche marketers understand their customers so well that customers willingly pay a premium. Attractive niches are characterized by the following:

- Customers in the niche have a distinct set of needs.
- They will pay a premium to the firm that best satisfies their needs.
- The niche is not likely to attract other competitors.

- The nichers gain certain economies through specialization.
- The niche has size, profit and growth potential.

Patterns of Market Segmentation

Market segments are built up by taking into account preference segments. The following three different patterns emerge: homogeneous, diffused and clustered preferences.

- **Homogeneous preferences:** Markets where all customers have roughly the same preference. The market shows no natural segments
- **Diffused preferences:** Consumer preferences are scattered throughout the space – consumers vary widely in their preferences. The first brand to enter the market is likely to position itself in the centre to appeal to the most people. A brand in the centre minimizes the total customer dissatisfaction.
- **Clustered preferences:** The market reveals distinct preference clusters – natural market segments. The first firm to enter the market has three options:
    - Position in the centre to appeal to all groups. It will develop only one brand; competitors would enter and introduce brands in the other segments
    - Position in the largest market segment – concentrated marketing
    - Develop several products positioned in a different segment

Effective Segmentation

Even after applying segmentation variables to a consumer or business market, marketers must realize that not all segmentations are useful. For example, table-salt buyers could be divided into blonde and brunette customers, but hair colour is not relevant to the purchase of salt. Furthermore, if all salt buyers buy the same amount of salt each month, believe all salt is the same, and would pay only one price for salt, this market would be minimally segmentable from a marketing perspective.

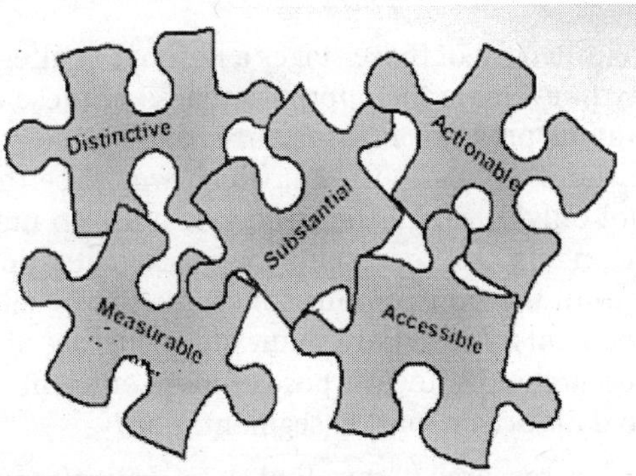

To be useful, market segments must be

- **Measurable:** The size, purchasing power and characteristics of the segments can be measured.
- **Substantial:** The segments are large and profitable enough to serve. A segment should be the largest possible homogeneous group with a tailored marketing programme.
- **Accessible:** The segments can be effectively reached and served.
- **Differentiable:** The segments are conceptually distinguishable and respond differently to different marketing mixes. If two segments respond identically to a particular offer, they do not constitute separate segments.
- **Actionable:** Effective programmes can be formulated for attracting and serving the segments

MARKET SEGMENTATION IN TOURISM

Tourism is a unique services sector where the tourists (consumers of tourism services) are not one homogeneous group of individuals who seek the same benefits from a destination, have similar expectations, undertake similar vacation activities and perceive the same activities as attractive. It is not possible to customize a tourism product for each tourist and, hence, it becomes all the more important to segment the tourism market as per distinct groups of tourists who share common needs, and have similar expectations from a tourism activity and destination.

As discussed in the previous sections, market segmentation is a fundamental practice in marketing research, involving the process of dividing the markets into smaller groups and further subgroups that share common characteristics. What follows is a brief description of the various market research techniques used in studying the tourism sector and the variables used to segment the tourism market.

Market segmentation research has a long history in tourism research. Both a priori or commonsense and post hoc, or a posteriori, or data-driven, segmentation studies have frequently been undertaken to gain an in-depth understanding of parts of the tourism market in order to improve the possibilities of target marketing activities towards attractive sub-markets. The basic idea underlying market segmentation is to identify or define groups of tourists who are similar with respect to the construct of primary interest – for instance, travel behaviour, travel motives and patterns of expenditure.

Data-driven segmentation studies are exploratory in nature and consist of a number of steps that are crucial to the quality of the solution derived. These steps include the following stages:

- Data collection stage
- Data pre-processing stage (if needed)
- Segmentation stage
- Validation stage

Within each of these stages a number of alternative options exist, and it is the researcher's responsibility to evaluate the appropriateness of these options for the problem at hand, and choose the optimal way to proceed. For instance, during the segmentation stage the researcher needs to decide which distance measure to use, which would be the most appropriate algorithm (as algorithms are known not only to reveal the structure, but also impose it on the data), how to determine which number of segments best represents the market situation, and finally, which of the many possible solutions (even within the same number of segments) to select, and whether to inform the tourism industry that the segments derived are naturally occurring distinct groups of tourists or artificially constructed by the researcher for the purpose of more efficient target marketing, both of which are legitimate approaches to data-driven market segmentation.

A research shows that data-driven segmentation studies are essentially limited to behavioural and psychographic segmentation bases, with psychographic constructs being used as grouping criterion in three quarters of all studies. Psychographic constructs typically include segmentation bases such as benefits, motivations and preferences. Only 3 per cent did not use either behavioural or psychographic criteria, instead they chose a mixed approach including variables of different nature.

Specific techniques that are in use for segmentation in the tourism industry are discussed as follows:

- **Factor-cluster segmentation:** This is a basic, widely used technique in the tourism sector to classify/group tourists into various segments. This enables tourism marketers to position their products to specific segments, thereby increasing their potential profits and reducing the risks associated. The research is based on gathering data based on motivational factors for an activity/destination and then clustering them into groups. The clustering approach can be either bottom-up (the ones that build up clusters) or top-down (those that break down a market into clusters). Factor-cluster segmentation was developed in tourism research in the very early years of data-driven market segmentation. Since then, it has been used widely. However, there are arguments against the use of this technique, as discussed by Sara and Bettina in their paper *Challenging Factor-Cluster Segmentation*. It is highly probable that different clustering techniques result in different solutions (contradictory segments within the same data set, if the technique requires subjective inputs from the researcher).

- **Common-sense segmentation:** This technique uses the classical segmentation variables to segment the tourism market — geographic, psychographic, demographic and behavioural.
  - **Geographic:** Segregating a market into different geographical units such as country, region, state and city
  - **Psychographic:** Segregating a market on the basis of consumer values, attitudes, opinions and personality
  - **Demographic:** Segregating a market on the basis of demographic variables such as age, gender, income, family life cycle, family size, occupation, education, religion and nationality
  - **Behavioural:** Segregating a market on the basis of consumers' knowledge, attitude, benefits and responses with regard to a product or a service
- **Importance-performance approach:** This approach is specifically useful in catering to tourists visiting natural and protected parks, segmenting them into categories and adopting strategies accordingly. This technique is particularly useful for firms having scarcity of funds and lacking market-research expertise.

  This technique helps in understanding the tourists who are visiting the destination and then classifying them into segments that could be catered to in an effective manner, thereby improving the offerings. This technique has been discussed in detail by Derek J. Wade and Paul F. J. Eagles in their paper *The Use of Importance-Performance Analysis and Market Segmentation for Tourism Management in Parks and Protected Areas: An Application to Tanzania's National Parks*.
- **Involvement-based segmentation:** Involvement is a state of mind/behaviour, which can be described as an outcome of the culmination of motivation, arousal and interest. When a

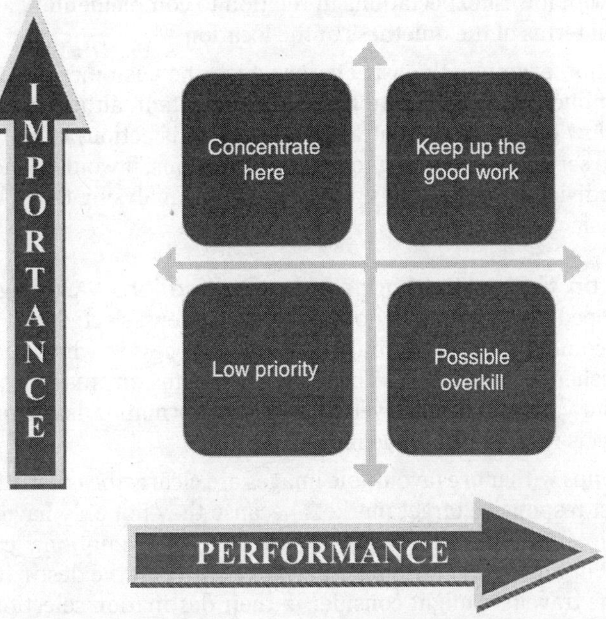

consumer gets involved with a product, it directly affects his decision making; this very involvement forms the basis of segmenting tourists. This helps in predicting the behaviour of consumers (tourists) and can be very effective in segmenting them into various categories and devising relevant strategies to lure them. The level of involvement indicates the seriousness, motives and expectations of consumers.

- **Special segmentation techniques:** It is generally felt that in case of tourism, the traditional methods of segmentation are not very effective. Hence, researchers over the years have developed quite a few special bases for segmentation, which are primarily based on consumer benefits, expectations and perceptions. These are being discussed in detail in the following section.

Special Bases for Tourism Segmentation

Tourism segmentation is based on customer expectations and customers' images of a destination.

Segmentation Based on Customer Expectations. Customer expectations have received the most thorough treatment in the customer satisfaction and service quality literatures. Customer expectations are dynamic – they can change from one consumer to another and from one situation to another for the same individual, or can even vary for different attributes of a single service. They basically depend on:

- Explicit and implicit promises made to the market by the organization
- Word-of-mouth communication
- Personal needs or requirements
- Service intensifiers (personal factors such as personal-service philosophies)

To illustrate, tourists could be segmented based on the following groups:

Group 1: Individuals who have the highest expectations about the complementary activities to be made in the area (sporting and leisure activities)

Group 2: Individuals who do not expect as much as Group 1 from the complementary activities and do not expect much regarding the quietness of the location

Group 3: Individuals with lowest expectations in relation to complementary activities, but at the same time they expect most in terms of the quietness of the location

In the above segmentation example, the aspects for which the customer has the highest expectations are usually those that influence his satisfaction to a greater extent, although anomalous situations (for example, aspects with low expectations that affect overall satisfaction) can arise. Hence, once people have been classified into segments according to their expectations, it would be advisable to obtain a deep understanding of the individuals that make up each group by analysing the effect of different elements of the offer on their satisfaction.

Segmentation Based on Customers' Images of a Destination. An image can be described as "a mental construct developed by the consumer on the basis of a few selected impressions among the flood of total impressions; it comes into being through a creative process in which these selected impressions are elaborated, embellished and ordered." The traveller creates an image by processing information about a destination from various sources over time. This information is organized into a mental construct that, in some way, is meaningful to the individual.

Apparently, the groups with more favourable images are clearly the most attractive segments. These segments form the most responsive target markets because they not only have a favourable image, but also have the greatest intention to visit or tour. By directing a promotional campaign at such places, destination marketers can further enhance the image in a way that the destination becomes favourable over other areas that the travellers might consider in their destination selection process. This pinpoint approach of targeting the most responsive target markets will likely increase the effectiveness and efficiency of the destination's promotional dollar.

Application of Segmentation Variables in Tourism

Having discussed the various segmentation techniques, we can analyse the various segmentation variables that and can be used as effective tools for segmentation of the tourism market.

The major segmentation variables commonly used in categorizing tourists into smaller subgroups are shown in the table below.

Even after having discussed a number of alternatives for segmenting the tourism market, there is always a scope for further refinements through

- Identification of new market segments based on why at all people travel and their desires, wants and needs, motivations, behaviours, etc.

Geographic	
Region	North India, South India, etc.
City	Delhi, Lonavala, Jaipur, Agra, etc.
Demographic	
Age	Kids, teenagers, middle-aged, old-aged, etc.
Family size	Newly married, nuclear families, joint families, etc.
Gender	Male, female
Income	Low, middle, high, etc.
Occupation	Students, salaried, businessmen, etc.
Education	Illiterates, engineers, scientists, etc.
Race	Religion, caste, sect, etc.
Psychographic	
Socio-economic classification (SEC)	Sec A1, A2, B1, B2, C, D, E1, E2, and R1, R2, R3, R4
Personality	Compulsive, gregarious, authoritative, etc.
Behavioural	
Occasions	Honeymoon, summer vacations, Christmas, etc.
Benefits	Service, affordability, etc.
User status	First-timer, regular traveller, etc.
User rate	Frequent travellers, one-timers, etc.
Loyalty status	None, medium, strong, absolute, etc.
Readiness	Aware, informed, interested, etc.
Attitude	Enthusiastic, positive, indifferent, negative, etc.
Special bases for tourism market segmentation	
Customer expectations	High, low, personal service philosophies, etc.
Customer image	Favourable image, neutral image, negative image, etc.
Trip descriptors	Recreational, visiting friends/relatives, business, etc.

- Propagation of strong messages that these potential segments would want to hear
- Development of an understanding of the methods and benefits of segmentation among the destination marketers

TARGETING

Once the market segments are identified and evaluated, the immediate step is the creation of a specific tourist package to fulfil the needs as well as market conditions of each specific target segment. So, the logical sequence of action after choosing a market segment is to choose a generic competitive strategy. At this point, it is also necessary to review the selected strategy across segments and explore general strategic approaches. In some cases, it might become apparent that a counter-segmentation strategy is applicable. In other cases, the development of distinct mixes for each segment uncovers inconsistencies or lack of resources at the corporate level, and so it is necessary to revert to the segment evaluation stage.

According to Philip Kotler, the only sustainable generic strategy in a segmented market is differentiation. He explains that the only other generic competitive-strategy alternative (low cost) is not sustainable in a segmented market. In addition, a strategy successful at differentiating must generate tourist value, provide perceived value and be difficult to copy. At this point in the process, the operators need to select those ways through which they will distinguish themselves from competitors.

Selecting and Entering Market Segments

Having evaluated the different segments, any operator can consider five patterns of target market selection, as shown in the following figure. There patterns are described below.

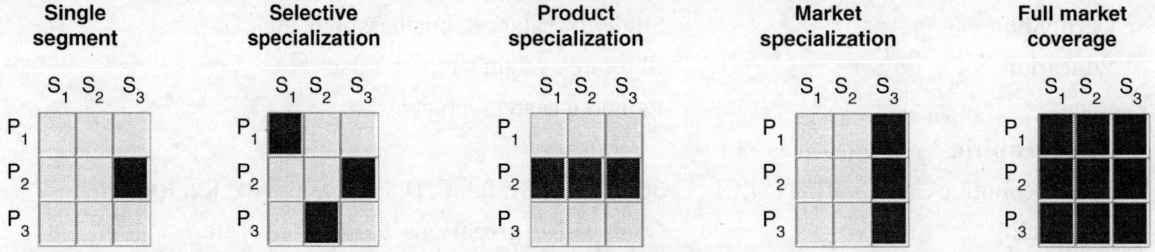

Single-segment Concentration: Many operators concentrate on a single segment. Through concentrated marketing, the firm gains a thorough understanding of the segment's needs and achieves a strong market presence. Furthermore, the firm enjoys operating economies by specializing its production, distribution and promotion; if it attains segment leadership, it can earn a high return on its investment.

However, concentrated marketing involves higher than normal risks if the segment turns sour because of changes in buying patterns or new competition. For these reasons, many operators prefer to operate in more than one segment.

Selective Specialization: Here, the operator can select a number of segments, each objectively attractive and appropriate. There may be little or no synergy among the segments, but each segment promises to be a moneymaker. This multi-segment coverage strategy has the advantage of diversifying the firm's risk.

Product Specialization: Another approach is to specialize in making a certain product for several segments. Through a product specialization strategy, the firm builds a strong reputation in the specific product area. The downside risk is that the product may be supplanted by an entirely new technology.

Market Specialization: With market specialization, the firm concentrates on serving several needs of a particular customer group. An example would be a firm that sells an assortment of products, including microscopes, oscilloscopes and chemical flasks, only to university laboratories. The firm gains a strong reputation in serving this customer group and becomes a channel for further products that the customer group could use. The downside risk is that the customer group may have its budgets cut.

Full Market Coverage: Here, a firm attempts to serve all customer groups with all of the products they might need. Only very large firms can undertake a full market coverage strategy. Large firms can cover a whole market in two broad ways: through undifferentiated marketing or differentiated marketing.

- In undifferentiated marketing, the firm ignores market-segment differences and goes after the whole market with one market offer. Focusing on a basic buyer need, it designs a product and a marketing programme that appeals to the broadest number of buyers. To reach the market, the firm uses mass distribution backed by mass advertising to create a superior product image in people's minds. The narrow product line keeps down costs of research and development, production, inventory, transportation, marketing research, advertising and product management; the undifferentiated advertising programme keeps down advertising costs. Presumably, the company can turn its lower costs into lower prices to win the price-sensitive segment of the market.
- In differentiated marketing, the firm operates in several market segments and designs different programmes for each segment. Differentiated marketing typically creates more total sales than undifferentiated marketing. However, the need for different marketing programmes also increases the firm's costs for product modification, administration and promotion. Since differentiated marketing leads to both higher sales and higher costs, we cannot generalize regarding this strategy's profitability. Still, companies should be cautious about over-segmenting their market. If this happens, they may want to use counter-segmentation to broaden their customer base.

Targeting Multiple Segments and Super Segments

Very often, companies start out by marketing to one segment, and then expand to others. In targeting more than one segment, a company should examine segment interrelationships on the cost, performance and technology side. A company that is carrying fixed costs, such as a sales force or store outlets, can generally add products to absorb and share some of these costs. Smart companies know that economies of scope can be just as important as economies of scale. Moreover, companies should look beyond isolated segments to target a super segment, a set of segments that share some exploitable similarity. For example, many symphony orchestras target people with broad cultural interests, rather than only those who regularly attend concerts. Still, a company's invasion plans can be thwarted when it confronts blocked markets. This problem calls for mega marketing, the strategic coordination of economic, psychological, political and public relations skills to gain the cooperation of a number of parties in order to enter or operate in a given market.

POSITIONING

After selecting target markets, the next step involves developing positioning objectives and then developing these into a detailed marketing mix. However, developing the positioning objective needs to be done only after the brand identity and value proposition has been developed with the help of a successful differentiation strategy. In exploring the idea of positioning, it is useful to understand Aaker's definition of positioning as "the part of the brand identity and value proposition that is to be actively communicated to the target audience and that demonstrates an advantage over competing brands." Philip Kotler refers to it as the unique selling proposition. In other words, the positioning statement is the point where the bundles of attributes join to form one concept that aims at capturing the essence of what the target tourists seek in the tour package offered. These two concepts (differentiation and positioning) will be dealt with in greater detail in the next chapter.

PROMINENT GENRES IN INDIAN TOURISM

The segmentation techniques and variables discussed help categorize contemporary Indian tourism into a host of genres listed in the following table. The segmentation variables (geographic, demographic, psychographic and behavioural) along with a couple of special bases become the guiding tools for classification of the tourism industry into genres that have an identity of their own. Each of the following genres has a uniqueness of its own and follows the basic rules of segmentation – measurable, substantial, accessible, differentiable and actionable.

Prominent Genres: Indian Tourism

Tourism Genre	Key Offerings/ Features	Hot Spots/ Destinations	Segmentation Bases
Adventure Tourism 	Trekking, water sports, skiing, mountaineering, rafting, safaris, paragliding, backwaters, aero sports, mountain biking, scuba diving, and snorkelling	Jammu & Kashmir, Uttaranchal, Assam, the North East Goa, Andaman & Nicobar Islands, Kerala, Rajasthan, Tamil Nadu, Arunachal Pradesh, Sikkim, Lakshadweep	**Geographic** Region **Demographic** Age, gender **Psychographic** Personality **Behavioural** Attitude, user status **Special Basis** Trip descriptor
Ayurveda and Spa Tourism 	Yoga, spa, meditation, steam bath, ayurveda, and herbal treatment	Goa, Kerala, Uttaranchal	**Geographic** Region **Demographic** Age, family size, gender, income, occupation **Psychographic** Socio-economic, personality **Behavioural** Benefits, user status and rate, readiness, attitude **Special Basis** Customer expectation

Tourism Genre	Key Offerings/ Features	Hot Spots/ Destinations	Segmentation Bases
Beach Tourism 	Relaxing and refreshing, quiet walk barefooted, watching the sun rise and set far in the horizon, swimming along with the waves, diving deep into the water, surfing, cruising in the ocean water	**Popular Beaches** Anjuna beach, Kovalam beach, Varkala beach, Juhu beach, Baga beach, Colva beach, Pondicherry beach circuit **Destinations** Goa, Maharashtra, Andhra Pradesh, Andaman & Nicobar Islands, Lakshadweep, Orissa	**Geographic** Region **Demographic** Age, family size, gender, income, occupation **Psychographic** Socio-economic, personality **Behavioural** Occasions, benefits, user status and rate, readiness, attitude **Special Basis** Customer expectation, trip descriptor, customer image
Culture Tourism 	Handicrafts, festivals, history, music, dance, languages, pilgrimage, cuisine	Jammu & Kashmir, Kerala, Goa, Lakshadweep, Rajasthan, Arunachal Pradesh, West Bengal, Maharashtra, Uttar Pradesh, Himachal Pradesh, Madhya Pradesh	**Geographic** Region, city **Demographic** Age, gender, race **Psychographic** Socio-economic, personality **Behavioural** Occasions, user status and rate, readiness, attitude **Special Basis** Customer expectation, trip descriptor
Ecotourism 	Ancient cities, hill stations, remote villages, desert areas, wildlife parks	Andaman & Nicobar Islands, Lakshadweep, Uttaranchal, Himachal Pradesh, Jammu & Kashmir, Rajasthan, Madhya Pradesh, Kerala, Andhra Pradesh, Assam, Sikkim, West Bengal, Bihar	**Geographic** Region **Demographic** Age, occupation, education **Psychographic** Personality **Behavioural** Readiness, attitude **Special Basis** Trip descriptors

Tourism Genre	Key Offerings/ Features	Hot Spots/ Destinations	Segmentation Bases
Heritage Tourism 	Heritage forts, palaces, temples, monuments, caves	Taj Mahal, Agra Fort, Ajanta and Ellora caves, monuments of Mamallapuram, Konark Sun Temple, monuments of Fatehpur Sikri, monuments of Hampi, Khajuraho temples, Valley of Flowers	**Demographic** Age, education **Psychographic** Personality **Behavioural** Occasions, readiness **Special Basis** Customer image, trip descriptors
Pilgrimage Tourism 	Religious sites, sacred trips, temples	Amarnath cave, Vaishno Devi, Haridwar, Badrinath, Gangotri, Kedarnath, Yamunotri, Shirdi, Chardham Yatra, Rishikesh, Poanta Sahib, Ajmer Sharif, Mathura, Puri, Tirupati, Golden Temple	**Demographic** Age, education, race **Psychographic** Personality **Behavioural** Occasions, user rate **Special Basis** Trip descriptors
Train Tourism 	Heritage train travel	Palace on Wheels, Heritage on Wheels, Deccan Odyssey, Royal Orient, Fairy Queen, Shimla–Kalka Express, Darjeeling toy train	**Demographic** Age, income, education **Psychographic** Personality **Behavioural** Occasions, benefits, attitude **Special Basis** Trip descriptors
Wildlife Tourism 	Wildlife trips, explorations of forest/park interiors	Corbett National Park, Nanda Devi Wildlife, Valley of Flowers (Uttaranchal), Periyar Sanctuary (Kerala), Ranthambore Park, Bharatpur Bird Sanctuary (Rajasthan), Kanha Wildlife (Madhya Pradesh), Sunderbans Wildlife (West Bengal), Gir National Park (Gujarat)	**Demographic** Age, occupation, education **Psychographic** Personality **Behavioural** Attitude, readiness **Special Basis** Trip descriptors

Tourism Genre	Key Offerings/ Features	Hot Spots/ Destinations	Segmentation Bases
MICE (Meetings, Incentives, Conferences, and Exhibitions) Tourism 	Meetings, conferences, exhibitions, conventions, launches	**Places** Hyderabad, Delhi, Cochin, Noida, Mumbai, Pune, Chennai, Agra, Bangalore **Hotels** The Ashok, New Delhi; Hyderabad International Convention Centre, Hyderabad; Le Meridian, Cochin; The Taj Palace, Mumbai	**Demographic** Income, occupation **Psychographic** Personality **Behavioural** Benefits, occasions, loyalty status, readiness **Special Basis** Trip descriptor
Medical Tourism 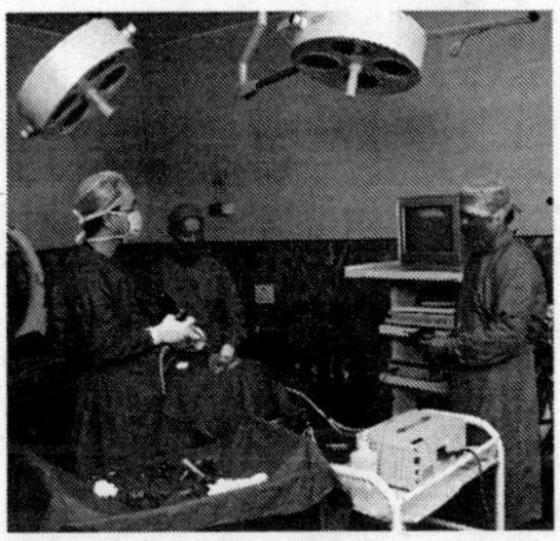	Rejuvenation, treatment, surgeries, healthcare, well-being	Apollo Hospitals, All India Institute of Medical Studies, Ram Manohar Lohia Hospital, Escorts Heart Institute (New Delhi); CMC, (Vellore); Leelavati Hospital, Tata Memorial Hospital (Mumbai)	**Demographic** Age, income **Psychographic** Socio-economic **Behavioural** Benefits, loyalty status **Special Basis** Customer expectation

Case Study: Mcleodganj and Triund — An Exciting Experience as a Tourist

In May 2006, we, a group of seven people planned to make a memorable trekking trip. The first choice that came to my mind was Triund because I had been there before as well. It is 9 km uphill McLeodganj in Himachal Pradesh. McLeodganj itself is around 10 km from Dharamshala. McLeodganj, also known as Upper Dharamshala, was so named in the 19th century after David McLeod, the lieutenant governor of Punjab at that time. During the British rule in India, the town was a hill station where the Britishers spent the hot summers. It is very famous for Tsuglagkhang or Tsuglag Khang, the Dalai Lama's temple. It has statues of Shakyamuni and Avalokitesvara, and a statue of Padmasambhava (Guru Rinpoche).

We reached McLeodganj on a Saturday afternoon after a tiring journey that started on Friday night. We left from Delhi in a train to Pathankot, from where we took the state roadways bus to McLeodganj via Dharamshala. We were there by 2 p.m. in the afternoon, when we decided to take some rest. We toured the monastery on the same day, after which we headed for a famous waterfall. We reached there after a small but arduous trek of around 45 minutes. When we reached the foot of the waterfall, it was dusk and getting darker. So, most of the people had left. The most amazing part there was that there was a tea stall that served us hot tea while we took fun dips in the ice-cold water. We spent

Case Study: *(Continued)*

Triund Trek

around 40–50 minutes there. Getting back to the hotel, we took rest as we had a long day ahead.

Our plan was to start from McLeodganj early morning, for which we had already hired a guide and tents, sleeping mattresses and bags. We left on time, and took some breakfast on the way itself. As per the time, we reached Triund by 2 p.m. It took us around seven hours, including all the food and rest breaks.

On the way, the guide told us about another place that is 5 km uphill of Triund, known as Illaqa. And he assured us that we could be on the snow if we went there. We had already trekked arduous kilometres to reach Triund, and it only took us a while to decide that we were going further ahead to Illaqa. However,

the challenge was that we had to reach there and come down again to Triund by 6:30 p.m., before it got really dark. So, we dropped all our camping stuffs there itself with one of our friends escorting it, as he was too tired to go further.

The journey thereafter was more exciting, but proportionally more challenging. We managed to reach Illaqa at 4:30 p.m. That was the first time that I was on an ice-covered mountain and, I think, so was everybody else. We were all so excited that we played with snow for around 45 minutes, before the guide warned us that if we did not leave, we would get stuck on the way down, which could be fatal for us. We left for Triund. Most part of it was downhill and we reached Triund by 6:30 p.m. There, our guide started to put on the tents for all of us. There was a small food stall at the top which served us *rajma chawal*, *dal chawal*, *maggi*, and tea and snacks. We had a lot of food and fun. The temperature by that time had gone below 15 degrees (even in the month of May) but we had expected that, and had taken sufficient number of woollens along. We camped the night on the hilltop, where the speed and sound of wind was so much that one felt scared and it was difficult to sleep. Despite all these fears, we did get some sleep and as the day broke out, the view out of our camps was just unimaginable. We all probably had seen the best scenic view of our lives. We waited till the food-stall person opened his stall. We grabbed some breakfast and returned downhill. This ended what I would call one of the most splendid tours of my life.

Camps at Triund

Unsung Tourist Destination: Renuka Lake

The Renuka Lake (660 m) is regarded as the embodiment of Renukaji, the wife of sage Jamadagini and the mother of Parashurama, one of the ten avatars of Lord Vishnu. Shaped like the profile of a woman, the lake has a circumference of 2.5 km and is the largest in Himachal. This placid stretch of water is fed by underground springs, and the surrounding hills are padded by lush forests that support a large variety of plant and animal life. Boating and trekking are additional attractions of Renukaji, whose natural beauty has to be seen to be believed. This is a perfect year-round destination that beckons every traveler

Renuka Temple

Renuka Lake

How to Reach Renuka Lake

By road: It is 315 km from Delhi. The nearest railheads are at Ambala (95 km), Dehradun (105 km) and Chandigarh (95 km). The nearest airports are at Chandigarh and Dehradun. Taxis/buses are available for Renukaji at all places.

Places to See Around

Legend has it that when the evil Sahasarjuna killed the sage Jamadagini and tried to abduct his wife Renuka, she flung herself into the water. The god restored her to life, and this lake is regarded as her embodiment. There is a row of temples along its banks, and a track encircles the water.

Parashurama Tal and Renuka Temple (100 m): Situated at the base of the Renuka Lake, this large pool is considered to be embracing Lord Parashurama, who wished to spend all eternity at his mother's feet. Reportedly built overnight by an invading force of Gurkhas in the early 19th century, the original temple of Renukaji is here. Both mother and son are reunited every year at a celebratory fair held in November.

Jamu Peak (8 km): Above the lake is the peak where Rishi Jamadagini is said to have meditated. A footpath leads to the peak. There is a small temple on this peak, which offers an excellent view of the lake and the surrounding area.

Mini Zoo (2 km): One can boat across the lake or drive to this zoo, which has Asiatic lions, spotted deer, lion-tailed macaques, nilgai methuen, barking deer and Himalayan black bears.

Lion Safari (2 km): Adjoining the zoo, an armoured van enters the large enclosure allowing for a close glimpse of the lions within.

Jataun (5 km): The dam of the Giri Hydel Project is here, and angling for mahaseer (river carp) may be done.

Best Time to Visit Renuka Lake

In winter, the climate is pleasant and light woollens should be taken along. Summer temperatures are high and cottons are recommended. The best season to visit Renuka Lake is April to June and September to November.

Accommodation

The Himachal Pradesh Tourism Development Corporation's hotel Renukaji is just by the side of the lake. A small town Dadahu which is around 2 km from Renuka Lake has some low-budget private hotels along with PWD and Forest rest houses.

SUMMARY

- Marketing is more effective when marketers target their markets. Target marketing involves three activities: market segmentation, market targeting and market positioning.
- Markets can be targeted at four levels: segments, niches, local areas and individuals.
- Market segments are large, identifiable groups within a market, with similar wants, purchasing power, location, buying attitudes or buying habits.
- A niche is a more narrowly defined group.
- Markets are segmented in a three-step procedure of surveying, analysing and profiling.
- The major segmentation variables for consumer markets are geographic, demographic, psychographic and behavioural, to be used singly or in combination.
- The major segmentation variables for consumer markets are geographic, demographic, psychographic and behavioural, to be used singly or in combination.
- Business marketers can use all of these variables along with operating variables, purchasing approaches, situational factors and personal characteristics.
- To be effective, market segments must be measurable, substantial, accessible, differentiable and actionable.
- Once a firm has identified its market-segment opportunities, it has to evaluate the various segments and decide how many and which ones to target.
- In evaluating segments, managers look at the segment's attractiveness indicators and the company's objectives and resources. In choosing which segments to target, the company can focus on a single segment, selected segments, a specific product, a specific market, or the full market.

FIELD EXERCISES

1. For your region, segment the market on basis of customer expectation and explain how you will target the segment and techniques used.
2. For a destination, you have recently visited or are planning to visit, analyse how the segmentation and targeting for that region has been done. Prepare a report mentioning the process and techniques.

REFERENCES

Bloom, Jonathan Z. (2004), "Tourist Market Segmentation with Linear and Non-Linear Techniques," *Tourism Management*, Vol. 25, pp. 723–733.

Díaz-Martín, Ana M., Víctor Iglesias, Rodolfo Vázquez, Agustín V. Ruiz (2000), "The Use of Quality Expectations to Segment a Service Market," *Journal of Services Marketing*, Vol. 14, No. 2, pp. 132–146.

Dolnicar, Sara (2007), "Management Learning Exercise and Trainer's Note for Market Segmentation in Tourism," *International Journal of Culture, Tourism and Hospitality Research*, Vol. 1, No. 4, pp. 289–295.

Dolnicar, S. (2006), "Data-driven Market Segmentation in Tourism – Approaches, Changes Over Two Decades and Development Potential," Conference Paper, 15th International Research Conference of the Council for Australian University Tourism and Hospitality Education (CAUTHE), Australia.

Kotler, Philip and Kevin Keller, (2003), Marketing Management (A South Asian Perspective), Prentice Hall.

Leisen, Birgit (2001), "Image Segmentation: The Case of a Tourism Destination," *Journal of Services Marketing*, Vol. 15, No. 1, pp. 49–66.

Web Sites

Official Indian tourism portal: www.incredibleindia.org/; www.tourisminindia.com/

Machu Picchu (Peru)

CHAPTER 8

Differentiation and Positioning in Tourism

ABOUT THE DESTINATION

Popularly known as the "Lost City," it was built high in the Andes by Pachacuti Inca Yupanqui of the Incas. It was rediscovered by Hiram Bingham in 1911 and is one of the world's most impressive archaeological and civil engineering sites.

OBJECTIVES

- To learn the basics of differentiation and how it is done in the services, specifically tourism, industry
- To learn the basics of positioning and its process and errors
- Differentiation and positioning of three Indian states as popular tourist destinations

INTRODUCTION

Have you ever been to a restaurant? Definitely yes, is it not? All people have a distinctive choice about food (say, someone likes Chinese cuisine very much and generally goes to a Chinese restaurant) and whenever someone is eating out, they generally goes with their choice. Now, think of one cuisine (Indian/Chinese/Thai/Continental/Mexican or whatever else you like) that is your favourite; and then, think of the names of four or five of your favourite restaurants that serve this cuisine. It will not be very difficult for you to rank these in descending order; now, the trick comes — do you find any vast difference in the qualities of food across these restaurants? Possibly, there is a little chance that the food differs widely in quality across these restaurants. So, what makes you choose a particular restaurant as number one? Probably the ambience, the service or the music played by the live band? Restaurant is a typical example of a continuum of product and services, where the product (food) is about 20–40 per cent of the total experience and the rest is service and experience. Similar is the case in tourism. The service and overall experience is as necessary as the product (Taj Mahal in Agra or the sea beaches in Goa). So, what makes a destination clearly stand apart? Take the popular tourist destinations of Malaysia, Singapore, Thailand, Hong Kong, Goa or Kerala — what differentiates them? One may say all have different tourist attractions. True, and yet, it is also necessary to find out why someone likes Singapore more than Bangkok or vice versa. While the tourist attractions are the product part of the overall tourism industry which clearly differentiates two distinct places, the service and experience part helps in positioning the destination.

Differentiation and positioning are two very important aspects of marketing. Differentiation tells what features of the product or service one needs to focus on, while promoting the product or service, and positioning tells how the product or service is to be placed in the consumer's mind. A detailed discussion on these two is given in subsequent sections of the chapter.

DIFFERENTIATION: BASIC IDEA

In marketing, differentiation is the process of distinguishing the differences of a product or service offering from others to make it more attractive to a particular target market. This involves differentiating it from competitors' products or services as well as from one's own product or service offerings.

Differentiation is a source of competitive advantage. Although research in a niche market may result in changing a product or service offering in order to improve differentiation, the changes themselves are not differentiation. Marketing or differentiation is the process of describing the differences between products and services or the resulting list of differences. This is done in order to demonstrate the unique aspects of a product and to create a sense of value. Marketing textbooks are firm on the point that any differentiation must be valued by buyers. The term "unique selling proposition" refers to advertising to communicate a product's differentiation.

In economics, successful differentiation leads to monopolistic competition and is inconsistent with the conditions for perfect competition, which include the requirement that the products or services of competing firms should be perfect substitutes.

Brand differences are usually minor; they can be merely a difference in packaging or an advertising theme. The physical product need not change, but it could. Take the case of Malaysia and Thailand. Both have similar products (that is, similar tourist attractions) for tourism, but they differentiate on the cultural value. Malaysia portrays itself as a country rich in culture. Differentiation is due to consumers perceiving a difference; hence, the causes of differentiation may be functional aspects of the product or the service, how it is distributed and marketed or who buys it. The major sources of product differentiation are as follows.

- Differences in quality, which are usually accompanied by differences in price
- Differences in functional features
- Ignorance of buyers regarding the essential characteristics and qualities of goods or services they are purchasing
- Sales promotion activities of sellers and, in particular, advertising
- Differences in availability (e.g., season of the year)

The objective of differentiation is to develop a position that potential customers see as unique.

Differentiation primarily impacts performance through reducing directness of competition. As the product or service becomes more different, categorization becomes more difficult and, hence, draws fewer comparisons with its competition. A successful differentiation strategy will move your product from competition based primarily on price to competition on non-price factors (in case of tourism, such as the exoticness of the locations and the uniqueness of various experiences).

Most people would say that the implication of differentiation is the possibility of charging a price premium; however, this is a gross simplification. If customers value the firm's offer, they will be less sensitive to aspects of competing offers; price may not be one of these aspects. Differentiation makes customers in a given segment have a lower sensitivity to other features (non-price) of the product.

Stages in Differentiation

It is a three-step process as explained below:

- **Defining the customer-value model:** The company first lists all the product and service factors that might influence the target customers' perception of value

- **Building the customer-value hierarchy:** Four factors come under this head. Consider a fine restaurant:
  1. *Basic:* The food is edible and delivered in a timely fashion
  2. *Expected:* There is good china and tableware, a linen tablecloth, a napkin, etc. (These factors make the offering acceptable but not exceptional)
  3. *Desired:* The restaurant is pleasant and quiet, and the food is especially good and interesting
  4. *Unanticipated:* The restaurant serves a complimentary sorbet between the courses and places candy on the table after the last course is served
- **Deciding on the customer-value package:** Now, the company chooses a combination of tangible and intangible items, experiences and outcomes designed to outperform competitors and win the customers' delight and loyalty

Differentiation Tools

Differentiation is the act of designing a set of meaningful differences to distinguish the company's offerings from those of competitors' offerings.

The Boston Consulting Group (BCG) Competitive Advantage Matrix: The BCG has distinguished four types of industries on the number of available competitive advantages and their size.

A product-based company can differentiate their product along five dimensions — product, services, personnel, channel and image.

		Number of approaches to achieve advantage	
		Few	Many
Size of the advantage	Large	Volume	Specialized
	Small	Stalemated	Fragmented

BCG Competitive Advantage Matrix

Services Differentiation

When the physical product cannot easily be differentiated, the key to competitive success may lie in adding value-added services and improving their quality. These hold particularly true for the tourism industry. The main service differentiators include ordering ease like booking tickets or hotels through a Web site, delivery and customer consulting.

Many authors have argued that the marketing concept in tourism is based on a long-term commitment to the satisfaction of travellers' needs and motives and calls for a more strategic approach to marketing, instead of relying on operational measures such as marketing communication. There are three approaches to the strategy that may be used by the travel and tourism industry.

The consumer-oriented approach dominates most current discussions on international marketing strategies. Another approach focuses on competition. However, these two approaches (or a blend of them) may be insufficient for them to neglect the role of intermediaries in travel and tourism. Hence, a third approach to strategy, the trade-oriented focus on intermediaries' desires, problems and demands, needs to be investigated.

The Consumer-Oriented Approach. Within the scope of this consumer-oriented approach, organizations can focus on two core marketing strategies:

1. An undifferentiated marketing strategy (full product/market coverage)
2. A differentiated marketing strategy (product specialization, market specialization or product/market specialization)

Undifferentiated strategic marketing focuses on the average expectations of target markets — marketing efforts concentrate on the common interests of the target segments' needs and behaviour rather than their variances. In contrast, differentiated strategic marketing aims to identify the characteristics of diverse consumer groups through the use of marketing instruments directed at specific targets in order to create and implement a marketing approach and programme that suits particular segments' needs and expectations. The extent of differentiation varies depending on prevailing market conditions.

The Competitor-Oriented Approach. The next approach to strategy concentrates on competition. The travel and tourism industry is undergoing a period of rapid change and uncertainty, with new technologies and more experienced consumers being some of the opportunities and challenges facing the industry. The role of a competitive marketing strategy is to develop, maintain or defend the position of an organization. Public and private travel and tourism organizations may either strive for an overall cost/price leadership or differentiate themselves to gain a product-quality leadership. Furthermore, a concentration on market niches may lead to a successful strategic position.

The above two strategies together give rise to the approach of product differentiation and positioning. The third approach given below incorporates the significant role played by the intermediate organizations handling the organization of the entire national tourism industry.

The Trade-Oriented Approach. The third approach to strategy focuses on intermediaries and appears to be particularly relevant to the travel and tourism industry. The distribution of travel and tourism products/services is a most important activity along the tourism chain. There are two main considerations that need to be distinguished – first, the degree to which organizations become involved in organizing and structuring the overseas distribution channel and, second, organizations' reactions and responses to marketing and distribution strategies of intermediaries in overseas markets. As a result of organizations' activeness or passiveness with regard to these two considerations, four trade-oriented strategies are possible – by-passing, cooperation, conflict or adaptation.

A *by-passing strategy* means travel and tourism organizations or airlines would relinquish any collaboration with the distribution channel. The appropriateness of this strategy for public and private travel and tourism organizations seems very limited, considering the current importance of intermediaries in most overseas marketplaces. However, *cooperation strategies* are widely adopted in vertical marketing. These interactive forms vary on a continuum from very loose cooperative forms with fairly unrestrained degrees of binding forces or commitments based on, for example, flows of information to very strictly regulated distribution systems. In contrast to the cooperation strategy, active reactions in organizing and structuring the distribution channel can lead to a *conflict strategy* whenever the marketing communication strategies and activities of the trade are not given sufficient attention or are even ignored by travel and tourism organizations or airlines. That is, travel and tourism bodies attempt to bring about or enforce their own interests against the resistance of the trade in order to gain marketing leadership in the distribution system. The *adaptation strategy* is characterized by a passive reaction of public and private travel and tourism organizations to the marketing strategies of intermediaries in terms of organizing and structuring the distribution channel. That is, initiatives of these organizations are very scarce. Such passive behaviour would not apply to a marketing-oriented organization and will, therefore, not be followed further in this research. In brief, all the three approaches of consumer-oriented, competition-oriented and trade-oriented may fit into an overall strategy with varying degrees of emphasis that are not yet known with precision.

POSITIONING: BASIC IDEA

In marketing, positioning has come to mean the process by which marketers try to create an image or an identity in the minds of their target market for their product, brand, service or organization. It is the relative competitive comparison their product or service occupies in a given market as perceived by the target market.

Re-positioning involves changing the identity of a product or a service, relative to the identity of competing products or services, in the collective minds of the target market.

De-positioning involves attempting to change the identity of competing products or services, relative to the identity of your own product or service, in the collective minds of the target market.

The growth of high-tech marketing may have had much to do with the shift in definition towards competitive positioning.

Definitions. Although there are different definitions of positioning, probably the most common is: "A product's position is how potential buyers see the product or service and is expressed relative to the position of competitors."

Positioning is a concept in marketing which was first popularized by Al Ries and Jack Trout in their bestseller book *Positioning: The Battle for Your Mind*. They iterate that any brand is valued by the perception it carries in the prospect's or customer's mind. Each brand has, thus, to be positioned in a particular class or segment. For example, Malaysia is positioned as a heritage-tourist destination, whereas Dubai is positioned as a place for shopping extravaganza.

The position of the brand (here, brand meant as a destination) has to be carefully maintained. This differs slightly from the context in which the term was first published in 1969 by Jack Trout in the paper "*Positioning is a game people play in today's me-too market place*" in the publication *Industrial Marketing*, in which the case of the typical consumer is studied who is overwhelmed with unwanted advertising and has a natural tendency to discard all information that does not immediately find a comfortable and empty slot in his/her mind. It was then expanded into their ground-breaking first book, *Positioning: The Battle for Your Mind*, in which they defined positioning as an organized system for finding a window in the mind. It is based on the concept that communication can only take place at the right time and under the right circumstances.

What most will agree on is that positioning is something (perception) that happens in the minds of the target market. It is the aggregate perception the market has of a particular company, product or service in relation to their perceptions of the competitors in the same category. It will happen whether or not a company's management is proactive, reactive or passive about the ongoing process of evolving a position. But a company can positively influence the perceptions through enlightened strategic actions.

So, positioning can be defined as the act of designing the company's offering and image to occupy a distinctive place in the target market's mind.

The end result of positioning is the successful creation of a market-focused value proposition, a cogent reason why the target market should buy the product.

Consumers' Perceptual Space

In marketing terms, there are no such things as a product or a service that exists by itself in space, independent of the customer. For a product or a service to exist, it must find a place in an individual consumer's perception of the world of products around him or her. And this perception is subjective, governed by the individual consumer's values, beliefs, needs, experiences and environment.

It can be shown by a relevant example. Suppose you want to position your hometown in the customer's mind with a particular message. How can you do it? It is very important to remember that how your position decides who will be your closest competitor(s). Generally, for positioning, a two-axis perceptual map or 3 × 3 matrix is created choosing any two parameters you think are important for the success or failure of the service you are offering (here, your hometown). For tourism, one of the two most important factors is connectivity — that is, how well the destination is connected with other parts of the country and the world.

Another attribute, the weather, may be chosen. Places where the weather is always good or normal are ideal as throughout-the-year tourist attractions, and where weather is extreme — for example, Shimla or Darjeeling in India, which are basically hill stations and have sub-zero temperatures in winter season — the place is good only for a particular season.

The two parameters are chosen arbitrarily. It has to be chosen as per the marketer's choice.

An arbitrary perceptual map is developed in Figure 8.1 to illustrate the concept. Now, you need to fit your hometown into this two-dimensional space and then have to look which place is the nearest competitor. Suppose your hometown is well connected and also has very pleasant weather — in that case, your nearest competitor will be Goa. You can fill the space with more places, and you have to choose the parameters that seem to be important to you.

After the identification of the closest competitor, you need to differentiate your hometown from the competitor (here, Goa) and then position it according to the differentiation. Suppose your hometown has

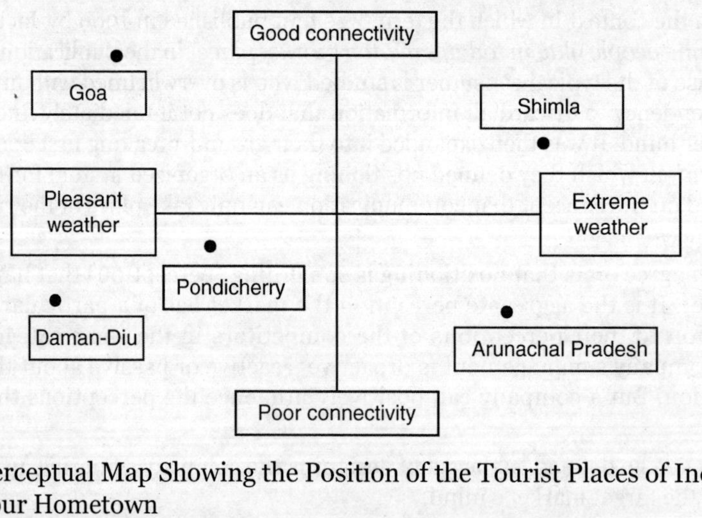

Fig. 8.1: Perceptual Map Showing the Position of the Tourist Places of India in Relation to your Hometown

some beautiful old temples and monuments; then, it can be positioned as a place to experience the rich culture of the bygone era.

The 3 × 3 matrix method is almost similar, where on the two chosen parameters you create a 3 × 3 matrix and fill the nine cells of the matrix with the destinations – it is not necessary to fill all the nine cells – and then decide how to position your hometown.

Positioning Process

First, we will discuss the positioning process for a product and then we will gradually shift our focus to services. Generally, the product positioning process involves

- Defining the market in which the product or brand will compete (who the relevant buyers are)
- Identifying the attributes (also called dimensions) that define the product "space"
- Collecting information from a sample of customers about their perceptions of each product on the relevant attributes
- Determining each product's share of mind
- Determining each product's current location in the product space
- Determining the target market's preferred combination of attributes (referred to as an ideal vector)
- Examining the fit between
    a. The position of your product
    b. The position of the ideal vector
- Positioning

The process is similar for positioning a company's services. Services, however, do not have the physical attributes of products – that is, we cannot feel them or touch them. In tourism, though, we do have one advantage – we can show nice pictures of the places of attraction. It is very important in tourism that you ask your customers first and then yourself: what value do clients get from my services? How are they better off by coming to your place? Is there a characteristic that makes my services different?

Write out the value that customers derive and the attributes your services offer to create the first draft of your positioning. Test it on people who do not really know what you do or what you sell, watch their facial expressions and listen to their response. When they want to know more because you have piqued their interest and started a conversation, you will know you are on the right track.

A competitor has four strategic alternatives.

1. The first is to strengthen its own current position in the consumer's mind.
2. Grab an unoccupied position
3. It can be argued that, in an over-advertised society, the mind often knows brands in the form of product ladders, such as Dubai-Goa-Darjeeling. The top place is remembered best. The marketer should identify an important attribute or benefit that a place can convincingly own
4. The fourth strategy is the exclusive-club strategy – for instance, the idea that it is one of the "big three"

Marketers essentially deal with communication strategy for positioning or re-positioning a brand in the consumer's mind. Yet, they acknowledge that positioning requires that every tangible aspect of product, price, place and promotion must support the chosen positioning strategy.

How Many Differences to Promote?

Each company must decide how many differences (e.g., benefit, features) to promote to its target customers. Many marketers advocate promoting only one central benefit – a company should develop a unique selling proposition (USP) for each brand and stick to it. Each brand should select an attribute and tout itself as "number one" on that attribute.

Number-one positioning includes

- Best quality
- Best service
- Lowest price
- Best value
- Safest
- Fastest
- Most customized
- Most convenient
- Most advanced technology

Not everyone agrees that single-benefit positioning is always the best. Double-benefit positioning may be necessary if two or more firms claim to be the best on the same attribute.

There are even cases of successful triple-benefit positioning. Smith Kline Beecham promotes its Aquafresh toothpaste as offering three benefits – anticavity protection, better breath and whiter teeth. The challenge is to convince consumers that the brand delivers all three. In doing this, Beecham "counter-segmented"; that is, it attracted three segments instead of one.

Positioning Errors

There are four major positioning errors:

1. **Under positioning:** Some companies discover that buyers have only a vague idea of the brand. The brand is seen as just another entry in a crowded marketplace
2. **Over-positioning:** Buyers have too narrow an image of the brand. Most Indians have an idea (though it is slowly changing) that a foreign tour is overtly expensive – even in the case of Malaysia or Bangkok
3. **Confused positioning:** Confused image of the brand resulting from the company making too many claims or changing the brand's positioning too frequently
4. **Doubtful positioning:** Buyers may find it hard to believe claims in view of the product's features, price or manufacture

POSITIONING OF THREE INDIAN STATES

India is a country of such dimensions that positioning the country in the tourists' mind map is far away from practicality. It would be wise, then, to choose some particular state and then try to find out how to position it. With this purpose, three states, which attract major tourist attractions and are geographically far away from each other, have been chosen. The size and population of the states are comparable enough to many Asian countries. The chosen three states are Uttarakhand – formerly known as Uttaranchal and one of the newest states of India, created in November 2000 – Kerala and Goa. These three states have different landscape and naturescape and are major attractions for tourists.

Uttarakhand borders Tibet to the north, Nepal to the east and the states of Himachal Pradesh and Uttar Pradesh (of which it formed a part before 2000) in the west and south, respectively. The region is traditionally referred to as Uttarakhand in Hindu scriptures and old literature, a term derived from the Sanskrit for "northern country" or "northern section." The provisional capital of Uttarakhand is Dehradun, which is also a railhead and the largest city in the region.

Kerala is located at the southern part of the Indian peninsula. It is bordered on the north by Karnataka, on the south and east by Tamil Nadu and on the west by the Arabian Sea. Thiruvananthapuram, the capital, Kochi and Kozhikode are the major cities. The principal spoken language is Malayalam, though other languages are also spoken. Kerala is one of the most densely populated states in India and ranks 12th among states in terms of population.

Goa is situated in the west coast of the country at the shore of Arabian Sea and very popular among Indian as well as international tourists as a beach destination. Goa has some amazing beaches and also some great churches.

The positioning is done for these three states creating some points in view as explained below.

- What is the duration of time generally spent by people visiting the state?
- How is the attitude of locals towards tourists?
- How costly do people perceive the tourism of the state to be?
- How safe tourists perceive the state to be?

To find out what the majority of tourists think on these parameters, a survey was conducted. The duration of the visit is important as domestic tourism in India has inclined towards the following three trends.

1. Visiting any place over a weekend (Saturday and Sunday) by combining the weekend with a holiday on Friday or Monday in such a way that it would be a holiday trip for 3–5 days typically
2. Taking a week off and then visiting a place for 7–10 days (combining both the weekends). This is a prevalent trend for tourism in the time of Dussehra or Diwali
3. Visiting a place for 10–15 days during the summer vacation or winter vacation in schools

Depending upon the duration of the stay, the state can be positioned as a weekend destination, etc., and advertisement and other promotional activities can be utilized heavily during that time.

Uttarakhand

Leisure, adventure and religious tourism play a prominent role in Uttarakhand's economy, with the Corbett National Park and Tiger Reserve and the nearby hill stations of Nainital, Mussoorie, Almora, Kausani, Bhimtal and Ranikhet being amongst the most frequented destinations of India. The state also contains numerous peaks of interest to mountaineers, although Nanda Devi, the highest and the best known of these, has been off limits since 1982. Other national wonders include Valley of Flowers, which along with Nanda Devi National Park form a UNESCO World Heritage Site.

Nainital in Uttarakhand

To Uttarakhand – long called "abode of the gods" (*Devbhumi*) – belong some of the holiest Hindu shrines, and for more than a thousand years, pilgrims have been visiting the region in the hopes of salvation and purification from sin. Gangotri and Yamunotri, the sources of the Ganga and the Yamuna, respectively, fall in the upper reaches of the state and together with Badrinath (dedicated to Vishnu) and Kedarnath (dedicated to Shiva) form the Chardham of Uttarakhand, one of Hinduism's most spiritually auspicious pilgrimage circuits. Rishikesh near Haridwar is known as the pre-eminent yoga centre of India, while the spectacular view from Hemkund is of special significance to Sikhs.

In the survey on Uttarakhand, 79 per cent of respondents said that they were there for 4–7 days. It clearly emphasizes that the state can be positioned as a weekly destination and people can go there during Diwali and Dussehra. There are many towns in Uttarakhand where tourists visit, such as Dehradun, Rishikesh, Nainital and Mussoorie, and each for different purposes. The visit to Dehradun and Nainital is for nature tourism, while it is a religious journey that is oriented with adventure sports for Rishikesh. So, the state may be promoted as a destination where you can have all the blends of tourism like mountaineering, trekking, nature tourism and religious tourism. Two important factors are safety and local attitude which have been found to be of enormous implication as far as revisit and recommendation are concerned. In both the parameters for Uttarakhand, 84 per cent respondents rated either very good or good. The revisit and recommendation parameters were also rated high for Uttarakhand. So, the positioning for Uttarakhand can be as a destination for short trips (7–10 days) during festival holidays or during Christmas. The differentiation strategy can be the destination mix it offers for all kinds of tourists – religious, trekker, mountaineer, nature lover or jungle lover (from the survey, it was seen that 56 per cent went to the state for nature holiday), but it is recommended to go for an undifferentiated marketing strategy to attract people with varied interests.

Kerala

Kerala, situated on the lush and tropical Malabar Coast, is one of the most popular tourist destinations in India. Named as one of the "10 paradises of the world" and "50 places of a lifetime" by the *National Geographic Traveler* magazine, Kerala is especially known for its ecotourism initiatives. Its unique culture and traditions, coupled with its varied demographics, has made it one of the most popular tourist destinations in the world. Growing at a rate of 13.31 per cent, the state's tourism industry is a major contributor to its economy.

Until the early 1980s, Kerala was a relatively unknown destination; most tourist circuits focused on North India. Aggressive marketing campaigns launched by the Kerala Tourism Development Corporation, the government agency that oversees tourism prospects of the state, laid the foundation for the growth of the tourism industry. In the decades that followed, Kerala's tourism industry was able to transform the state into one of the niche holiday destinations in India. The tagline "Kerala – God's Own Country," originally coined by Vipin Gopal, has been widely used in Kerala's tourism promotions and soon became synonymous with the state. In 2006, Kerala attracted 8.5 million tourist arrivals, an increase of 23.68 per cent over the previous year, making the state one of the fastest growing destinations in the world.

Padmanabhapuram Palace

Popular attractions in the state include the beaches at Kovalam, Cherai and Varkala; the hill stations of Munnar, Nelliampathi, Ponmudi and Wayanad and the national parks and wildlife sanctuaries at Periyar and Eravikulam National

Park. The backwaters region, which comprises an extensive network of interlocking rivers, lakes and canals that centre on Alleppey, Kumarakom and Punnamada – where the annual Nehru Trophy Boat Race is held in August, also sees heavy tourist traffic. Heritage sites, such as the Padmanabhapuram Palace and the Mattancherry Palace, are also visited. Cities such as Kochi and Thiruvananthapuram are popular centres for shopping and traditional theatrical performances. During early summer, the Thrissur Pooram is conducted, attracting foreign tourists who are largely drawn by the festival's elephants and celebrants.

For Kerala, it is suggested that the state can be positioned as an ideal place for honeymooning. Major tourists go there for an average duration of 10–15 days; so, it is well suited with the image of a leisurely and luxurious honeymoon destination. Again, the variety of product mix can be a winning point on differentiation; the major differentiation, though, would be the backwater as this is unique in India and will give tourists a feel of "rural Venice of east."

Goa

Goa is a major tourist attraction and every year it attracts 12 per cent of the total international tourists coming to India. Variously known as "Pearl of the Orient" and a "tourist's paradise," the state of Goa is located on the western coast of India in the coastal belt known as Konkan. The magnificent beauty and the architectural splendours of its temples, churches and old houses have made Goa a firm favourite with travellers around the world. But then, Goa is much more than just beaches and sea. It has its unique history and rich culture and some of the prettiest natural sceneries that India has to offer. Much of the real Goa is in its interiors, both inside its buildings and in the hinterland away from the coastal area. Legends from Hindu mythology credit Lord Parashurama (an incarnation of Lord Vishnu) with the creation of Goa.

Basilica of Bom Jesus, Goa

The state of Goa can be positioned as an ideal place for fun and frolic. People may come over there for a weekend – 80 per cent respondents say that they visited Goa for a period of 3–5 days. It was a bit surprising to see that people do not perceive it as much of a honeymoon destination compared to Kerala or Uttarakhand. The differentiating factors for Goa can be its exotic beaches, the tourist-friendly culture, the beautiful churches – with a dash of westernized civilization and also the famous carnival.

A Beachside View of Goa

In the survey, an important fact observed about Indian tourists was that most of them had firsthand as well as detailed information from their family and friends; the Internet, magazines, travel guides, TV programmes, etc., played a less significant role. The state tourism departments' Web sites for these three states were assessed to

Case Study: Singapore's Positioning as a Tourist Destination

The city-state of Singapore has seen remarkable growth in tourism considering its size and limited supply of cultural and natural resources. Such an achievement can be attributed to a variety of factors, not the least being the heavy investment in infrastructure and product development, and it is likely that marketing has made a contribution as well. The subject of this case is the most recent promotion involving a new brand entitled "Uniquely Singapore" and examines the initiative within the framework of the country's destination branding and tourism development strategies.

Tourism in Singapore

Singapore was a British colony until it gained independence in 1965, and it is an island of about 626 sq km, frequently referred to as a city-state. It is highly industrialized and urbanized and has a population of over 4 million comprising Chinese (75.6 per cent), Malays (13.6 per cent), Indians (7 per cent) and others like Eurasians. Rapid economic progress and resultant prosperity have been credited to the government of the People's Action Party, which has been in office since 1968. Safety and security are selling points, and Changi Airport provides international access by air. An interesting mix of attractions and activities is on offer related to the colonial and wartime eras, multiculturalism and the ethnic quarters, parks and gardens, the arts and food, shopping and other assorted events. Business travellers of different types constitute a key segment, particularly those attending conferences, and increasing emphasis is being devoted to healthcare tourism. Most visitors originate within the region, although Europeans and Americans are sizeable markets, and their average length of stay is comparatively short – for example, the duration was 3.2 days in 2004.

Promoting Singapore

Singapore's distinct political system and the regime's intervention in many aspects of life are regularly remarked upon. The constraints it has imposed are the subject of censure from certain quarters, a chewing gum ban and fines for not flushing public toilets being often quoted by the overseas media in more frivolous examples. It is not the intention to explore the merits or otherwise of Singapore's political system and the veracity of international reporting on it, but it should be recorded that there has been some relaxation in regulations and there are signs of change as the second generation of political leaders takes charge and society evolves. The labelling of Singapore as "funky" in *Time* magazine, with a cover headlined "Singapore swings," was hailed as evidence of this shift and welcomed by the authorities. There is, nevertheless, a tension between "meeting the demand for greater social freedom and efforts to maintain social order," the anticipated solution being "cautious steps to extend social freedoms while ensuring that debate on purely political issues remains largely out of bounds." Putting such questions of politics aside, it can also be observed that the distinctive conditions in Singapore have afforded advantages such as security and efficiency with regard to the presentation of facets of destination images likely to be attractive and reassuring to many tourists and investors. However, they have also led to perceptions of Singapore as "staid, restrictive, boring, conservative, too strict with nothing much to do on a tiny island" and an unexciting vacation choice. Tourism marketers, thus, face the challenge of breaking through what might be seen as misconceptions and convincing potential visitors of the wealth of attractions and experiences to be found in Singapore. At the same time, the shortage of space, the confined stock of traditional tourism resources and other realities cannot be overlooked. Responses to the challenge are partly reflected in the ways the Republic of Singapore has been promoted to overseas visitors, albeit with a set of recurring motifs. An early marketing slogan was that of "Instant Asia," employed in the 1970s and suggesting that visitors could sample

Case Study: *(Continued)*

Asia's principal cultures in multiracial Singapore. The theme gave way to that of "Surprising Singapore" in the 1980s, and this promised a fascinating blend of the exotic oriental and Western-style modernity. These characteristics were echoed in "New Asia – Singapore," which was introduced in the late 1990s and was perhaps the fullest scale-branding campaign up to that point, disclosing how tourism officials wanted the world to see late 20th-century Singapore. The brand personality was that of cosmopolitan, youthful and vibrant modern Asia, with reliability and comfort and designed to tell a "story of how a young nation emerged from an uncertain future to become what it is today." It spoke of a bold, visionary approach in revolutionizing traditional ways of doing things and applying them successfully to the situations generally faced. The intention was to propagate an image of a stimulating but well-organized place with a distinctly Asian population who were sophisticated members of a global society and where the visitor would feel safe. A strong destination brand encompassing these messages is seen to generate economic gains, and tourism branding is sometimes one element of a broader scheme by authorities that aspire to position their locality or country and present it to the world as an excellent venue for all kinds of business. Considerable resources are being invested in these initiatives and consultants employed to proffer expensive advice, resulting in campaigns of varying degrees of sophistication and impact. However, success is not easy to attain or measure. As previously noted, destinations are unusual entities, and their characteristics and complexities may defy productive efforts at branding. The imperative of re-branding, observable in business generally, can lead to brand fatigue or confusion if conducted regularly and could be an inefficient use of scarce resources. In addition to spending on marketing, heavy investment in an enhanced tourism infrastructure and attractions could be necessary if the visions conveyed and the expectations inspired are to correspond with the realities of visitor experiences. Commitment is demanded from all those involved in order to deliver the promises of the brand, and branding is perhaps best attempted as part of a long-term plan that provides strategic direction to the tourism industry. The tendency towards convergence and similarities in brands and supporting campaigns, possibly encouraged by a common stance and mode of operation among consultants, is also to be guarded against. Brands are launched with great enthusiasm, but energy must also be devoted to monitoring and evaluation to permit properly informed judgements about outcomes. These represent daunting challenges and suggest that there are certain disadvantages to destination branding which must be acknowledged to ensure a balanced debate on the subject of its merits and contribution to tourism marketing.

see how effective the information-gathering process was. For Goa, it was found that only some generic information was given. Transportation detail is provided only for travelling to Goa from other places and that too by air; nothing is given in terms of rail or road transportation or transportation within the state. Details about accommodation facilities and from where to book them are not available on the Web site. One cannot book rooms into government resorts or hotels over the Internet, and no phone numbers are given either. Worse is the case for Uttarakhand, with no Web site from the government's tourism department. There are a couple of non-government Web sites, but they are not very catchy and are rather ill informed. The Web site of the tourism department of Kerala is a rare exception (www.keralatourism.org) where the information about hotels and tour operators is given along with their phone numbers and mail IDs. Also, a tourist having any grievance can interact with the tourism secretary over the Web site itself. The Web site is available in Hindi, Malayalam, French, Dutch, Italian and Spanish languages, apart from the default English. Seems that state governments of India need to be more net savvy and can learn a lesson from Kerala!

Case Study: Positioning of West Bengal Using Durga Puja

It is now becoming a common practice to position a place in a very particular manner in the customers' black box by using a local festival of that place. Brazil has used the carnival of Rio de Janeiro to position the place as well as the country as a place for fun and frolic. Goa has used its carnival in the same manner. Kerala has used the Onam festival to position itself as a traditional tourist destination as well as to promote the back waters to tourists.

A Durga Puja Pandal in Kolkata Duplicating Taj Mahal

Durga Puja is the biggest festival for the residents of the state of West Bengal, and it can be used to position the state – especially Kolkata, the main city and capital of the state – differently in people's mind. The art value of the pandals and idols of Goddess Durga is invaluable. The pandals on the street depicting various themes or monuments look so real that international tourists tend to think that they are permanent. Kolkata can be positioned as a place to experience art traditionally during Durga Puja. The pandals – made mainly of thermocol and jute, though to bring variety anything from iron straps to safety pins are used – are so realistic that tourists find it hard to believe that these will be destroyed once the festival is over. The state government never looked into the aspect of promoting this festival to attract tourists. One possible explanation is that during evenings, the heavy rush on roads may act as a deterrent to tourists' activities. Proper planning is required to properly position this festival in tourists' minds. Readers are requested to think and chart down possible positioning strategies for West Bengal using Durga Puja as main differentiator.

Case Study: Medical Tourism in India

India is one of the leading countries for 'medical tourism', and it is a popular choice for patients from Western countries for cheap and quality medical services. This holds true for Indian patients also as they travel far for a reliable medical facility. India's national health policy declares that treatment of foreign patients is legally an "export" and deemed "eligible for all fiscal incentives extended to export earnings." Government and private-sector studies estimate that medical tourism to India is growing by 30 per cent a year, and this could bring between US$ 1 billion and $ 2 billion into the country by 2012. India's top-rated education system is churning out not only computer programmers and engineers but also an estimated 20,000 to 30,000 doctors and nurses each year.

The largest of the estimated half-dozen medical corporations in India serving medical tourists is Apollo Hospital Enterprises, which treated an estimated 60,000 patients between 2001 and spring 2004. It is Apollo that is aggressively moving into medical outsourcing. Apollo already provides overnight computer services for U.S. insurance companies and hospitals and is also working with big pharmaceutical corporations on drug trials.

Apollo's business began to grow in the 1990s, with the deregulation of the Indian economy, which drastically cut the bureaucratic barriers to expansion and made it easier to import the most modern medical equipment. The first patients were Indian expatriates who returned home for treatment; major investment houses followed with money, and then patients from Europe, the Middle East and Canada began to arrive. Apollo now has 37 hospitals, with about 7,000 beds. The company is in partnership with hospitals in Kuwait, Sri Lanka and Nigeria. One more popular destination is Christian Medical College (CMC), Vellore. These hospitals attract not only foreigners, but also Indian patients, especially from the eastern and north eastern parts of the country. As the food habits in South India – where these hospitals are situated – are quite different from those in other parts of the country, some restaurants have come up in the vicinity of the hospitals to cater to food choices of the relatives of patients. There are cheap hotels available nearby so that patients' relatives can stay. Western patients usually get a package deal that includes flights, transfers, hotels, treatment and often, a post-operative vacation from the various tour operators, whereas there is nothing such as a package for Indian patients till now.

CONCLUSION

In conclusion, destination marketing is becoming more complex as tourists consume regions as experiences, often ignoring that tourism products consist of a great number of individually produced products and services. Global competition and industry concentration throw up new challenges. In this sense, destination marketers have to achieve the strategic objectives set through stakeholders' analysis and match the appropriate demand with supply, by using the entire range of marketing tools for communicating with consumers and suppliers. Global competition and the new, experienced, demanding and sophisticated travellers reposition destination marketing to be the main interface between consumers and local principals. Consumers are increasingly following special interests and regard their trips as both recreational and educational experiences. Therefore, destination themes and their interpretation become more important for the future. Training of human resources as well as cooperation between competing and complementary destinations enable regions to learn from each other and adapt to demand requirements. Innovative marketing led by research and using new technologies will be the only way to manage and market competitive destinations in the future for the benefits of their stakeholders.

Unsung Tourist Destination: Ghatshila (Jharkhand)

Ghatshila, also spelt as Ghatsila, is a census town in Purbi Singhbhum (East Singhbhum) district in the state of Jharkhand, India. The city is located on the banks of Subarnarekha River and is situated in a forested area. It contains a station on the main line of the South Eastern Railway. Ghatshila was formerly the headquarters of the rajas of Dhalbhum.

Ghatshila is connected to most of the important stations in Bihar and Jharkhand through a rail and road network. Jamshedpur is at a distance of 45 km by road and 37 km by railroad, west of this town. Trains from Kharagpur that go west in the direction of Jamshedpur mostly have stoppages here. The distance between Ghatsila and Kharagpur is 98 km.

How to Reach Ghatshila

- **By rail:** Ghatshila is a railway station on the Kharagpur-Tatanagar stretch of the Howrah-Mumbai track, 215 km from Howrah. It is well connected to three metros in India — namely, Mumbai (by Bombay Express), Kolkata (many trains ply between 6 a.m. in the morning until 1.15 p.m. in the afternoon) and New Delhi (by Neelachal and Utkal Express). There are many local passenger trains connecting Jamshedpur and Kharagpur with Ghatshila. For timings and schedules, one may check with Indian Railways.
- **By road:** Ghatshila is about 240 km from Kolkata. Those travelling from Kolkata first have to take NH 6 to Baharagora and then the road to Jamshedpur. Buses plying between Kharagpur and Jamshedpur pass through Ghatshila. Buses going from Kolkata to Jamshedpur and Ranchi also pass through Ghatshila. By road, Jamshedpur is 42 km away and frequent bus service is available.

Places to See Around

There are many tourist attractions here, the major one being *Subarnarekha River*. Subarnarekha means "the golden line." It is said that gold grains can be found in the sand besides the river. There is Rukmini mandir and the old palace of Dhalbhum rajas, which are of historical importance.

The Burudih, or Burundi, dam situated by Dimna Lake is a natural reservoir and a good picnic spot. This is the world's second largest earthen dam. There are small hillocks and water falls also. Earlier, this place was famous as a destination for ill patients to regain their health; many ill people used to come here and stay for 2–3 months. Now, tourism has taken a backseat, though.

Subarnarekha River in Ghatshila

Accommodation

There is no dearth of hotels in Ghatshila. There are a plenty of hotels ranging from mid price to budget hotels and guest houses.

Best Time to Visit

The temperature varies between 25°C to 38°C in summer and it falls to 10°C to 20°C during winter season. Best time to visit Ghatshila is between October to April.

SUMMARY

- Differentiation is the process of distinguishing the differences of a product or service offering from others to make it more attractive to a particular target market.
- In services differentiation, especially in travel and tourism industry, there are three main approaches – the consumer-oriented approach, the competitor oriented approach and the trade-oriented approach.
- To make a successful differentiation in travel and tourism industry, a firm may adopt any of the three strategies, viz. by-passing strategy, cooperation strategy or adaptation strategy.
- Positioning means the process by which marketers try to create an image or identity in the minds of their target market for its product, brand, service or organization.
- The main purpose is to create an image on customer's perceptual space or black box.
- Positioning is an eight-step-process where any firm has four alternative strategies to be chosen from.
- A firm can do re-positioning or de-positioning of its products or services.
- Error in positioning can end up in over-positioning or under-positioning or doubtful positioning or confused positioning.

FIELD EXERCISES

1. How will you differentiate and position your city as a tourist destination using perceptual map? Make a group of four people and choose the service differentiation strategy you would use for tourism industry of your city.
2. Analyse the positioning of Singapore as a tourist destination. Is there anything that India could learn from Singapore? Discuss with your colleagues.

REFERENCES

Bhatia, A.K. (2006), "The business of tourism: Concepts and strategies," New Delhi, Sterling.

Buhalis, D., (2000), Marketing the Competitive Destination of the Future, *Tourism Management*, Vol. 21, No. 1, pp. 97–116

Graham, Hankinson (2005), "Destination Brand Images: A Business Tourism Perspective," *Journal of Services Marketing*, Vol. 19 No. 1, pp. 24–32

Kotler, Philip (1995), "Marketing Asian places: Attracting investment, industry and tourism to cities, states and nations," The Free Press, New York.

Ksela, Atila Yu and Olcay Akgu (2007), "Postcards as Affective Image Makers: An Idle Agent in Destination Marketing" *Tourism Management*, Vol. 28, No. 3, pp. 714–725

Kotler, Philip et al, "Marketing Management: A south Asian perspective," Pearson Education, New Delhi.

Riege, Andreas M. (2000), "National Marketing Strategies in International Travel and Tourism," *European Journal of Marketing*, Vol. 34, No. 11/12.

Sengupta, Subroto (1990), "Brand Positioning: Strategies for competitive advantage," Tata McGraw Hill, New Delhi.

Web Sites

www.incredibleindia.org

www.india-tourism.com/EN

http://www.tourismofindia.com/

www.ssrn.org

www.wikipedia.com

www.goa-tourism.com

www.keralatourism.org

http://www.indiamedicaltourism.net

www.mapsofindia.com

Great Wall of China

CHAPTER 9

Tourism Product Development and Packaging

ABOUT THE DESTINATION

A series of fortifications in northern China, built during various successive ancient Chinese dynasties, to protect the northern borders of the Chinese Empire from attacks by nomadic tribes. It extends for about 8,850 kilometres (5,500 miles).

OBJECTIVES

- To understand tourism product development and the stages in its development
- To determine the essentials for a successful tourism product destination
- To highlight various methods to bring an experiential feeling among tourists
- To understand tourism product differentiation, positioning and packaging

INTRODUCTION

Tourism is an experiential product. It is a continuum of both tangible and intangible elements. Tangible being the souvenirs, or the services being provided in terms of hospitality and travel. Intangible elements being the pleasure derived due to the ambience of the destination or due to the warmth of the people. It is always difficult to map minute factors which make a tourist happy, indifferent or disappointed. In case of historical monuments certain arrangements can be done, which make the visit to the monument, a memorable one. For this, multiple small experiential products like light and sound show can be developed. On the other hand, if a specific region decides to design and establish a tourist destination of repute, then all the factors need to be taken into consideration for developing a tourist product.

Today when the tourism industry is getting into new dimensions and when different bodies are doing a considerable amount of research to develop new products it becomes essential to learn the fundamentals of tourism product development. It is also important to understand that the new era belongs to man-made modern destinations of tourism.

TOURISM PRODUCT

There are several ways to define tourism products. In general, a product is any offering that can satisfy needs or wants of consumers. It may consist of one or a combination of components, including physical goods, services, experiences, events, persons, places, properties, organizations, information and ideas. A tourism product includes a combination of those components that contribute to the satisfaction of travellers.

Box 1: MakeMyTrip

MakeMyTrip offers a combined and exhaustive package of such services. MakeMyTrip provides the chance to customize tours by deciding one's own favourite destinations and the number of days one wishes to stay in a particular destination. With the makemytrip service, one can make one's own trips with individual choices and preferences. It also offers the advantage of choosing location, areas of attraction, duration, luxury or economy level, thereby giving a complete range of choices. For more information, refer to Web site www.makemytrip.com.

Tourism products can be broadly divided into attractions and facilities. Attractions are those natural and man-made features and events that stimulate people to visit a destination. For example, a historical place may act as the key attraction enticing historians to a destination. Facilities, on the other hand, provide necessities to both residents and tourists, and include roads, railways, airports, parking areas, hospitals, police, water and power services, and accommodation. Together, the mix of destination, attractions and facilities creates a set of intangible subjective experiences for tourists known as a tourism product. For wildlife viewing, the product might be made up of attractions such as the opportunity to view unique species and a related festival, while the facilities they might use are the roads, informal restaurants, campgrounds and other basic services.

While the main component of the tourism product is generally the experience, other factors are important and may even serve as attractions for viewers. For example, information is often a component of the wildlife-viewing product since many viewers seek education about the species and habitats being observed. Wildlife festivals and other events also can attract wildlife viewers and can, therefore, be considered an important part of the tourism product being offered. Additionally, through their interactions with customers, persons, such as guides and outfitters, can enhance or harm the experience. Their actions can have a profound impact on the quality of the tourism product (Keane, 1996). For instance, a wildlife-viewing outfitter with a great sense of humour and a vast amount of wildlife-related knowledge could greatly enhance the wildlife-viewing experience. Organizations like wildlife preservation societies could also be part of the product.

Tourism Product Development

The stages for a tourism product development can be shown diagrammatically. For example, if we consider a wildlife tourist place product development, the following stages can be thought of.

- **Stage 1 – Generic development:** To develop and promote several natural features of a destination as the generic component. The tourism industry should offer packages that include a variety of outdoor activities rather than focusing on just one. Destinations should focus on providing pre-trip information about the variety of high-quality natural resources and associated activities that they have to offer to tourists and other outdoor enthusiasts.
- **Stage 2 – Unique features development:** To develop and promote tourism-viewing products that focus on species that are unique to the destination or would be unique to potential visitors. Develop and promote unique tourism products that will attract domestic travellers. For instance, many city dwellers may not normally get to see flora and fauna, and may be attracted to areas that offer such viewing opportunities. Likewise, people who live in land locked places may be attracted to view marine or estuarine tourism. Develop and promote unique tourism products that will attract international travellers. Many wildlife species in some areas are quite different from species found elsewhere in the world. By highlighting species that are not seen in other parts of the world in tourism products, destinations may be able to attract more foreign tourists.

- **Stage 3 – Segmentation based on age:** Develop tourism products to accommodate tourists of all age groups. Once the area has been developed with unique characteristics, the focus shifts to providing services to all age segments. It needs to be ensured that services and facilities adequately meet the needs of all ages. For example, easy walking and hiking trails should be developed so that children and seniors may enjoy them. Younger adults could tackle trails that are more difficult.
- **Stage 4 – Segmentation based on income:** Destinations should ensure that services and facilities range from very affordable to high-priced luxury. Accommodation should range from budget (campgrounds, inexpensive motels, cabins, bed and breakfasts) to luxury (high quality, expensive hotels and breakfasts). This has to be done to accommodate tourists from different income segments.
- **Stage 5 – Customized products:** Efforts should be made to attract tourists by offering affordable short-duration getaways. Trips during summers are most common among tourists. Offering shorter getaways during the shoulder seasons could help alleviate some of the seasonality problems associated with tourism. With an area's specific climate in mind, many communities could potentially offer products during shoulder seasons.
- **Stage 6 – Product design:** Weekend trips should be offered throughout the year to entice those tourists who work during the week or who wish to travel with school-aged children. High-value mid-week trips should be offered round the year to attract retired tourists or those who do not work during the week.

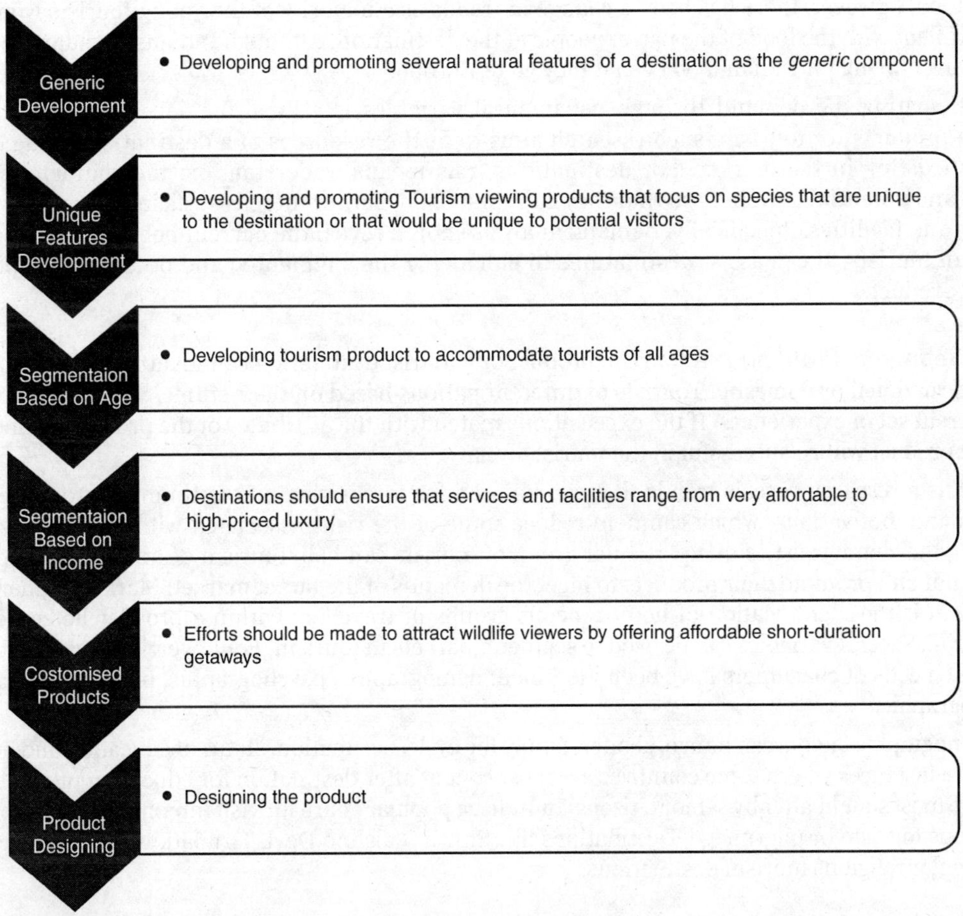

Essential Requirements In Product Development

The essential requirements in product development can be clubbed as below.

Need Gap Analysis. International tourism arena is full of interesting tourist destinations which can make a guest's holidays most memorable. Inspirations can always be drawn from there for either developing something new or improvising on something existing. At the same time each region has some inherent socio-cultural characteristics. These, along with the natural fauna and flora give leads for developing a particular genre of tourism destination. Finally another lead can be derived from the outgoing tourists' statistics. The most popular international tourist destination for the outgoing natives speaks volumes about the latent needs of the domestic tourists. Need gap analysis throws light on such issues which otherwise lie unattended. As the time progresses a relook into the need gap, probably the ever increasing need set, becomes necessary for the marketer or the CEO of the destination. For instance, for a destination to be attractive for a family it may need to satisfy adventure needs, shopping needs, aesthetic needs and many more.

Behavioural Trends. Tourists generally would like to behave differently when they go out for tourism. This is a major factor which should always be kept in mind while designing a tourism product or destination. Two factors which remain constant is the attachment towards native language and native food. In case of food, however, there has been a change in trends as a majority of the young tourists would like to experiment with the food of the native people at the destination. Although Indians are supposed to be still having craving for Indian food even if they go to Europe.

Anticipating the demand through behavioural variables is critical for developing appropriate tourism products. In tourism, such research aims to fit the resources of a destination to the opportunities existing in the market. For destinations, this means understanding the characteristics of current and potential travellers so that they can establish whether there is sufficient demand for new services and facilities. Specifically, demand analysis should reveal the current behaviours and expectations of tourists. It can assist destinations in enhancing the augmented and potential components of their product.

Target Segments Profiling. A tourism product or a tourist destination cannot attract all the tourists, be it international or domestic. Tourists of different nations based on their ethnicity and exposure look for different set of experiences. If the expectations match with the attributes of the product, chances are that the product will be successful in the tourist arena.

Tourism research reveals trends that can be used for forecasting and outlining customer characteristics and motivations, which can help reduce some of the risks associated with making decisions. Knowing the characteristics of a particular group of tourists can help tourism destinations more effectively tailor and promote their products to meet the demands of the target market. Market segmentation in tourism is the identification of homogeneous groups of travellers within a broader heterogeneous population. Several variables can be used to segment markets in tourism. Four overriding categories that shape the needs of consumers have been identified: demographic, psychographic, behavioural patterns and geographic.

Demographic factors can be age, gender, family life cycle, occupation, status of education and income. There are instances where some countries are most sought after destination for education purposes, and some are most sought after by senior citizens. In India, a popular genre for visit (among domestic tourists) is religious tourism or pilgrimage. Destinations like Shirdi, Vaishno Devi, Tirupati, Ujjain, Haridwar are very popular religious tourism destinations.

Psychographics examine the motivations behind the travel behaviour. Psychographic characteristics are created on the basis of psychological/personality traits, values, or lifestyle and interests, and contribute to differences in customer needs. These variables primarily reflect the influence that social forces can have on the consumption process. Tourists who are demographically the same may differ significantly in their value orientation, which may result in distinct preferences.

Attitude, aspirations and goals in life mark the behaviour of any individual. The same then translates into the type of destinations they would like to visit. For instance, previous trip characteristics are often examined in order to determine probable future travel patterns. Additionally, such information can help reveal the travel preferences of the tourists.

Finally, tourism markets can be segmented geographically. Such segmentations can reveal information about travellers' locations of origin and destination, and whether they are rural or urban. This is important because consumer preferences and habits vary across regions, different countries and different states in these countries.

Since the market for tourism is massive, it is more dynamic and cost effective to identify several minor groups of people with similar attributes. The chosen segment becomes the target market segment. The goal of target marketing is to position a business/destination within a product market so that it gains a comparative advantage. This comparative advantage is gained when the business offers products with attributes that are both unique and important to the customer. To be useful, these markets should be segmented by attributes that can apply to the product or the service. The first step in the market segmentation process is to group customers based on a criterion, such as traits, and then discover which demographics, lifestyle forces and usage factors set them apart from other customers.

Analysing Supply. In order to meet the demands of customers, tourist destinations need to have a good understanding of their supply of key product attributes. This will help them determine if they should alter or increase the number or types of tourist-viewing products that they offer. The features, advantages and benefits of the tourism product should meet the expectations of tourists and have the ability to augment the product. The features are physical characteristics of the product; advantages are those that are offered by or included in the features and benefits are what can be gained from those advantages.

In the tourism industry, the key to effective marketing of products is emphasizing experiences and benefits. For tourism products to be successful, it is important to consider demand characteristics and incorporate them into the products' features, advantages and benefits offered. Thus, these destinations will augment the product being offered.

Once the demand and supply information for the destinations has been acquired, they need to apply that knowledge to develop tourism products. We will briefly review how this information can be used by destinations by throwing light on product differentiation, branding and positioning in the subsequent sections.

CREATING EXPERIENCE SET

The word "experiences" is used a lot in the tourism industry and can be a source of confusion. Yet, businesses that are not able to understand the importance of experiences for the market, and fail to provide in a way that matches holidaymakers' expectations, are being left behind in the competition for tourists. It is all because of our rapidly changing world that the tourists' needs have changed. Extensive research on changing consumer behaviour shows that visitors/tourists want holidays that enable them to make a connection with the places of visit and the local people – holidays that change one in some way.

It is the prospect of a temporary new life that motivates tourists – not just in terms of places to see and things to do, but also in terms of learning, personal development and gaining genuine social and cultural insights. Experiences that deliver a sense of exhilaration and vitality, whether through active adventure or passively acquiring new skills, are on the top of the wish list.

Experiences Are Different from Activities

An activity is usually focused on the physical action, with minimal connection to the meaning or significance of the place in which it occurs, or the local story. Examples are sightseeing, bushwalking, or swimming. An experience, however, goes beyond an activity to provide a higher level of engagement with the sense of place and local people, and access to a greater depth of involvement with and understanding of both.

People (not just tour guides but all frontline personnel) play a key role in an experience. The quality of the relationship between the visitor and those involved in providing the experience is critical.

How Does It Work?

Experiences have the power. They

- Spark the imagination
- Engage the senses
- Stimulate the intellect
- Invoke an emotive response
- Enliven the spirit

They can do this in wide-ranging settings – from an underground mine to an eco-cruise, from a wildlife night prowl to a mountain lake. One's role as a tourism operator is to create an environment for the experience – to provide the ingredients and set up the circumstances so the visitor can be an active part of what happens, as in the case of shucking their own oysters as part of a marine farm tour, or going with the chef to buy vegetables as part of a food tourism experience.

An experience is not only what happens when a visitor arrives for the tour, attraction or adventure, but is a managed process that starts from initial communication, such as an advertisement, brochure or Web site, and can continue even after the visitor leaves, through follow-up, reinforcement or marketing of allied products.

Experiences apply at all levels of tourism – from products, businesses and destinations to the role of local government and regional tourism bodies. Everyone has an important role to play in order to achieve the goal.

Experiences, Not Destinations

The trend internationally is seeing a shift from marketing of destinations towards marketing of experiences developed across destinations. That means destinations are positioning and delivering their offerings based on one or more sets or groupings of themed experiences.

PRODUCT DIFFERENTIATION

A sound understanding of consumers' demand allows businesses and destinations to achieve differentiation. Product differentiation can be defined as the process of distinguishing the differences of a product or offering from others, to make it more attractive to a particular target market. Specifically, segmentation can identify critical attributes that can be used to differentiate competitive offerings. For instance,

Box 2: Tourist Experiences

I had been to Kullu-Manali in early February 2008 with a few of my friends, and it had been a remarkable experience. To give an overview of the destinations, they are among Himachal Pradesh's best-known hill stations and offer a great destination for those who love the hills. The beautiful hills (some of which are snow-capped), the fascinating Beas, pine forests, bustling new Manali and foreign tourists' haven of old Manali – all combine to make Manali a great holiday destination.

We began our journey from Hyderabad and reached Delhi by flight. Now, one can reach Kullu from Delhi in two ways. Either take a flight from Delhi or take a bus that will complete the journey in around 15 hours. We chose the latter option because the flights from Delhi to Kullu usually get cancelled or delayed. We were lucky to carry a shawl because the AC was quite chilling. We arrived Manali at 11 p.m. and were surprised to see the Mall area, the centre of the town, bustling with tourists enjoying shopping and busy eating joints at that hour. Manali town can be considered in two parts. One is the Aleo New Manali town that is on the left bank of the Beas river. New hotels and resorts are available on the road to Nagger. The other part is the old Manali village that lies on the east of the Manalsu nallah (water stream), which in its present form looks more of a hippy enclave. There are lots of temples and monasteries that are tourist attractions in Manali. We spent and enjoyed the entire day visiting these places, which are not very far from the centre of the town. There is also a famous temple that we visited. It is that of the local deity Hadimba, wife of the Pandava prince Bhim. The temple dates back to 1533 and is famous for its four-storey pagoda and exquisite wooden carvings. A major festival is held in Manali in the month of May. The place is also famous for its Buddhist monasteries, or gompas. Famous among them is the Gadhan Thekchhokling gompa, built in 1969. The monastery is well maintained with donations from the local community, and they sell hand-woven carpets made in the temple workshop. Manali is also famous for being among the popular adventure-sports destinations in India. We went for mountaineering, trekking, paragliding, skiing, white-water rafting and mountain biking.

Hadimba Temple, Manali

The visit to Manali is incomplete if you do not go to Rohtang Pass, the highest point in this area, at 3,900 metres above sea level. Rohtang is at a distance of 51 km from Manali. All vehicles stop over at Marhi, 17 km before Rohtang, for refreshments. It takes about two hours to reach Marhi. Marhi is a landscape offering extensive views of the valley and mountains. We later visited Kullu valley and were mesmerized by the scenic charm of the peaceful wooded glades and the rivers through the rocks. After spending three days, we picked up the bus back to Delhi, which started at 9:00 a.m., and then took the connecting flight to Hyderabad.

Overall, it was a remarkable experience and a great holiday destination.

market segmentation could reveal that newlywed couples have a different preference of tourist destination compared to children, who would prefer more of theme parks like Disney World.

Walt Disney World Resort — A Tourist Destination with a Difference

The Walt Disney Company was founded in 1922, and has become a world leader in family entertainment. Today, the company is operating on a multinational level, and has over 66,000 employees worldwide. The company developed tourism after having done research on what the target customer wanted. Today, its Walt Disney World Resort is the most visited and the largest recreational resort in the world, containing four theme parks, two water parks, 23 themed hotels, and numerous shopping, dining, entertainment and recreation venues. Owned and operated by the Walt Disney Parks and Resorts segment of the Walt Disney Company, it is located southwest of Orlando, Florida. The property is abbreviated as *Walt Disney World, Disney World, or WDW.*

Magic Kingdom Florida, USA

Walt Disney has been able to find a very distinctive niche in the industry. It has product attributes that are quite unique, complicated and not easy to copy. It would be impossible for someone other than Walt Disney Company to duplicate a Disney World, thus giving Disney substantial market power in the amusement and theme park industry. The primary target customers have been children. As Disney pretty much dominates the family entertainment market, it will be very difficult for a new organization to develop brand recognition/identification and product differentiation. Hence, the entrance barriers are high. Not surprisingly, Disney is regarded as the most aggressive pricier in the industry.

Disney Character, Disneyland, USA

PRODUCT POSITIONING

Positioning has come to mean the process by which marketers try to create an image or an identity in the minds of their target market for their product, brand or organization. It can be defined as "relative competitive comparison" the product occupies in a given market as perceived by the target market. A destination's product position is established by focusing marketing strategies on a particular target market having specific product preferences. In particular, tourism destinations may attempt to position their products so that their products seem to possess the characteristics most desired by the target market.

More generally, there are the following types of positioning concepts:

- Functional positions
- Solve problems
- Provide benefits to customers
- Get favourable perception by investors and lenders
- Symbolic positions
- Self-image enhancement
- Ego identification
- Belongingness and social meaningfulness
- Affective fulfilment
- Experiential positions
- Provide sensory stimulation
- Provide cognitive stimulation

For instance, the Kerala backwaters emphasize that they are the perfect location for soothing oneself, away from the hectic day-to-day life. In customer-oriented positioning, organizations attempt to separate themselves from major competitors by serving one or a limited number of market segments. Strategies to strengthen a product or a destination's image can be divided into two categories – repositioning and strengthening. Repositioning involves changing the generic or expected components of the product being offered. Future changes in demand could justify a company to shift its position in the market. For instance, changes in demographics, such as age or income, could affect tourist viewers' demands for a certain type of product.

The second strategy by which destinations can be positioned to enhance their image is by strengthening their current position. Destinations can accomplish this by constantly monitoring the demands of target customers and ensuring that the demands are satisfied.

PRODUCT DEVELOPMENT AND SUSTAINABLE TOURISM

Several opportunities for product development can be looked into based on the factors defined above. As stated in the beginning, tourism has the potential to affect the socio-economic and ecological foundations of destinations. Destinations should, therefore, keep the principles of environmental sustainability in mind while developing tourism products. Environmental sustainability principle includes protecting life-support systems (air, water and land), enhancing and protecting biodiversity, and using natural resources carefully and efficiently. Following these principles will help ensure that the historic monuments and places are preserved for their own sake, and they will be enjoyed by future generations of tourists as well.

TOURISM PRODUCT PACKAGING

A package combines two or more products so that the purchaser (and the market segment being targeted) is advantaged compared with buying the items separately.

Time is a valuable commodity for today's travellers. Some families find it difficult to schedule vacation time; family members often have activities that conflict; or, an individual's job makes long vacations impractical. As a result, more families and individuals are taking holiday vacations or long weekends, or extending business trips into short getaway vacations. Packaging is a technique used for attracting these customers because packages make travel easier and more convenient.

Box 3: Chardham India Pilgrimage Tours

Chardham India Pilgrimage Tours is an adventure pilgrimage tour based in Uttaranchal. The tour operators provide all kinds of travel services including Chardham package tours, Hemkund Sahib and Sri Badrinathji pilgrimage package, Sri Amarnathji Yatra and Mata Vaishno Devi pilgrim package, honeymoon packages, trekking/biking tours, white-water rafting packages/courses, wildlife adventure packages, water skiing packages/courses and snow skiing packages/courses.

In the tourism and hospitality industry, packaging is a process of combining two or more related and complementary offerings into a single-price offering. A package may include a wide variety of services such as transport, accommodation, meals, attractions, entertainment, entrance fees to attractions, guide services and other similar activities, which can be carefully combined into a complete packaged experience that provides the customer with either greater convenience or a more competitive price.

Packaging Benefits

Travel packages have become increasingly popular. They are attractive because they benefit not only the customer, but also participating businesses; packaging provides convenience and value to the customer and added profit for participating businesses.

Benefits to customers have to be seen in the light of their convenience, providing greater economy, ease of payment and planning, and causing low stress. These are described as follows:

- **Convenience:** Trips can be time consuming and difficult to arrange. Several letters or telephone calls may be required to arrange for tickets, reservations, accommodations and other components of a trip. A package allows the customer to arrange various components of a trip. This reduces time and money spent in locating the key product and facilitates booking a destination with one call or a letter and one payment, saving the customer time and money.
- **Greater economy:** Businesses that package can purchase tickets, meals and other package components at wholesale prices. The business can add in the cost of packaging and can still provide a competitive price to the customer. Thus, it is more economical to buy the package than to purchase the package components individually.
- **Ease of payment and planning:** Packages include most of the components a customer must pay for during the tour. The customer pays only once and has a good idea of the trip's total cost. Travel arrangements are generally pre-paid and confirmed prior to travel, or handled by tour staff/guides.
- **Low stress:** This relieves travel anxiety of new and older travellers, and satisfies their need for security, reliability and companionship. Travellers are relieved from the various tensions of making arrangements and can really enjoy the trip.

Benefits to participating businesses have to be judged on the basis of profitability, smooth business patterns, shared marketing opportunities, specialized products and target marketing.

- **Profitability:** During peak or high-demand periods, packaging can be used to add value to an existing product. Purchasers may be required to stay a prescribed time period or purchase a combination of goods and services. Packaging may also allow organizers to price a product at a premium by adding special goods and services.
- **Smooth business patterns:** During low-demand periods, packaging can be used to add attractive features to the business's service or product, thus generating additional business. Other businesses may also be ready to give discount on their services during this time to increase the revenue. Adding this type of services to the existing product mix may generate new business.
- **Shared marketing opportunities:** Packaging can allow a business to market their products that cannot be marketed otherwise due to cost constraints. This also allows the business to start a new programme by joining with one or more businesses to conduct marketing or advertising programmes. This strategy can be especially effective if the businesses involved have similar customers, which is generally applicable for tourism products.
- **Specialized products:** Packaging can be used to highlight specialized products by developing services appropriate to the time period or the theme. New Year, Valentine's Day and Mother's Day are some holidays that can be used to develop special programmes for parties, couples or family gifts.
- **Target marketing:** Packaging can be an effective way to generate tourism and travel products for specific target markets. Examples can be sports, adventure sports or theatre weekends. A proper market research is required to find an appropriate mix of tourism and travel services that will meet the needs and desires of a target group of customers.

TOURISM PACKAGING FACTORS

The tourism packaging factors incentives, communication, branding and pricing are discussed as follows:

Incentives

The best packages provide customers something they would not get, if they purchased package elements separately. Sometimes, this benefit could be the offer of value, but in other cases, it is some component that is not easily available to individual customers. This might involve some special experiences, a speciality of the place, incorporating special lectures or appearances, unique dining experiences or other activities.

Some other incentives like a clear policy on refunds/cancellations and complete information on all package elements included in the price can also be given, which will create positive vibes for the product.

Communication

After creating a good tourism product and even after packaging it well, it may not succeed in the market because of invisibility to the customers. So, it becomes very important for the organizers to communicate about the package in an effective way. A package should be designed in a way that creates some curiosity about the place in the customer's mind. Communication should be able to establish a relationship with the customers.

Branding

Every tourist destination in the world has an image. If developed carefully, the image/brand serves to differentiate a destination from competing destinations. However, some destinations do not have a brand strategy, and are supported by inconsistent advertising, creating a confused image for customers. Image should be controlled by a clear projection of brand identity.

Box 4: Incredible India Programme

The Incredible India Programme of department of tourism, government of India, helps you plan your Indian holiday with destination information and holiday themes that cover adventure sports, cool retreats, ecotourism, beaches of India, pilgrimages and spirituality, royal retreats, wildlife, heritage sites and medical tourism.

When consumers decide on a destination for a holiday, several brands compete for attention. A strong brand has several strong advantages when compared to others, and has an attractive appeal for consumers. In tourism, while some factors such as cost of travel, convenience and quality of facilities are important, the most important motivator is image which puts a destination up in the consumer's shopping list and creates an emotional appeal, and enhances that destination's chances of being chosen over others.

Developing a strong image for any product requires a carefully planned strategy with

- Selection of the positioning strategies
- Themed product development
- Consistent and appropriate advertising and promotion
- Careful brand guardianship

Pricing

Pricing is one of the most important factors for a successful tour package. The package should provide good value for money and be competitive in the market. Customers should not be able to purchase individual items in the package for less than the package price. This can be easily arranged by using the discounts attained for the bulk purchase of package components. While packaging can be used to implement different strategies, the basic motive is to generate additional business using product packaging. Evaluation of the package's financial feasibility should be done by applying a break-even analysis to help determine how many packages a business must sell for earning profit.

Case Study: Barnawapara Sanctuary

People participation is paramount for the success of any scheme concerning wildlife conservation and education. But it is very difficult to achieve it, especially when the villagers are uneducated, poor and dependent on forest. Considering the uncertainty of their income and the fact that their main livelihood is agriculture, which is rain-fed, it becomes difficult to seek people's cooperation for protection and conservation of forests and wildlife. The correct meeting grounds for the implementation of any new project must be found with this perspective in mind.

Barnawapara Sanctuary, Raipur

In this case study, the inception of ecotourism in Barnawapara Sanctuary in the state

Case Study: *(Continued)*

of Chhattisgarh is discussed. We also look into its implementation with the help of joint forest-management committees, with an overall assessment of its success in the prevailing condition.

Sanctuary Profile

Barnawapara Sanctuary is situated in the mid-northern part of Raipur District. It is 125 km away from Raipur, the state capital of Chhattisgarh. The name of the sanctuary is derived from Bar and Nawapara forest village. The sanctuary lies between the parallels of latitudes 21° 18′ 45′ and 21° 30′ 0′ north, and meridians of longitudes 82° 22′ 30′ and 82° 37′ 30′ east, at an elevation of 213–597 metres above mean sea level. It consists of 244.66 square km of reserved forest. The sanctuary is under the administrative control of territorial division, Raipur.

One of the oldest scientifically managed forest reserves, the sanctuary has diverse habitat and fauna. The sanctuary houses sal (*Shorea robusta*), saja (*Terminalia tomentosa*), teak (*Tectona grandis*), tendu (*Diosphyros melanoxylon*), bija (*Pterocarpus marsupium*), karra (*Cleistanthus collinus*), harra (*Terminalia chebula*), baheda (*Terminalia belerica*), lendia (*Lagerstroemia parviflora*), bamboo (*Dendrocalamus strictus*), haldu (*Adina cordifolia*), dhaora (*Anogeissus latifolia*), salai (*Boswellia serrata*) and other miscellaneous species. Tendu leaves, mahua (*Madhuca indica*), aonla (*Embelica officinalis*), char (*Buchanania latifolia*), honey, medicinal plants, sal seeds, grasses, mahul leaves (*Bauhinia vaillai*) and kulu gums (*Sterculia urens*) are among the major non-timber forest produce. The area is a well-known home for wild ungulates, bovids, carnivores and avian fauna. The wildlife species found in the sanctuary include tiger (*Panthera tigris*), panther (*Panthera pardus*), spotted deer (*Axis axis*), sambhar (*Cervus unicolor*), nilgai (*Boselaphus tragocamelus*), gaur (*Bos gaurus*), barking deer (*Muntiacus muntjak*), wild dog (*Cuon alpinus*), cobra (*Naja naja*) and peafowl (*Pavo cristatus*). The sanctuary has been one of the most popular resorts for wildlife viewers in this region. Also, the sanctuary is geographically very conveniently located, and has immense potential for wildlife tourism, conservation and education.

Socio-Economic Status of Forest Dwellers

There are 22 forest villages inside the sanctuary. The forests are put under pressure by the villagers residing inside the sanctuary. These villages were settled inside to address the demand for labourers for forest workings (extraction of timber). The reserve forest was declared a sanctuary in 1976. Each of the families who had settled there has 2.5 hectares of agricultural land today. The majority of forest villagers are scheduled tribes – the main tribes are Gond, Bhujia, Binjwar, Kamar and Sawara.

Predominantly, the people here are farmers; they cultivate paddy as main crop, and some also grow wheat and vegetables as per their needs. Excess quantity, if any, is sold in the market. They also work as labourers as the landholdings do not give enough to meet all their needs. They make baskets with bamboo and brooms with grasses.

People living near the periphery of the sanctuary are mostly dependent on the forest for fuel wood, small timber, fodder, etc. Thus, the forest is central to their life-support system. In the lean period, people are solely dependent on forestry works, mahua flowers, tendu leaves, mahul leaves and aonla collection.

Threats to Protected Area and Wildlife

The following were threats to the protected area and wildlife:

- Grazing inside the protected area
- Illicit felling of trees and selling of bamboos for profit
- Fire – for mahua flower collection
- Poaching for sale of skin, bones and meat

Case Study: *(Continued)*

Factors Responsible for Threats

The following factors were responsible for these threats:

- Poor agricultural productivity
- Small landholdings
- Lack of irrigation facility
- Lack of electricity
- Practicing inefficient animal-husbandry methods
- Lack of communication
- Lack of income-generating activities
- Ban on timber, bamboo, firewood harvesting

Establishment of Ecotourism Network

The year 2002 was declared as the International Year of Ecotourism (IYE). the tourism industry being the world's largest industry, with nature tourism the fastest-growing segment, the idea of nature tourism or ecotourism in Barnawapara sanctuary took root. In November 2000, the creation of Chhattisgarh state provided a lot of opportunity in this regard. With Raipur becoming the capital of Chhattisgarh, it gave more advantage to the sanctuary, as it was the nearest tourist spot and could be nicely developed.

Considering the needs of the people living inside the protected area and keeping in view such activities that would help generate revenue for them, a talk with the JFM society of Barnawapara for promoting ecotourism was started. These activities were sought to generate revenue, which could benefit the rural communities of the sanctuary for upgrading their livelihood, which in due course would help in forest conservation and education. A proper and planned ecotourism network was started by the forest department, and the active involvement of local people was sought.

Facilities Provided to Tourists

The JFM society members were in charge of accommodation and camp arrangements of the tourists. An eco-centre has been set up at Deopur Forest department, where there is infrastructure for training villagers in forestry and other income-generating activities. The facilities available were utilized for sensitizing tourists about the forest department's work. The tourism programme has been scheduled in a way to help tourists appreciate the diverse values of protected areas and cultural-heritage sites.

Backyard Activities

Before initiating tourism, a tourism route was to be developed. The government of India was reached for funds. This mobilized the people of the sanctuary – they were given the work of upgrading roads, thus generating employment. The state government, too, provided funds for repairing and furnishing the tourist huts. The old government buildings were converted into tourist huts, thus providing employment to the villagers. Solar power in these tourist huts was provided by the Department of Alternate Energy Resource (CREDA). A fund from district administration was provided for development of waterholes. Thus, with collaborative efforts from the national and state governments, sufficient money was pooled in for the development of the sanctuary for tourism.

Achievements

Today, tourism has helped generate money for the common people – money that otherwise usually goes to outside people in other protected areas. The sanctuary set precedence by determining that no government money is being wasted in future tourism infrastructure, as the society is going to maintain the buildings, accommodation facility and food facility without any establishment costs. The funds would be diverted for the development of the sanctuary and the people residing in it, who in a way also get a market now for the sale of handicrafts, honey, bamboo articles, grass articles, etc., at their doorstep. Local youngsters can get employment as guides, cooks, drivers, caretakers, etc. More funds can be pooled in for employment of firewatchers, anti-poaching squads, habitat management staff, etc., which will help in the protection and development of the sanctuary.

Since the tourism started, it has been seen that incidents of fire, timber theft and poaching have come down. Improvement in the forest roads has aided in frequent movement. Information network and monitoring of wildlife have become more effective after the introduction of feedback information, which is collected from the visitors. Guides act as effective tools in conservation education,

Case Study: *(Continued)*

and littering inside the sanctuary is checked by them. Thus, ecotourism in Barnawapara Sanctuary has started giving fruitful results.

Future Programmes

There is a need to make tourism and conservation sustainable with proper assessment and planning for the future. Some of the requirements and efforts aimed at a better future are as follows:

- Carrying capacity of tourists staying day and night in the sanctuary should be assessed and controlled. Regulation of this can be done by providing limited entry passes.
- In order to tackle international tourists, guides and caretakers should be educated.
- Habitat development can help improve wildlife sightings.
- Accommodation and other facilities need to be upgraded for encouraging international tourists to visit.
- An interpretation centre and a nature's trail are planned in the near future.
- Emphasis on more local handicraft marketing is to be stressed.
- Increase in facilities such as post offices having telephone, primary healthcare centres with medicines, greater frequency in bus services, more teachers and educational institutions can help in development.
- Immunization of all the cattle and limiting of unproductive cattle are also planned. This will reduce grazing pressure in the sanctuary.
- Providing alternatives sources of fuel for the villagers is an urgent requirement. Currently, they still largely depend on the forest for meeting their basic requirements of fuel wood.

To achieve the above management concept as a major conservation strategy for the future, it is necessary to re-orient and train villagers and forest staff in the right direction. The concept of ecotourism has taken roots in the sanctuary and is expected to produce positive results. The objective is not only to enable the local people but also to motivate visitors to learn about the local environment and culture. It is believed that this process will create employment and improve standards of living by stimulating the local economy and providing incentives for conservation.

Unsung Tourist Destination: Mirzapur

Mirzapur is a city in the heart of North India, nearly 650 km between Delhi and Kolkata, and also equidistant from Allahabad and Varanasi. Situated in the state of Uttar Pradesh, the name of the district is derived from the goddess Lakshmi, who had emerged from the sea. The word Mirza is formed of two words – mir meaning "sea" and ja meaning "outcome," with the additional pur standing for "town."

Places to See Around

Vindhyachal: This is a large agricultural town about 11 km west of Mirzapur, and is connected by road. The place is famous for the Vindhyavasini Devi temple, which is one of the holiest temples for Hindus in India. The temple is dedicated to Goddess Durga. Goddess Durga after eliminating the demon Mahishasura decided to reside on the hills of Vindhyachal, and, thus, she came to be known as

A Queue of Devotees at Vindhyavasini Devi Temple

Unsung Tourist Destination: *(Continued)*

Vindhyavasini. While residing here, she continued to eliminate several other demons.

Ashtabhuja Temple: It is located at a distance of 3 km from the Vindhyavasini Devi temple, amidst the serenity of Vindhya hills. The Ashtabhuja temple is another place of religious importance. According to myth, the mother goddess was born from the womb of Yashodha. Kans intended to kill her considering her to be the eighth child of Devaki. The baby child got rid of the shackles of the devil Kans and through the aerial path settled at Vindhyachal hills as the incarnation of Shakti.

Kali Khoh: Among the three divine manifestations of Adi Shakti, Mahakali is said to be settled in the cavern of Kali Khoh, 3 km south from the Vindhyavasini Devi temple. The temple premises are a favourite place of sojourn for *tantriks* from all over the country. Dense greenery and beautiful streams flowing over the pebbles of Vindhya rocks surround the temple.

Kali Khoh, Mirzapur

Chunar: This historic place is 32 km east of Mirzapur and is connected by rail and road. Chunar has an immense fort overlooking the Ganga. Since 1540, this place has been the scene of battles, when Sher Shah took it from Humayun. Akbar recaptured it in 1575. In the mid-18th century, it was appropriated by Awadh and, subsequently, the British. The fort has a sundial and a huge well, and offers a splendid view of the Ganga.

Chunar Fort, Mirzapur

Windham Fall: Situated at a distance of 16 km from Mirzapur, it is a place of great natural beauty.

Sirsi Dam and Fall: It is situated on the river Sirsi at a distance of 45 km from Mirzapur. The waterfall here has a great height. One can very well relax at this place and feel free from the tensions of day-to-day life.

Sirsi Waterfall, Mirzapur

Siddhanath Dari: It is almost 20 km from Chunar. This pleasant and beautiful place is considered to be the worship place of Siddhanath Baba and, thus, got the name Siddhanath Dari. There is a small temple of Siddhanath situated inside a cave adjacent to the waterfall. Apart from these places of interest,

Siddhanath Dari, Chunar

Mirzapur also has the famous carpet industry. However, most of the carpet products are exported due to lack of carpet markets in India.

How to Reach Mirzapur

- **By air:** Nearest airport is Babatpur (Varanasi) located at a distance of 60 km from Mirzapur. It has flights to and fro from Delhi, Agra, Mumbai, Lucknow and Kathmandu.
- **By rail:** The Mirzapur station has direct rail link to all major cities of India. Some important trains are Kalka Mail (Delhi–Kalka), Purshottam Express (New Delhi–Patna), Magadh Express (Delhi–Patna), Ganga Tapti, Triveni Express (Lucknow–Chopan), Mahanagri Express (Varanasi–Bombay), Howrah–Bombay Mail (Bombay–Howrah).
- **By road:** Mirzapur is well connected to the rest of the country with good motorable roads. There are frequent bus services available from Mirzapur to major parts of the state.

Best Time to Visit

The maximum temperature in summer rises upto 42°C and in winters it drops to 7°C. The best time to visit Mirzapur is between October to March.

Accommodation

A lot of hotels have mushroomed in Mirzapur over the last few decades. The popular ones being the Galaxy Hotel and Rahi Tourist Bungalow.

Product Development

Some of the places like Vindhyavasini temple are already very famous. However, other places like Sirsi dam, Windham Fall and Chunar fort can be developed by providing better road and rail connectivity as well as infrastructure. Also, the places are known only locally and not well-known outside. So, proper promotion of these places needs to be done in order to attract tourists.

Packaging

Mirzapur is well connected to Allahabad and Varanasi, which already attract huge numbers of foreign and domestic tourists, and hence, they can be targeted as potential customers. However, hotels, roads and other infrastructure facilities should be improved in Mirzapur to make the stay of tourists comfortable.

SUMMARY

- Tourism is an experiential product with both tangible and intangible elements. For developing new destinations it is important to keep both types of elements in mind.
- With the ever-increasing significance of new tourist destinations the process of tourism product development becomes significant.
- Product development involves generic development, unique features development, segmentation based on age, segmentation based on income, customized products and product design.
- To create a unique experience for the travellers would require the tourist product to spark an imagination, engage the tourist senses and enliven their spirit.
- Product positioning and differentiation are the keys to success, for example, Disney World that has carved a niche for itself in the theme resort and entertainment industry. Therefore, it is important to understand the market forces and importance of various factors to bring out a successful tourist product.

FIELD EXERCISES

1. Find out five tourist destinations attracting the highest number of tourist visits and analyse how many of them are creating and focussing on experiences. What are that experiences? Discuss with colleagues.
2. Visit, three to five most popular places, resorts or parks in your city meant for family entertainment. How are they different from each other? Devise a strategy for development, of the place you liked most, as a tourism product.

REFERENCES

Kotler, Philip, Keller Kevin, Koshi Abraham and Mithileshwar Jha, "Marketing Management (A South Asian Perspective)," Prentice Hall, New Delhi

Masip, Jordi Datzira (2006), "Tourism Product Development: A Way to Create Value," IV International Doctoral Tourism and Leisure Colloquium. ESADE, May 2006

Web Sites

www.ceeweb.org/members/capacity/academy_II_ST/Topic10Tourism_product_development.pdf

www.disneyworld.com/

http://extension.ait.ac.th/documents/brochures/Tourism-2008.pdf

www.fao.org

www.iimcal.ac.in/imz/imz-archive/article.asp?id=bhatt_tourism, Professor C. Panduranga Bhatta

www.kerala-hub.com/gods-own-country/

http://www.keralatourism.org/tourismvision/VisionIndex.htm

www.keralatourism.org/business/incentive.php

www.mirzapur.nic.in

www.tpdco.org/dynaweb.dti?dynasection=tourismenhancement&dynapage=proddiver

www.tourismofchhattisgarh.com/wildlife-tourism-of-chhattisgarh/barnawapara-wildlife-sanctuary.html

CHAPTER 10

Tourism Promotional Mix: An Integrated Marketing Communication (IMC) Approach

Sydney Opera House

ABOUT THE DESTINATION

A multi-venue performing arts centre on Bennelong Point in Sydney, it was conceived and largely built by Danish architect Jørn Utzon. Its unique sail-like design makes it one of the most photographed buildings in the world.

OBJECTIVES

- To understand the communication process – its use and significance
- To define the role of marketing communications in tourism
- To elaborate the steps involved in developing an integrated marketing communication for a tourist destination
- To define long-term and short-term communication objectives
- To define the various stages in design of communication strategies for tourism
- To define the tools used in tourism marketing communication

INTRODUCTION

After developing a product, or a tourist destination the task of tourism marketer does not finish. The essential part of marketing at this stage is to communicate to the target audience. More importantly the communication should be touching those objects which are essential priority wise from the target customer perspective.

Integrated Marketing Communications (IMCs), according to The American Marketing Association, is a planning process designed to assure that all brand contacts received by a customer or prospect for a product, service or organization are relevant to that person and consistent over time.

Promotion is, according to Pickton and Broderick (2001), usually replaced by the term marketing communication that also describes one of the key areas of marketing. To define marketing communication: *"marketing communication is a conversation between a brand and its audience and it is the collective term for all the communication functions used in marketing a product or service"* (p. 165) (ibid). Keller (2001) has further defined marketing communication as: *"the means by which firms attempt to inform, persuade, incite and remind consumers-directly-or indirectly about the brands they sell"* (p. 819)

Communication is the mechanism through which human relations exist and develop – all the symbols of the mind, together with the means of conveying them through space and preserving them in time. It includes the expression of the face, attitude and gesture, the tones of the voice, words, writing, printing, railways, telegraphs, telephones and whatever else may be the latest achievement in the conquest of space and time. All these taken together, in the intricacy of their actual combination, make up an organic whole corresponding to the organic whole of human thought; and everything in the way of mental growth has an external existence therein. The more closely we consider this mechanism, the more intimate its relation will appear to the inner life of mankind, and nothing will more help us in understanding the latter than such consideration.

No field of study has a more important implication for our lives in contemporary society than that which looks systematically at the process of human communication. Everything we do, from making friends to governing a nation would be impossible if human beings were unable to communicate with speech and language. It is no exaggeration to say that communication is at the heart of human existence. Indeed, all the great advances in civilization that have occurred since prehistoric times (in government, law, science, education, religion, the arts and many others) depended on improved systems of communication. About 40,000 years ago, our direct forbears, the Cro-Magnon, developed the ability to speak. Earlier hominids, such as the Neanderthal, were unable to do so because of the physiological structure of their tongue, facial muscles and voice box. Developing speech and language separated the Cro-Magnon from other hominids and from related animal species. With the ability to think, reason and communicate in complex ways, the human species went on to invent writing, then printing, and in modern times to develop our sophisticated electronic media. It was those long and often difficult changes — constantly extending our ability to communicate more swiftly, widely and accurately — that enabled us to advance far beyond the level of our primitive forebears.

The Communication Process

Task of the marketing communication activity is to create a message and then send the same to the receiver through different channels. This has been referred by Duncan (2002) as the interactive communication process. But it has to be noted here that such a process takes place in an environment where disturbances, termed as noise, might affect the message and its transmission to be received differently than intended by the sender (ibid).

There are many models theorized to capture the communication process. In all cases of communication, a successful communication process occurs when the receiver understands the message just as the sender wants it to be understood.

Figure 10.1 shows a communications macro-model with nine elements. The elements of the communication process are: input, sender, channel, noise, receiver, output and fields of response.

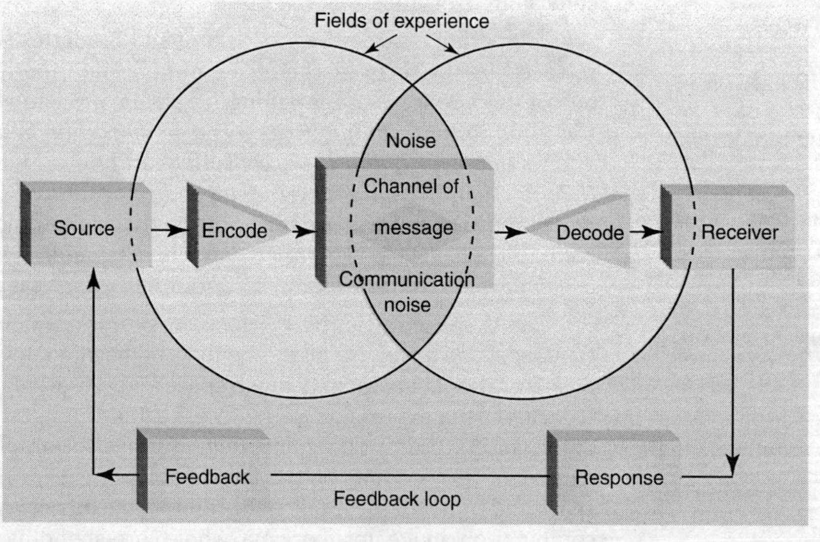

Fig. 10.1: Communication Process Model

- **Input:** The sender has an intention to communicate with another person. This intention makes up the *content* of the message.
- **Sender:** The sender encodes the message. Thus, he gives expression to the content.
- **Channel:** The message is sent via a channel, which can be made of a variety of materials. In acoustic communication, it consists of air, and in written communication, of paper or other writing materials.
- **Noise:** The channel is subjected to various sources of noise. One example is telephone communication, where numerous secondary sounds are audible. Even a solid channel such as paper can be crushed or stained. Such phenomena are also regarded as noise in the communicative sense.
- **Receiver:** The receiver decodes the incoming messageo or expression. He translates it and thus receives the message.
- **Output:** This is the content decoded by the receiver.
- **Fields of response:** In the process, the relevance of a code becomes obvious. The codes of the sender and the receiver must have at least a certain set in common in order to make communication work. That frame of reference is the sum of experiences in the form of each person's knowledge, beliefs and values. Our frame of reference is also greatly influenced by the culture to which we belong. On the basis of that body of personal knowledge, each member of the audience decodes the message. As members of the audience differ, so will their interpretations of what they hear.

Written communication such as ancient texts is a linear process in which there is no feedback loop to allow for correction. Also, given the factors of culture, history, geography and language, the more the receiver shares in these elements, the higher the probability of a successful communication process. When the sender and the receiver do not share the same culture, historical time period, geographical location or language, the probability of a successful communication process is low.

Types of Attention

The marketing communicator's ultimate objective is to encourage the consumer to choose his product rather than the competitor's offering. In terms of tourism, this would mean encouraging the consumer on to visit the location at hand rather than a different location. Capturing the end user's attention, then, becomes critical in this regard. Attention simply means to focus on and consider a message to which one has been exposed. There are three basic types of attention: involuntary attention, non-voluntary attention and voluntary attention.

- **Involuntary attention:** Requires little or no effort on the part of the receiver and the marketing tool intrudes upon the person's consciousness. Loud music or dramatic videos on television advertising a location are an example of this.
- **Non-voluntary attention:** Also called spontaneous attention, it occurs when a person is attracted to a stimulus and continues to pay interest because it holds its interest. The "Incredible India" campaign with magnificent pictures of Kerala or of the Bengal Tiger seeks to capture the consumer's attention via these means.
- **Voluntary attention:** It occurs when a person wilfully notices an advertisement. This happens when the consumer is specifically planning his/her vacation and is seeking information regarding various tourist destinations.

INTEGRATED MARKETING COMMUNICATION

Integrated marketing communication can be defined as a strategic combination of select tools of advertising and promotion with an aim to achieve communication objectives. This in turn focuses on supporting the selected positioning of the brand. Finally, all communication irrespective of mode should convey the same message to the target audience. The concept of IMC is very similar to that of an orchestra. There are so many musical instruments that are played together. But each of the member plays according to a plan in a cohesive and well-coordinated manner. This synchronization produces a wonderful affect which is known as music. There is a very thin line which demarks noise and music. Similarly, there are multiple vehicles for taking the message to the customer, but then, each conveys the same message about the brand as well as the organization.

TOURISM MARKETING COMMUNICATION (TMC)

From a tourist destination perspective, it is essential to first understand the thought process of the tourists. For instance, domestic tourists will have a completely different set of priorities and concerns than international tourists. Based on this, a proper communication strategy has to be designed.

Definition. Marketing of tourism is simply applying the appropriate marketing concept and planning a strategy to attract a visitor to a destination, whether it is a resort, a city, a region or a country. Marketing can be seen as a process of planning and executing a conception, pricing, promotion and distribution of ideas and services to create exchanges that satisfy the individual and organization goal. While selling is an important part of promotion, there would be no long-term gain for a city to focus only on convincing people to visit, without first making sure that the city offers the experience they desire. This definition can further be extended to mean that the exchange should also meet the needs of both the city and the people who live there. Therefore, the development of a city as a tourist destination should be undertaken if economic benefits improve the quality of life of city residents as well.

Significance of Tourism Marketing Communication

Customer satisfaction in tourism is greatly influenced by the way in which the service (hospitality) is delivered and also by the physical appearance and personality of the business. It is critical that these elements be communicated in the best possible manner to convince people to come and experience what your business or community has to offer. Equally important is the ability to generate repeat business. Thus, marketing communication becomes the mode to reach potential visitors. It has a vital part of tourism marketing.

Relevance of Tourism Marketing Communication

Marketing brings the five major sectors of the tourism industry together, namely — the market demand in the area of origin, the product supply at the destination, the transportation or physical access to destinations, the distribution organizations and travel organizers. There is no automatic harmony between what customers want and will pay for and what producers are able or willing to provide. In practice, there is usually a continuing tension between a producer's need for profit and the efficient use of assets and the consumer's search for value and satisfaction.

Marketing managers often have to use judgement in balancing the conflicting needs of the parties and do so with imprecise knowledge about their customers and about the decisions of other destinations marketing competitive products. Their judgement is expressed in the communication and distribution, upon which the bulk of the marketing expenditure is spent. The better the balance between the interests of the two parties, the smaller the marketing expenditure will need to be as a proportion of sales revenue.

Influence on Tourists

It can be generally said that marketing influences visitors' demands, but not all visitors are influenced by marketing activities. For example, domestic travellers who travel by private car and stay with friends and relatives may not have been influenced by marketing. Marketing comprises the following elements: the attitudes and decisions of customers (target market) concerning the perceived utility and value of available goods and services, according to their needs, wants, interests and ability to pay. It also comprises the attitudes and decisions of producers concerning their production of goods and services for sale in the context of their business environment and long-term objectives. Lastly, it includes the ways in which service providers communicate with customers, before, during and after the point of sale and distribute or provide access to their services.

Implications of TMC

Marketing is about systematically and thoughtfully coming up with plans and taking actions that get more people to buy more of a supplier's product and services more often and at higher prices, so that more money is made. Marketing is not about creating an image; having an image just means that people know who you are, but it does not motivate them to do anything. Although small businesses still account for the largest part of travel and tourism services, the marketing practices of large organizations will be increasingly influential. Such organizations will tend to dominate customer expectations, service design, prices and marketing techniques. The emergence of these corporations has greatly added to the surplus capacity available that exceeds the basic propensity to consume. However, competition between large corporations tends to leave gaps and niches, too small to be profitable for big firms.

Applications of TMC

The four basic controllables are the tourist package according to the changing needs of target customers; pricing, which is used to manage the volume of sales; promotion to make potential customers aware and favourably disposed towards buying it and the place, which includes the location of the facility and all the points of sale that provide access to the product (tourist package) and services to prospective customers. These are discussed as follows:

Product. The inclusive tourism package is a themed experience that provides an immediate context to its visitors, but is primarily confident on stimulating the senses of sight and sound. The key to success for the tourism industry is to customize its package offering to meet the needs of the defined target market.

People. Hospitality is often described as people's industry. All of the people who play a part in the service delivery influence the buyer's perception of the service itself. A service is performed and not handed over as in the case of a manufactured item, and people form part of the process and delivery by means of friendliness, helpfulness and efficiency.

Price. Marketers should consider the external factors when making pricing decisions including the nature of the demand for the offering, consumer perceptions, price elasticity and competition. The quality of the offering must meet the expectation that the price has generated in the customer's mind.

Promotion. Consumers have a choice, and marketers must give them a reason, other than price, for deciding to buy their products and services. Various promotional tools available with the marketer are advertisement and public relations.

- **Advertisement:** One of the important tools for creating awareness in the mind of the customer is advertising. Advertising is the non-personal communication in which a message is delivered through a paid medium for the purpose of influencing the buying behaviour of the tourist.
- **Public relations:** In tourism, public relations assume special significance because of the peculiar nature of the product. Here, the need for making complete information (the facts) available to both potential and actual tourists assumes special significance.

Brochures and other printed sales literature represent a distinctive group of paid-for marketing communications that exclude commercial publications such as directories, maps and guidebooks sold through bookstores.

Analysis of Situations in which TMC Suits Best

At the centre of marketing orientation lie questions about consumer demand and the measures that are necessary to identify, influence, satisfy and manage it profitably. While a destination, an attraction and an accommodation product share some similarities, differences in market characteristics and consumer profiles must be taken into consideration in suggesting marketing approaches for each.

Broadly speaking, while marketing communications is an essential feature for all tourist destinations, there are certain situations where it suits the best – for example, when the location has a potential but is relatively unknown. When the organization or travel agency is offering a different tourist package, it needs to be marketed to grab the attention of the potential tourist.

COMMUNICATION OBJECTIVES

Communication is the foundation of all human relationships and concerns exchange of information, ideas or feelings. Marketing communications is a collective term for all communication functions used in marketing a destination and is defined as the process by which the marketer develops and presents an appropriate set of communications stimuli to a defined target audience with the intention of eliciting a desired set of responses. The purpose of marketing communications is to add persuasive value to a product or a service for customers.

Traditionally, the distinct tools of the marketing-communications mix are advertising, public relations, sales promotion, direct marketing, personal selling, and over recent years, Internet marketing and sponsorship. Each component has a specific task to achieve, and the message is greatly enhanced if it is reinforced by other tools in the mix. Each element, thus, has a different capacity to communicate and to achieve different objectives.

Long-Term Objectives

Long-term objectives include creating interest and reinforcing the brand.

- **Create interest:** From the awareness stage, motivating a prospective tourist to buy a tourist package presents a significant challenge. It is very essential that tourists (customers) first are able to recognize as to what are their needs. Identifying and clearly establishing the latent need in the

An Advertising Campaign Appealing to the Charm of Reconnecting with Family minds of the customer is an endeavour of any marketing communication strategy. This has been done on the basis of various personality traits / characteristics such as emotion, aspirations and ambitions.

- **Reinforce the brand:** Once a purchase is made, a marketer can use promotion to help build a strong relationship that can lead to the tourist becoming a loyal customer. For instance, many service providers now ask for a customer's email address so that follow-up emails containing additional information or even an incentive to purchase other similar tourist packages can be sent in order to strengthen the customer–marketer relationship.

Short-Term Objectives

Short-term objectives include building awareness, providing information and stimulating demand.

- **Build awareness:** New destinations are often unknown to a market, which means initial promotional efforts must focus on establishing an identity. In this situation, the marketer must focus on promotion to effectively reach customers and tell the market who they are and what they have to offer.
- **Provide information:** Some promotions are designed to assist customers in the search stage of the purchasing process. In some cases, when a destination is novel, the information is simply intended to explain what its main attractions are. In other situations, where there are many similar destinations, informational promotion may be used to help with a positioning strategy. Marketers may use promotional means, including direct comparisons with other destinations or tourist packages, in an effort to get customers to mentally distinguish the destination from other destinations.
- **Stimulate demand:** The right promotion can drive customers to make a purchase. In case of destinations that a customer has not previously visited or has not visited in a long time, the promotional efforts may be directed at getting the customer to try the destination. For destinations with an established customer base, promotions can encourage customers to increase their visits to those destinations. For example, a pre-holiday newspaper advertisement may remind customers about the destination or the tourist package.

STAGES IN DESIGNING COMMUNICATION STRATEGY

The stages in the design of communication strategies supporting the realization of promotional objectives are summarized below: identification of target audience; determining communication objectives; determining communication objectives, designing the message, selecting communication channels, establishing promotional budget, deciding on the promotional mix and measuring promotional results. These stages form the steps in the design of a promotional campaign when it comes to the launch of a new or re-designed or re-branded destination. However, many organizations are also interested in maintaining awareness and a positive attitude to their product or service. In these cases, each stage remains important; however, they will not necessarily follow the same order as shown below. The purpose of each of the stages is described in further detail in the following sections.

Identification of Target Audience

The first stage is to characterize the target audience. This target audience may include the complete market segment for the destination or the organization, or a specific promotional strategy may be targeted more narrowly at a niche within the broader segment. Accordingly, the messages and channels may be selected, although with caution not to alienate other groups in the market with the message associated with a niche strategy. In order to create the right message, it is important to understand the characteristics of the audience. This refers to the type of message likely to be disposed by the audience (for example, customers' priorities concerning quality or price) as well as the awareness of the audience about the current image of the company and its product or service.

Determining Communication Objectives

The objectives of the communication strategy are derived from the objectives of the promotional strategy. The objectives can further be categorized based on the model of the communication process. Four different models of the communication process with different stages are illustrated in Fig. 10.2. Each model can be identified as having three different stages: the cognitive stage during which potential customers become aware of the destination; the affective stage during which customers form opinions and attitudes concerning the destination and the behaviour stage when customers take actions, such as making the purchase on the basis of their experience in the first two stages.

As can be viewed in Fig. 10.2, communication objectives typically refer to how the communication should affect the mind of the target audience – that is, generate awareness, attitudes, interest or trial. The most frequently used of these models is the AIDA model, which includes four stages. These stages are attention – where the customer becomes aware of the destination; interest – where an interest in the destination develops; desire – where the customer has developed a sense of wanting the destination and finally, action – where a purchase is made.

When designing communication strategies, it is important to identify whether the objective is to draw attention, develop interest, stimulate desire or provoke action. Furthermore, the communication objectives should be quantified in terms of success/failure and timescale. This is to ease the control

Stages	Models: AIDA model	Hierarchy-of-effects model	Innovation-adoption model	Communications model
Cognitive stage	Attention →	Awareness → Knowledge →	Awareness →	Exposure → Reception → Cognitive responce →
Affective stage	Interest → Desire →	Liking → Preference → Conviction →	Interest → Evaluation →	Attitude → Intention →
Behaviour stage	Action	Purchase	Trial → Adoption	Behaviour

Source: Marketing Management, 13th edition, Philip Kotler.

Fig. 10.2: Communication Objectives

as actual results can be measured against quantified objectives. Moreover, the objectives of the previous year and corresponding results help make the planning job a little easier, as previous experience provides a better idea regarding the realistic objectives for the future. Objectives should be S.M.A.R.T: specific, measurable, actionable, realistic and time-specific. In addition, establishing clear objectives is necessary to give a focus to the organization. Clear objectives also give direction to the following creative efforts.

Designing the Message

A message that is consistent with its communication objectives is important in each communication strategy. Moreover, the unique selling proposition (USP) is the unique set of benefits that marketers believe is provided by their destination. In addition, promotion that focuses on brand or corporate image or identity forms the basis of the marketing message. Furthermore, the message consistency between different campaigns must be taken under consideration in order to promote a consistent image through all of its separate campaigns. In order to achieve a consistent message, the content (what to say) and the structure (how to say it logically and symbolically) are significant. In addition, the format and source – who should say it and who should act as the spokesperson – are all of major importance.

Selecting Communication Channels

Communication channels can be divided in terms of personal and non-personal communications. Personal communication channels are those in which two or more people communicate with one another. Word of mouth is the primary way of communication, although other media, such as e-mail, are growing in significance. Personal communication channels can be divided into three types: advocate channels, expert channels and social channels and consultants.

- Advocate channels, such as exhibitions where salespeople can interact with customers, often supplemented by leaflets, posters and possibly videos and samples
- Expert channels, such as independent experts
- Social channels and consultants, such as friends, professional colleagues and professional networks

Non-personal communication channels occur through some medium other than person-to-person. These are listed below:

- The press including national and regional newspapers and magazines, although most significantly for the information industry, trade, professional and technical journals
- Television, including satellite and cable television. This medium is expensive and, therefore, an option only for major advertisers
- Radio offers a wide range of competitively priced promotional options. This medium usually has less potential impact than television due to the lack of visual image
- Posters can be placed in many different environments, from billboards at the roadside to the underground and other public places
- Leaflets and publicity material are important takeaways and can act as a reminder of products and contact points

Eye Catching Tourism Promotion Campaign run by Government of Kerala in Sunday Supplement of Leading National Newspapers

Establishing Promotional Budget

The calculation of a promotional budget has different potential approaches. To establish the promotional budget considerations of what is affordable, the budget is set as a percentage of revenue from tourism. Furthermore, the budget can be set on the basis of seeking to achieve "share-of-voice" parity with competitors, and set as the result of an analysis of the desired objectives and tasks required to achieve those objectives.

Deciding on the Promotional Mix

When establishing an appropriate promotional mix, which consists of a selection of strategies from more than one of the communication tools, some issues that need to be taken under consideration are: the available budget, marketing message, complexity of the tourism package offered, distribution of the service and competition. Furthermore, the communication mix is composed differently, depending on the focus of promotional activities. It can be focused on intermediates, recognized as push-strategy, or directly on end users, known as pull-strategy. The appropriate channels of communication are very different and the decision to use push or pull strategy determines whether the focus is on intermediaries or end-user consumer marketing.

Measuring Promotional Results

When measuring promotional results, it can be difficult to differentiate between the effect of promotion and that of the other elements of the marketing mix. However, it is important to observe the effects of promotion by looking at sales figures and any measures of reputation available.

TOOLS OF COMMUNICATION

The following are the tools of communication:

- **Advertising:** Advertising is often seen as TV commercials, radio commercials and print ads in magazines, newspapers, books and brochures. In addition, advertising is also seen as tourist boards, travel guides, telephone directory and third-party and outdoor advertising.
- **Direct marketing:** Direct marketing includes direct mail, catalogue marketing and telemarketing.
- **Personal selling:** Personal selling is direct-sale contact, face-to-face sales or telephone sales.
- **Public relations:** Public relations is often seen as service publicities, press relations, internal communications, open houses and information packages.
- **Sales promotion:** Sales promotion includes items such as discounted prices and extra incentives offered within the sales promotion.
- **Trade shows:** Trade shows are usually composed of periodic gatherings with potential groups of buyers such as tourists and intermediaries.
- **Internet:** The Internet can facilitate communication through banners, chat rooms and booking online. For example, Government of Dubai has established a new portal on the Internet for promoting tourism by showing the attractions that Dubai has to offer to tourists. For more detailed information visit www.dubaitourism.ae.
- **Sponsorship:** Sponsorship is a communication tool including sponsors for sports teams, cultural programmes and the arts.
- **Point of purchase:** It includes design and improvement of ambience, posters and other materials at point-of-purchase of service.
- **Word of mouth:** An example of word-of-mouth communication is messages spread via rumours or friendly recommendations.

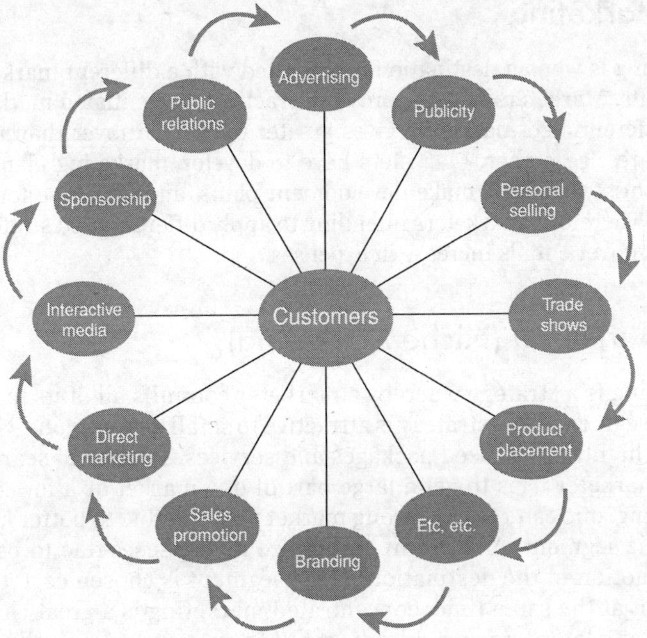

Integrating Different Channels of Communication with the Needs of Customers

DEVELOPING AN IMC MIX FOR DIFFERENT TYPES OF TOURISM

A tourism firm can use one of the following strategies:

- Undifferentiated marketing strategy
- Differentiated marketing strategy
- Concentrated marketing strategy (niche marketing)

Undifferentiated Marketing

Undifferentiated marketing is when a destination is marketed to all its customers with a single marketing mix. Sometimes, it is also called mass marketing. It was much more commonly used in the past. While using undifferentiated strategy, a tourism firm ignores different market segments and proposes one tourist package for the whole market. It pays attention to what is common in the consumer needs which unites them, and not to what differentiates them. Such a firm makes the marketing plan to embrace as many numbers of customers as possible. There are fewer expenses in undifferentiated strategy. Absence of segmentation also defines low expenses level for marketing researches and development of new tourist packages and services. Today, however, we have a big competition in the tourism market, which is why specialists do not recommend using an undifferentiated approach. It is very difficult to develop a destination or a trademark that will fit everyone or at least a major part of the consumers. When a few firms are directing their efforts on the largest market segment, there will inevitably be strong competition. Moreover, large segments can be less profitable because of more marketing expenses, including the possibility of price decline. Realizing this problem, a lot of firms take aims at smaller segments and at niches with differentiated products.

Differentiated Marketing

Differentiated marketing is when a destination is marketed with a different marketing mix designed to satisfy smaller segments. Marketers may be forced to practice differentiated marketing to remain competitive. As a rule, differentiated marketing gives greater tourist turnover than undifferentiated marketing, but expenses are also higher. Marketers have to develop marketing plans, conduct marketing researches, analyse tourist turnover, make development plans, and advertise for each trademark and each market segment. Therefore, marketers intending to apply differentiated strategy have to know that increase in product turnover entails increase in expenses.

Concentrated Marketing (Niche Marketing)

Concentrated marketing is a strategy whereby a marketer commits all of its marketing resources to serve a single market segment. This strategy is attractive to small destinations with limited resources, and to firms offering highly specialized packages and services. Instead of searching a small part of the big market, the marketer tries to get a large part of one market or a few small markets. Using concentrated marketing, one can reach a strong market position due to better knowledge of customers' needs in a specific segment. A firm can economize its expenses due to package specialization and placing and promotion of the destination. If the segment is chosen correctly, a firm will enjoy great profitability. But at the same time, concentrated marketing is a great challenge. The selected market segment may at a later stage prove to be small therefore economically unviable. Because of such reasons, most agencies try to operate on two or more markets at the same time.

While determining what strategy to choose, an agency should take into account the following factors: resources, homogeneity of the tourist packages, homogeneity of the market and strategies of competitors.

- **Resources:** If a firm has limited resources, the most effective strategy will be concentrated marketing.
- **Homogeneity of the tourist packages:** The most effective strategy for homogeneous packages is undifferentiated marketing. Products that differ in design more befit a strategy of differentiated marketing. It is also important to take into account the life-cycle stage of the destination. When a firm introduces a new destination to the market, it is reasonable to start with only one version. The most effective marketing type here will be undifferentiated or concentrated marketing.
- **Homogeneity of the market:** If tourists have the same taste, they would prefer to go to destinations offering similar experiences; and if they have the same reaction to marketing, undifferentiated marketing is appropriate.
- **Strategies of competitors:** If competitors segment the market, then undifferentiated

Marketing Communication by Tour Operator in New Zealand Directed at the Niche Customer Segment of Adventure-Sports Enthusiasts

marketing would be highly hazardous. On the other hand, if competitors use undifferentiated marketing, then a firm can obtain advantage by applying differentiated or concentrated marketing strategy.

Tourists visit different types of places and for different purposes. Tourism can be classified into the following six main categories: extreme tourism, cultural or cognitive tourism, ecological tourism, medical tourism, recreational tourism and business tourism.

- **Extreme tourism** engages people who are interested in sport or original extreme tourism. This target market usually includes young and active people.
- **Cultural or cognitive tourism** is the tourism accomplished with the purpose of studying the culture and way of living of some nationalities. These trips are carried out for the need of expanding knowledge.
- **Ecological tourism** attracts travellers to the untouched, sometimes remote, places of the world. It is similar to ethnic tourism. The trips accomplished with the purpose of "communication with nature" mainly have a geographical character. On offer are pedestrian trips or trips on horses, mountaineering, swimming on a canoe, residence in small towns and villages, photographing of wonderful types of nature, etc.
- **Medical tourism** is based on the need of health improvement. Tourists in this target market go to sanatoriums and use medical features of the nature.
- **Recreational tourism** refers to the trips accomplished with the purpose of rest. It includes sunbathing, swimming, social contacts in a quiet situation and participation in the sporting games. Such areas of rest are often located on the sea or in the mountains with wonderful views.
- **Business tourism** refers to the trips undertaken with the purpose of participation in congresses, seminars and other important business events. The trips accomplished with business aims can be combined with other types of tourism.

An Example of Communication for Connecting with the Medical Tourists

Different tourist centres can attract tourists from different sectors of the market. For example, Las Vegas, the famous American centre of gambling business, besides holding a steady position in the market for recreational tourism, is also known as a large centre of Congress business. The main factors determining the attractiveness of a tourist region are:

- Availability of region
- Nature and climate
- Attitude of local population towards visitors
- Infrastructure of region
- Standard of prices
- Level of retail shopping
- Sporting, recreational and educational possibilities
- Cultural and social descriptions

The last factor attracts tourists on the strength of various reasons such as work, national clothes, architecture, handicrafts, history, language, religion, education, traditions, rest, painting and music.

Many international travellers are interested in the economic state of one or another country, industry, trade, welfare of people, etc. Tourist companies are able to organize special tours on factories and plants of a country. Such measures in tourist centres are supported by the local chambers of commerce, hotels, restaurants and other organizations.

The chambers of commerce can organize group tours for establishment of close contacts with potential markets and calling attention to the commodities. Other interested organizations are shopping centres and large shops that want to sell as many commodities as possible to the tourists. The agriculture of a country can also attract guests. In some countries, there are organized special group tours for workers from agricultural industry for getting acquainted with achievements of colleagues from other countries.

An important expression of a country's culture is its cuisine. Tourists taste national dishes and drinks with pleasure. The cultural legacy of a region is expressed in its historical monuments, and some tourist centres are directly related to history. Having interest in the history of a region can become the strongest motivation for visiting it, and, consequently, this aspect forms a considerable segment of the market. Painting, sculpture, architecture, music and dances characterize the unique cultural view of a country. This can serve as an important motivational force for having a special-purpose segment. In tourist centres, hotels actively use creations of local artists and sculptors, enabling the guests to become acquainted with the culture of another country.

Another market segment is formed by religious pilgrims, for example, Muslims go to Mecca; Catholics actively visit Vatican and most journeys to Israel bear a religious import. Well-educated people, as a rule, want to know at least two languages, and interest in the language of another country can serve as motivation for undertaking a journey to the country. Very noticeable is the segment of students making trips for the improvement of their linguistic knowledge. In many instances, universities, institutes and colleges attract tourists from different countries, in addition to regular students, as they are located in picturesque places. In addition, campuses and other educational institutes are visited by foreign guests for participation in conferences and meetings organized by international scientific and educational organizations.

A potential traveller interested in scientific achievements of another country can visit museums of sciences, planetariums, zoos, aquariums, and also research centres of space and atomic stations. People interested in policymaking and nature of political problems and lawyers studying socioeconomic problems in different countries make another target market.

CONTEMPORARY AVENUES IN TOURISM MARKETING COMMUNICATION: BLOGS

Significance of marketing communication has been highlighted and accepted by many destination marketing organizations. It is essential that proper communication mix is engaged to reach the desired target market segment and achieve the business objectives within the available budget. Here a noteworthy point is that in tourism the prospective customers or tourists have access to only virtual destination experience. This makes the task of the communicator more critical and strategic in nature. With the onset of the Internet now it is possible to communicate with everyone at any part of the day or night. The Internet has proved to be effective even in tourism. One of the components of Internet communication has been Internet blogs.

Blogs

Peter Merholz (1999) had propounded this terminology. Blogs create a high-tech consumer-to-consumer communication. An important feature of this is that the communication is not under the control of a corporate entity but is run by the consumers themselves. In terms of categories the following four types of blogs have been classified by Smudde (2005): personal blogs, industry blogs, publication-based blogs and corporate blogs.

Personal Blogs: Personal convictions, expressions, observations are expressed here.
Industry Blogs: Also known as topic blogs. They contain expressions related to specific industry or topic.

Publication-based Blogs: This contains expressions from editors, reporters, freelancers, on contemporary issues in media.
Corporate Blogs: These are basically hybrids of personal blogs. The views here are expressed by corporate executives with a sole aim of getting their communication out to their organization.

Blogs can be used in tourism in various ways. Firstly, while deciding on which destination to visit a glance through the personal blog regarding experience in a specific country or destination may influence the decision making. Similarly, with the help of the company blog one can come to know about the principles and standards which say a cruise company would like to set for itself.

It has to be, however, kept in mind that the strongest influence remains in word-of mouth-publicity. In tourism, a satisfied and happy tourist always plays the role of the advocate for the destination.

Case Study: Promoting San Gimignano

San Gimignano is a small walled medieval hill town in the province of Siena, Tuscany, in north-central Italy at an elevation of 324 m and having an area of 138 sq. km. It is famous for its medieval architecture, especially its towers, which may be seen from several kilometres outside the town. There are many churches in the town housing a wide representation of artworks from some of the main Italian Renaissance artists. The Communal Palace is currently home of the Town Gallery, with works by Pinturicchio, Benozzo Gozzoli, Filippino Lippi, Domenico di Michelino, Pier Francesco Fiorentino and others. The heart of the town contains the four squares or piazzas.

The colour of its stone, a warm ochre, which radiates a golden lustre in the afternoon light, its twisted and winding streets, its convivial piazzas, its cool and solemn Duomo, churches, cafès and restaurants can take you back in time in a way that few other places can. And, from the top of the famous towers, you can see a rolling, green and verdant Tuscany.

San Gimignano: A View from one of the Piazzas

How to Get There?

Take a flight to Rome or Milan. From there, one can take the Roma-Milan expressway and head south if approaching from the north, and vice versa. After reaching Siena, take the Florence and cuts across borders effortlessly. Details of this village would obviously be up on the official Web site for Italy. In addition, local authorities might want to set up a Web page of their own with keywords ranging from as wide as "Italy" to as small as "village" to attract potential customers. Google AdWords provides an excellent opportunity in this regard due to its well-developed algorithms that direct interested tourists to necessary Web sites – not to mention, they are cheap too. Advertising on other tourism-related Web sites is also a must, especially in those sections of the Web site, which cover Italy in general or Tuscany in particular. This brand of advertising would address the customer who is basically looking for a filler destination to spend some time at before (Firenze)-Siena Dual Carriageway and exit at Poggibonsi Nord. From there, one can follow the road signs for San Gimignano.

Since the location under study is a small city, the integrated marketing approach adopted or proposed cannot be as broad-based as the kind we see in

Case Study: *(Continued)*

Malaysia with its "Truly Asia" campaign or in India with its "Incredible India" campaign. Such a city requires a far more focused approach in order to attract potential tourists. To do this, one must first understand the market and the kind of people that are likely to visit this ancient village. As this particular village is self-sustaining, it does not have the resources at hand to market its uniqueness around the world by means of publishing advertisements or distributing pamphlets. In addition, for most, if not all, of the people who would potentially visit Sam Gimignano, the purpose of the trip would not be a sole visit to the village; instead, it could at best be a last-minute add-on – a pit stop between other well-known destinations such as Florence, Pisa or Rome. Thus, it makes little sense to market in other countries through the forms of print media or audio-visual media. This leaves us with two options, first of which is the Internet. This is a cheap source of marketing the next big city.

Second, we would also want to target those tourists who are already in Italy. Pamphlet distribution at airports and visa office with an eye-catching ad could easily prompt the tourist into considering the village as a pit stop. Cities that should be targeted are those that are nearby, namely, Florence and Siena. Here, marketing would become a little trite with boards on bus stops, and on buses, cabs and light posts. However, focus here should be on the things that make this village special, such as the abundance of towers, the spirited daily performance of a local band, the archaic appeal of the village, its World Heritage Site status and its long history. Print media could be utilized during the holiday season with ads in newspapers and magazines and distribution of pamphlets.

We also find that a number of Asians coming to Italy are via travel agencies that have predefined tours through certain big cities. These tours almost always omit smaller locations such as the village in question. Thus, finally, it might be possible for the local authorities to include Sam Gimignano as a historical location, for which a certain commission could be paid to the travel agencies. Such payment would be more than compensated for by the business generated for the locals.

Case Study: Incredible India Campaign

Until 2002, Indian tourism was promoted through delegates at the Indian tourist offices located globally. These promotional campaigns were not too effective as the approach was unorganized, varied and limited by the skills and capabilities of the delegates. Realizing the need for a consistent approach, the Tourism Department of India appointed Ogilvy and Mather (O&M), Delhi, to develop a print campaign, and Enterprise Nexus, Mumbai, to create a television commercial. The media account was handled by WPP Group's Maximize India, and Grey Interactive was briefed to work on the official Web site (www. tourismofindia. com). In September 2002, the Tourism department unveiled a new campaign called "Incredible India" to promote Indian tourism globally. The first phase of the campaign, for a period of three months, was jointly funded by the government of India and Experience India Society, an association of travel agents in India. The campaign focused on the Himalayas, wildlife, yoga and ayurveda and was widely promoted in the print media, television and the Internet. The television campaign was telecast on CNN, BBC and other popular channels across the world. In the Asia-Pacific and European countries, BBC, CNN and Discovery channels were used to promote the campaign. In the United States, the commercial was aired on Travel channel. CNN was used also to advertise the campaign in Africa and the Middle East. The campaign focused on yoga, ayurveda, meditation and spirituality. It was widely advertised across Southeast Asia, Australia, Britain, France, Italy and Germany.

The Americas were not extensively focused upon as the government felt that Americans would visit India only for very short stints. To support the campaign, the infrastructure was improved, airports were upgraded and "Tourist Police" were posted at bus terminals,-

Case Study: *(Continued)*

Incredible India: An Integrated Marketing Campaign for Promoting India as an Attractive Tourist Destination with a Range of Attractions

airports and railway stations to guide the tourists. The Tourism department measured the effectiveness of the "Incredible India" campaign through hits on its Web site and also from feedback given to Indian tourism offices in 13 countries. The campaign was so successful that Conde Naste Traveler, one of the leading magazines on the travel industry, rated India as one among the top-10 tourist attractions in the world in its British edition's Annual Readers' Travel Awards 2003. India was preferred for its diversity, hospitality and value for money. Revenues increased and the mood of the industry also changed for the better. The second part of the campaign was launched in January 2003. The campaign changed its positioning and focused on the "Spiritual India" theme. O&M developed the campaign for the government. Lavanya Anirudh, an account director at Ogilvy and Mather (India), said, "Yoga, we own it but have never flaunted it. Bali, etc., are flaunting yoga and meditation with their spas. But we had it for centuries and centuries. And the real ayurveda is in India. We decided to showcase all of that and we layered the entire campaign with spirituality."

The "Incredible India" ad campaign demonstrated the beautiful locales, the culture, the traditions and the spirituality of India. O&M's sources claimed that the focus shifted to "Spiritual India" as westerners were attracted by the spiritual offerings of India. It also highlighted the diversity of India that caught customers' attention. The campaign was released in leading airlines, news and travel publications such as Conde Naste Traveler, Tutotourismo, Geo, Vogue, Tattler, Financial Times and The New York Times.

The Tourism department resorted to other promotional media beyond television, print and the Internet. Pictures of elephants, peacocks and women in traditional attire were painted on taxis to grab tourists' attention in England. In Paris, buses were painted with the "Incredible India" slogan. The Tourism department entered into joint ventures with local tour operators in Spain to promote "Brand India." "We felt our campaigns needed more punch. All that was required was to get creative, put in a little money, get private – public partnership, and get going," said tourism

Case Study: *(Continued)*

minister Renuka Choudhury. The Tourism department also resorted to niche marketing promotions for certain special-interest groups, under which specific promotions such as adventure tourism, spiritual tourism and focus on the flora and fauna or beaches of India were undertaken. For instance, a Buddhist Circuit Trail was conceived to attract a larger number of tourists from Southeast Asia, China and Japan. These promotional efforts over 3 years have paid rich dividends. India's tourism revenues rose to \$4.3 million during the period January – November 2004, as compared to \$3.1 million during the same period in 2003.

Unsung Tourist Destination: Chail (Himachal Pradesh)

At a height of 2,250 metres and about 45 km away from Shimla, Chail is a small mountain resort with the splendour and elegance of a princely preserve. The 19th-century palace and the pretty cottages are part of Chail Holiday Resorts. It is also well known for having the highest cricket pitch in the world. Chail has lovely walks and trails that meander through the dense pine forests — the home of the barking deer, the wild bear, the pheasant and a variety of birds.

Best Time to Visit

During winters, the temperature can drop below freezing point in Chail, while in summer, the climate is mild and light woollens/cottons are recommended. The best time to visit Chail is between May to July and September to November.

Accommodation

Chail has 16 hotels, 9 paying guesthouses, and 7 resorts with 467 rooms and 767 beds in the study area. There is only one travel agency operating in the area. Two resorts in Naldehra, 4 in Kufri and 1 in Chail are under construction. Most of the upcoming accommodations are for relatively higher income people. In the recent past, there has been a spurt in construction of hotels in the area due to incentives provided by the department of tourism under the Incentive Policy (DOT, 2000). Under the policy, hotel units, especially the resorts, are eligible for luxury-tax concessions and power-tariff freeze for a period up to 10 years.

Tourism in the Chail area is dominated by domestic tourists, with 89 per cent tourists being Indian nationals. A majority of the domestic tourists visiting the area (65 per cent) are from Punjab, Haryana, Chandigarh and Delhi due to their proximity to the area. The share of Maharashtra and Gujarat is 17 per cent, while that of West Bengal is 7 per cent. Ten per cent are from the rest of the country. Among the foreign tourists, Europe accounts for 65 per cent of the total arrivals, followed by Asia at 20 per cent and America and Canada at 11 per cent.

How to Reach Chail

Chail is connected by road. It is 45 km from Shimla via Kufri and via Kandaghat it is 61 km. Kalka is 86 km away. Regular buses for Chail leave from Shimla, Chandigarh and Delhi. The closest airports are at Chandigarh (120 km) and Shimla (63 km).

There are two very distinct allied activities that have come up as a result of tourism in this area. These are gift shops and mule/yak operators. Gift shops mostly store handloom and handicrafts items, art pieces and souvenirs, as well as sundry things like soft drinks, chips, biscuits and sweets. Mule/yak operators provide joyride facilities up to the adjoining sightseeing places at rates ranging from INR 10 to INR 150 per ride. There are no guides because there are no museums or historical buildings in the area for which guide services would be required. However, outdoor photographers registered with the state tourism department provide service to the tourists.

Chail can be promoted as the new tourist destination using a mixed strategy of infrastructure development and communication. The place can be promoted as an attractive ecotourism option that is easily accessible from New Delhi. Chail already boasts of a wildlife sanctuary with species such as ghoral, kakkar, sambhar, red jungle fowl, and khalij and cheer pheasants. The infrastructure development has to be primarily in the area of accommodation availability.

There should be enough availability of both onsite and offsite accommodations. Onsite accommodations

Unsung Tourist Destination: *(Continued)*

Chail: An Unsung Tourist Destination for Nature Lovers

may be relatively primitive, such as camping in remote areas or staying in paying guesthouses in remote villages. These can be located inside the sanctuary area as well. Since these do not involve much capital, locals can develop these very easily. Through this, tourists will come in closer contact with the local population, use local products and also taste local cuisines. Offsite accommodations, like the present resort areas, will be more comfortable for those taking day tours to the nature-tourism areas. The communication strategy needs to be developed around the following key areas: niche tourist place, easy accessibility and co-branding strategy.

- **Niche tourist place:** The promotional communication needs to be constructed so as to promote Chail as an ecotourism option. The intent behind this message is to reduce major variation in the seasonality of tourist visitors so that the resources can be better utilized. Further, promoting it in the niche category of "ecotourism" will reduce competition from other more developed and recognized destinations in surrounding locations in Himachal Pradesh.
- **Easy accessibility:** The communication message needs to focus on promoting Chail as a weekend getaway easily accessible from New Delhi. Most of the foreign tourists land in New Delhi and, hence, a location that is easily accessible from New Delhi will add to the attraction of the place for foreign tourists.
- **Co-branding strategy:** The brand of Shimla, a better-known tourist destination, can be leveraged to promote Chail. The state tourism department can use Shimla to promote Chail in its promotional campaigns. The state government can further promote some discounted packages for visiting Chail to the visitors coming to Shimla. This will create initial footfalls, and the good experience of the visitors will further boost word-of-mouth publicity for the place.

SUMMARY

- Communication is the mechanism through which human relations exist and develop—all the symbols of the mind, together with the means of conveying them through space and preserving them in time. A successful communication process occurs when the receiver understands the message just as the sender understood it.
- The elements of the communication process are input, sender, encoding, channel, noise, receiver, decoding, output and fields of response.
- Attention simply means to focus on and consider a message to which one has been exposed. In terms of tourism, this would mean encouraging the consumer to visit the location at hand rather than a different location. There are three basic types of attention: involuntary attention, non-voluntary attention and voluntary attention.
- Tourism marketing is simply applying the appropriate marketing concept and planning a strategy to attract a visitor to a destination.
- Customer satisfaction in tourism is greatly influenced by the way the service (hospitality) is delivered and by the physical appearance and personality of the business.
- Marketing brings the five major sectors of the tourism industry together: namely, the market demand in the area of origin, the product supply at the destination, the transportation to destinations, the distribution organizations and the travel organizers. Marketing managers often have to use judgement in balancing the conflicting

needs of the parties, and do so with imprecise knowledge about their customers, and about the decisions of other destinations marketing competitive products.

- While a destination, an attraction and an accommodation product share some similarities, differences in market characteristics and consumer profiles must be taken into consideration in suggesting marketing approaches for each.
- Marketing communication is the collective term for all communication functions used in marketing a destination. Traditionally, the distinct tools of the marketing-communications mix are advertising, public relations, sales promotion, direct marketing, personal selling and over recent years, Internet marketing and sponsorship.
- The long-term objectives of tourism marketing are to create interest and reinforce the brand. The short-term objectives are to build awareness, stimulate demand and provide useful information.
- The stages in the design of communication strategies are identification of target audience, determination of communication objectives, design of the message, selection of communication channels, establishing promotional budget, deciding on the promotional mix and measurement of promotional results.
- The various tools of communication are advertising, direct marketing, personal selling, public relations, sales promotion, trade shows, the Internet, sponsorship, point of purchase and word of mouth.
- In developing an IMC mix for different types of tourism, a tourism firm can use one of the following strategies: undifferentiated marketing strategy, differentiated marketing strategy and concentrated marketing strategy.
- While determining what strategy to choose, an agency should take into account some factors: resources, homogeneity of the tourist packages, homogeneity of the market and strategies of competitors.
- Tourism can be classified into the following six main categories: extreme tourism, cultural or cognitive tourism, ecological tourism, medical tourism, recreational tourism and business tourism.
- The main factors determining the attractiveness of a tourist region are availability of region, nature and climate, attitude of local population towards visitors, infrastructure of region, standard of prices, level of the retail shopping, sporting, recreational, and educational possibilities and cultural and social descriptions.

FIELD EXERCISES

1. Visit a monument in your city and try to figure out the factors that tourists considered before visiting this place, regarding the destination's attractiveness. Find out, are their responses in any way affected by the communication strategy used for marketing that destination.
2. Choose any unsung destination in India and develop a communication strategy for that destination. Share your strategy with colleagues and gather their responses.

REFERENCES

Duncan, T . (2002), IMC-Using Advertising and Promotion to Build Brands, New York, McGraw hill

Philip Kotler and Kevin Keller (2003), "Marketing Management (A South Asian Perspective)," Prentice Hall, New Delhi

Lynne Dore and Geoffrey I.C. (2003), "Promoting destinations: An exploratory study of publicity programmes used by National Tourism Organizations," *Journal of Vacation Marketing*, Vol. 9, p. 137

Marsha D. L, N. William and F.B. Kenneth (2007), "Advertising and Publicity: Suggested New Applications for Tourism Marketers," *Journal of Travel Research*, Vol. 45, p. 259

Pickton, D. and A. Broderick (2001), Integrated Marketing Communications, Chicago, Prentice Hall

Rhonda W.M., E.B. Julia and P. Bing (2008), "Believe it or not: Credibility of Blogs in Tourism," *Journal of Vacation Marketing*, Vol. 14, p. 133

Angkor Wat (Cambodia)

CHAPTER 11

Destination Branding: Building Brand Equity

ABOUT THE DESTINATION

Angkor Wat (Khmer: "Holy City Temple"), built by King Suryavarman II, is the single largest religious structure in the world. The temple complex consists of over a thousand Hindu and Buddhist temples.

OBJECTIVES

- To study and understand destination branding and building brand equity concepts
- To study and understand the strategic brand management process for destinations
- To study the application in Indian context by analyzing a promoted destination in India
- To try to replicate or extend the model to a popular non-promoted destination and an unsung location

BRANDING

A brand is a symbolic embodiment of all the information connected to a company, product or service. A brand serves to create associations and expectations among products made by a producer. It often includes an explicit logo, fonts, colour schemes, symbols and sound, which may be developed to represent implicit values, ideas and even personality. The key objective of the brand is to create a relationship of trust.

The brand, branding and brand equity have become increasingly important components of culture and economy, now being described as cultural accessories and personal philosophies.

Although the historical roots of branding can be traced back to the late 19th century with the development of branded consumer products such as Gillette and Quaker Oats, researchers have only recently considered branding a destination.

Destination Branding

Destination branding is a new way of thinking about the development of places — cities, regeneration areas, towns and major developments. It combines commercial brand strategy, marketing and communications, detailed destination planning, spatial and master planning, identification of attractors, infrastructure planning, service specification and development management.

A destination brand is more than its identity, which is, in turn, more than a logo or a mark or a strapline. It is an expression of the planned offer of value and experience that a destination provides to target consumers in priority markets — investors, businesses, institutions, residents and visitors. A destination brand provides a key to what the place is about, what it offers and the kind of experience it provides. A successful destination brand is a promise delivered and it is the uniting bond between the experience on offer in the destination and all the people, who live, work or visit there.

Branding Country, Region and City

Nation branding is a field of theory and practice which aims to measure, build and manage the reputation of countries (closely related to destination branding). It applies some approaches from commercial brand-management practice to countries in an effort to build, change or protect their international reputations. It is based on the observation that brand images of countries are just as important to their success in the global marketplace as those of products and services. Increasing interconnectivity through advances in information technology, coupled with an increasing importance of the symbolic value of products, has led countries to emphasize their distinctive characteristics. The branding and image of a nation-state and the successful transference of this image to its exports, are just as important as what they actually produce and sell.

Often the most visible aspect of a country's brand, tourism is usually also the biggest spender and the most competent marketing force. The touristic idea of the nation creates a visual image of the country, which can impact many other areas of the nation's performance – foreign investors, for example, may well be influenced in their choice of country by tourism images, so this particular aspect of the nation's identity needs to be seen as rather more than a simple sales channel. In a deeper sense, nation branding also provides a way for newer, smaller and poorer countries to establish and broadcast their true cultural, social and historical identities and carve out a perceptual niche for themselves in the global community.

Increasingly, cities and urban regions compete with other places for attention, investment, visitors, shoppers, talent, events and the like. Accelerated and intensified globalization has led to a situation where the main competition is no longer the city down the road or the town across the bay, but one where competitors are places half a world away. And this global competition is no longer limited to the capital and big cities, it now directly affects all cities and concentrations of urban settlements. A city brand is its promise of value, a promise that needs to be kept.

The Principles of Destination Branding

Destination brands have developed a set of destination-branding principles that we believe should guide any destination-branding programme.

Purpose and Potential. Destination branding creates value for a city, region or country by aligning the messages that the place already sends out, in accordance with a powerful and distinctive strategic vision; by unlocking the talent of the people who live there and stimulating investment to reinforce and fulfil this vision; and by creating new, powerful and cost-effective ways to give the place a more effective and memorable voice and enhance its international reputation.

Truth. Destinations often suffer from an image that is out-of-date, unfair or unbalanced. It is one of the tasks of destination branding to ensure that the true, full and contemporary picture is communicated in a focused and effective way and to never compromise the truth or glamorize it irresponsibly.

Aspirations and Betterment. The destination brand needs to present a credible, compelling and sustainable vision for its future — firmly in the context of our shared future. This will support the overall aim of a real increase in the economic, political, cultural and social well being of the people who live in the place, while contributing in more than a token way to the well being of other people in other places.

Inclusiveness and Common Good. Destination branding can and should, be used for achieving societal, political and economic objectives. Inevitably, a workable strategy will favour certain groups or individuals over others and this creates an inalienable responsibility to ensure that they are supported in other ways.

Creativity and Innovation. Destination branding should find, release and help direct the talents and skills of the population and promote the creative use of these in order to achieve innovation in education, business, government, environment and the arts. Furthermore, only creativity of the highest order can square the circle of translating the complexity of a place into a purposeful, distinctive and effective brand strategy.

Complexity and Simplicity. The reality of destinations is intricate and often contradictory; yet, the essence of effective branding is simplicity and directness. It is one of the harder tasks of destination branding to do justice to the richness and diversity of places and their people and still be able to communicate this to the world in ways that are simple, truthful, motivating, appealing and memorable.

Connectivity. Destination branding connects people and institutions at home and abroad. The clear and shared sense of purpose, which a good brand strategy engenders, can help unite government, the private sector and non-governmental organizations; it stimulates involvement and participation among the population; externally, it helps build strong and positive links with other places and people.

Things Take Time. Destination branding is a long-term endeavour. It need not and should not, cost more than any place can comfortably afford, but is neither a quick-fix nor a short-term campaign. Devising an appropriate place-brand strategy and implementing it thoroughly takes time and effort and wisdom and patience; if properly done, the long-term advantages, both tangible and intangible, will outweigh the costs by far.

Benefits of Destination Branding

The benefits of branding related to tourism destination products (TDPs) are

- Branding helps to reduce the choice
- Branding helps in reducing the impact of intangibility
- Branding conveys consistency across multiple outlets and through time
- Branding can reduce the risk factor attached to decision-making about holidays
- Branding facilitates precise segmentation
- Branding helps to provide a focus for the integration of producer's effort, helping people to work towards the same outcome

DESTINATION BRAND POSITIONING

The substitutability of tourism destinations allows tourists search most types of experiences through a wide range of choices. As a result, the need for destinations to create a unique identity, so as to differentiate themselves from competitors, is more critical than ever.

Brand managers differentiate their products by stressing attributes they claim will match their target markets' needs more closely than other brands and then they create a product image more consistent with the perceived self-image of the targeted consumer segment. There is an increased focus among marketers on differentiation through loyalty and emotional appeal of brands, rather than through discernible, tangible benefits. Within this context, destination marketers are faced by a number of key challenges in differentiating their destinations, namely:

- Limited funding as compared to consumer goods and services — need to outsmart rather than outspend
- Politics — balance between cutting-edge brand promotions and the management and bureaucratic red tape of local, regional and national politics
- An unstable external environment — global, regional and national conflicts, disasters and economic changes
- Changing consumer preferences (from products to emotional experiences) need to package destinations to make them living experiences
- Tourism competition — finding a point of differentiation that is credible and that competitors cannot surpass

In applying this concept to tourism destination brands, we can see that at first the market is small, and many places become popular in spite of (or due to) their lack of advertising activities because the destination is new and exclusive. Its visitors are trendsetters who, although few in numbers, are influential opinion formers. Yet, as the destination becomes famous and loses its cutting-edge appeal, these tourists move on to the next new destination, since they do not want to be seen somewhere that has become popular. In this phase, a destination brand's consumers are loyal and affluent, but at any time the destination's brand values may become irrelevant to them; hence, the ongoing need for them is to remain fresh and appealing. If the destination fails to remain contemporary, it will drift into the familiar zone where everyone knows about the destination, but it has lost its appeal. Becoming familiar can ultimately lead a destination to evoke a sense of fatigue – a place that finds it difficult to attract lucrative market segments. If it becomes very badly damaged, a destination brand's core values will need to be reassessed and its relevance to target markets redefined and revitalized.

DESTINATION BRAND EQUITY

Destination brand equity refers to the marketing effects or outcomes that accrue to a destination with its brand name, compared with those that would accrue if the same destination did not have the brand name. And, at the root of these marketing effects is consumers' knowledge. In other words, consumers' knowledge about a brand makes them respond differently to the marketing of the brand. The study of brand equity is increasingly popular, as some marketing researchers have concluded that brands are one of the most valuable assets of a company.

As a consequence of the international mobility of people and information in the present era, destination supply and the resulting competition are greater than ever before. Creating and managing ownable, trustworthy, relevant, unique and distinctive brand equity for destinations – the process of destination branding has emerged as an imperative of destination marketing in practical recognition of the fact that product superiority alone may not guarantee success. Each destination adopts a different set of reasons to initiate a branding project. Some seek better visibility and understanding; others wish to modify themselves or add elements of surprise to keep their image vivid and exciting and some even drastically change their public persona. There are destinations that wish to expand their world image, associating their identity with additional attributes or more effective ones. No matter where they go, all destinations seem to agree that their global perception is very important in terms of building and sustaining brand equity. A country's or a city's destination brand is ever-evolving, while mass media are constantly producing new trends, the competition remains fierce, destination supply is greater than visitors' demand and people are hungrier for new experiences than ever before.

DESTINATION BRANDING: EVOLUTION

Destinations have personality (concept of brand personality) and they speak to the user. The theory of brand equity postulates that the value of a brand is derived from four main factors: brand awareness, perceived quality of the brand, brand associations and brand loyalty. The characteristics of strong brands include consistent advertising and reinforcing a differentiated brand message.

The concept of destination branding (DB) has, therefore, evolved and is considered a potent marketing tool. It can be defined as selecting an element mix that is consistent to identify and distinguish a destination through positive image building and can be considered synonymous with (re)positioning, image building and image reconstruction of a destination.

Destination marketers face a challenge since they are dealing with something more complex than general goods or products. The marketers' problems are further increased because they may not have full control over the product experience. First, destinations exist as holistic entities or nuclear products and as collections of contributory elements or individual services and facilities. Second, a visitor can uniquely assemble the destination product from his own experiences of a chosen set of elements of that place. Third, destinations provide multiple functions. A single destination may offer historical buildings, shopping facilities, sports facilities and entertainment venues to a visitor. Destination branding results in a consistent, attribute-based image across multiple communities (in mountain cooperative sites) as perceived by tourists, but it builds stronger linkages of the image to the brand identity and more favourable affective and attitude-based brand associations for a region than for individual communities.

In the competitive tourism marketplace, destinations have to adopt branding techniques to differentiate themselves from other destinations and create an identity of their own, with the elements representing the uniqueness of the place. But one has to overcome a few constraints that any destination will have. A marketer does not have any control over the marketing mix of the place and also has a limited budget. One way to overcome this constraint could be the creation of brand saliency. Brand saliency here means an emotional relationship between the destination and the customer, built by effective communication strategies and providing lifetime experiences to the consumer. This can also be termed as mood marketing and is an efficient and effective way to overcome some of the problems associated with a destination.

There are several studies that have extended the role of branding to conceptualize the relationships that consumers form with brands. Instead, the literature on destinations marketing can be found in several academic areas; it is most systematically defined in two major domains: urban planning and tourism, and vacation marketing. However, these two domains take very different approaches: urban planning perspective and tourism, and vacation marketing perspective.

- **The urban planning perspective:** The urban planning literature focuses on the nature of the destination product, its historical development and the marketing implications of its distinctive features. The destination product can be viewed to be dualistic and one can distinguish the "nuclear" product — the destination as a holistic entity — from the product's contributory elements — the services, activities and features of which the destination is constituted. One can also think of a destination product to be divided into three levels: the individual good or service, for example, a tourist attraction; clusters of related services, for example, urban tourism; and urban agglomeration, referring to the collection of goods and services that make up the place.

- **The tourism and vacation marketing perspective:** To the tourism marketer, the location is a destination, a place that people and organizations visit. As such, tourism is a distinctive aspect of economic development of a location. The literature in this area emphasizes the importance of establishing a balance between competing objectives and environmental objectives relevant to the tourists.

Apart from these two major domains, a destination can be conceptualized as a communicator, a perceptive entity and as a relationship. These three main streams of destination brand conceptualization have been defined below. They are destination brands as communicators as perceptive entity and as relationships.

- **Destination brands as communicators:** The core objective of destination branding can be defined as the production of a consistent and focused communication strategy, based upon the selection of a collection of core intangible values existing in the mind of the consumer. A communicator perspective can be combined with a relationship perspective in which tangible attributes play an important supporting role within the communication framework, providing reasons for the consumer to believe. Increasing product parity requires destinations to create unique identities in order to differentiate themselves from their competitors. In addition, one can set out a brand equity that includes the development of a personality, as the focus of consumer relationships with the brand.
- **Destination brands as perceptive entity:** Brand images or perceptual perspectives dominate the literature. The literature on destination images includes studies of specific destinations and studies identifying common attributes across a sample of destinations at regional, national and international levels. Destination image has a key role for tourism marketers; several researchers have illustrated that destination image and tourist's purchase decisions are positively correlated. According to the general model of traveller destination choice, the intentions to visit reflect a destination's level of traveller awareness, its propensity to become part of the choice set and its affective associations or level of perceived emotional attraction. Therefore, destination image is an important issue in an individual's travel purchase-related decision-making and the individual traveller's (dis)satisfaction with a travel purchase depends on a comparison of his expectation from the destination or a previously held destination image and his perceived performance of the destination.
- **Destination brands as relationships:** A destination's environment influences the formation of stereotypical images of the kinds of people typically visiting the destination. The propensity to visit is due to a match between the destination visitor image and the tourist's self-concept. The destination brand equity can be analysed in the relationship perspective, arguing that the role of brands is to build a meaningful relationship with the consumer in order to secure higher profits. The conceptualization of brands as relationships is arguably part of the increasing acceptance of the relational paradigm of exchange. The relational-exchange paradigm characterizes exchange as a continuous process focused on the creation of value through relationships with all stakeholder groups, not just the consumers. These include employees, suppliers, alliance partners, shareholders, government agencies and so on. This conceptualization puts brands at the centre of marketing activities. It also widens the focus of branding activities beyond communications to include behaviours – a focus of considerable relevance to destination branding.

In the increasingly competitive global tourism market, many tourist destinations can act as substitutes and it is becoming increasingly essential to create a brand destination offering a unique identity to tourists. The results of a study indicate that tourists ascribe personality characteristics to destinations and destination personality can be described in three dimensions: sincerity, excitement and conviviality. The dimensions were found to be reliable and valid, with sincerity and excitement as the two main factors.

Destination-Brand Models

Destinations are amalgams of tourism products, which offer an integrated experience to the consumers. Tourists consume this amalgam of tourist products and services during their period of stay. There are various destination-branding models that have been researched. A destination marketer can use these models for branding a new destination and also to have a better understanding of an already branded destination. Some of these models that are described here are Kaplanidou and Vogt model, Cai's model and relational network brand model (Hankinson model)

Kaplanidou and Vogt Model. Kaplanidou and Vogt identify a destination-brand model to create and manage the place value in the tourist's perspective. This model incorporates many components that work together to form the destination-brand concept. The core of this model is the defining and building of brand identity. This is how brand strategists want the brand to be perceived. Destination brand identity is founded by a set of unique brand associations – these associations imply a promise to customers from organization members. Brand identity should be able to establish a relationship between the brand and the customer by generating a value proposition involving functional, emotional or self-expressive benefits. In this framework, five bases are defined to manage the destination-brand identity: brand image, brand personality, brand essence (or soul), brand character and brand culture.

Moreover, the main studies on destination-marketing literature, which explain destination-brand models define the core brand value or brand identity as a promise to a customer and it examines

- the process that communicates this value or identity to the tourists
- the role of all business local players and internal/external stakeholders creating and managing this value or identity

Cai's Model. This model considers destination branding as a recursive process that revolves around the central axis formed by brand-element mix, brand identity — the core of the model and brand-image building. The process described in the model starts with carefully choosing one or more brand elements to serve as trademarkable devices. These factors distinctly identify the destination and begin the formation of strong and consistent brand associations that reflect the attribute, affective and attitude components of an image (3 A's of the model). This makes it possible to assess the gap between the perceived and the projected. The assessment then provides input in building the desired image that is consistent with brand identity, through marketing programmes, marketing communications and managing secondary associations (3 M's in the model). Moreover, Cai defines four components on the model's outer circle specifying the contextual preconditions (4 C's) in which destination branding takes place: existing induced image, destination size and composition, positioning and target market and existing organic image. Therefore, the model is recursive, centring on building destination identity through spreading activation, which results from dynamic linkages among brand element mix, image building, brand associations (3 A's) and marketing activities (3 M's). The model also specifies that spreading activation takes place under the four conditions of existing organic image, existing induced image, destination size and composition and positioning and target markets (4 C's).

The Relational Network Brand Model (Hankinson Model). This model is represented by a brand core and four categories of brand relationships (Fig. 11.1). These relationships are dynamic and evolve over time. Stakeholder partners may also change as the brand develops and repositions. The "brand core" represents a place's identity – the blueprint for developing and communicating the place brand. It may be the vision of one or a number of organizations and it can be defined by three elements: brand personality, brand positioning and brand reality.

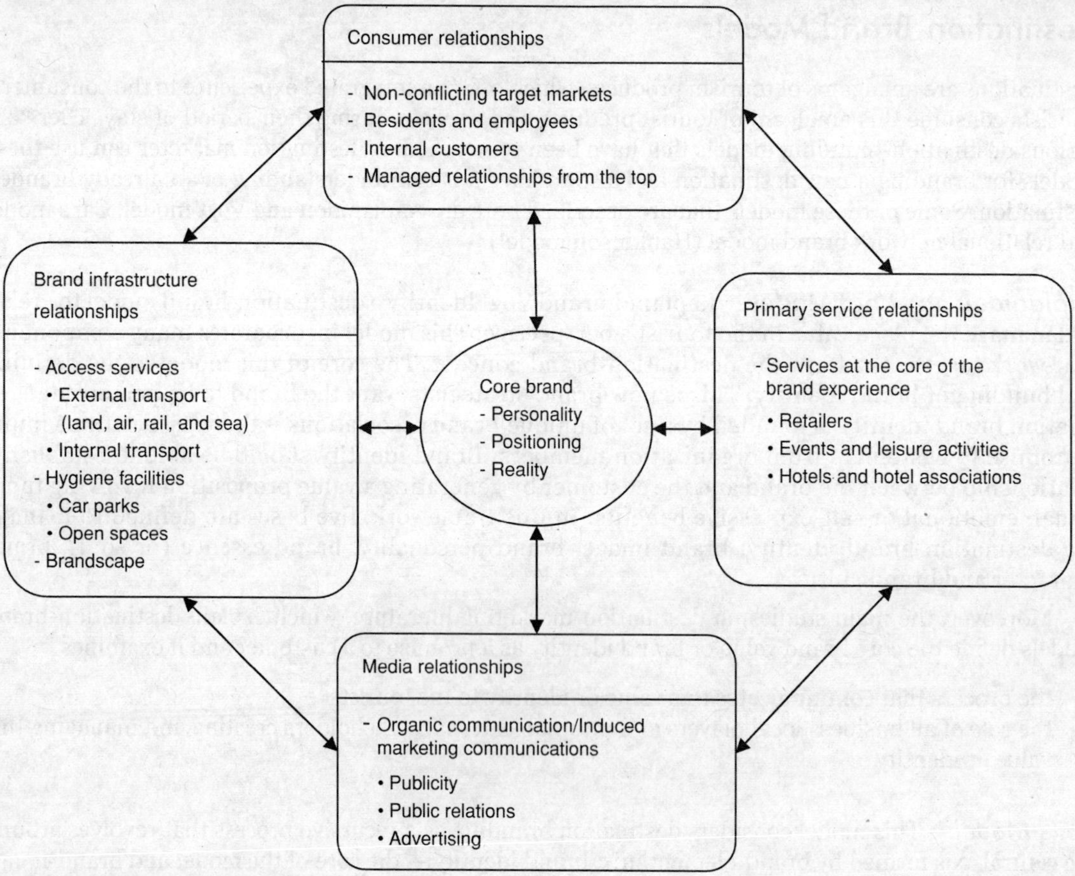

Fig. 11.1: The Relational Network Brand Model (Hankinson Model)

1. **Brand personality:** This is characterized by functional attributes, symbolic attributes and, most importantly in the context of tourist destination products, experiential attributes.
2. **Brand positioning:** This defines the brand's point of reference with respect to the competitive set by identifying the attributes that make it similar to other places and then identifying the attributes that make it unique within that set.
3. **Brand reality:** Developing the core brand is not about creating an image that presents a highly selective identity like a means of selling the place and it is also not a sales pitch that sees the place through rose-tinted spectacles.

Places as Relational Brand Networks

Brands-Box Model. De Chernatony and McDonald identified the roles of brands as non-verbal communication tools; for example, to communicate messages about the user to others, to reinforce group membership or to obtain information about the people or the environment around them. Using carefully chosen brands as badges, consumers advance towards their idealized self-concept by communicating associated values to themselves (a feel good factor) and to the reference groups to which they aspire.

Marketing managers need to ensure that the associated values required by the target segment form the core of the brand's personality.

De Chernatony and McWilliam seek to apply the Brands-Box model developed for physical goods to the context of tourism brands. The model is a four-cell matrix based on two dimensions of a brand: the representationality dimension and the functionality dimension. The methodology of an interview survey of a random sample of the general public was replicated as far as feasible, including the sample size, with adaptations in the Likert statements to allow for the replacement of physical goods by tourism brands. The choice of tourism brands was tested against an evaluation exercise using a convenience sample; all six brands were recognized as in Oxford for having the representationality and functionality dimensions of six tourism brands and to suggest possible explanations for the pattern alongside implications for marketing practice. The emerging Brands-Box matrix suggested that the brands were high on both dimensions, although there was some indication that the representationality dimension varied more than the functionality dimension.

Marcello Risitano's Destination Branding Model. The most important phases of destination branding processes are to define and communicate to the tourists the main brand value driver of a place. To achieve these aims, the first step of branding strategy is the definition of destination brand identity and identifying the principal elements that compose it. Moreover, to strategically manage the place value proposition, it is indispensable to analyse and to measure the destination brand knowledge of the tourists; this is related to the cognitive representation of the destination brand. Based on these statements, the destination branding model proposal in this paper represents two kinds of brand equity analysing: (1) the brand identity, through the element of projected brand equity defined by policymakers, development agency and so on and (2) the brand knowledge, through the components of perceived brand equity

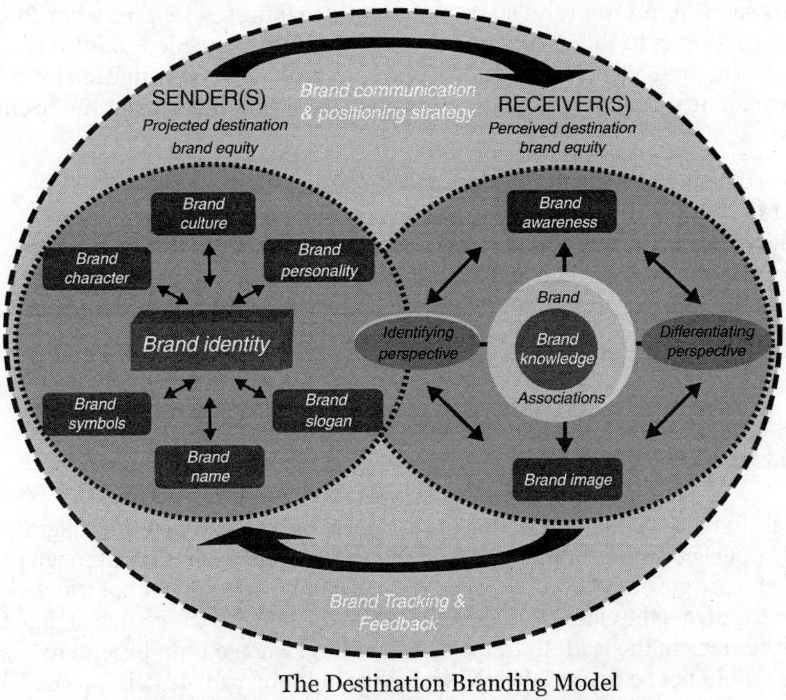

The Destination Branding Model

Source: The role of destination branding in the tourism stakeholders system. The Campi Flegrei case by Marcello Risitano, University of Naples Federico II.

on consumer-based perspective. In the case of destination, the analysis of resources, competences and capabilities of the place is the ground to define its brand identity. In the destination branding model proposal, the brand identity is based on six elements: brand culture, brand character, brand personality, brand name, brand logos (and symbols) and brand slogan.

CHOOSING A DESTINATION

A study was conducted to find out the ranking of important factors for choosing a destination both for short-term and long-term holidays. The characteristics to study about a destination typically are safety, friendliness, avenues for relaxation, connectivity, excitement, fun activities, comfortableness, good restaurants, good accommodation, natural beauty, quietness, good shopping and nightlife.

- **Short-term holidays:** For short-term holidays (between 2 and 4 days), safety was considered as the most important characteristic for choosing a destination. The other characteristics that were given more importance were comfort, fun and excitement. The least important characteristic was quietness.
- **Long-term holidays:** For long-term holidays (duration of more than 4 days), safety of the location was again considered as the most important deciding factor. The tourists looked forward to the friendly nature of the destination and the extent of relaxation they can get at the destination.

DESTINATION BRAND PERFORMANCE MEASUREMENT

Destination brand performance evaluation is vital to the success of the destination brand. It enables brand owners to see where the brand's strengths and weaknesses lie and what forces are driving these, which in turn points to the nature and level of investment needed to fulfil the brand's potential. Measuring destination brand performance is an integral part of destination brand management. The following are some of the questions that can be used while measuring the brand performance of a destination:

1. How did you come to know about this destination?
2. Do you want to travel to this destination? Why?
3. What are the key attractions of this destination?
4. What time of the year would you like to visit the location?
5. If already visited, does the promotion reflect the major attractions of the location?

Based on the data from the responses, analysis can be done to find out whether the branding exercises fetch a fitting result.

BRAND VALUE SUSTENANCE

Marketers struggle to enhance the satisfaction of customers only to find that they migrate to competitors. The long-lasting appeal of various brands does remind us time and again that although products and services are mortal and are governed by a life cycle – which can be delayed but not avoided, various brands can sometimes escape from the clutches of time. It is this resistance to the course of time that sees certain countries or destinations in the lead. In terms of accounting, when a brand is entered as an asset in the balance sheet, it should not be depreciated. Nevertheless, a brand can also disappear. If badly managed, any brand is doomed. A brand is not a once-and-for-all construction, but the aim of a constant effort to build the added value.

Box 11.1: Measuring Brand Performance – A Kerala Survey

Destination brand performance of Kerala was measured by conducting a survey among people in India and abroad, featuring countries such as Spain, France, Denmark, Italy and Belgium. The total number of participants in the survey was 36.

People Who Have Not Visited Kerala. A majority of the survey participants came to know about Kerala by word of mouth. People associated Kerala with the tagline "God's own country." Many of them found the place to be attractive and wanted to visit the destination in the near future.

People Who Have Visited Kerala. People who had already visited Kerala were asked about their travel experience. A majority of the respondents agreed that the destination met their expectations and they had a memorable experience in Kerala. The survey respondents associated Kerala with coconut trees, boats, backwaters, elephants and massage.

These findings show that the Kerala Tourism Development Corporation has promoted its state very effectively among potential tourists.

Effective marketing strategies to undertake market research to identify and assemble a highly attractive product should be developed to differentiate from competing tourist destinations. In case of India, an Indian tourism brand position should be created by focusing on what makes India an unmatched destination. Market research should be carried out to establish the present image of India as a destination in relation to its competitors. Tourist-centric products and issues relating to price, security, health, safety and quality should be studied. Digital technology can be applied to enable tourism organizations to promote their destination projects on Internet and other multimedia platforms. Failure to build and sustain destination brand equity or the value of the brand in the minds of potential visitors and investors, can lead to economic decline. The image of a place directly relates to how it is perceived and how it competes for visitors, investors, trade, talented people, media attention and relevance.

Case Study: Destination Branding in Kerala

Destination branding is about discovering the true essence of a place – city, state and nation, developing its core competency by incorporating all the attributes associated and communicating the same to the target audience in a favourable manner. In this section, let us try to understand how the Kerala brand has been implemented and managed.

A Houseboat in the Backwaters Near Alleppey in Kerala

Background

Kerala, a state situated on the tropical Malabar Coast of southwestern India, is one of the most popular tourist destinations in the country. Kerala is famous especially for its ecotourism initiatives. Its unique culture and traditions, coupled with its varied demography, have made Kerala one of the most popular tourist destinations in the world.

Case Study: *(Continued)*

Major Attractions

Beaches. Flanked on the western coast by the Arabian Sea, Kerala has a long coastline of 580 km (360.39 miles), all of which is virtually dotted with sandy beaches. Kovalam beach near Thiruvananthapuram was among the first beaches in Kerala to attract tourists. Rediscovered by backpackers and tan-seekers in the 1960s and followed by hordes of hippies in the 1970s, Kovalam is today the most visited tourist destination in the state. Other popularly visited beaches in the state include those at Cherai, Kappad, Kovalam, Fort Kochi and Varkala. The Muzhappilangad beach at Kannur is the only drive-in beach in India.

Munnar in Idukki District of Kerala

Backwaters. The backwaters in Kerala are a chain of brackish lagoons and lakes lying parallel to the Arabian Sea coast – known as the Malabar Coast. Kettuvallam (Kerala houseboats) in the backwaters are one of the prominent tourist attractions in Kerala. Alleppey, known as the "Venice of the East," has a large network of canals that meander through the town. The Vallam Kali (the snake boat race) held every year in August is a major sporting attraction. The backwater network includes five large lakes (including Ashtamudi Kayal and Vembanad Kayal) linked by 1,500 km of canals, both manmade and natural, fed by 38 rivers and extending through virtually the entire length of Kerala state. The backwaters were formed by the action of waves and shore currents creating low-barrier islands across the mouths of the many rivers flowing down from the Western Ghats range.

Hill Stations. Eastern Kerala consists of land encroached upon by the Western Ghats; the region, thus, includes high mountains, gorges and deep-cut valleys. The wildest lands are covered with dense forests, while other regions lie under tea and coffee plantations or other forms of cultivation. The Western Ghats rises on an average to 1,500 m above sea level. Certain peaks may reach to 2,500 m. Popular hill stations in the region include Munnar, Nelliyampathi, Ponmudi, Wayanad and Kottanchery Hills.

Wildlife. Most of Kerala, whose native habitat consists of wet evergreen rainforests at lower elevations and highland deciduous and semi-evergreen forests in the east, is subject to a humid tropical climate. However, significant variations in terrain and elevation have resulted in a land whose biodiversity registers as among the world's most significant. Most of Kerala's significantly biodiverse tracts of wilderness lie in the evergreen forests of its eastern-most districts. The state also hosts two of the Ramsar Convention-listed wetlands: Lake Sasthamkotta and the Vembanad-Kol wetlands are noted as being wetlands of international importance. Silent

Lion Tailed Macaque

Case Study: *(Continued)*

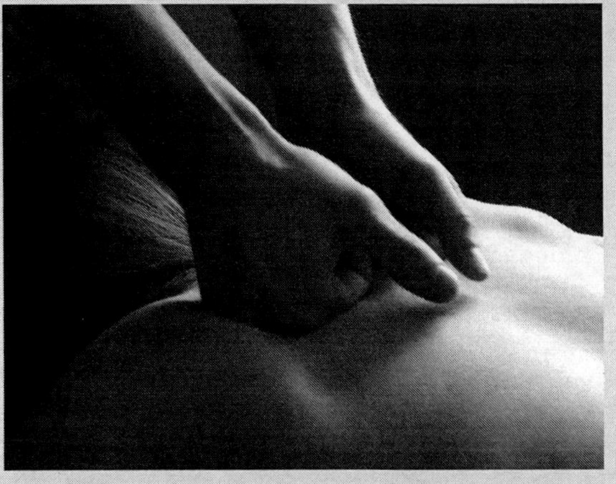

Traditional Ayurveda Treatment Given in Kerala

Valley National Park in Palakkad is home to the largest population of lion-tailed macaque. They are among the world's rarest and most threatened primates.

Ayurveda. Medical tourism in Kerala, promoted by traditional systems of medicine like ayurveda and siddha, draws increasing numbers of tourists. A combination of many factors has led to the increase in popularity of medical tourism: high costs of healthcare in industrialized nations, ease and affordability of international travel, improving technology and standards of care.

Brand Evolution. God's Own Country

Until the early 1980s, Kerala was an unknown destination, with most tourism circuits concentrated around the north of the country. In the early 1990s, advertisements featuring the tagline "God's Own Country" began appearing in the print and electronic media in India. This campaign was run by Kerala Tourism Development Corporation (KTDC).

The advertisements projected Kerala as the place to be, by marketing every aspect of the state – from the towns, cities, beaches and backwaters, to cultural heritage, food and wildlife. These aspects of Kerala, which were identified as the state's unique selling propositions, were packaged in a professional way by KTDC. Apart from these marketing initiatives, the government of Kerala made an effort to professionally manage the state's tourism industry. The state's tourism agenda promotes ecologically sustained tourism, which focuses on the local culture, wilderness adventures, volunteering and personal growth of the local population. Over the next few years, the organization's efforts to sell Kerala to Indians as well as foreigners began paying off. The state reportedly became one of the places with the highest brand recall, thanks to its unique positioning and targeting efforts. The advertisements helped Kerala stand out as the "destination of choice" in India and tourist arrivals began to increase significantly.

In the past, although many other states, such as Goa and Rajasthan and places such as Agra, Khajuraho and Kanyakumari were famous all over the world, India did not feature anywhere in the top tourist destinations of the world. Today, Kerala tourism is a global superbrand and regarded as one of the destinations with the highest brand recall.

Advertising Campaigns

Kerala tourism is noted for its innovative and market-focused ad campaigns. These campaigns have won the tourism department numerous awards, including the government of India's Best Promotion Literature, 2004 Best Publishing, 2004 and Best Tourism Film, 2001.

Catchy slogans and innovative designs are considered to be a trademark of the brand Kerala tourism. Celebrity promotions are also used to attract more tourists to the state. The Kerala tourism Web site is widely visited and has been the recipient of many awards. Recently, the tourism department has also engaged in advertising via mobiles, by setting up a WAP portal and distributing wallpapers and ring tones related to Kerala through it.

The earlier advertisements (before 2005) offered a platter of Kerala experiences, while the new campaign focuses on theme-based ads, which is a part of Kerala's evolution as a tourism brand. The ads are typically 30-second commercials that promote Kerala's core tourism offerings such as beaches, backwaters, culture, hill stations and ayurveda. The

Case Study: *(Continued)*

new commercials are market focused and have enabled Kerala tourism to target the interests of specific travel markets. For example, the ad film that promotes ayurveda is used in markets such as Germany, while the television commercials that focus on beaches are used in Russia.

The Kerala government saw an opportunity in the marketing initiatives of other states as well. In 2002, it entered into a cross-promotional deal with Maharashtra to jointly attract domestic and foreign tourists and to apprise tourists of the attractions and specialities of the other state.

Awards for Tourism Initiatives

The state has won numerous awards for its tourism initiatives. Highlights include

- Nominated as one among the three finalists at the World Travel and Tourism Council's "Tourism for Tomorrow" awards in the destination category, in 2005
- Das Golden Stadttor Award for Best Commercial, 2006

Kerala has also won various awards from

- Pacific Asia Travel Association
- Pacific Asia Travel Writers Association
- Outlook Traveller, TAAI
- Federation of Indian Chambers of Commerce and Industry
- Galileo, Express Travel and Tourism

Tourist Statistics

- Number of foreign tourist arrivals to Kerala during the year 2007 was 515,808. It shows an increase of 20.37 per cent over the previous year.
- Number of domestic tourist arrivals during the year 2007 was 6,642,941. It shows an increase of 5.92 per cent over the previous year.
- Foreign-exchange earnings for the year 2007 was INR 26409.4 million, which recorded a growth of 32.82 per cent over the previous year.
- Total revenue – including direct and indirect – from tourism during 2007 was INR 114330 million, showing an increase of 25.28 per cent over the last year's figure.
- Considering the district-wise foreign tourist arrivals in 2007, Pathanamthitta district showed the highest variation of 58.09 per cent over 2006.
- Considering the district-wise domestic tourist arrivals in 2007, Kollam district showed the highest variation of 18.31 per cent over 2006.

Earnings from Tourism

Year	Foreign-Exchange Earnings (INR, in million)	Percentage of Increase	Total Revenue Generated from Tourism – Direct and Indirect (INR, in million)	Percentage of Increase
2001	5350.0	1.85	45000.0	9.58
2002	7056.7	31.90	49310.0	20.42
2003	9833.7	39.35	59380.0	12.83
2004	12667.7	28.82	68290.0	15.01
2005	15523.1	22.54	77380.0	13.31
2006	19884.0	28.09	91260.0	17.94
2007	26409.4	32.82	114330.0	25.28

Source: www.keralatourism.com

Box 11.2: Travel Experience in Switzerland

Switzerland means the Alps, pine trees, lush-green countryside, lakes, waterfalls, glaciers and Swiss chocolates. I decided to experience a variety of these in four days, which was not offered by any tour company as a four-day package. So, I, along with a couple of my friends, planned our own trip including hotel, flight bookings and Swiss pass purchase. Though it is a packed tour, we never regretted; after all, it is the number-one travel destination.

We took flight from the London airport to Geneva. We had a work permit of the United Kingdom, because of which we did not require tourist visa to Switzerland. However, it is always advisable to confirm with the nearest Swiss embassy. In Geneva, we just had a night stay in a hotel, close to the Geneva main railway station. Though we stayed there only for the night, we will cherish forever the lavishness and the comfort of the traditional Swiss room.

The next day, we took a train from Geneva to Interlaken, part of the journey by the scenic train named Golden Pass Line. The colours of the buildings add more beauty to the picturesque and breathtaking places. On arriving at Interlaken, we checked in at a nearby hotel I had booked. We immediately took the train to the peak Jungfraujoch (pronounced as *yungfrau yo*), the topmost point of the Alps and also the whole of Europe. We had a Swiss pass, but the Jungfrau train was not free. We could have availed a 25 per cent discount. We realized that we paid extra only after boarding the train. At the next station, ticket-checking staff took me to the ticket counter and the extra money was refunded immediately. I was amazed at their service and kindness.

The entire route to Jungfrau was unimaginably wonderful and breathtaking. It was a marvel to lay tracks with tunnels and stations at heights of around 10,500 feet. The route had a nearly 15 km long tunnel to reach the Jungfrau. To keep you entertained during this time, there are in-train screens playing documentaries about Jungfrau. Also, the train halts at two stops before reaching the top, just for passengers to view the perennial snow and take photos of the same. Then, we went into the ice palace, where even the floor was made of ice. Inside Jungfrau, there are five restaurants apart from shopping areas. I was surprised to see one of the restaurants named as Bollywood and we went in, out of curiosity. It was a complete Indian restaurant with wallpapers of famous cine stars and after a long time we enjoyed good indian food. Apart from Jungfrau, there are a couple of notable peaks and excursion points like Mt'Rigi, Mt'Pilatus and Mt'Titlis.

Next morning, we travelled by Golden Pass Line Interlaken to Lucerne. The window extends to the top to view the high-rise mountains. It was a beautiful route passing through many lakes and hills. On the way to hotel in Lucerne, we peeped into a Big Chocolate shop, where even chocolates like Big Chocolate fountains were made.

We had planned to visit Rhine Falls, which is along the Swiss–German border. We took a train to Zurich, where the main railway station is very big and even has cloakroom facilities. From Zurich, we took a train and reached a small station called Schloss Laufen. We were able to see the falls from the station itself. There are two paths from the station and either way the beauty of Europe's biggest falls can be seen. To enjoy the absolutely stunning countryside, we were advised to get down 2 or 3 stations before Schloss Laufen. In spite of the

Lakeside at Lucerne

Box 11.2: *(Continued)*

crowd at the Rhine Falls, it looks very calm and really marvellous. The waters were flowing at great speed, were slowing after falling down. It is usually quoted as second best to Niagara Falls.

On the same day, we rushed back to Zurich and stayed in a hotel directly facing the lake. From the room, we had a beautiful view overlooking the lake and the snow mountains in the background. The lake was very calm and tempted me to take a walk. Overall, Zurich is a small, calm and peaceful town – a perfect place to relax at.

The next morning, we had a quick breakfast and took the shuttle to reach railway station, where the much-awaited Glacier Express was waiting to start. Glacier Express and Bernina Express are considered to be the best scenic trains in the Swiss out of the 7 or 8 trains available. The train goes to a place called Chur and then deviates towards Brig. This route is considered to be the best of the scenic routes among tourists. It was green on one side and we could see amazing glaciers on the other. Not to miss is the beauty of a parallel river and a road that stretches along the entire route. There was a beautiful restaurant inside, serving western food with rice and vegetable cutlet. It was the most wonderful dining experience. From Brig, we took a direct train to Geneva airport and then back to London.

We were speechless most of the times looking at the stunning natural beauty, especially the countryside and the train routes of Switzerland. I think Switzerland has got the best train services. There are a variety of trains and I wonder how they could maintain such high precision in train timings. The maximum deviation from the expected time was 20 seconds. Even ordinary local trains and trams were superb, well maintained and very comfortable.

Unsung Tourist Destination: Velankanni

Velankanni is one of the most visited pilgrim centres in India. It is a town situated on the shores of Bay of Bengal, about 14 km from Nagapattinam in Tamil Nadu. The renowned basilica of Our Lady of Health draws pilgrims from all over the world. Not only Christians, but also people of other faiths come to this church to pray at the shrine of Our Lady of Health. In 1560, Virgin Mary is said to have appeared to a shepherd, asking him for milk to quench the thirst of baby Jesus. When the shepherd returned to his master, after performing the good deed, the pitcher kept on filling up with milk. Consequently, a small thatched chapel was built at the site. At the end of the 16th century, Virgin Mary appeared again in front of a lame boy, who regained the use of his limbs. The actual church was constructed after the incident. The tradition is to offer Our Lady of Health a candle in the shape of the respective ailment – for instance, a heart in case of cardiac complications, a liver in case of jaundice and lungs in case of tuberculosis.

Velankanni Church

Unsung Tourist Destination: *(Continued)*

The basilica has been extended at the back of the original church, and it has two floors, where services are held every day. The Gothic style of architecture is a unique feature of the church. The church itself is an imposing building with inspiring architecture. The museum situated opposite to the basilica has a very rich variety of exhibits which tells about the numerous miracles that have taken place after praying in this church. The precious offerings made by the devotees are on display here. Biblical incidents are depicted on both sidewalls. Festivals are celebrated here with pomp and gaiety. Every year on August 29, the feast of Our Lady commences with the hoisting of the flag. The 10-day festival ends on September 8 and the flag is lowered. The pilgrims also follow the Hindu tradition of tonsuring their heads as an offering, perform ear-boring ceremony and walk on their knees or roll up to the shrine as rituals. This is a religious centre where Hindus, Muslims and Christians from all over India congregate in large numbers and worship in harmony.

How to Reach Velankanni

- **By air:** Nearest airport to Velankanni is at Tiruchirappali at distance of about 165 kms. It is well connected to Chennai airport by regular flights. Taxi services are available from Tiruchirappalli to Velankanni for a fare of about Rs. 2000.
- **By road:** Velankanni is connected by buses to all the major towns and cities in Tamilnadu and also connected to cities in Kerala, Karnataka and Andhra Pradesh. Regular bus services are available to Madurai, Kanyakumari, Chennai, Trichy, Pondicherry, Trivandrum and Thanjavur. Deluxe tourist buses operate between Velankanni and many major cities of South India.
- **By train:** Nearest railhead to Velankanni is Nagapattinam, which is just 12 km away from the holy city of Velankanni. Nagapattinam is well rail connected to all major cities in India through Chennai and Tiruchirapalli. Taxi services can be availed from Nagapattinam to Velankanni for a charge of about Rs. 250.

Accommodation

Popular Velankanni hotels are Bethesda Inn MGM, Picnic Hotel, Sea Gate Hotel, Sea Gate Resorts, Golden Sand Hotel.

Best Time to Visit Velankanni

Velankanni, being in the coastal belt, has a humid climate all through the year. Summers (March to May) are hot with the temperature hovering around 28°C to 38°C. But evenings are pleasant with the cool sea breeze. Tourists mostly avoid hot summer days in April and May months.

Monsoons (June to September) have temperate climate accompanied with mild to medium rainfall. The place looks pretty good in monsoons. The beach wears a deserted look during monsoon season.

Winters (December to February) are pleasant with moderate climate. During winters the temperature falls in the range of 30°C to 21°C.

Best season to visit Vailankanni is October to March.

SUMMARY

- A brand is a symbolic embodiment of all the information connected to a company, a product or a service. A brand serves to create associations and expectations among products made by a producer. The key objective of the brand is to create a relationship of trust.
- Destination branding is a new way of thinking about the development of places – cities, regeneration areas, towns and major developments. A destination brand provides a key to what the place is about, what it offers and what sort of experience it provides.
- Brand managers differentiate their products by stressing attributes they claim will match their target markets' needs more closely than other brands and then they create a product image more consistent

with the perceived self-image of the targeted consumer segment.

- Brand equity refers to the marketing effects or outcomes that accrue to a product with its brand name, compared to those that would accrue if the same product did not have the brand name.
- The emphasis of the various studies done on destination branding and the models has been to understand the techniques that can be adopted by a destination marketer to differentiate a destination from other competing destinations, which can easily act as substitutes. A marketer has to understand that he cannot have much control over the contributory elements of the place and so he should select the appropriate branding strategy.
- Brand performance can be measured by taking a survey among the past and potential tourists for the various parameters and the resulting characteristics of the destination in the order of preference can be derived.
- A brand is not a once for all construction, but the aim of a constant effort to reconstruct the added value.

FIELD EXERCISES

1. Visit the official Web site of Switzerland tourism (www.myswitzerland.com) and find how it is different from a traditional product Web site?
2. Find out the world's most favourite tourist destination and figure out how it has been established as a brand.

REFERENCES

Cai, L. (2002), "Cooperative Branding for Rural Destinations," *Annals of Tourism Research*, Vol. 29, pp. 720–742

Ekinci, Yuksel and Sameer Hosany (2006), "Destination Personality: An Application of Brand Personality to Tourism Destinations," *Journal of Travel Research*, Vol. 45, p. 127

Hankinson, Graham (2004) "Relational Network Brands: Towards a Conceptual Model of Place Brands. "*Journal of Vacation Marketing*, Vol. 10, No.2, pp. 109–21

Jackie Clarke (2000), "Tourism brands: An Exploratory Study of the Brands Box Model," *Journal of Vacation Marketing*, Vol. 6, No. 4. pp. 329–345

Sirgy, M. and C. Su (2000), "Destination Image, Self Congruity, and Travel Behaviour: Toward an Integrative Model," *Journal of Travel Research*, Vol. 38, May, pp. 340–352

Sleipen, W. (1988), "Marketing van de Historische Omgeving," Research Institute for Tourism, Breda, Netherlands,

Park, Sun-Young, James F. Petrick (2006), "Destinations' Perspectives of Branding," *Annals of Tourism Research*, Vol. 33, No. 1, pp. 262–265

Pritchard, Annette, Nigel Morgan (1998) , "Mood marketing'—The new destination branding strategy: A case study of 'Wales' The Brand," *Journal of Vacation Marketing*, Vol. 4, No. 3, pp. 215–229

Van Den Bergh and E. L. Braun, (1999), "Urban Competitiveness, Marketing and the Need for Organising Capacity," *Urban Studies*, Vol. 36, pp. 987–999

Walker R.H., and D.J. Hanson, (1998), "Green Marketing and Green Places: A Taxonomy for the Destination Marketer," *Journal of Mark eting Management*, Vol. 14, pp. 623–639

Woodside A G, and S. Lysonski. (1989), "A General Model of Traveller Destination Choice," *Journal of Travel Research*,Vol. 27 No. 4, pp. 8–14

Stonehenge, Wiltshire

CHAPTER 12

Information and Communication Technology in Tourism Marketing

ABOUT THE DESTINATION

One of England's greatest national icons symbolizing mystery, power and endurance, it is composed of earthworks surrounding a circular setting of large standing stones. The purpose of this monument has remained a mystery although several theories have been proposed by archaeologists.

OBJECTIVES

- To understand the categories in tourism ICT
- To understand the channel linkage of information and communication technology with tourism
- To understand the key role of an e-community in tourism marketing
- To visualize benchmarking factors which can be used for evaluating tourism promotion Web sites

INTRODUCTION

As the world is being ushered into the information age, adoption of the information and communication technology (ICT) is rapidly increasing. The Internet has transformed the world into a global village that can be navigated at the click of a mouse. It provides potential tourists with immediate access to textual and visual conformation on destinations throughout the world. The Internet has also become an essential tool in business to business (B2B) and business to consumer (B2C) transactions, the distribution of products, networking of business partners and is an instantaneous means of accessing knowledge on all kinds of subjects including travel and tourism information. The Internet can be accessed through mobile telephones, cable television, fixed telephones using traditional personal computers and laptops. Information is readily available 24/7, and the resulting cost transparency enables consumers to make more informed choices (Sinha, 2000). This ease of access and depth of information have stimulated the emergence of a new breed of travel consumers who are independent and prefer to search for holidays themselves online, rather than through travel agents. And the majority of the people connected to the Internet happen to be from the world's top three tourism spending markets – Germany, the United States and UK. The Internet is already the primary source of tourist destination information in these major markets. It has outpaced traditional sources of information on tourist destinations within the short period of its existence. Its audiovisual presentation of information on destinations outdoes the glossiest and most colourful print, and the quality of the presentation plays a decisive role in the end-consumer's choice of one destination over another.

The Internet also offers tourism destination and businesses the means to make information and booking facilities available to millions of consumers around the world at a relatively low cost, while at the same time enabling them to cut down drastically on amounts invested in the production and distribution of promotional materials. Travel and tourism are fast becoming the largest category of products sold on the Internet, which must therefore be seen as the new marketing battlefronts for tourism destinations in Asia-Pacific. Apart from the Internet, technological advances gave rise to other electronic distribution platforms such as interactive satellite television and mobile devices. The expected proliferation of satellite TV and m-commerce will gradually intensify competition among intermediaries who will have to reengineer their business processes and evolve new business models in order to survive and remain competitive (Buhalis & Licata, 2002)

ROLE OF INFORMATION AND COMMUNICATION TECHNOLOGY (ICT) IN TOURISM

With the increasing acceptance of e-commerce as a primary medium for business, information and communication technology (ICT), in general, and Web sites, in particular, have become inevitable for all business entities. ICT can be considered to have broadly four different categories of services. They are

- Web site
- Mobile communication
- Smart cards
- Management information system (MIS)

Applications of ICT in Various Activities in Tourism

1. Selecting and developing tourism site	Geospatial information technologies
2. Marketing	Inbound (market research), outbound (advertising, promotions, etc.)
3. Customer relationship management	Home–destination–home Turn prospects into customers Book-travel-lodging-tours-miscellaneous Trip management: Pre-during-post
4. Operations	Buying managing services and supplies Managing value chain
5. Managing and monitoring tourism site	GIS, GPS

Web Site

While we shall give a brief description of each of these components in this section, primarily we will be concentrating on the Web site as we believe it is the most important ICT tool a company can have. In the Internet age, it is imperative for all the companies to have a Web site of their own. It is not only an aesthetic accessory but also a significant medium for carrying out their businesses. A Web site, today, forms the basis of a bulk of the marketing campaigns of the company and, thus, is the primary source of attracting consumers worldwide to the company's products.

Thus, it is prudent for any business entity to spend appropriate time and efforts in building an effective Web site. In order for a company's site to be effective, it needs to have the following features:

- Viewers should be able to find the site easily
- Viewers should be able to navigate through the site conveniently
- Viewers must be able to extract relevant information with ease
- Viewers must attach appropriate credibility with the site

Though a lot of these points overlap each other, these essentially ensure that a Web site effectively serves its purpose. Let us now take each of the points individually.

Viewers Should be Able to Find the Site Easily. Most of the people find a Web site through a search engine. While it is a commonly accepted myth that once a site is built it will figure in the search engine's results, the truth is far from it. The possibility of a site figuring in the search results is a function of the traffic that the site receives. An effective means to manage and develop the traffic on one's site is to use search engine optimization (SEO).

Viewers Should be Able to Navigate Through the Site Conveniently. A Web site should be properly structured so as to give viewers a clear idea as to where they can find the relevant information. The layout of the site should be in sync with the purpose it intends to serve. There is a possibility that a majority of the viewers in our country do not use high-speed broadband connection. Hence, the site graphics should not be too heavy so as to make the site run slowly. Information display should be clear enough to make things easy for someone with vision impairment.

Viewers Must be Able to Extract Relevant Information with Ease. A Web site has to be usable to its viewers. More than 83 per cent of the viewers are likely to leave a Web site if they do not find it easy to extract relevant information (Arthur Anderson). More than 58 per cent of the viewers who find navigation problems with a site do not come back to it (Forrester Research).

Viewers Must Attach Appropriate Credibility with the Site. Once the company has ensured that viewers visit its site, it needs to also ensure that the viewers stay on the site. Users are unlikely to stay on a site if they do not find it credible (Stanford-Makovsky, 2002). More than 46 per cent of the credibility that a site earns comes from its overall design (Stanford-Makovsky, 2002). The same study goes on to say that information design and structure amount to almost 28 per cent of the credibility earned by the site.

While all of the above-mentioned pointers hold value for any commercial site, their significance increases manifold when it comes to tourism sites. This is because most of the times, a potential tourist has very few sources of information about the concerned location. One of these and an important one at that is the destination's Web site. Moreover, if the tourist is not satisfied with the Web site, there is a high chance that he/she will shift to some other location. Thus, Web site holds a crucial role in tourism marketing.

Mobile Communication

Another important ICT tool is the mobile phone, which has facilitated convenient communication media and information database in all possible corners of the world. Mobile communication is increasingly becoming a significant medium of communication for modern businesses. Companies market their products/services via SMSs, confirm receipt of payment via the same or provide various other services through the mobile phone.

Smart Cards

Smart cards are basically an advanced version of what we understand as plastic money. A smart card is primarily a convenience tool that gives you the liberty to use only one piece as the payment medium for all your purchases. Especially for an international tourist, such facilities become supremely important as there is a limit on the foreign currency that a tourist can carry. It also brings convenience in petty purchases like tickets for intra-city transport and entry tickets for various parks/monuments/museums/other amusement activities in the city. Thus, by using ICT to provide such facilities, destinations can attract tourists. This is why smart cards are believed to be an important ICT tool today.

Management Information System (MIS)

As the name suggests, MIS is primarily an information database that helps the consumer (the potential tourist in this case) scan through scores of tourist destinations and choose the one that gives the maximum value to him. A well-built MIS can work wonders as far as the marketing of a destination is concerned.

ICT AND TOURISM MARKETING: INFINITE AVENUES FOR GROWTH

Information and communication technology is fast becoming the buzzword of the day when it comes to the tourism industry. Entities are finding more and more innovative means of using various ICT tools such as the Internet and other PC-based facilities in providing a higher order of convenience to the consumers.

In the cut-throat competition of today, business entities are looking for ways to provide more value to the consumer. One of the best ways to do so is to increase the convenience of purchase and use of one's product/service by effective application of ICT tools such as the Web site.

Broadly, we shall try to cover the following aspects in this chapter through the next three sections:

- Key trends for the use of ICT, in general, and for tourism, in particular
- Key roles for ICT/e-business in destination marketing and tourism
- Specimens of good ICT applications in India and worldwide

KEY TRENDS FOR USE OF ICT

In this section, we focus on some significant trends that have been observed in the past few years. This will set the stage for all our further discussion pertaining to ICT and destination marketing. Let us have a look at some charts.

As is clearly evident from Figures 12.1 and 12.2, Internet user population has grown exponentially in the last decade, notably so in the Asia-Pacific region. This shows the importance of ICT in marketing campaigns for all industries, in general, and the tourism industry, in particular.

Not only are the number of Internet users increasing, the number of potential tourists going through the Web site of a particular destination before planning a visit have also increased significantly. Gone are the days when people used to seek opinions of acquaintances in choosing a destination for their vacation (Figure 12.3).

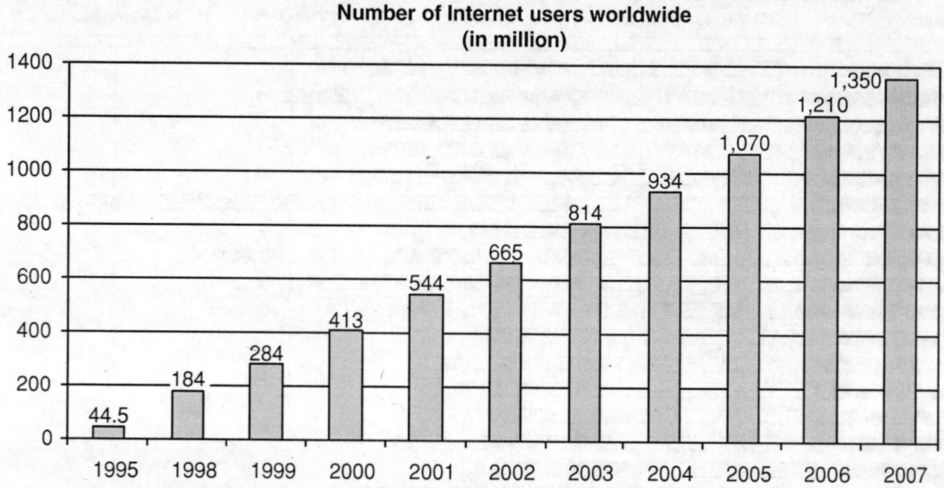

Source: Computer Industry Almanac; December 2002.

Fig. 12.1: Number of Internet Users Worldwide

Keeping in mind these trends, it becomes all the more essential that one spends a substantial amount of time and efforts on the destination's Web site. This shows that the first step towards the selection of a tourist destination for a majority of consumers is visiting the Web site of the destination. Hence, it is essential to keep in mind the points mentioned in the first section while making a site.

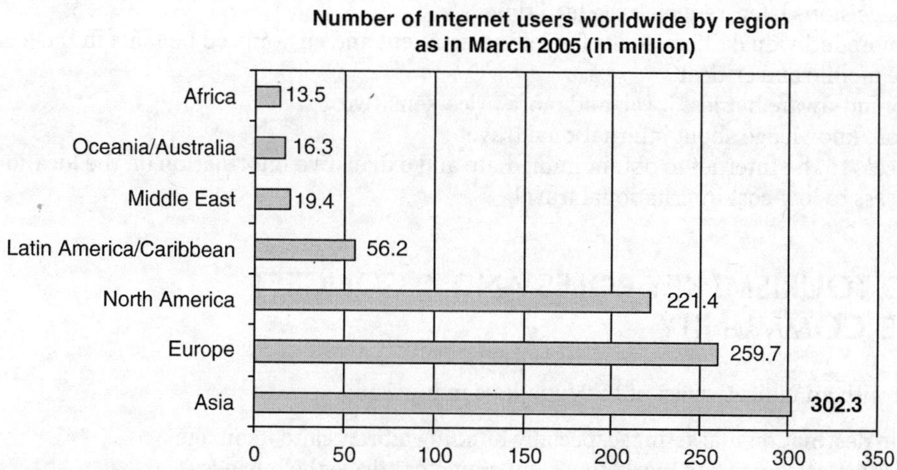

Source: Internet World Stats, March 2005.

Fig. 12.2: Number of Internet Users Worldwide by Region

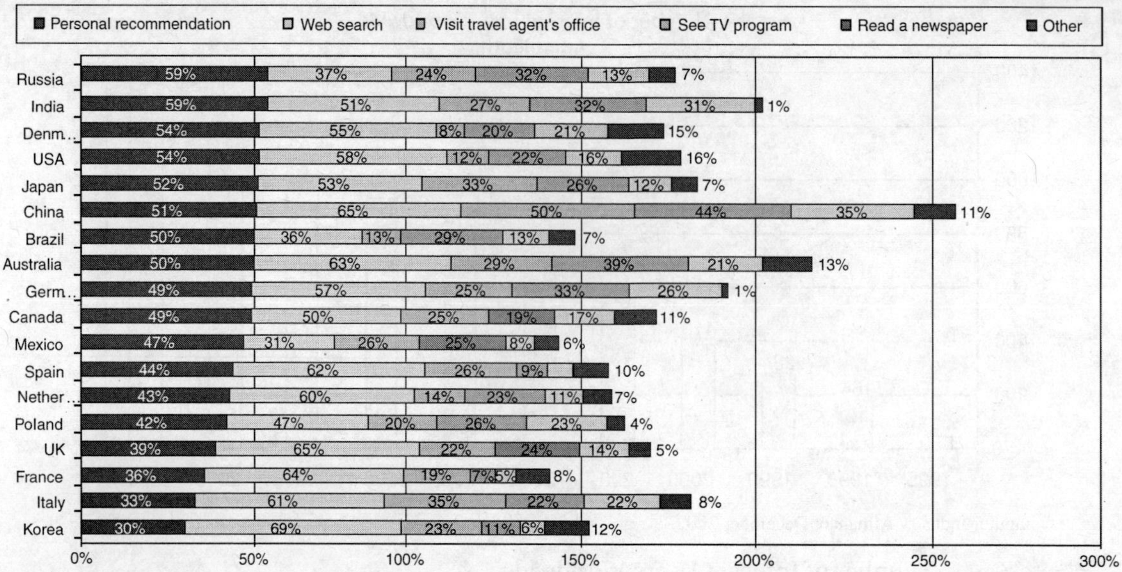

Source: Global Market Insight (GMI) survey, June 2005.

Fig. 12.3: Sources of Information for Tourist Destination Selection

In addition to the Web sites, tourists also indulge in online booking through various agencies. Figure 12.4 gives a clear indication of the same.

To sum it up, we can mark out the changes in consumer behaviour in the context of the tourism industry in the following manner:

- Consumer today takes shorter holidays and with greater frequency
- Makes decisions later, reducing the lead time
- Seeks more individual offers, looks for self-enrichment and customized benefits in the location
- Is more mobile and critical
- More brand-aware but less loyal, and more price-sensitive
- Has more knowledge about international travel
- Has access to the Internet to obtain immediate and exhaustive information on the location
- Has access to low-cost international travel

ICT AND TOURISM: KEY ROLES AND A CONCEPT OF AN E-COMMUNITY

Let us start with an indicative list of ICT functions in tourism:

- Helps in destination marketing, especially building a brand and its image
- Provides a platform to run marketing campaigns that drive the business
- Its a medium of providing unbiased information to the consumer
- Facilitates the operations of booking transportation and accommodation with ease
- Destination coordination and management to ensure the quality of experience of tourists

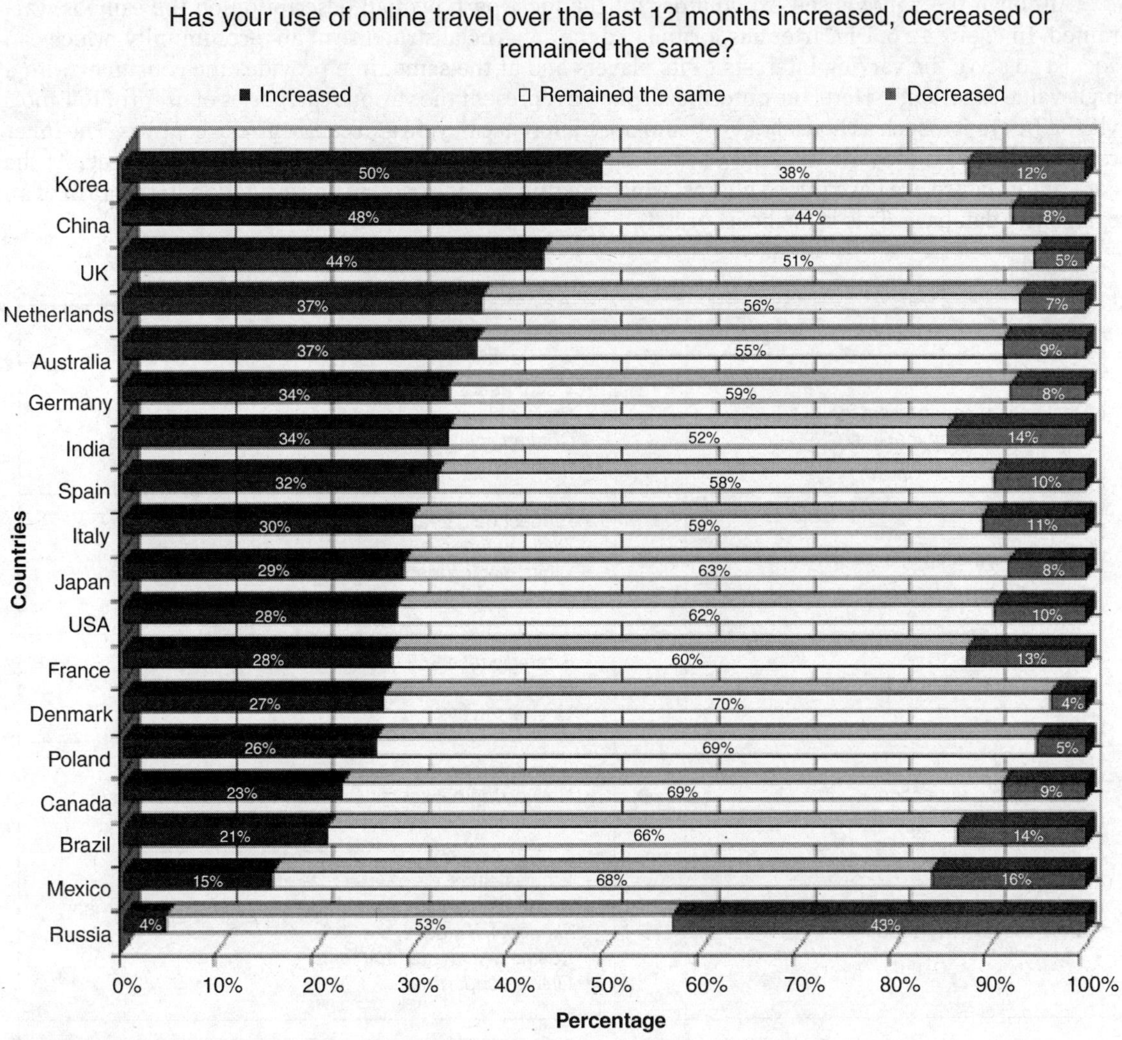

Source: Global Market Insight (GMI) survey, June 2005.

Fig. 12.4: Status of Online Travel Bookings by Tourists of Different Countries

- Visitor information and reservations for accommodation and various activities
- Event management and development

Figure 12.5 sums up the needs of a modern tourist and his/her linkages with ICT.

The destination represents the focal point of all the players in tourism whose interests are interdependent – government, residents, suppliers, carriers, major corporations, intermediaries and consumers. One of the core functions of ICT in destination marketing is to bring together all of them to ensure a meaningful experience to the consumer. The ICT tools provide key media for all these players to participate in a unified effort for destination marketing and branding. A symbolic representation of the destination e-community as described here is shown in Figure 12.6.

Although the figure is self-explanatory for the most part, a small description on the same is warranted. In Figure 12.6, Dr Carter has formulated the superficial structure of an e-community, which can coexist to serve the varying interests of its players and at the same time provides the consumer with a high-value experience. Here, the outermost spheres represent the various categories of users of ICT tools via the Internet – such as household consumers, conference buyers and call-centre executives. The inner rounds of spheres indicate the kind of information that these consumers would intend to seek. At the core of this figure, we have three spheres, which contain all the concerned information in the form of an exhaustive database. This is the heart of ICT.

Function		e-Business supported activity
Destination management for visitor 'quality of experience'	➔	• Visitor needs/ satisfaction research • Project planning/ management • Communication network for destination partnership • Problem alert system
Visitor information and reservations	➔	• Product data search and presentation • Reservations • Digital audio/video guides • Information centre management
Strategy, research and development	➔	• Strategic research, including impact assessment • Evaluation • Online surveys
Training and education	➔	• Distance learning • Networking between institutions to share resources • Practitioner input
Business advice / support	➔	• E-newsletters • Knowledge bank–research, plans, case studies, advisory handbooks/ videos, etc • Business management tools • Online support
Product 'start-ups'	➔	• Business planning tools, case studies, knowledge bank (as above) • Start-up online advisory support, including financial advice
Events development and management	➔	• Market analysis • Project planning and management • e-Marketing • Business management tools • Online support
Attractions development and management	➔	• Market analysis • e-Marketing • Business management tools • Online support

Fig. 12.5: The Needs of a Modern Tourist and Linkages with ICT

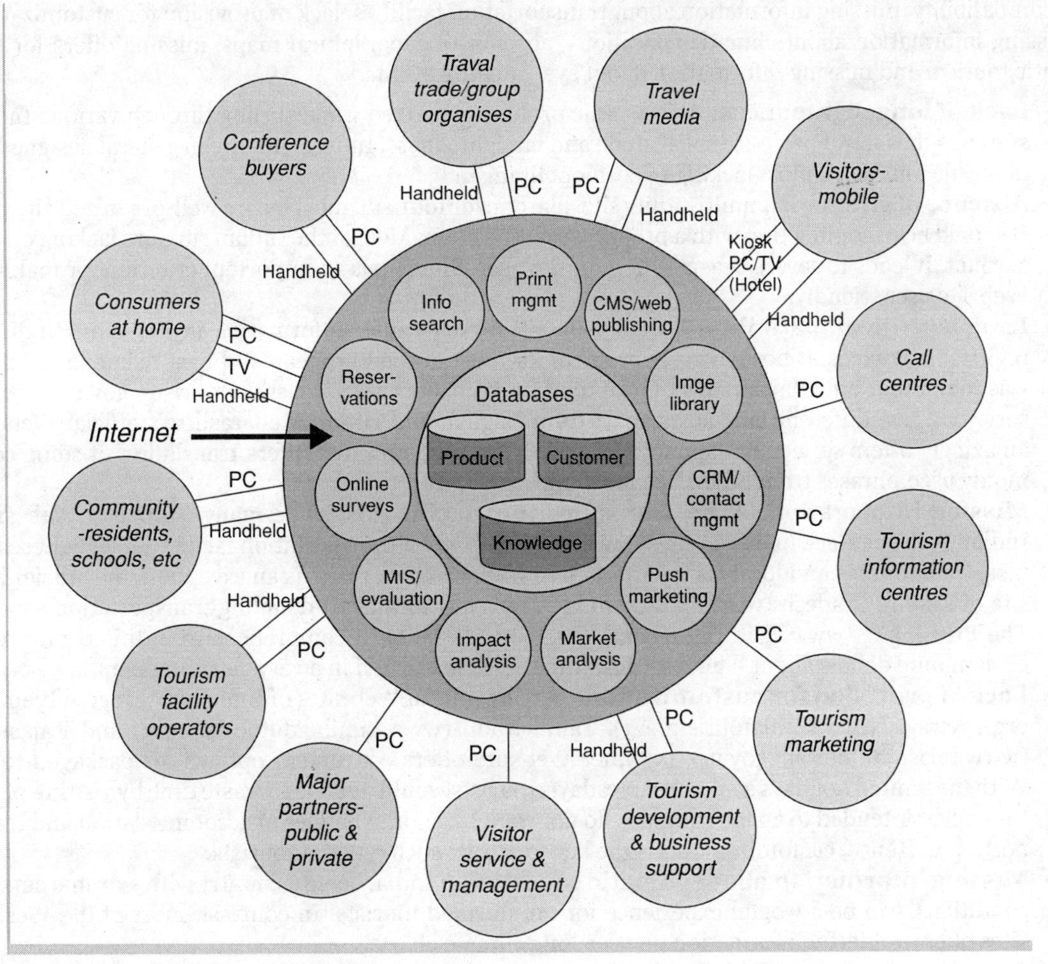

Source: Dr Roger Carter, UN Affiliate, June 2005.

Fig. 12.6: Symbolic Representation of the Destination e-Community

Comparison of Indian Tourism Web Sites with Their Global Counterparts

Here, we shall try to give an Indian perspective to the discussion and assess the avenues for improvisation in various tourism Web sites in India.

The Andaman and Nicobar Islands Web site (http://tourism.andaman.nic.in) received "the best Web site award for tourism" in 2007. Apart from catchy colours and vivid animation, it provides a searcher with all details starting from the history of the place to basic travel tips. Every link provides contact information and special features that an enthusiast can look for in Andaman. The photo gallery and the video gallery are marvellously organized to give a peek into the beautiful world underwater.

While the above-mentioned is an example of a well-built Web site, there are quite a few shortcomings in the Indian tourism infrastructure. They are lack of long-sightedness, absence of sitemap, language incompatibility, missing information about transportation facilities, lack of provision for customization, missing information about climatic conditions, absence of geographical maps, missing offers for thematic tourism and missing information about eye-catching events.

- **Lack of long-sightedness:** A very basic problem observed while surfing through various Indian sites was the lack of professional attitude and farsightedness. Indian sites are in general designed for domestic tourists, almost lacking in cosmopolitanism.
- **Absence of sitemap:** A multi-utility site, like one for tourism, must have a well-organized sitemap. It should be in conjunction with a proper "search" option. Most of the Indian sites are lacking on this account. It leads to severe exasperation for the user. Sitemap is an important criterion for making a Web site user friendly.
- **Language incompatibility:** Indian Web sites mostly offer information in English, Hindi and regional languages. It poses a great problem for most of the European and East Asian nationals. It was found that only Rajasthan's official tourism Web site (www.rajasthantourism. gov.in) – offers service in five different languages apart from English and Hindi. Maharashtra's official Web site amazingly offers service in Japanese as well. It has one link that offers translation of some commonly used phrases from English to Marathi.
- **Missing information about transportation facilities:** Unlike many European Web sites, Indian Web sites lack in providing detailed information on transportation facilities like flight schedules, train timings and local transportation. In what can be termed as an exception, the official Web site of Andhra Pradesh (www.aptourism.in) displays a nice chart detailing transportation aspects. The British site (www.visitbritain.com) was found to be most comprehensive in this regard, with even minute details about flights, trains, trams, etc., presented in a very clear manner.
- **Lack of provision for customization:** Barring official Web sites of India (www.incredibleindia. org), Kerala (www.keralatourism.org), Tamil Nadu (www.tamilnadutourism.org) and Rajasthan (www.rajasthantourism.gov.in), no other Web site offers convenient options for packaged tours. With the limited holidays available nowadays, tourists would not like to waste time by visiting places they never intended to go to. They also do not want to get into hassles of accommodation and transportation. Hence, customized tour is the key to attract such types of tourists.
- **Missing information about climatic conditions:** India, being a country with extreme climatic conditions, can be a woeful experience for uninformed tourists. In contrast, most of the Western sites offer wonderful information on year-long climate charts.
- **Absence of geographical maps:** These maps can be a great help for someone coming to India for the first time. The Japanese Web site (www.jnto.go.jp) offers an animated country map that can be used for various purposes such as distance estimation, finding rail routes and understanding area topology. Similar is the case with the German Web site (www.germanytourism.de)
- **Missing offers for thematic tourism:** This is an almost invariable feature of all the European sites and is, perhaps, a higher state of customization. It helps a potential tourist to clearly identify his reason to travel. He can decide which specific facet of the particular country he wishes to experience. For example, the French Web site (www.franceguide.com) offers tourism in different sectors, viz. health and fitness, folk, new millennium and adventure. Hence, a person can choose immediately according to his predilections.
- **Missing information about eye-catching events:** European Web sites present up-to-date information about forthcoming cultural, religious and adventurous events such as rose show, canoeing, skiing, annual chocolate competition and opera. This information is always put up on the home page with eye-catching invitations and punch lines. A few remarkable Web sites are those of the United States (www.usatourism.ca), Italy (www.en.cnta.gov. in) and Canada (www.canadatourism.ca). The Chinese Web site (www.en.cnta.gov.in) has also leveraged well on the country's rich cultural diversity. This information can help in attracting enthusiastic tourists throughout the year and can sustain demand even during lean periods.

Unsung Tourist Destination: Chitrakot (Chhattisgarh)

Chitrakot waterfall is located at a distance of 38 km to the west of Jagdalpur, which is about 350 km from the state capital Raipur. The approximate height of the waterfall is 100 feet. The maximum width during rainy season is around 1,000 feet. The rainbow colours of Chitrakot waterfall have all the capacity to mesmerize tourists at the very first sight. So, Chitrakot waterfall could become the prime attraction for tourists. Its water looks muddy brown in rainy season due to high laterite contents in the soil. This, in a way, is a contrast to the Jog falls, which has water that looks white during monsoon.

Chitrakot is worth a watch especially in the rainy season, between the months of July and October. Tourists can also enjoy the beauty of Chitrakot waterfall at night because it is one of the few such natural features in the country to be floodlit. Chitrakot is also considered as mini Niagra Fall because of its horseshoe shape.

Chitrakot Waterfall: A Potential Tourist Destination

The Bastar region of Chhattisgarh state, with its picturesque valleys, green forests, caves and spectacular waterfalls, is an untapped destination for tourists. Bastar, a region populated largely by tribals, has a rich cultural heritage that dates back to prehistoric times. The people of Bastar plateau, criss-crossed by rivers such as Indravati, Sabari, Kholab and Mahanadi, proudly tell stories of the rise and fall of numerous kingdoms, some dating back to the time of the Hindu God Rama. Tiratgarh waterfall, Danteshwari temple, Bastar palace, Kanger Valley National Park and Kutumsar and Kailash caves are other tourist attractions in the area. The landscape is dotted with caves, and Bastar is also a geologist's dream-come-true, as rocks in the region are said to be 3,000–3,300 million years old. The region has vast deposits of iron, tin, granite, uranium and even diamonds.

Chitrakot Waterfall

Hurdles on the way to Prominence

As already discussed, Chitrakot waterfall has all the potential to become a widely accepted tourist destination due to its uniqueness. However, before accomplishing that, certain impediments will have to be removed:

- Connectivity is a major issue as the region is not connected to any rail link. NH-49 serves as the only connectivity up to Jagdalpur, a nearby small town. The closest metropolitan is Raipur, which is about 350 km away. The only mode of transportation is bus, which is inconvenient and unreliable.
- Proper tourism infrastructure is lacking in the region. There are a few government lodges and these are allotted on first-come-first-serve basis. Also, getting quality food is a big problem.
- Tourism and shopping go hand-in-hand, but these resources are yet to be harnessed here. Bastar region is well known for its exquisite handicrafts, which are displayed in many national and international fairs. There should be proper marketing for it.
- Then, there is the problem of Naxalism – a problem that is perhaps the root cause of all the other ones mentioned above. Until and unless a region is socially stable, it cannot be developed on any dimension. But one thing is for sure: the regional development (absence of which is the purported cause for internal violence) can have a curative effect on this problem. The onus lies with both the centre and state governments.

SUMMARY

This chapter introduces one of the latest ways of tourism marketing – the usage of information and communication technology. There are several avenues ranging from Web sites and mobiles to smart cards that are used by tourism departments to provide customers with hassle-free tours. With the advent of globalization and the proliferation of technology, the number of people using ICT as a platform to make decisions on tourist spots and availing of its features has been on the rise. Although the increased number of ICT users is predominantly from developed countries, others are also catching up. The chapter also discusses certain features on which Indian Web sites (the main element in ICT marketing) are are still lacking in comparison to foreign counterparts. Lastly, this chapter endorses Chitrakot as one of the sites worth seeing for any tourism enthusiast.

FIELD EXERCISES

1. Visit official tourism Web site of India and Singapore and figure out the differences on basis of appearance and effectiveness from a tourist's perspective.
2. Search the Internet for information about Chitrakot as a tourist destination and prepare a report on relevance and effectiveness of information for tourists.

REFERENCES

Fodor, Oliver, Hannes Werthner (2004) "Harmonise: A Step Toward an Interoperable E-Tourism Marketplace," *International Journal of Electronic Commerce*, Vol. 9, No. 2, pp. 11–39

Fogg, B.J., T. Kameda, J. Boyd, J. Marshall, R. Sethi, M. Sockol and T. Trowbridge (2002) "Stanford-Makovsky Web Credibility Study 2002: Investigating what makes Web sites credible today." A Research Report by the Stanford Persuasive Technology Lab & Makovsky & Company Stanford University

Sinha, Manoj Kumar and Satish A.V. (2000). Recent advances in information technology and its application in library and information services: an appraisal. In Excellence in information technology: Dr. S.P. Sood testschrift volume (Eds. Vyas, S.D. Usha Pawan and Swain, N.K.) Raj Publishing House, Jaipur, p. 269

Stockdale, Rosemary (2007), "Managing Customer Relationships in the Self-Service Environment of E-Tourism," *Journal of Vacation Marketing*, Vol. 13, pp. 205

Web Sites

http://www.forrester.com/rb/research

http://tourism.andaman.nic.in/

http://www.aptourism.in/

http://www.visitbritain.com/

http://www.incredibleindia.org/index.html

http://www.keralatourism.org/

http://www.tamilnadutourism.org/

http://www.rajasthantourism.gov.in/

http://www.jnto.go.jp/

http://www.germany-tourism.de/

http://us.franceguide.com/

http://www.usatourism.com/

http://www.canadatourism.ca/

CHAPTER 13

Tourism Marketing: Planning, Implementation and Control — A Holistic Approach

Pyramids & Sphinx, Giza

ABOUT THE DESTINATION

They have fascinated travellers and conquerors in ancient times and continue to inspire wonder in tourists, mathematicians and archaeologists. They are a brilliant evidence of the architectural and technical capabilities of the Egyptian civilization.

OBJECTIVES

- To understand tourism marketing at a macro-level
- To learn how to develop a business vision and mission in tourism
- To understand the extended marketing mix
- To understand marketing strategy formulation and role of planning in tourism marketing.

INTRODUCTION TO TOURISM MARKETING

Tourism emerged as the largest global industry of the 20th century and is projected to grow even faster in the 21st century. For India, since the opening up of the economy in 1991, the government has advanced several incentives to promote infrastructural growth in the tourism sector. India has significant potential for becoming a major global tourist destination. Travel and tourism industry is the second highest foreign-exchange earner for India, and the government has given export-house status to organizations in this industry. The industry is waking up to the potential of domestic tourism as well, with an estimated 4.7 billion domestic trips in 2001. Tourism spending within India in 2001 was US$ 22 billion. There is considerable government presence in the travel and tourism industry. Each state has a tourism corporation, which typically runs a chain of hotels/motels and operates package tours, while the central government runs the India Tourism Development Corporation (ITDC). Divestment of these state-run tourism corporations has either already taken place or is in process. Incoming foreign tourist arrivals have shown a 6 per cent compounded annual growth rate over the last 10 years. Current investments are likely to see hotel room capacity increase by 20 per cent over the next 3 years, with several international hotel chains entering the industry. Similar growth is anticipated in air-travel capacity (Source: *http:// meaindia.nic.in/ indiapublication/Tourism.htm*).

India has immense possibilities of growth in the tourism sector with its vast cultural and religious heritage and varied natural attractions, but, so far, the country has only found a comparatively small role in the world tourism scene. From this standpoint, India should have been a tourism haven as the country is blessed with destinations and products catering to the tastes and preferences of tourists and travellers of all ages and economic backgrounds. There is no doubt that tourism, frequently referred to as "the world's largest industry," is big business. Tourism is, without doubt, one of the major social and economic phenomena of modern times.

Tourism is primarily a services-based industry – the principal products provided by tourism businesses are experiences and hospitality. These are intangible products and more difficult to market than tangible products such as cars. The intangible nature of services makes quality control difficult but crucial. It also makes it more difficult for potential customers to evaluate and compare service offerings. But as long as the inherent sense of curiosity and adventure dwells in the hearts of human beings, the desire to travel and experience new things under different environments will grow. In addition, instead of the product moving to the customer, the customer must travel to the product, that is, the area and/or the community.

The last few years have seen considerable growth in India's tourism and hospitality sector. Driven by a surge in business traveller arrivals and a soaring interest in India as a tourist destination, 2006 turned out to be the most productive year till then. India is probably the only country that offers various categories of tourism. These include history tourism, adventure tourism, medical tourism (ayurveda and other forms of Indian medications), spiritual tourism and beach tourism (India has the longest coastline along the east). Thus, there is a need for establishing a strong business relationship between the ministry of tourism and the tourism industry.

In the following sections, we shall try to cover the major aspects of tourism marketing principles that include strategy, micro-environment, prevailing market environment, tourism potential in India; and planning, implementation and control aspects and we will take up a case study on tourism marketing.

STRATEGIC CONTEXT

Corporate Vision

Corporate vision is a short, succinct and inspiring statement of what the organization intends to become and achieve at some point in the future, often stated in competitive terms. Vision refers to the category of intentions that are broad, all-inclusive and forward thinking. It is the image that a business must have of its goals before it sets out to reach them. It describes aspirations for the future, without specifying the means that will be used to achieve those desired ends. It should contain commitments to create value for customers and a new experience and a brand for the tourism organization as a whole.

Corporate statements of a few top companies are:

- **GE:** We bring good things to life
- **Ford:** To become the world's leading consumer company for automotive products and services
- **Microsoft:** To enable people and businesses throughout the world to realize their potential

Along these lines, the tourism vision statement can be: "To give people a unique experience so that they visit us again and again and have us as their first choice for their holiday dreams."

Corporate Mission

The overall goal of an organization, often called its mission, is the reason for its existence. A mission statement is an organization's vision translated into written form. The mission describes the organization's vision, its shared values and beliefs and its reason for being. In other words, it is nothing but the organization's official goal. The primary purpose of a mission statement is to serve as a communication tool. It should represent the combinations of purpose, strategy, values and behavioural standards of an organization and incorporate the core tasks an organization intends to carry out in order to achieve the corporate purpose within the constraints of corporate vision. According to Kotler, an organization's mission statement should include reference to industry scope, its breadth of products and applications, its core competence and its market segment.

For an organization in the tourism industry, the corporate mission should be to provide industry leadership locally, create awareness of the value of tourism within the community and facilitate a unique experience and a royal treatment for the customers, which they will cherish throughout their lifetime.

Here are some mission statements of international tourism companies:

- **The Puerto Rico Tourism Company:** "Our mission is to set the standard of excellence with the implementation of our world-class tourism policy through the commitment of our people to pursue the common goal of making Puerto Rico the first choice for world travellers and business in the Caribbean."
- **Tourism Malaysia:** "Marketing Malaysia as a destination of excellence and to make the tourism industry a major contributor to the socio-economic development of the nation."
- **Ecotourism Australia:** The association's mission is about growing, consolidating and promoting ecotourism, and other committed tourism operations to become more sustainable, through approaches such as
    - developing and adopting standards for sustainable practices
    - increasing professionalism among those working within the tourism industry
    - streamlining policies and processes that have in the past complicated operations in protected areas
    - assisting operators to improve the quality of interpretation offered about the places they visit
    - improving positioning and financial viability for operators who adopt sustainable practices
    - contributing to conservation solutions and projects; involving and providing benefits to local communities
    - marketing the principles of sustainability to increase awareness across the tourism industry

Corporate Goals and Objectives

A corporate goal can be what an organization plans for a longer time range, aiming for a specific period. It is not mentioned in the corporate mission. It reflects the reason for the organization's existence, and its activities should be directed to the achievement of this goal/purpose. It ought to set strategic planning to perform activities that ensure reaching the goals through operational planning.

Corporate goals provide guidance about the operations to the management of the tourism organization. Objectives set out more specifically the goals of the tourism organization. According to Copper et al. (1998), objectives need to be SMART, which means they are

- Specific, in that they should be focused on the results required
- Measurable for each objective set
- Achievable, in that they are set against trends and market position constraints are assessed fully
- Realistic, by taking into consideration the given resource constraints of time, money and personnel
- Time-specific, in that targets are set as to when the objectives should be met

ANALYSIS OF THE TOURISM ENVIRONMENT

As a precursor to planning for tourism marketing, it is necessary to assess the prevailing environment as it is dynamic and affects and guides future actions. Formulation of tourism marketing plans would be governed by the hierarchical level of the organization envisaging these plans. If the planning is being carried out at the national level, the market environment that needs to be analysed would

Box 1: Few Strategic Questions to Ponder

While formulating the overall strategy, questions that may come to mind are

- What is the status of the existing industry?
- What is the unexplored potential?
- What are the developed tourist destinations around?
- What is the status of the socio-economic infrastructure in the area?
- What will be the benefits to the local economy after implementation of these plans?
- What are the environmental issues specific to the region?
- What are the expansion possibilities for the industry that the region provides?

stretch beyond the country's boundaries, while that at the state or local levels would envisage developing regional areas and ensuring their synchronization with the overall national-level plans (Box 1). For business entities, this planning would be further limited to their areas of interest, kind of competition in that region, category of clientele they are targeting and the requirement of infrastructure for implementation of the plan.

Strategic/Macro-Environment

The Petronas Towers in Kuala Lumpur, Malaysia

Tourism has a far wider range of direct and indirect impacts than other economic sectors. At its simplest, tourism can be seen to be a temporary addition to the population of a given location, with tourists having all the needs and impacts that the permanent population does. Tourism activity involves direct contact with the local population. Government planning, regulation, etc., are therefore needed; yet, tourism is an economic activity executed by the private sector. Tourism, then, involves a triumvirate of destination interests: state, private sector and community. As such, tourism planning for development and marketing is unlike any other economic sector and requires special approaches, procedures and institutions.

For marketing purposes, strategic planning is the process by which an organization first analyses its strengths and weaknesses in its current and prospective markets – "where are we now?"; second, identifies its aims and the opportunities it seeks to develop – "where do we want to get to?" and third, defines the strategies and programmes of activity to achieve these aims – "how do we get there?." Strategic decisions are always focused on the longer run. For example, Malaysia has consciously developed its infrastructure, designed to match the modern tourist destination it is developing into.

Marketing strategy is designed to produce future sales revenue through the specification of market segments to be targeted, products to be developed and focused on and associated action programmes to realize the potential identified in these targeted product and market segments. Business strategy is not only about marketing; all strategy for a commercial organization depends on its ability to persuade sufficient customers to buy enough of its products to secure a surplus of revenue over costs in the long run and to produce customer satisfaction. The key components of marketing strategy are goals and objectives, images, positioning and branding, strategies and programmes, budget and review and evaluation.

- **Goals and objectives:** The position or place in its chosen markets that an organization seeks to occupy in a future period, defined in terms of sectors of business, target market segments, sales volume, product range, market shares and levels of profit
- **Images, positioning and branding:** Where the organization wants to be in terms of the market's (trade and consumer) perceptions of its products and values, including image and branding in relation to competitors
- **Strategies and programmes:** The specification of actions, including product development and investment, needed to achieve the goals and objectives set
- **Budget:** What resources (human, technical and financial) are required to realize the goals
- **Review and evaluation:** Procedures and systems permitting the appraisal of the extent to which goals were met in the context of overall market conditions and external factors

If we look at the emerging tourist markets in the Asia Pacific region, we find that the major destinations such as Thailand, Malaysia, Singapore, Dubai and Sri Lanka are developing their tourist industry based on their core potential and competencies. They have a targeted approach towards the international tourists they would like to attract. While Thailand has its culture, beaches and leisure industry at the core of its tourism programmes, Sri Lanka's tourist attractions are its lush-green tea gardens, beaches and lagoons. Malaysia, in addition to its serene beaches and islands, is developing infrastructure that is equivalent to the best in the world. It is also developing other tourist avenues such as adventure sports, resorts, water sports, theme parks and shopping festivals that provide ample options to the international tourists in terms of enjoyment and leisure activities. Singapore and Dubai have crafted their USP in terms of man-made attractions for tourists, and, of course, their famous shopping festivals add to the overall charm of visiting those countries. Coupled with the world-class infrastructure, most of these destinations are attracting hoards of foreign tourists every year. Having made their packages affordable for the middle-income groups of people of Asian origin, they are also witnessing a lot of traffic from the countries around them, including India.

Burj Al Arab, Dubai, World's Second Highest Hotel

According to Middleton and Clarke (2001), "Strategy is essentially proactive in the sense that it defines and wills the future shape of the organization as well as responding to changing industry patterns, technology, market conditions, and consumer needs."

The strategic market-planning process should involve the functions that answer some direct questions that provide the necessary inputs for the development: market audit, vision and goals, strategy formulation, action plan and implementation and control.

- **Market audit:** What is the current state of the community of the destination and how does it compare to places in similar situations? What are the community's strengths/weaknesses and opportunities/threats?
- **Vision and goals:** What do the planners want the community to be?
- **Strategy formulation:** What broad strategies will help in achieving these goals?
- **Action plan:** What specific actions must be undertaken to carry out the strategies?
- **Implementation and control:** What must the community do to ensure a successful implementation?

The Indian tourism industry has also awakened to the vast potential that it possesses and is thriving towards increasing its share of tourism revenue in the region. With the opening of the Indian economy and its growing convergence with global businesses, a vast pool of business travellers have also been added to the number of foreign visitors to the country. In addition to the oriental charm that the Indian industry used to depend on for attracting Western tourists, the Indian government has started working towards reviving heritage sites and developing infrastructure in terms of rail/road networks, airports and hotel industry, while also identifying alternate ways of boosting its tourism revenues. India has developed a vast resource of highly qualified physicians and medical practitioners and has also developed world-class medical infrastructure that provides high-quality medical services at nominal prices. This has resulted in an ever-increasing number of medical tourists and is also becoming a major source of revenue for the tourism industry. At the same time, a vast pool of target market for the Indian tourism industry lies within the country itself.

Along with the country's economy, the Indian middle-class has also been growing affluent at a rapid pace. A huge part of this population in the country is constituted by the younger generation, who are earning well enough to aspire for luxurious lifestyles. They are also ready to splurge rather than save and are growing up amid the globetrotting corporate culture now quite commonly witnessed in the country. This target group, however, prefers to holiday abroad due to relatively insufficient tourism infrastructure, facilities and attractions in India.

Another potential target group is the large section of government employees who are provided leave travel concessions (LTCs) once every 2years to visit any place within the country (Box 2). However, a majority of this population prefers to avoid utilizing this facility on a regular basis for want of an organized industry sector that could devise packages that are custom-made for their requirements. Although the Indian Railways has now come up with certain travel packages that cater to this target group, there is still considerable untapped potential for the Indian tourism industry within the country.

Box 2: Alternatives to Boost Domestic Tourism

Following are the possible alternatives for the Indian Government and the tourism industry to boost domestic tourism in the country:

- Develop packages aimed at the domestic middle-class traveller with end-to-end facilities
- Explore the possibility of extending travel insurance to individuals and their families for accidents, thefts and other likely mishap/loss during travel
- Develop a system of benchmarking-associated services such as hotel, transport and guides who are a part of the packages provided to tourists. A code of conduct in the form of minimum service standards may be formulated and implemented within the industry
- Government certification for the service providers may be mandatory till the industry comes forward to govern such activities by themselves
- More economy and low-budget hotels may be opened without diluting the basic service standards. The model of "Ginger" hotels can be a case in point
- The domestic-circuit travel packages introduced by the Indian Railways may be expanded and developed to provide exquisite holiday experiences
- Improvement of basic amenities such as motels, clean toilets, eateries and service stations en route to major tourist spots should be carried out on a countrywide scale.
- Consider policy innovations to encourage government servants to make use of the LTC facility provided to them along with their pay and perks, for tourism purposes

Tactical/Micro-Environment

Tactical decisions are always focused on the short run in which specific marketing campaigns are planned, implemented and evaluated. Tactics respond to market conditions and particularly to competitors' activities. Tactical or operational marketing plans include

- **Objectives and targets:** Specified, quantified, volume and sales revenue targets and other specific marketing objectives to be achieved
- **Mix and budget:** Decisions on the marketing mix (product, price, promotion, place) and marketing budget
- **Action programmes:** The implementation of marketing programmes and coordination of promotional activity to achieve specified targets
- **Monitoring and control:** An effective system of monitoring the results of the marketing and the application of control procedures related to the agreed targets

Some of the typical characteristics of the short-term issues that need to be kept in mind while planning are fragmented supply, interdependence within tourist services, supply rigidity, intangibles, price elasticity of demand, seasonality, experience feedbacks and importance of intermediaries.

- **Fragmented supply:** The tourist product is a composite one, a combination of attractions, transport, accommodation, entertainment and other services. In most countries, there are many separate suppliers of these various components — airlines, hotel companies, tour-excursion organizers, etc.
- **Interdependence within tourist services:** It follows that the various tourist products and services are interdependent and complementary. This leads to the marketing policies and actions of one enterprise directly influencing other enterprises. A country with a liberal charter policy and/or an airline with an aggressive pricing policy may result in the attraction of low-budget tourists, something that could damage the high-quality image central to the marketing of a five-star hotel chain at the destination.
- **Supply rigidity:** The variation in tourism demand cannot be easily or quickly adjusted in the short term. A hotel, for example, cannot add or remove rooms in line with demand. This relative lack of flexibility has obvious operational and economic implications. When demand falls below capacity, waste of resources occurs; when it exceeds capacity, the industry fails to maximize its revenue. This "short term" can extend to years if the rigidity is caused by prolonged apathy towards development of infrastructure.
- **Intangibles:** Tourism mainly comprises "expectation-experience-memory." Tourist products (except items like souvenirs) are services rather than goods. The tourism product is subjectively perceived – each destination or individual tourist operation is a mental concept for each individual prospective tourist.
- **Price elasticity of demand:** Most forms of tourism demand involve the use of what economists call personal discretionary disposable income and free time. As a result, tourists are highly sensitive to price, and generally their demand for tourist services exhibits a significant degree of price elasticity.
- **Seasonality:** It is a characteristic of most tourism markets that demand fluctuates over the course of the year. The principal determinant is the climate — either in the destination or the tourist-generating markets. Residents of northern parts of the European and North American continents tend to take domestic or intra-regional holidays in the summer months of June-September, and long-haul, inter-regional holidays in the winter mostly when the climate at home is generally cold and wet.
- **Experience feedbacks:** In tourism, the customer is part of the product. The experience of those who have been to a destination affects the decision of the ones planning to visit the very same place. Feedback from previous tourists, therefore, influences their decisions also.

- **Importance of intermediaries:** A distinguishing characteristic of tourism is the relatively dominant role played by travel intermediaries. Tour operators or wholesalers and travel agents are all traditionally important in product design, pricing, distribution and promotion. However, with the proliferation of such services through the Internet, the role of these intermediaries has somewhat diminished.

Analysis of Market Environment

The next step in developing a marketing plan is to assess the impact of environmental factors such as economic, social and political on present and future markets. Changes in these factors can create marketing opportunities as well as problems. An assessment of these trends is important to understand how they will likely affect the business or the community. For example, some of the important trends that are being studied in the United States are:

- population growth and movement
- rural community growth compared to metropolitan areas
- number of adult women employed outside the home
- growing number of households, especially non-family and single-parent households, but family size is decreasing
- the impact of two-wage-earner households on real family income
- the number of retired persons with the financial ability to travel
- better health to an older age
- continued ageing of the population (the United States is becoming a middle-aged society)
- **Economic conditions:** Overall economic conditions can have a significant impact on recreation and tourism markets. A marketing strategy that is effective during periods of low-unemployment rates may have to be significantly adjusted if unemployment increases. Businesses and communities should monitor and assess the likely impact of factors such as unemployment rates, real family income, rate of inflation, credit availability and interest rates. Consideration should also be given to the prices of complementary products, such as lodging, travel costs and recreations. As a complex industry, tourism is significantly affected both positively and negatively by laws and by actions of governmental agencies. For instance, rulings on such things as liability issues or decisions regarding building and health codes may change or possibly prevent the construction of a proposed facility. If a public facility changes the prices of its services, it could affect the service offerings of associated private businesses. These actions may have both positive and negative effects on the marketing efforts of the business and the community.
- **Technology:** Technological developments are rapid and change business environments equally rapidly. New recreation products and services provide new ways for people to satisfy their likes and preferences. Changing production technologies and materials offer ways to recreation and tourism businesses to reduce costs and improve the quality of their products/services. Advances in telecommunications will continue to create new promotional opportunities. Technological innovations, in relation to jobs and livelihood, have resulted in increased leisure time for many people. Businesses and communities must identify and analyse existing and potential competitors. The objective of the analysis is to determine the strengths and weaknesses of the competition's marketing strategies.

Analysis of Internal Environment

Marketing services for recreation and tourism differ from marketing tangible products. Recreation and tourism businesses must direct as much attention to marketing to customers onsite as to attract them. In this respect, internal marketing is important because dissatisfied customers can effectively cancel out an otherwise effective marketing strategy. The success of internal marketing is dependent on creating an atmosphere in which employees desire to give good service and sell the business/community to visitors. To create such an atmosphere requires the following four important elements: hospitality and guest relations, quality control, personal selling and employee morale.

- **Hospitality and guest relations:** An organization-wide emphasis on hospitality and guest relations, including a customer-oriented attitude on the part of the owners and managers as well as the employees.
- **Quality control:** Programmes that focus on improving both the technical and functional qualities (the standards associated with how the customer receives the service). All employees who come into contact with customers should receive hospitality training.
- **Personal selling:** Training the staff in the selling aspects of the property, business or the community. This also includes rewarding them for their efforts. By staying informed about the marketing objectives and their role in accomplishing those objectives, they can help in increasing sales.
- **Employee morale:** Programmes and incentives aimed at maintaining employee morale. The incentives can be both monetary and non-monetary. A customer-oriented atmosphere usually results in customers who are more satisfied, do less complaining and are more pleasant to serve. This helps to build employee morale, their desire to provide good service and their efficiency.

Marketing Budget

Successful marketing requires that sufficient money and personnel time be made available to implement activities comprising the marketing strategy. A marketing budget is a financial plan that shows the total amount to be spent on marketing during different times of the year and how it is to be allocated among alternative activities. Separate marketing budgets should be developed for each marketing mix strategy. Separate budgets should then be aggregated to develop an overall marketing budget. If the total amount is too high, it will be necessary to modify the overall objectives and the target-market objectives, and narrow down or drop target markets, or adjust marketing mixes. The final budget should be realistic given your objectives. When deciding on a marketing budget, consideration should be given to the job that needs to be done as defined by the objectives. Basing marketing budgets on some percentage of sales or what the competition spends is likely to lead to over-spending or under-spending. Decisions should also be based on the costs, projected revenues and desired profitability of different activities, not just costs alone. Successful marketing activities will generate additional revenues, which can be projected based on the marketing objectives – such as decreasing off-season rates by 5 per cent.

Although budgets should be viewed as flexible plans, every effort should be made to adhere to them. Revisions in the budget should only be made after a careful consideration of the likely impact of change on the marketing mix and the accomplishment of your objectives.

Strength Weakness Opportunity Threat (SWOT) Analysis

For assessing the efficacy of a destination in attracting tourists, one should always undertake the process of assessing its strengths and weaknesses. The SWOT analysis is a tool to analyse the strengths and weaknesses of a destination and, the opportunities and threats emanating from the same. This will further lead to marking out opportunities and threats. This facilitates efficient and strategic planning on the part of the marketer.

In assessing a destination's competitive position, an "outsider-in" approach is needed in order to identify which of its characteristics represent

- a major strength
- a minor strength
- a minor weakness
- a major weakness

Competitive positions are determined both by "outside factors" beyond local/regional influence and "location characteristics" that specific local actions can influence. The destination's long-term strategic approach should be to seek to maximize the leverage of its major strengths and to improve its notable weaknesses. The hard and soft factors in the strengths-and-weaknesses assessment can be presented in a matrix form according to the five-scale degree of importance.

The next step is to identify a destination's opportunities and threats. An opportunity is where the destination has "a fairly good chance to achieve a competitive advantage" (Kotler et al., 2002), while threats come from unfavourable trends or developments in the environment which would erode its competitiveness. Each opportunity and threat has to be evaluated according to the probability of occurrence and the degree of advantage/harm its occurrence would have for the destination. By assembling a picture of the major opportunities and threats facing a specific destination, its overall attractiveness can be assessed:

- **Ideal:** High in opportunities and low in threats
- **Speculative:** High in both major opportunities and threats
- **Mature:** Low in major opportunities and threats
- **Troubled:** Low in opportunities and high in threats

MARKETING STRATEGY FORMULATION AND PLANNING

The formulation of marketing strategy follows the identification of markets as the next logical step. The marketing strategy has got certain specific objectives that need to be formulated and prescribed. The marketing strategy can be formulated to meet certain specific objectives like increase in the tourist traffic as well as increase in the foreign-exchange receipts. The tourism marketer should keep in mind that these objectives should go hand-in-hand with the characteristics of the market and the capacity of the tourist "plant" and facilities available. Thus, the first important step in the formulation of marketing strategy is to assess the potential market regarding its size, conditions and trends in a realistic manner.

Generic Strategy Options

According to Porter, marketing strategy can be classified into three broad categories for any industry: overall low-cost leadership, differentiation and focusing.

- **Overall low-cost leadership:** The tourism services like hotel rooms, airline bookings and transportation can be provided at competitive rates as compared to competing destinations
- **Differentiation:** A tourist destination can achieve differentiation through several ways like creating unmatched new avenues, providing a safe environment or proper infrastructure.
- **Focusing:** A tourist marketer should understand the needs of the particular market segment and formulate low cost or product differentiating strategy.

Cost leadership still remains a benchmark among competing tour operators and travel agents, while destinations use the concept of differentiation to create interest among potential tourists — an example is the "Malaysia — Truly Asia" campaign. A third strategy is to develop strong relationships with actual or potential market segments. Organizations need to focus on mixed strategies rather than individual ones to achieve success.

Market Position

A very important aspect in formulating strategy by any tourist organization is to determine its current market position as a leader, a follower, a nicher or in terms of what it aspires to be. In any particular tourist block, for example, in Southeast Asia, there are various tourist destinations such as Singapore and Malaysia, and they have created a market position for themselves in the minds of world tourists. In fact, various states in India to some extent and facilities within a destination are subdivided as well.

Push or Pull Approaches to Marketing Strategy

There are many intermediaries in the tourism business including tour agents and operators. In managing the intermediaries, the organization must decide how to use the "push versus pull" strategy of marketing. A push strategy uses the firm's sales force, trade promotion money or other means to induce intermediaries to carry, promote and sell the product to end users. In a pull strategy, a firm uses advertising, promotion and other forms of communication to persuade consumers to demand the product from intermediaries, thus inducing them to order it. The latter strategy is appropriate when there is a strong brand loyalty. An efficient tourism marketing company must use both the strategies skilfully. The intermediaries play a vital role in creating and sustaining demand for the tourist products. They can collaborate with the tour operators, potential and actual markets. There are two aspects to this: first, how much are the organizations actively involved in marketing and distribution strategies together with the intermediaries, and, second, what are their reactions to the marketing and promotion strategies used by the intermediaries. As a result of an organization's activeness or passiveness with these two considerations, four trade-orientation strategies are possible: bypassing, cooperation, conflict and adaptation.

- **Bypassing:** It completely ignores the distribution channels.
- **Cooperation:** The organization works in tandem with the intermediaries having a very precisely defined distribution channel. This forms a part of vertical marketing. This type of cooperation may vary from loose to binding.
- **Conflict:** In this case, organizations try to enforce their own interests under resistance from the trade bodies in order to gain market leadership.
- **Adaptation:** This is characterized by the passive reaction of tourism organizations towards marketing strategies of intermediaries in terms of organizing and structuring of distribution channels.

Marketing Objectives

An organization needs to establish its exact marketing objectives to be pursued. The marketing objectives especially focus on two important aspects: product-market decisions, and means by which such decisions shall affect achievement of corporate objectives. Ansoff's model can be used here for the analysis of strategic choices. There are two variables employed here, products and markets. The matrix demonstrates potential areas in which an organization can deploy core competencies and generic strategies (Fig. 13.1).

Segmentation, Targeting and Positioning

Market Segmentation. The first step that a marketing organization needs to carry out is to identify its market(s). It may be done in connection with a particular geographical area or in connection with a particular type of service or product. Thus, we can define the market as a collection of present or potential buyers of a particular service or product within a particular geographic area during a given period of time.

Market segmentation is the process of identifying groups of buyers of a total market into various useful categories on the basis of different buying desires, lifestyles, and motivational characteristics.

	Destinations existing	Destinations new
Markets existing	Market penetration (increased marketshare)	Destination development
Markets new	Market development	Diversification

Fig. 13.1: Product–Market Decision Model

An organization, however big, may not cater to the entire market due to financial and manpower limitations. Thus, it makes economic sense to subdivide the market into proper segments and target them on one-to-one basis. The main objectives of the market segmentation are as follows:

- Developing new markets for product variations or new product
- Developing defence against competitors by differentiating one's own product from their product, and matching it closely to the requirements of the consumers in the particular market segment chosen by the organization
- It has to be made sure that the expenditure on the marketing activities is utilized effectively, especially with regard to the communication part
- The marketing plans and budgets should be prepared in accordance with the expected response from the consumers in the particular segment

The following types of information are required to accomplish the segmentation of tourist markets:

- Income distribution of overseas travellers and, particularly, correlation between income and distance travelled as well as travel expenditure
- Travel expenditure data, that is, distribution of per-head expenditure on travel
- Discretionary income of households correlated with other characteristics, enabling targets to be identified closely
- Historical trends in travelling in different socio-economic categories
- Survey data on overseas travellers regarding attitudes and motivations of both the tourists and the locals in relation to them
- Data on how the potential customers are distributed geographically within the market
- Membership of clubs and associations associated with other characteristics, which identify particular groups as potential customers
- Influence of intermediaries (travel agents, tour operators, carriers, etc.) on destination choice in a particular market
- Relative importance of particular intermediaries in a particular market
- Whether the particular group has some religious or historical bondage with the tourist destination

Market segmentation is carried out on the basis of certain factors. The most commonly used bases of market segmentation are: geographical segmentation, demographic segmentation, socio-economic segmentation, behavioural and product-based.

- **Geographical segmentation:** Operational areas — for example, sales regions, sales districts such as provinces, cities and political administrative zones.

- **Demographic segmentation:** Age groups, sex differences, ethnic origin, marital status, religious affiliations.
- **Socio-economic segmentation:** Levels of income, types of occupation, social class, educational level, level of economic activity.
- **Behavioural:** Patterns of purchase, response to changing trends, brand loyalty, benefits/ recognition sought.
- **Product-based:** Travel purposes, types of holiday, average length of stay, type of accommodation, mode of travel, arrangements of travel, individual/group travel.

One of the early steps in marketing tourism is to divide the present and potential markets on the basis of meaningful characteristics, and then concentrate on promotion, supply and pricing efforts to serve these prominent segments of the market. These are the target markets.

In the tourism sector, segmentation can be carried out within each of the segments discussed above. The segments include vacation, business and common-interest tourist.

- **The vacation tourist:** This is the most popular and common form of tourists. He is easily influenced by aggressive marketing efforts and is very much price sensitive. This form of tourism is also highly seasonal.
- **The business tourist:** Such tourists are least price sensitive. Thus they cannot be influenced by promotional strategies. The demand depends on the type and nature of business and is mostly big city oriented or oriented towards places of commercial significance. The visits are of shorter duration and relatively frequent. The trade fairs, conventions, exhibitions, conferences and similar other events attract this kind of tourist.
- **The common-interest tourist:** This segment comprises visits to relatives and friends and visits for the purpose of pilgrimage or education, etc. The demand for this type of tourist will be relatively price elastic. These types of tourists cannot be influenced much by promotional activities. The length of stay shall be longer, and they are less likely to see tourism commodities and services such as hotels.

The identification of potential buyers through segmentation is the first step in the formulation of marketing strategy. The information available through market research and segmentation gives the dimensions of the market and determines which markets are crucial. The information also assists in creating a meaningful promotional strategy.

IMPLEMENTATION: THE TOURISM MARKETING MIX

Once it is decided that what will be the marketing objective and the strategies to achieve them, the need for an effective marketing plan emerges. An effective plan enables achievement of the objectives in proper time.

Implementation

Many well-designed marketing plans fail because they are poorly executed. Businesses, agencies and communities can increase the likelihood of successful implementation if they:

- Identify specific tasks that must be accomplished
- Assign people or departments with specific responsibility for different tasks
- Provide employees with information on the marketing plan – rationale, objectives, strategies
- Develop time lines and deadlines
- Adhere as much as possible to the budget
- Regularly monitor and evaluate progress

This section should incorporate target markets, especially those that are primary. Consider the four P's: product, price, place (distribution) and promotion.

- **Product:** What is being offered to the tourist and how is it different from the competitors' destination. The visitors may be offered a range of services such as extensive coverage of the tourist spots, and places of entertainment for all age groups may be specifically mentioned. Availability of basic amenities and infrastructure may be mentioned.
- **Price:** Destination product pricing and its justification.
- **Place (distribution):** Who delivers the tourism service and what are the touch points e.g. travel agents, tour operators who facilitate the consumption. Any destination can strategically use them to gain a competitive advantage.
- **Promotion:** It includes the promotional strategy for the destination products. This section includes our advertising, publicity, sales promotion, and public-relations strategies. Our media schedule should be included in this part of the marketing plan. Media planning is an important constituent of the marketing plan.

Since tourism is mainly a service, three additional P's of service marketing can always be included.

- **People:** In tourism, the quality and attitude of people delivering the services speaks to success.
- **Process:** Clarity and transparency in process always earns goodwill and motivates positive word-of-mouth.
- **Physical evidence:** Attributes like cleanliness, pollution free environment, proper town planning and marketing communication, highlighting these issues form the physical evidence for any tourism destination. This is very essential to have a lasting impact in the minds of tourists. It also plays a big role in justifying the price paid by tourists.

Marketing plan must include:

- Key result areas.
- Time frame for getting results
- Schedule of activities
- Vision statement

The Marketing plan must get translated in terms of brochures, marketing communications through electronic media or through Web site management. Finally, financial implications should be laid out. A proper marketing plan should lay out a marketing budget which is in sync with sales forecast.

The Prescott Area Coalition for Tourism (PACT), a regional destination-marketing organization, has developed itineraries to effectively market the Prescott area's natural beauty, outdoor recreation options, historical attractions and the extensive offerings of special events and festivals.

Based on the Prescott area's assets, PACT has successfully identified and implemented a creative marketing theme titled "History Lives On." Its marketing message is selected to appeal to an array of key target markets. No matter what your interests are, Prescott, Arizona, offers something for everyone: museums, art galleries, six golf courses, lodging and accommodations, five lakes, boutiques, fine dining, theatre and 450 miles of hiking and recreational trails. There is a fun-filled calendar of events scheduled to delight, entertain, educate and amuse. Many of the events are free and the others are extremely reasonable, making a trip to Prescott affordable for everyone. Families enjoy the friendly hotels, bed and breakfasts, restaurants and attractions.

The message resonates with consumers who have a fascination with the excitement, romance and mystique of the Old West – which extend beyond the bounds of the United States to a worldwide audience. The Prescott area recognizes the need to capitalize on the Western heritage and broaden the appeal to include more regional products. Its ads and collateral materials feature images of contemporary cowboys and incorporate copy points on special events and itineraries throughout the region such as golf, hiking, shopping and back-road adventures where history is literally living on.

Each Prescott area advertisement features copy, the motto "History Lives On!," and representative images associated with the traditional west or a featured itinerary. Based on reader-response cards, the Prescott message gets the readers' attention. More than 16,000 requests for Prescott information were received in FY 2004. Nearly 43,000 leads were received through reader-response mechanisms in FY 2005. The first 7 months of FY 2006 generated 12,000 leads (Source: *www.visit-prescott.com*)

Their tourism marketing activities include:

- Magazine advertising
- Newspaper advertising
- Web-based promotional programmes
- Itinerary/events collateral pieces
- Extensive public relations to obtain positive media coverage

Extended Marketing Mix

This section includes plans and procedures for tracking each type of marketing activity that an organization is engaged in. Tracking helps monitor the effectiveness of each marketing activity and is especially helpful in overall programme evaluation. Here are some types of media along with ideas for tracking their effectiveness. The techniques will vary depending on the product type and the market: display advertising, direct marketing, TV or radio ads, internet marketing, promotions, events, trade shows, database, data analysis and storage.

- **Display advertising:** With traditional consumer publications, tracking can be done through the use of different phone numbers, special offers – specific to that advertisement or publication or reference to a specific department to call for information. When those calls come in, the call-centre staff must be prepared to record the information so the results can be tallied for that publication.
- **Direct marketing:** With postal mailings, tracking is relatively simple. Include on the mailing label a code (called a key code or a source code) that corresponds with the mailing list, so we know which list is producing, and instruct the call-centre staff to record the information by asking the customer for the code.
- **TV or radio ads:** These require tracking methods similar to those for consumer publications. They can be tracked through the use of unique phone numbers, special offers – specific to that advertisement or reference to a specific department to call for information. Again, when those calls come in, the call-centre staff must be prepared to record the information so the results can be tallied for that particular spot.
- **Internet marketing:** Usually, this is easily tracked because it is based on click-through or page impressions. The Web administrator should be able to provide reports that indicate the number of click-throughs that actually led to the purchase of a product. Also, unique URLs that direct to the Web site track user's response to a specific promotion or campaign.
- **Promotions:** Most closed promotions are basically "self-tracking" because they require the customer to do something, such as fill out an entry form (tractable), turn in a coupon, return a rebate slip (tractable) or log on to a Web site to claim a prize (also tractable). Open promotions, such as sales, require a little more work to track, although they can be tracked in a general way by noting increased sales for that time period, store or region, or whatever the parameters are of the sale.

- **Events:** An event is slightly tricky to track. We know how many people attended, but do we know how many sales occurred as a result? We can issue coupons at the event that can be tracked, offer other special deals or even allow attendees to join a special club. One has to be creative in order to track the true sales results of a big event.
- **Trade shows:** A trade show's effectiveness can be tracked by collecting the right information at the show and following up on it. These results must also be tallied and recorded. The success of trade-show attendance can be measured by the number of consumers who requested information from the booth or the number of tour operators or travel agents who requested specific information on the destination or business.
- **Database:** Before the marketing plan is kicked off, make sure you have the database structure in place to record information. Use codes for every level of information so that these can be sorted by various specifications. This takes a lot of planning, as well as training for the staff. Setting up the records with drop-down boxes for selecting preset information such as product number, list codes, publication codes or department codes will make the records much more consistent and usable.
- **Data analysis and storage:** The tabulated results and customer information are very valuable. We should routinely back up the system where these data are kept and keep copies in safe places. The customer data are extremely valuable to future direct-marketing efforts and must be keyed in correctly and accurately.

Example. Bisbee review its objectives twice a year to evaluate the achievement of its goals. In addition, Bisbee monitors the monthly attendance figures for the Bisbee Visitor Centre and the two most attended attractions: the Queen Mine Tour and the Bisbee Mining & Historical Museum. It monitors its Web site hits and the amount of time people spend on the site. It monitors the monthly and yearly tax-revenue figures for accommodations (bed tax), food and beverage, and retail sales as well as total taxable sales. The figures are compared on a monthly basis as well as a yearly basis. On a comparative monthly basis, it looks at what happened the year before; how did it market the destination this year as opposed to last year; what special events occurred to spur an increase (or decrease), and if the weather might have been an influence. When its numbers go up, either on a month-to-month basis or on a yearly basis, it cautiously feels its marketing efforts have been successful. It hopes to have an increase of 10 per cent per year in all tax revenues and 10 per cent in attendance figures to call its efforts a profitable success.

MARKETING CONTROL

Evaluation

This section addresses the manner in which achievement of objectives will be measured. Although often overlooked this section is essential for determining the outcome of marketing effort. It also assists in reporting return on investment (ROI) to members, constituents, etc. Methods for evaluation of marketing efforts are different for each type of marketing project. The selected method of tracking helps in evaluation. As an example, for print placement the number of leads generated by a magazine or a newspaper advertisement can be measured. For a Web site, the number of page views or the number of Web-based requests for products or services can be measured. Public relations efforts can be measured by the number of articles written about host community or business in newspapers and magazines and the residual media value. The success of trade-show attendance can be measured by the number of consumers who requested information from the booth, or the number of tour operators or travel agents who requested specific information on host destination or business. Additional evaluation techniques include attendance at an event from year to year or a visitor research study to determine who is visiting and what did they find about the destination.

An evaluation may include the following: leads generated through the marketing programme – direct marketing efforts, Internet leads and number of enquiries as a result of advertising efforts, travel trade shows, familiarization (FAM) tours and number of visitors, hotel occupancy rates or hotel sales-tax revenues.

Control

Control is applied to arrest deviation from the planned outcome. A good schedule and budget should make it easy to monitor progress. When things fall behind schedule, or costs overrun, one needs to be ready to do something about it and to adapt their plan accordingly.

From time to time, one needs to stand back and ask whether the plan is working. What can we learn from our mistakes? How can one use what he/she knows to make a better plan for the future?

The most important questions that should be asked for the control processes are:

- Did the destination reach its goal?
- Was the marketing campaign successful?
- Was the destination able to determine return on investment?
- Did the efforts result in conversion? In other words, was the marketing team able to convert an enquirer to a visitor?
- Can the database be utilized for survey, capture additional information or establish a "customer relationship management" programme?

A good marketing plan achieves the following goals:

- Sets clear, realistic and measurable targets, for example, increasing visitor/tourist attendance by 10 per cent
- Includes deadlines for meeting targets
- Provides a budget for each marketing activity
- Specifies who is responsible for each activity

Poorly thought-out objectives will cause problems. For example, one might set a target for the number of new enquiries. But if none of these enquiries turns into actual visitation, then costs are incurred without any benefits.

A plan will not happen by itself, one needs to make someone responsible for monitoring progress and following up on overdue activities. Reviewing progress will also help in learning from mistakes so that one can improve his/her plans for the future.

Terrorism and Tourism

Extreme events such as terrorism have a deep impact on an industry such as tourism (Ritcher and Waugh 1986, Ryan 1993). For developing any tourist destination, absence of terror or violence is the precondition (Israeli and Reichel 2003). In the last few decades all around the world, prominent tourist destinations have been threatened by terrorism and acts of violence. These events can be considered a handicap for development of the industry since tourist have over a period shown marked preference for peaceful and tranquil social environments (Neumayer 2004; Reisinger and Mavondo 2005). Tourist destinations have been struggling to recover from the adverse affects of terrorist attacks. Destination recovery strategies have been studied in depth and recommendations given by Beirman (2002); Berno & King (2001); Blake & Sinclair (2003); Cassedy (1992); Fainstein (2002); Henderson (1997); Richter (1999) and Wall (2005).

Terrorism Prevention

Since terrorist strikes have a deep impact on the psyche of the tourists for a long time, it is necessary that a robust mechanism to tackle this menace is developed. For prevention of terrorism and devising an anti-terrorism strategy, the role of destination management organization (DMO) becomes very critical. Generally, it is the government-run departments that are the DMOs. However, with the growth in risk of terrorist strikes, there is a need to bring in more professionals in this structure. It is necessary to create a terrorism prevention cell which may have representations from DMO, regional/state tourism departments, hotel associations, travel agencies, security agencies, intelligence agencies and also some private bodies as well as individuals with expertise in this area. A pertinent issue always will be a smooth coordination among all the stakeholders in the cell. Without a proper coordination, such cells will only exist on paper and will never be operationally effective.

Tasks for Terrorism Prevention Cell

Tasks for such a cell cannot be sacrosanct and will have to be tweaked based on the geopolitical as well as socio-economic scenario. Any such activity cannot be effectively executed without local support and weak intelligence and execution system. Tentatively following can be a list of probable tasks which can be taken up for setting up robust anti-terrorism mechanism:

1. Formation of terrorism prevention cell: Who qualify to be the members for such group?
2. Gauging the destination risk: What is the risk of terrorist attack to the destination in question?
3. Incident preview scanning: If the destination faces such an attack, what will be the consequences?
4. Socio-cultural and geopolitical study: Which factors will deter and which facilitate such an act?
5. Anti-terrorism strategy: How can such an event be prevented?
6. Strategy execution plan: How to implement the strategy so that it is effective in achieving its goal?
7. Control mechanism: What will be the monitoring mechanism and review process?
8. Disaster plan: If despite all efforts such an incident happens, what should be the systems in place to minimize the impact?

Any anti-terrorism strategy has to always include the local public. For this, it is also necessary that the DMO takes into consideration the local issues. Such issues can be in terms of employment, sanitation, local infrastructure or avenues of further growth. It has generally been found that if local interests are catered to, there are chances that scope for such negative activities can be minimized to a great extent.

Case Study: Croatian — Tourism Marketing Issues

Croatian Tourist Spot Brela

Brela is a source of beauty in Croatia. Thanks to nice beaches, clear seawater and sources of potable water, Brela has been known for decades as one of the most attractive seaside resorts in Dalmatia. Luxuriant pine forests, located close to attractive pebble beaches, add to its charm. Brela also offers a nicely arranged coastal promenade and a number of excellent restaurants serving seafood.

Product

Croatia is a potential tourism destination primarily because of the unique natural, cultural and historical heritage of Brela. It is mostly recognized for the

Case Study: Croatian — Tourism Marketing Issues *(Continued)*

Adriatic coast and the natural resources – 1,800 km of coastline and over 1,000 islands have been demarcated both by tourism bodies and policy-makers. TOMAS research (2001) found that over 90 per cent of foreign tourists come to Croatia for sun and sea. Such an image, both projected by tourism bodies and perceived by foreign tourists, does not bear the danger of the gap between the two, which usually results in disappointment and future avoidance of the destination and dissemination of the negative image (Gitelson and Kerstetter, 1994). However, it underestimates the other potential tourist destinations within the country (national parks, health tourism, sport tourism, cultural and historical heritage, etc.), limits the tourist season to only a few summer months and makes it less profitable than it could be. Another correlated problem is the bed structure – only 40 per cent of tourist beds are in hotels and resorts, and the rest are camping sites and private rooms and apartments, which are to a large extent neither officially registered nor standardized, and often a part of the grey market.

Price

The relative price of competing tourism destinations can have a significant influence on the choice of destination by potential customers – tourists (Dwyer et al., 2000), especially within the trend of increased price sensitivity. Thanks to its geographical position, Croatia is an attractive and a relatively easily reachable destination for both Western and eastern European travellers. During the past few years, 500 million Euro have been invested in the tourism industry, and a large part of it went towards modernization of roads and travelling infrastructure in general. The major problem concerning price competitiveness is to reposition Croatia to the middle and upper classes as a cheap destination of mass tourism. The other problem considering prices in Croatian tourism is that it is not used as an additional marketing tool. Croatian tourism managers seem to be very stiff and inflexible in their price decisions. For example, last-minute travel options with lower prices were introduced only in the year 2008.

Promotion

Promotion activities carried out on both national and local level can significantly contribute to tourism-product repositioning. The Croatian National Tourism Board budgeted $11.352 million on advertising for 2006 and $660 million was allocated for investment in hotels, campsites and holiday resorts in the same year (*Source:* Euro monitor International). Promotional activities on national level are created by National Tourism Association and Ministry of Tourism and mainly directed towards the most important foreign markets. The following major activities are included:

- Participation in major international tourism fairs throughout the year (75 in 2003), including being a "partner country" in some of them, giving press conferences and presentations and organization of "Croatian evenings."
- Printing of brochures and handouts with general tourism information and distributing these in foreign tourist offices, as well as special brochures on sailing in Croatia, Croatian cultural heritage, hunting in Croatia, etc.
- "Croatian angels," the tourist 24-hours-a-day toll-free service information during the summer months
- Official Croatian tourism Web site (www.croatia.hr) with multimedia contents of 600 tourism destinations and possibility for online registration and booking
- Advertising in print, electronic and other media in 20 countries where most tourists come from
- TV advertising through CNN, Eurosport, TW1 and ORF
- Info-kiosks and welcome service for tourists at major airports and border crosses
- Hands-on promotional projects by tourism offices in 16 major emitting markets
- Organization of study tours for tourism journalists (633 in 2003) and foreign travel agency representatives (from 17 countries in 2003), as well as numerous activities on local level

Distribution

Product distribution systems in tourism are complex and affected by many factors. Increased accessibility

Case Study: Croatian — Tourism Marketing Issues *(Continued)*

of information and destinations significantly impacts traditional distribution systems and calls for new technologies and know-how in the area of distribution. On the destination level itself, provision of infrastructure is complicated and problematic for a few reasons:

- Tourism is highly seasonal, which makes it difficult to maximize returns on investment in assets, especially for private investors
- There is significant involvement of government agencies on both national and local level.

Although there were significant investments in infrastructure improvement, it is still often incapable of supporting the supra-structure growth. Thus, transportation, water and electricity supply and other services are under enormous pressure during peak summer months to satisfy the demand density.

Research

A pilot survey of 273 foreign tourists who had spent their 2003 summer holidays in Poreč, Istria, wascarried out. Istria is a peninsula and the most developed tourism region in Croatia and accounts for about 40 per cent of total tourism turnover in Croatia. The town of Poreč is a top tourism destination in Istria and had won the "Champion of Tourism Award" for 4 years in a row. Analysing the situation in Croatia, Poreč is one of the rare places that have managed to define a high-quality tourism destination image combining natural resources, cultural heritage, sporting activities and numerous events.

Our sample consisted of 273 foreign tourists from 16 countries: 36.3 per cent from Germany, 20.1 per cent from Austria, 12.5 per cent from Great Britain and 9.2 per cent from The Netherlands – altogether 78.1 per cent. The other countries included Russia, Sweden, Slovenia, Hungary, Czech Republic, Italy and Poland. In the sample, 54.9 per cent were male and 45.1 per cent were female. The majority of the sample fell in the age group of 26–60 years (62.6 per cent); 24.5 per cent were older than 60 and 12.8 per cent were 25 or younger. Further, 63.7 per cent were employed, 26 per cent were retired, 7 per cent were students and 3.3 per cent were unemployed. For over 40 per cent of the sample, this was their first visit to Croatia, and 39.2 per cent had already been to Croatia for holidays. Only 20.1 per cent of the sample regularly spent holidays in Croatia.

They were asked to evaluate their holidays in general, as well as the specific aspects of Poreč as a tourism destination. On five-point Likert scale, the average mark they gave to the holidays in Poreč in general was 3.83. The specific aspects were marked as follows:

Natural resources (beauties) got the highest average mark of 4.05; hospitality got the second best mark of 3.95; food got 3.90 and accommodation 3.81. Entertainment and fun possibilities got the lowest mark of 3.45. In more detail, 72.5 per cent of the respondents had evaluated the accommodation as above average (marks 4 and 5); 78 per cent evaluated natural beauties and hospitality above the average and 70.7 per cent have evaluated food as above the average. Only 51.6 per cent of respondents had marked entertainment possibilities above the average, while 14.5 per cent had marked it either below average or even totally unsatisfactory. In all other categories, marks below the average were given by less than 6 per cent of the respondents. Among the sample, 31.1 per cent spent more than 100 kunas (about 15 Euro) per person daily. Interestingly, 60.8 per cent of them claimed that they spent most of their money on food and drinks and 25.6 per cent on excursions; only 9.9 per cent had bought souvenirs and things to take home. Finally, 47.6 per cent of the sample considered holidays in Croatia comparative to other Mediterranean countries; 34.4 per cent found it less expensive than other Mediterranean countries; and 12.8 per cent considered it more expensive in comparison to other Mediterranean countries. Among those who consider holidays in Croatia price competitive were 60.6 per cent tourists who have visited Croatia several times. Generally, it seemed that those who visited Croatia for the first time were more critical and gave lower marks to most of the criteria.

Strategic Implications

According to the Ritchie and Crouch model of competitive destination (Ritchie and Crouch, 2000), it seems that Croatian tourism has its major strengths in core resources and attractions and supporting fac-

Case Study: Croatian — Tourism Marketing Issues *(Continued)*

tors and resources, while the destination management, policy, planning and development are the weak points. However, it only accounts for the Adriatic coast area, while the continental resources and possibilities are very much underestimated. So, foreign tourists, when thinking about holidays in Croatia, associate it with Adriatic coast – that is, "sun and sea." If Croatia wants to improve its general tourism product, there will have to be a significant improvement of communication channels targeted at the potential tourists by National Tourism Association, ministry of tourism and travel agencies on two levels:

- to inform potential tourists about alternative destinations and holiday possibilities away from the coast and
- to emphasize other value-added connected to the "sun and sea" in order to create a new image of the destination.

These improvements should be aimed at defining the vision of "authentic Croatian experience" unifying tradition, natural resources and originality of different regions (Croatian Tourism Cluster, 2003). Furthermore, there is an evident lack of managerial know-how and a lack of strategic vision, especially at the local level.

Entrepreneurial activities are still at the starting point, which is due partly to lack of education and partly to macro-economic processes – that is, still uncompleted process of privatization. Marketing is another significant problem. In most of the cases in Croatian tourism, the product orientation is still being followed. In order to avoid the present mass-tourism destination image, it will be necessary to research and define the most important existing and emerging market segments, maximize their potential and stimulate the supply of differentiated specific tourism products to meet market requirements. For example, Australia has recognized backpackers as one of the key tourism-market segments and develops a whole range of specific products to satisfy their needs (Tourism Green Paper, 2003).

The analysis of Croatian tourism clearly illustrates the importance of the industry to the national economy's well-being. The strategic issue of Croatian tourism development is to reposition the product from being a low value-added "sun and sea" destination to a high-value, internationally recognized brand. In order to achieve this goal, the focus earlier had been on volume, but, in the future, tourism products will have to earn more from fewer international tourists. Thus, growth will need to be focused on yield, rather than profitless volume. A key factor to increasing Croatia's tourism export performance and competitiveness is better intelligence on the international market, and the distribution and utilization of that intelligence in effective international marketing and tourism management, and raising the standard and quality of tourism products and businesses.

CONCLUSION

By following a corporate strategy of planning, positioning and marketing properly, many smaller countries such as Singapore, Thailand and Malaysia have succeeded in providing customer value proposition and unique experience for the customers. Like any other product or service, tourism also needs to be marketed properly to achieve the desired returns. If able to achieve that, tourism would provide a huge boost to the economy of a country. A country like India, which has thousands of years of history, various cultures that are unique and heritage sites of great interest worldwide, can benefit immensely from proper development and marketing of the tourism industry. While a great amount of awareness has already been witnessed regarding this aspect both in the government and the industry, a lot is still left to be achieved. Apart from the places of historical and religious interest, the country needs to develop tourism facilities for leisure, adventure, eco, medical and corporate tourism and any other new aspects that can be thought of. For this to be possible, relevant infrastructure in terms of travel, hotel rooms, roads, en route facilities and most importantly, policies and rules governing this business need to be reviewed from time to time.

If the tourism activities are planned and implemented properly, they provide not only unique experiences for the customers but also substantial direct and indirect employment for the local population.

India also has a vast potential for the development of the domestic tourism industry. Presently, domestic tourism is primarily being handled by the unorganized sector of the industry. To give a boost to this vast resource of revenue generation, both government and the industry need to come up with better policies and infrastructure that are not only capable of supporting this concept but also attract and encourage the local population to avail of these facilities.

Customer satisfaction in tourism is greatly influenced by the way in which the service is delivered and by the physical appearance and personality of the business. It is critical that these elements be communicated in the best possible manner to convince people to come and experience what your business or community has to offer. Equally important is the ability to generate repeat business through these efforts. Thus, marketing is the only means to reach out to the potential visitors. It is a vital part of tourism management and can be executed effectively, with sophistication and tact, or it can be done poorly in a loud, crassand intrusive manner.

Unsung Tourist Destination: Ranchi

Ranchi is the capital city of the Indian state of Jharkhand. Ranchi was the centre of the Jharkhand movement for a separate state for the tribal regions of south Bihar, northern Orissa, western West Bengal and the present eastern Chhattisgarh. Jharkhand state was formed on November 15, 2000, by carving out the Bihar divisions of Chota Nagpur and Santhal Parganas. Ranchi is a prominent political, commercial, industrial and educational hub of eastern India.

The total area covered by Ranchi Municipal Area is about 110 sq km and the average elevation of the city is 2,140 feet above mean sea level. Geographically, Ranchi is located on the southern part of the Chota Nagpur plateau, which forms the eastern edge of the Deccan plateau system. The area surrounding Ranchi has been endowed with natural attractions, and it is referred to as the "City of Waterfalls." The most popular waterfalls are Dassam, Hundru, Jonha, Hirni and Panch Gagh, which are all active perennially. The Subarnarekha River and its tributaries constitute the local river system. Dams in Kanke, Rukka and Hatia have been built over these channels to cater to the water requirements of the local population. Ranchi has a hilly topography, and its combination with dense tropical forests ensures that it enjoys a comparatively moderate climate compared to the rest of the state.

Jonha Falls, a Popular Tourist Destination Situated 40 km from Ranchi

As per the 2001 India Census, Ranchi had a population of 846,454. According to the current estimates, the population of the city is now about 1,300,000. The city witnessed a sudden surge in population after the declaration of the new state of Jharkhand in the year 2000. Owing to the rising employment opportunities and the opening of numerous regional- and state-level offices, banks and marketing companies, the city witnessed an influx of migrants. Ranchi has always enjoyed a cosmopolitan environment and still boasts a good mix of people from different regions of the country. Ranchi is the largest city in Jharkhand and is well connected to all major Indian cities by air, rail and roads.

Unsung Tourist Destination: *(Continued)*

Places to See Around

Temples. Some important temples are as follows:

Rajrappa Mandir: For the worship of Goddess Kali, known as Chhinnamastika. About 65 km from Ranchi, it has great picnic spots
Pahari temple: Located at the heart of the city
Durga Badi: Near Firayalal Chowk at the heart of the city
Jagannathpur temple: Built in the architectural style of Puri temples; about 300 years old
Surya temple: 38 km from Ranchi on Ranchi-Tata NH
Bhawani Shankar Mandir, Ginjo Thakur Gaon: 25 km from Ranchi on Ratu road
Parasnath or Shikharjee: A major pilgrimage centre for the Jains; about 200 km from Ranchi in Giridih District
Ramakrishna Mission and Ashram: Morhabadi, Ranchi
Ramakrishna Mission Ashram and T. B. Sanatorium: Tupudana, Ranchi
Dewri temple: 58 km from Ranchi on Ranchi-Tata NH 33
Doranda Jain Mandir: 4 km from Ranchi
Headquarters of Yogoda Satsanga Society of India: Founded by Paramahansa Yogananda, it is situated about 200 metres from Ranchi railway station

Parks and Resorts. Important ones are

Nakshatra Van: Near Raj Bhawan (governor's house)
Birsa Zoological Park: 14 km from Ranchi
Night Safari: 14 km from Ranchi
Deer Park: 16 km from Ranchi on Ranchi-Khunti Road
Sidhu Kaanhu Park: Located at the heart of the city
Dr Zakir Hussain Park: Located at the heart of the city
Ranchi Hill-Pahari Baba Temple: Located at the heart of the city
Tagore Hill: Morabadi, 5 km from the centre of the city
Rock Garden: Kanke Road, 4 km from the centre of the city
Fun Castle: Ratu, 7 km from Ranchi
Crocodile Farm: Ormanjhi, 19 km from Ranchi

Water Resorts. Some of them are

Ranchi Lake: Located at the heart of the city
Rukka Dam: 16 km from Ranchi
Aqua World: Located at the heart of the city
Dassam Falls: About 40 km from Ranchi on Ranchi-Tata NH Road
Jonha Falls: About 35 km from Ranchi
Sita Falls: Near Jonha falls
Hundru Falls: 30 km from Ranchi
Hirni Falls: 90 km towards Chakradharpur
Panch Gagh: 50 km from Ranchi
Rani Fall (Soeko): 55 km from Ranchi
Perwaghagh (Torpa): 75 km from Ranchi
Ghaghri Fall (Bero): 45 km from Ranchi
Kanke Dam: 7 km from main road, Ranchi
Baghmunda (Basia): 100 km from Ranchi

There are many other places of tourist interest around Ranchi. Netarhat, a beautiful hill station, is situated close to the city. The national wildlife sanctuary in Palamau district is within visiting distance.

Accommodation

There are enough decent accommodation options in Ranchi and the scene is getting better every passing day. There are a number of hotels and other accommodation options catering to the needs of tourists coming to explore Ranchi or interesting in exploring the scenic region around.

Reasons for Ranchi Not Being a Successful Tourist Destination

The city could not be developed as a potential tourist destination in a big way due to certain socio-political and economic considerations. First, being in a poor region of India, it never got much attention in this regard. The city for a long time was disturbed by regional politics and protests regarding formation of the separate state of Jharkhand. Also, it witnessed conflicts between the local tribal population and the immigrants. After the formation of the state of Jharkhand, Ranchi had been developed more as an administrative and commercial centre than a tourist destination. Moreover, the influx of a huge population and the rising levels of pollution are slowly showing an adverse impact on its natural beauty and moderate climate.

SUMMARY

- Tourism marketing is an essential part of the development of the tourism industry in any country, quite like the marketing plan for any other tangible/ intangible product/ service, the marketing plan for tourism also needs to follow the normal principles of marketing.
- For the overall marketing plan to be successful it needs to have proper investment, training, implementation and control whereby the results assessed in relation to the goals and objectives that have been laid down. Necessary reviews of the plan needs to be undertaken based on feedback from evaluation system that are set in place.
- There is a need to focus attention and actions on the customer feeling and motivation, since the product offering in this industry is "a unique and exquisite experience", which is an intangible by itself.

FIELD EXERCISES

1. Figure out why India lags behind, if compared to top three global tourist destinations, in terms of marketing. Devise a strategic market planning to establish India as a global tourist destination.
2. Choose one tourist destination and analyse its tourism environment. Prepare a detailed report.

REFERENCES

Bhatia, A.K. (2006), The Business of Tourism: Concept and Strategies, Sterling Publishers.

Fyall, Allan and Bryan Garrod (2005), Tourism Marketing: A collaborative approach, Aspects of Tourism, Channelview Publications.

King, Brian, Michael McVey, David Simmons (2000), "A Societal Marketing Approach to National Tourism Planning: Evidence from the South Pacifi c," *Tourism Management*, Vol. 21, pp. 407–416.

Philip Kotler, Kevin Keller (2003), Marketing Management (A South Asian Perspective), Prentice Hall.

Negi, Jagmohan (2002), Marketing and Sales strategies for Hotels and Travel Trade, S. Chand and company.

Royo-Vela, Marcelo (2008), "Rural-Cultural Excursion Conceptualization: A Local Tourism Marketing Management Model Based on Tourist Destination Image Measurement," *Tourism Management*, Vol. 30, pp. 1–10.

Wang, Youcheng (2007), "Web-Based Destination Marketing Systems: Assessing The Critical Factors for Management and Implementation," *International Journal of Tourism Research*, Vol. 10, No.1, pp. 55–70.

Web Sites

http://www.visit-prescott.com

CHAPTER 14

Contemporary Avenues in Tourism

Nelson's Column

ABOUT THE DESTINATION

The column was completed in 1843 to commemorate the death of Admiral Horatio Nelson, the hero of the Battle of Trafalgar in 1805. The battle was the one of the most decisive British victories of the Napoleonic Wars (1803–15).

OBJECTIVES

- To understand various upcoming avenues in tourism
- To understand the potential of such contemporary avenues and challenges that lie in the path of their development

INTRODUCTION

In this chapter, we shall look closely at the various opportunities in the world of tourism – those that familiarize about tourist destinations in the world with certain unique features. In the previous chapters various marketing aspects in tourism have been discussed. This chapter focuses on various popular and upcoming avenues of tourism. The world is rapidly shrinking in terms of connectivity from place to place. The developments in technology and transport infrastructure have made tourism more affordable for the common man. Under such conditions, it is no wonder that more and more people are turning to global tourism as a leisure activity year-on-year. Tourists have higher levels of disposable income and greater leisure time; they are also better educated and have more sophisticated tastes. Tourism is a major money-spinner and vital to the economies of many countries like the United Arab Emirates (UAE), Egypt and Thailand. There are a lot of other related industries that depend on the success of the tourism industry in such countries. These include the transportation industry that includes cab services, package tours, etc., and the hospitality industry, which comprises hotels, resorts, etc.

The intention of this chapter is to make the reader aware of the current tourism situation in the world. This chapter serves to guide people on various upcoming and popular windows in the world of tourism. We shall go through some unique tourist destinations in the world, and then move on to a few popular options in contemporary world tourism, before taking up certain unsung tourism ventures as well as a case on the Dubai Shopping Festival.

TOURISM WITH A DIFFERENCE: SOME UNIQUE TOURIST DESTINATIONS

Buñol, Spain

Buñol is a town in the province of Valencia, Spain. It is a small town with an area of just around 112 sq km and a human population of close to 9,000. On the last Wednesday of August every year, things get lively in the otherwise quiet town of Buñol. And the reason for this is Tomatina de Buñol, the annual tomato-fight festival that draws in a crowd of over 30,000 from different parts of the world – more than thrice the population of Buñol itself! The tomato fight has been a strong tradition in Buñol since 1944.

The festival technically begins when one person manages to climb the top of a two-storey high, greased-up wooden pole and release the piece of ham placed at its top. The beginning of the fight is signalled by firing water cannons, and then the chaos begins. After exactly one hour, the fighting ends when the water cannons are fired once more to signal the end. In that single hour, over 110 tons of tomatoes are used up in throwing.

A Snapshot from the La Tomatina Festival

Though the tomato fight lasts only for an hour, Buñol has made the best use of the tourism potential of the occasion by creating a weeklong fest centred on the event. The festival features music, parades, dancing and fireworks. On the night before the tomato fight, participants of the festival even compete in a cooking contest.

Llanfairpwllgwyngyllgogerychwyrndrobwllllantysiliogogogoch, Wales

Please do not mistake the title to be some sort of gibberish or typographic error. This, in fact, happens to be the longest official place name in the United Kingdom and the third longest name in the world. Consisting of 58 letters, this name literally translates to "St. Mary's Church in the Hollow of the White Hazel near a Rapid Whirlpool and the Church of St. Tysilio near the Red Cave." Llanfair PG, as the place is commonly called, is a village on the island of Anglesey in Wales.

The Signboard Showing the Name, and Below it, the Correct Pronunciation of the Place Name

History has it that this is not the official name of the village, and that the name was artificially contrived in the 1860s as a sort of publicity stunt by bestowing upon the place and its station the honour of the longest name in the United Kingdom. In any case, the stunt has been quite effective as all round the year people from different parts of the world flock to the place to have photos of them taken under the station sign.

San Jose, California

San Jose is known to the world for many reasons, mostly technical and software related. But to tourists from around the world, it is famous for the Winchester Mystery House that was under construction continuously for 38 years and is allegedly haunted. The person behind this house is Sarah Winchester, the wife of eminent gun maker William Winchester. After the deaths of her husband and daughter, it somehow got it into her head that her house was haunted by ghosts of people who had died because of the Winchester rifles. The remedy for this told by a spiritual medium, as one story goes, was that she continually kept adding rooms to her house so as to confuse the ghosts! How the addition of rooms would confuse ghosts of all things is anybody's guess, but Sarah Winchester is said to have followed the instruction word for word and kept adding rooms until her death in 1922.

The result of Sarah's efforts can be seen today in the form of a four-storey tall house with about 160 rooms, now popularly known as the Winchester House. After Sarah's death, it has been said that even her ghost is roaming around in the house. To add to the ghostly element, Winchester considered the number 13 to be lucky, and, hence, 13 keeps appearing all around the house, like the chandelier with 13 candle-holders or clothes hooks in multiples of 13. A popular tourist attraction, the place stands today as a bizarre testimony to superstition and paranoia. Several tours are available to the house, special ones being on each Friday, the 13th and on Halloween.

The Winchester House

Ahmedabad, Gujarat, India

The International Kite Festival is held in Ahmedabad on January 14 of every year, to coincide with the festival of Uttarayan or Makar Sankranti – a harvest festival and a very auspicious event in India. Uttarayan is the day when the sun starts travelling northwards, marking the decline of winter. The whole of Gujarat celebrates this day as a kite-flying day, but the official festival is held at the kite capital, Ahmedabad.

Basically a Hindu festival, the festival started off as a ceremony of thanksgiving, marking the awakening of the gods from their six-month-long slumber. The belief goes that on this day the portals of heaven are thrown open again. The festival sees turnout from places like Japan, USA, Australia and the European countries every year. The day also witnesses the traditional food festival of Gujarat, giving the international crowd an opportunity to indulge themselves in authentic Gujarati food.

In the next sections various popular options of contemporary world tourism are discussed.

Reels of String on Sale for Uttarayan Kite Festival

ECOTOURISM

The International Ecotourism Society defines ecotourism as responsible travel to natural areas that conserves the environment and sustains the well-being of local people. Meanwhile, the World Conservation Union defines it as a visitation to relatively undisturbed natural areas having low negative visitor impact, and providing for beneficially active socio-economic involvement of local populations. Ecotourism is about uniting conservation, communities and sustainable travel.

Basic Principles

Given below are the basic rules that should be followed by people involved in ecotourism activities:

- Cause minimized impact on the locality
- Help build environmental and cultural awareness and respect
- Provide positive experiences for both visitors and hosts
- Provide direct financial benefits for conservation
- Provide financial benefits for the local people
- Sensitize people regarding the host countries' political, environmental and social environment profile of people who might be attracted to ecotourism

A Lion Camp in Kenya

The following is the profile of people who might be attracted to ecotourism:

- Educated travellers
- Travellers who are environmentally and socially conscious
- Travellers who enjoy cultural diversity and environmentally sound recreational activities
- Travellers who want to explore flora and fauna

According to the Program of Action of the Barbados SIDS Global Conference, "the mere availability of the requisite resources may not be sufficient to sustain either a viable ecotourism experience or a viable ecotourism business: those resources would need to meet a range of pre-requisite criteria."

The important strategic questions to ask about the development are the following:

- What has motivated the interest in and commitment to developing a strategy for ecotourism?
- What have been among the strongest influences?
- Who are the principal participants in ecotourism? Ecotourists?
- Should ecotourism be a standalone strategy, or an integral component of a broadly based tourism strategy?

Accessibility	• To the ecotourism region • To the site (access and circulation within the region)
Relationship	• Between ecotourism and other potential uses of the same resource • Complementarity, compatibility, integration and competition
Attractions	• Types of ecotourism experiences • IN (tropical forests, mountain areas) • OF (birds, trees, wild flowers, mammals) • BY (watching, filming, collecting)
Infrastructure	• Support infrastructure • Support services
Social interaction	• Level of interaction (with other ecotourists) sought, achieved • Level of interaction with local/host community sought, achieved
User prerequisites	• Prior knowledge • Prior skills • Equipment
Management	• Stakeholder involvement • Decision process

Assessment criteria for the development of ecotourism is as follows:

According to the circumstances of the ecotourism region, the tourism site, the degree of intensity of the development and the nature of that development, the above factors carry different weightage in the decision.

Below are suggestive steps that need to be taken to develop ecotourism:

- Limit tourist numbers in accordance with the area's carrying capacity
- Require permission to enter into the preserve
- Promote garbage reduction and cleanliness enhancement
- Encourage tourists to donate and contribute to the local place
- Set up a coordination centre
- Manage quality services

Box 1: Antalya (Turkey)

Tourism development, as a relatively new sector in the Turkish economy, started with the settlement of the five-year-fold economic development plans introduced by the government in the mid-1960s.

Antalya is located to the centre of Antalya Bay in the southwest coast of Turkey. The province of Antalya has a 657 km coastline, 42 km of which is within control of the greater city's municipality. Approximately, 10 km of coastline in the west side is under the authority of the state forestry department. The city of Antalya stretches along the bay bearing the same name and is built at 39 metres above sea level. Mostly, cliffs and caves constitute the coastline. Immediately to the north, Antalya is bounded by the Taurus Mountains rising to 3,086 metres above sea level, interspersed with valleys of

Box 1: (*Continued*)

varying sizes. Small and large streams emerge from the western side of the Taurus Mountains and waters the plains on their flow to the Mediterranean Sea. On the east and west parts of the Antalya plateau, large sandy beaches extend for km with high sand dunes covered by pine trees.

The plant life of Antalya is extremely varied and every kind of tropical plant can be found along the coast. Visitors to Antalya are struck by the size attained by different species of plants such as cacti. In particular, cotton, sesame, citrus and banana plants have a very diverse beauty of their own, and are hardly encountered to the same extent in other parts of the world (Uysal 1998).

The vast biodiversity and natural beauty coupled with active government support for the development have made Antalya a prime ecotourism destination in Europe and the Middle East.

The project, which incorporated the planning-programming-financing and operational stages in an integrated manner, aimed at creating a bed capacity of 65,500 by 1995 (which was slightly surpassed); generation of 20,000 jobs; setting up recreational facilities with a daily capacity to serve 200,000 people and achieving greatly improved infrastructure, health, and educational/training facilities for the local people.

SPORTS AND ADVENTURE TOURISM

Throughout the ages, the lure of sporting activities and the quest for adventure have proved to be great motivators for travel and tourism. Today, the adventure tourism sector is an approximately trillion-dollar industry. Commercial adventure tours make up a significant part of this sector. Adventure trends are, therefore, significant to the tourism industry as a whole.

Adventure sports as a category contain many different types of activities such as water sports, wildlife tourism, trekking, rock climbing, mountaineering, skiing and bungee jumping. Some of the categories are very well developed as tourist attractions, while others are at their evolving stages.

Profiles of people who might be attracted to adventure tourism are:

- Cash-rich and time-poor
- Reasonably fit
- Matured and experienced – they know what they want and what they can get at specific prices
- Relatively young people in the 16–35 years age group

Recent Trends

Below are some of the recent trends that have been observed in the adventure-tourism industry.

Increased Luxury: Tourists are demanding more luxury in adventure tours. For example:

- Backpacker buses are more comfortable.
- Wildlife, heli-ski and diving lodges have spas and massage therapists.
- Dive boats, surfboats and heli-ski operations offer private charters with especially luxurious facilities. Expedition cruise boats have suites with satellite phones, and sometimes even a helicopter

Adventure Destinations: The number of adventure-tourism destinations has increased greatly in recent years. Some of these are already developed tourism destinations and have added new products or changed their marketing strategies. Others are upcoming destinations seeking to develop tourism through a portfolio of adventure products.

Rishikesh: River Rafting

Retail Packaging: Many tour operators offer a portfolio of products at different destinations. They do not necessarily maintain an operational base at each of the destinations concerned. Many of these retail packagers develop a range of local tour products for the international clientele. Some specialist tour operators offer similar products or activities at multiple destinations.

Combination Products: Nowadays, almost all of the individual tour operators offer a range of different adventure activities at a single destination. These are often packaged as a discounted bundle of individual tours, marketed as a "combo" product. Some combo products simply involve syndicated marketing with on-ground activities operated by separate companies.

Flexible Itineraries: The tour companies also offer flexible schedules or itineraries as part of the adventure tour. This approach is used at both ends of the economic scale from overland buses to polar expedition cruises.

Copycats and Takeovers: Establishing a new adventure-tourism product requires considerable investment in product development and marketing. Once a new product is launched and becomes successful, other entrepreneurs often attempt to establish copycat products at lower/reduced prices. This problem is more severe for new products in developing countries.

Insurance: Because of litigation, especially in developed countries, adventure-tourism providers are very concerned about potential liability lawsuits. This has led to increasingly lengthy and complex pre-trip waivers and disclaimers, as well as much-increased insurance premiums.

Africa Safari Tours — An Example. Blessed with plenty of natural places where adventure tourism can be developed such as forests, coasts, mountains, lakes and deserts, Kenya developed various kinds of safari tours to cater to the tourism needs of people with different profiles.

Kenya Safari Tour

The different kinds of activities that Kenya actively promotes include trekking from the snowcapped peak of Mt. Kenya to the desert plains of the north; rock climbing; mountain biking; horse riding through herds in the wild; riding in camel trains that follow ancient routes through deep valleys and along winding dry river beds; boating, water skiing and windsurfing; and white-water rafting and kayaking.

ENTERTAINMENT TOURISM

We are entering an age when entertainment touches every aspect of our lives. We find entertainment at hotels and restaurants, shopping malls, television and radio, and also on Web sites, cellular phones and PDAs. There are museums, galleries, sporting events, theatres, nightlife entertainments, festivals, live music, dance, comedy, dining, shopping, antiquing, gambling centres and many such things that attract a lot of tourists across countries. For example, Disneyland attracts tourists from across the world, as mentioned in the next section.

Disneyland

Disneyland, one of the world's most well-known theme parks with presence in different countries, attracts tourists from all over the world. Disneyland offers magical experiences for the whole family, ranging from Broadway-style shows such as *Festival of the Lion King* and *The Golden Mickeys*, to hilarious 3D movie and musical adventures at Mickey's Philharmagic. There are also the signature Disney attractions, phototaking with favourite Disney friends, spectacular fireworks and a parade that is sure to enthrall the entire family.

Disneyland

Film Festival Tourism

A relatively recent phenomenon is film-festival tourism. It refers to the organized effort to use film festivals as a central incentive to attract cultural tourists or consumers (in addition to film professionals) drawn by the theme or the importance of the festival for the film industry. Film tourism also includes film-studio theme parks and screening of special block-buster movies at amusement parks.

Many cities hold film festivals that attract film buffs and fans to the event. Celebrities like actors, actresses and film directors have large numbers of fans and are able to draw huge crowds at the events where they appear. Occasions such as Cannes or Edinburgh film festivals attract thousands of people. The Bahamas International Film Festival and the annual 10-day Santa Barbara Film Festival are other examples.

Cannes Film Festival

There are off-location tourism options such as film studios and film-based theme parks. Paramount Studios in Hollywood runs guided tours of its site. Other Hollywood studios such as Universal and Warner Brothers have developed tourist-specific theme parks based on their hit movies like Jurassic *Park and Back to the Future*. New Zealand benefited from its holiday packages centring on the film set for the *Lord of the Rings* trilogy, the so-called "set-jetting phenomenon."

There are clear economic and political benefits derived from investing in cultural events since more visitors come to the venue of the festival and support the local economy through expenditures on lodging, meals, local products and other leisure activities.

Evidently, success of such ventures in film-festival destination tourism cannot be taken for granted. They may succeed if certain conditions are met. For one, the festival has to deliver quality programming since the individuals engaging in film-festival tourism tend to come from affluent and well-educated backgrounds with more refined cinematic tastes. Further, the location of the festival must reinforce the attraction of the fest, and the festival organizer needs to develop a comprehensive travel package in private-public sector partnerships.

Film Tourism in India

There are various opportunities for entertainment tourism development in India. Some of the avenues are already attracting a lot of tourists. India has tried to replicate the model of film festival in cities like Cannes with promotional strategies that include international film festivals in Goa, Mumbai and Trivandrum (present Thiruvananthapuram), which foster the tourism industry at these destinations. Another major highlight of entertainment tourism is Bollywood tourism, which involves daylong tours of shooting locations in Mumbai, Hyderabad (Ramoji Film City; discussed in the next section), etc.

Other entertainment tourism options include music fests and dance fests like the Chennai Dance and Music Festival, which attracts music and dance lovers from all over the world.

Ramoji Film City, Hyderabad, India. Ramoji Film City is conveniently located on the outskirts of the twin cities of Hyderabad and Secunderabad. It is one of the most comprehensive and professionally planned film-production centres in the world. Located at an hour's distance from Hyderabad, it is spread over an area of more than 1,000 acres. The place is popular among various film circles in the world not only for being a visual feast, but also for its multimedia and editing suit techniques.

Ramoji Film City, Hyderabad

Right at the entrance one will find a couple of three-star hotels called Tara and Sitara, where you will be given a royal treatment as a visitor. If one goes further, there are various gardens ranging from Japanese to tea gardens, temples sans idols, schools that turn into police stations at the drop of the board, colleges that double up as havelis and airports whose rear entrance is used for the hospital shot and side entrance for church. Sets like the airport and the hospital are astonishing.

The Film City tour takes you through a world full of surprises, scares and delights. You are taken in special buses first to Eureka, which is the beginning and also the end of the tour. Eureka is an architectural reproduction of a bygone era taking you across ornamental bridges and into the bowels of forts.

Conclusion

One of the major advantages of entertainment tourism like film festivals is that its economic benefit can be accrued throughout the year, without any inherent seasonality that is there in other tourism options. But there are problems such as exploitation of tourists by locals and increasing prices of entertainment industry. Also, the actual location may turn out to be different from what is being portrayed through advertisements or in films, resulting in consumer dissatisfaction. Access of tourists to the festivals, above and beyond the provision of travel, accommodations and passes or tickets is also to be taken care of. Proper destination (place) marketing, strategies and planning are very important to the success of tourism based on entertainment. Entertainment tourism serves basic consumer motivations like the desire to experience the imaginary pleasures that have been developed in the mind. The fun and frolic felt at the fairs and festivals can only be experienced rather than explained.

MEDICAL TOURISM

The hectic pace of life today has led to increasing incidences of lifestyle-related diseases. Increase in awareness about keeping oneself healthy, coupled with the rise in standards of living, has led to an increase in the demand for quality healthcare services. Increasing healthcare costs have resulted in patients in the developed world looking overseas for medical treatment. Under these circumstances, the healthcare services industry has emerged as one of the flourishing sectors in developing countries and is providing high standards of services.

In the past decade, the attempt to achieve better health while on holiday (through relaxation, exercise or visits to spas) has been taken to a new level with the emergence of a new and distinct niche in the tourism industry: medical tourism.

Some of the earliest forms of tourism were directly aimed at enhancing health and well-being, for example, the numerous spas that remain in many parts of Europe and elsewhere, which were common by the 18th century. With the partial exception of some spas, none of this had involved actual medical treatment, but merely provided incidental benefits in amenable, relaxing contexts. However, medical tourism as a distinct tourism niche has now emerged, satisfying the needs of a growing number of people, mainly in developed countries, benefiting both themselves and a growing number of destinations.

Some Third World countries like South Africa, Thailand and Malaysia were the first to try and tap medical tourism, and all of them geared their systems to attract the growing American clientele. India is also becoming a major destination for medical tourism owing to its high standards in medical care and service, and price competitiveness.

Reasons for the Success of Medical Tourism

The following are the reasons for the success of medical tourism:

- **Crowded conditions:** There is a long queue of patients for various treatments in developed countries.
- **Cost factor:** The cost of the treatment is much less in developing countries as compared to the rest of the world.
- **Demographic pattern:** In many developed countries, the proportion of population aged over 60 years is increasing, and is expected to still go up, as a result of which the healthcare infrastructure falls short.
- **A vacation:** Tourists from other countries have the dual benefit of a vacation and surgical treatments when they come to countries like India.
- **Infrastructure and medical technology:** Most of the countries promoting medical tourism have the latest infrastructure and medical technology, and offer the best treatment in modern medicine across medical divisions such as cardiology, orthopaedic surgery, eye care, gynaecology, cosmetics and dental surgery. India, in addition, also provides traditional methods of treatment such as ayurveda, homeopathy, naturopathy and yoga.
- **Qualified professionals:** Internationally, qualified and experienced specialists attract foreign patients from all over the world. Especially, Indian medical professionals are known for high-quality care.
- **Lack of healthcare services:** In some of the less developed countries, such as Bangladesh, specialized treatments are not available.

Medical Tourism in India: An Emerging Industry

The medical-tourism market in India is estimated at $333 million (Heath Care Sector Report, 2004) and is growing at 30 per cent per annum. According to a study by McKinsey and the Confederation of Indian Industry (CII), medical tourism in India can become a $1 billion business by 2012. It is estimated that nearly 15,000 foreigners have been treated in India in recent years.

Key Issues and Challenges. The major challenges that developing countries like India face in successfully promoting health tourism are as follows:

- Basic amenities need to be at par with international standards, especially air connectivity, road links, local conveyance and Internet connectivity.
- The issue of coordination between healthcare and tourism sectors is also critical.
- A major concern is about trained medical professionals who go abroad and settle down there. This is a major setback to the medical-tourism industry in India.

- Global accreditation of hospitals is also a major issue that the medical-tourism industry will have to respond to.
- Specifically for India, competitive cost advantage in healthcare is high in comparison to Thailand, Singapore and other healthcare destinations. But it has very poor visibility on the world healthcare-tourism map.

In conclusion, effective marketing as well as market research to segment the market with a view to tapping the full potential is absolutely essential.

LITERARY TOURISM

Literary tourism concerns itself with the places and events quoted in fictional texts, as well as the life of the author. The primary target market for such a venture is the literature enthusiast who is very keen to explore why such an environment inspired an author.

The culture of literary tourism can be traced back to the mid-19th century, with the promotion of Wordsworth's Lake District,[1] Dickens's London[2] and Hardy's Wessex,[3] among other imagined territories. Shakespeare's birthplace at Stratford-upon-Avon, which includes places of interest like Shakespeare's house, is another popular literary-tourism destination. The United Kingdom is considered to be the pioneer in the art of literary tourism, with their strategy of associating writers with countries. This strategy has been successful in promoting places like Cornwall, which is the home and theme site of various novelists including Thomas Hardy and Daphne du Maurier, and provides the backdrop to Winston Graham's Poldark series.

Shakespeare's House at Stratford-upon-Avon

Another interesting concept, popularized by the Irish Government is the Dublin Literary Pub Crawl, in which two actors give a pub tour introducing the writers in the process and performing scenes from their works. Mostly, famous writers from Dublin such as James Joyce, Samuel Beckett, the Behan brothers, Mary Lavin, Oscar Wilde, Eavan Boland and Paula Meehan are featured in the crawl.

In India, the practice of literary tourism has not caught as much attention as other avenues; however, the promotion of places like Shantiniketan and Tagore Hill, which are places associated with Rabindranath Tagore, proves that the culture of literary tourism exists in this country. Shantiniketan was the result of the great poet's vision of a world of peace and harmony (shanti = peace; niketan = house). Apart from Uttarayan, the complex where Tagore lived and now converted into a museum and art gallery, this "abode of peace" also houses Viswa Bharati University, which is now a centre for international studies and culture.

---

[1] Lake District: A village in northwest England known for its natural beauty, and popularized by its close association with Wordsworth. Wordsworth mentioned it in many poems, the most famous being "I Wandered Lonely as a Cloud."

[2] Dickens' London: London as popularized by Charles Dickens in his writings.

[3] Hardy's Wessex: Fictional names given by Thomas Hardy to different areas in the south and southwest of England, in various writings of his. For example, Hardy's hometown Dorchester was called Casteridge in the book *The Mayor of Casterbridge*.

Nearby destinations are Ballavpur Wildlife Sanctuary and Kenduli, which is the birthplace of the poet Jaydev.

Other destinations include Mussoorie, which is being promoted as the backdrop for a lot of Ruskin Bond's stories; the Thiruvalluvar statue at Kanyakumari which promotes the rich cultural heritage of the state; and Thonnakkal Asan Memorial and Tirur, which is the hometown of Thunjath Ramanujan "Ezhuthachan" – regarded as the first authentic writer (12th century AD) in Malayalam.

A popular ceremony that attracts tourists worldwide is "Ezhuthiniruthu," which is the ritual for initiating children into the world of letters. Popular writers and poets gather at the heritage site, and help children write the first letters of their life. This process is supposed to please the goddess of learning.

RURAL TOURISM

Rural tourism's emphasis is on creating an experience in rural setting. Worldwide, farming as an agricultural choice is getting highly mechanized and, therefore, requires less labour. This is causing economic pressure on the village, leading to exodus of innocent youths to urban centres. Rural tourism's focus is on participating in the rural lifestyle.

Rural tourism includes the following:

- **Agri-tourism:** There are various attractions in agri-tourism which pull tourists to rural areas. Some of the attractions are genuine rural atmosphere with farm accommodation, learning traditional crafts and skills from the hosts, and above all is enjoying homemade food and drinks. Visitors participate in agricultural operations, camel riding, buffalo riding, cooking and rural games like *gillidanda*[4] and *gotti*.[5] They can buy rural crafts, dress materials, farm gate-fresh processed food, and see animals, birds, farms, dresses and festivals. Tourism on the farms enables farmers to diversify their activities while enhancing the value of their products and property. Farm tourism also helps reconcile farming interests and environmental protection through integrated land management in which farmers continue to play a key role. Also, agri-tourism brings major primary sector agriculture closer to major service sector tourism, which is expected to create a win-win situation for both.
- **Heritage and cultural tourism in rural areas:** This kind of tourism includes temples and rural buildings, but may be extended to local features of interest including war remnants, monuments to famous literary, artistic or scientific people, historic remains, archaeological sites and traditional parkland.

Thiruvalluvar Statue at Kanyakumari

[4] Gillidanda: An amateur sport similar to cricket and popular among youth in the Indian subcontinent.

[5] Gotti: Game played using glass marbles in parts of India.

- **Ecotourism:** Many tourists visit rural areas for the purpose of bird and animal watching and learning about local flora and fauna. A rural tourist destination as a product is definitely very fragile in ecological, social and cultural sense. Its development requires very specific approach that could help it remain sustainable in the long term.

Rural Tourism Development

In developed nations, people prefer to take weekends off doing farming or visiting the countryside to de-stress and take a break from their office routines. Most of the European countries pay lots of attention to rural tourism. The growth of rural tourism is difficult to quantify because few countries collect statistics in a way that separate the purely rural from other forms of tourism. The concept of agri-tourism developed in the 1980s in Europe, and the participating farms have doubled in countries like Italy, the United Kingdom and France. The number of agri-tourism accommodation units exceeds 60,000. In the middle of the 1990s, 12 European countries (Belgium, Denmark, Greece, Netherlands, Portugal, Spain, Ireland, Great Britain, Italy, Austria, France and Germany) had more than 10,000 farm enterprises involved with different tourism activities. It is obvious that most of the European countries have a positive attitude towards rural tourism development because of the impact this strategy has on rural areas and their overall development. In America, rural tourism has great potential. A wide variety of tourist opportunities exist throughout rural America and continue to grow as increasing numbers of local entrepreneurs identify new ways to market previously untapped local resources and attractions, and bring tourists into their area.

Rural tourism is becoming important in developing countries like India also. It is especially true of nations where farming land is fragmented due to population growth and the farmer gets into the credit trap. In a country like India, where over 70 per cent of the population resides in the villages, the concept of rural tourism certainly holds a lot of significance. It leads to the dual benefit of tourism development and potential improvements in incomes and living standards of rural folk. Rural tourism will definitely add more to what a country earns in foreign exchange. Rural tourism will hasten the process of development and give a chance to the village folks to interact with the outside world. It will boost employment opportunities in rural areas, and the products of rural artisans will also find a ready market.

Rural Tourism in India

India is known as the land of villages. In 2001, more than 770 million farmers lived in 0.55 million villages . Agriculture contributed about 18.5 per cent of the national income in 2006–2007, as compared to a high 50 per cent in 1950. An estimated 85 per cent of the population of India still depend on agriculture. Hence, agriculture is not mere business but is the true culture of India. Rich in traditions of arts, crafts and culture, rural India can emerge as an important tourist destination. Those in the developed world who have a craze for imbibing knowledge about the traditional ways of life, arts and crafts will be attracted to visit rural India if the concept of rural tourism is marketed well. The government of India has initiated a competitive marketing programme for the new rural-tourism product, backed by the country's economic transformation and world recognition of India as a preferred destination. The union ministry of tourism in collaboration with the United Nations Development Programme (UNDP) has launched the Endogenous Tourism Project linked to the existing rural-tourism scheme of the government of India. The UNDP has committed $2.5 million for the project. The UNDP will help in areas of capacity building and work towards involvement of NGOs, local communities and artisans to help forge a strong community of private- and public-sector partnerships.

Project "rural tourism scheme" is now online, with a new Web site — www.exploreruralindia.org. The Web site showcases 31 unique villages in India where the ministry of tourism and UNDP have collaborated to promote sustainable livelihoods through rural tourism. Also, the government has decided to develop necessary infrastructure for facilitating rural tourism. It has identified 31 villages across the country as tourist spots. These are: Pochampalli in Nalgonda district and Srikalahasti of Chittor district of Andhra Pradesh; Durgapur in Golaghat district and Sualkuchi in Kamrup district of Assam; Nepura in Nalanda district of Bihar; Chitrakote and Nagarnar in Bastar district of Chhattisgarh; Hodka in Kachchh district of Gujarat; Jyotisar in Kurukshetra district of Haryana; Naggar in Kullu district of Himachal Pradesh; Banavasi in Uttar Kannada district of Karnataka; Aranmulla in Pathanamthitta district and Kumbalanghi in Kochi district of Kerala; Chaugan in Mandla district and Pranpur in Ashok Nagar district of Madhya Pradesh; Sulibhanjan-Khultabad in Aurangabad district of Maharashtra; Pipili and Raghurajpur in Puri district of Orissa; Rajasansi in Amritsar district of Punjab; Neemrana in Alwar district, Samode in Jaipur district, and Haldighati in Rajsamand district of Rajasthan; Lachen in North District of Sikkim; Karaikudi in Sivaganga district and Kazhugumalai in Thoothukudi district of Tamil Nadu; Kamlasagar in West Tripura district of Tripura; Bhaguwala in Saharanpur district of Uttar Pradesh; Jageshwar in Almora district and Mana in Chamoli district of Uttaranchal; and Ballabhpur Danga in Birbhum district and Mukutmanipur in Bankura district of West Bengal.

Challenges

The inflow of tourists in rural areas can generate social, cultural, economical and environmental problems. Rural areas are sparsely populated; they are predominantly set in a natural environment and based on preservation of culture, heritage and traditions. Proper control of tourist inflow should be ensured so that they do not disturb the tradition and culture of rural areas. Security of the tourists is another priority. Availability of amenities like hospitals, police stations and lodging facilities is a concern in rural areas. Support and participation of local government is especially important in the following areas: (i) funding for tourism development and promotion, (ii) creating and maintenance of infrastructure necessary for tourism, (iii) zoning and maintenance of the community so that it looks clean and appealing to tourists and (iv) educational support for farmers.

Conclusion

Rural tourism has a lot to offer to the world. Good planning is important for its development. The strength of rural communities is their strong personnel networks, but coordination and cooperation between the local government and the business community do not always occur easily. For tourism development and planning to work, coordination and cooperation between local government and entrepreneurs is crucial. Good planning for tourism development and promotion can help develop and support local businesses connected to tourism. Also, community support for tourism development and the attitudes and hospitality of local tourism workers are important.

MUSIC TOURISM

The rise of cultural tourism all over the world has led to the rise of various genres of tourism, and music tourism is one of the major upcoming niche tourism avenues. The link between music and tourism is a wonderfully pleasant association and has, therefore, inspired a lot of tourists to explore its possibilities, leading to an expansion of the boundaries and components of this form of tourism. Till sometime back, music tourism would have only featured Graceland, Elvis Presley's Mansion in Memphis. Today, it includes within its scope the musical genres including rock festivals, classical music festivals and traditional music promotion of almost all nations spanning the globe. The following sections cover these:

Graceland, Tennessee

Several hundred thousand visitors pay homage to Elvis Presley, the king of rock-and-roll, each year at his historic home, Graceland. For these visitors, Elvis is brought to life during audio tours that include his own voice as well as stories and memories of the house from his widow, Priscilla, and daughter, Lisa Marie.

Surprisingly, more than half of Graceland's 700,000 annual visitors are under the age of 35 years – people who have not heard him alive. And it is not just Americans who are fascinated with Elvis Presley. Graceland sees more international visitors from the United Kingdom (33 per cent) than from neighbouring Canada (29 per cent).

It is natural that over the 25 years that Graceland has been open to the public, a synergy has developed between the marketing of Memphis and Graceland. Graceland is the launching pad for music tourism in Memphis. Over the past 10 years, Memphis has grown into a three- or four-day destination to see everything from Sun Studio, where Elvis first recorded and was discovered, to Beale Street, whose blues bars influenced him, to the Smithsonian's Rock 'n' Soul Museum.

Trophy Room at Graceland

Traditional Music of Scotland

The government of Scotland has realized how traditional music will play an important role in promoting both tourism and culture at home and abroad.

Attempts have been made to disseminate ideas and examples of good practice gathered during the traditional music and tourism initiative, which ran throughout Scotland between 1998 and 2001. The project, a joint initiative by Scottish Arts Council and Visit Scotland, looked at ways in which the profile of traditional music could be raised within Scottish tourism. One key finding to come out of this innovative three-year study has been that visitors to Scotland expect to be able to hear traditional music, and overwhelmingly enjoy it when they do. One such survey showed that 78 per cent of visitors believed their holiday had been enhanced by local projects to promote traditional music, while 12 per cent reported that the sessions had influenced their decision to visit.

Accordingly, the Scottish Government has been focusing on promoting their traditional music forms to attract tourists.

Traditional Scottish Musical Instruments

Chennai Music Festival

The Chennai music festival is an event hosted in Chennai, India, every December–January, spanning some five weeks. The Music Season started in 1927 to mark the opening of the Madras Music Academy. Earlier it was be a traditional month-long Carnatic music festival, but over the years it has also diversified into dance and drama, as well as non-Carnatic art forms. The traditional role of the Music Season is to allow aficionados of Carnatic music to appreciate performances by renowned artistes, and also to provide a good opportunity for promising young artistes to display their talent and skills. During this time, a large number of *sabhas* (music halls) organize *kutcheris* (formal concerts). Artistes come from across the India and from among the international Indian diaspora to perform during the season. The event has grown over the years; there were over 1,200 performances by about 600 artistes in 2004–2005 (about 700 vocal, 250 instrumental, 200 dance, 50 drama and others). The Chennai festival is the world's largest cultural event, even larger than the Woodstock[6] festival. Curiously enough, an overwhelming majority of the population seems hardly conscious of its proportion and size. A possible explanation is that the social base of Indian classical arts, generally, and of Carnatic music, in particular, continues to be rather narrow. The festival does see some foreign nationals interested in Indian classical arts. Considering the popularity of Indian classical artistes such as L. Subramaniam, Pandit Ravishankar, Trilok Gurtu and L. Shankar, Indian classical music, if marketed properly, could be a major way of attracting music enthusiasts from all across the world.

TO CONCLUDE: SOME UPCOMING TRENDS

We have looked at various tourism options including ecotourism, sports and adventure tourism, music tourism, medical tourism and rural tourism. The nature of the tourism industry is dynamic, with new avenues cropping up from time to time. It is, indeed, surprising that the amount of innovation and creativity going into this industry over long periods of time has been consistent. People never seem to run out of ideas for promoting a particular town/region/state. This innovative nature is the backbone of tourism and fosters growth in the industry.

Tourism had one constraint till now, that is, geographic location. Now, the advent of space travel has opened another exciting avenue in the form of space tourism. Space tourism, dark and disaster tourism, and other new advents are discussed as follows:

Space Tourism

Sponsored space flight is not a new phenomenon. Tokyo Broadcasting offered to pay $28 million to the Russian Space Federation for flying one of its reporters, Toyohiro Akiyama, on a space mission. Akiyama gave a daily TV broadcast from orbit and also performed scientific experiments for Russian and Japanese companies. However, since the cost of the flight was paid by his employer, Akiyama could be considered a business traveller rather than a tourist. Dennis Tito, an American businessman and a former JPL scientist, is considered the first space tourist, as he was the first person to pay for his own flight. However, at this early stage of its development, space tourism is very expensive and risky. "Space Adventures" is the only company that offers such a service in association with Russian Soyuz media, and the cost for a space flight ranges from $20 to $28 million. Also, the process involves rigorous physical training and people need to wait for 5–6 years for their dream to become a reality. However, newly incorporated companies like Virgin Galactic promise to offer this service for $200,000 from 2009 onwards. As of November 2007, Virgin Galactic had pre-sold nearly 200 seats for their suborbital space-tourism

[6] Woodstock: A music festival that first happened in New York from August 15 to 18, 1969, featuring 32 of the best musicians of that time. There have been three more editions of Woodstock following the first one, the last being in 1999.

flights, according to the company's president. This is surely an indication that space tourism of the future is going to be an exciting and affordable affair.

Dark and Disaster Tourism

Other avenues like dark tourism and disaster tourism are catching on, an example being visits to places hit by the tsunami to appreciate the extent of the calamity. This would encourage people visiting the place to make some contributions to help rehabilitate the region and bring it back into the mainstream.

Other New Advents

Other new advents are tombstone tourism, war tourism and bookstore tourism. These are discussed below.

- **Tombstone tourism:** The practice of visiting the graves of famous people who are dead
- **War tourism:** Visiting war sites for sightseeing
- **Bookstore tourism:** Promotes independent bookstores as a group travel destination

Other specific areas include shark tourism and lion safari (promoted in Africa).

In summation, the inherent nature of the tourism industry is that of continuous innovation. What would be in vogue a decade down the line is something only time can tell. However, what we can be certain about is that whatever new initiatives crop up, tourism promoters would work tirelessly to create a value proposition for tourists to derive pleasure out of their travel experiences.

Case Study: Dubai Shopping Festival

History

Dubai is one of the seven emirates comprising the United Arab Emirates, and the most populous among all. Since the early 20th century, Dubai has been known as a trading hub of the Middle East, greatly benefitting from its geographical proximity to India. Following the infamous Iraqi invasion of Kuwait in 1990, the oil prices shot up, which benefitted all the Gulf countries alike. Since Dubai's major strength was trade (only 6 per cent of its revenues are due to oil, contrary to many other countries of the Middle East), it was encouraged to focus on free trade and tourism. There had been a free zone established in 1979, named Jebel Ali Free Zone, to promote unrestricted import of labour and goods. The success of this zone prompted the government to open new clusters of free zones.

Due to the low import duties, the goods were available at cheaper prices, and, hence, people from all over the world started visiting Dubai in increased numbers to buy things like jewellery. The Dubai administration saw this as a splendid opportunity for promoting their tourism industry as well, and came up with the path-breaking idea of having a shopping festival. Thus, was started the Dubai Shopping Festival (DSF) on February 15, 1996. This was a revolutionary approach as Dubai invited different nations to set up their shops in the DSF venue in their own cultural style, thereby giving the visitors a glimpse of various cultures while they bought the merchandise.

Facts and Figures

When DSF started in 1996, it was intended as a pure retail event. But Dubai has slowly and steadily built up its tourist attractions centred on the month-long festival to increase the number of visitors, and today it stands as an out-and-out tourism festival. For instance, DSF 2008 featured a fashion festival, a theatre festival, a food festival and musical shows by world-renowned artistes like A. R. Rahman, Zakir Hussain and Carlos Santana. There are also other mini-festivals organized in tandem with the main DSF throughout the month, so as to cater to tourists with esoteric interests. To quote an

Case Study: Dubai Shopping Festival *(Continued)*

A Glittering View of the Dubai Shopping Festival

example, the festival every year features a heritage village that shows the cultural traditions followed in Dubai, including even a real Arab wedding. This offers ample opportunity for people researching on Arab traditions. During the festival, the hotels in the city also provide special offers to the customers so as to further attract the tourists. The effectiveness of these efforts is clearly reflected in the exponential rise in the turnout for the event year-on-year. While DSF 1996 saw a 1.6 million-strong crowd spending about 2.15 billion dirhams, DSF 2007 saw it increasing to a massive 10.2 billion dirhams spent by 3.5 million visitors (*source:* www.mydsf.com).

Further Initiatives

Charged up by the huge success of DSF, the Dubai Government further came up with the idea of Dubai Summer Surprises, a summer counterpart of DSF, in 1998. This is a 10-week event aiming more at family-oriented entertainment. This fest was primarily introduced to prevent families in Dubai going abroad for summer vacations. By providing a variety of entertainment every year, this fest has also found its mark, with the 2007 edition seeing a turnout of 2.16 million people, spending 3.21 dirhams (*source:* www.mydsf.com).

Conclusion

DSF's success story is an ideal example of how a place can turn around its strength to promote tourism. The Dubai Government knew that their strength was as a prominent shopping destination, and they built on this reputation. The result stands tall for everyone to see. The fact that the 2007 edition of DSF was slated to earn a revenue close to 8 per cent of Dubai's GDP (*source:* http://www.ameinfo.com) in itself speaks volumes about the advantages of such revolutionary initiatives.

Unsung Tourist Destination: Wayanad, Kerala

Kerala has been traditionally credited with being God's Own Country, and tourism is a major source of business sustenance in parts of the state of Kerala. Yet, Wayanad district in north Kerala is a relatively unexplored region here which shows potential for being a great tourist destination.

Wayanad is a high-altitude district, and is of enormous historical and ecological significance. It presents a contrary picture to the rest of the state, in that its population density is only 369 people per square kilometre, compared to the state average of 819 per sq km. Wayanad is gifted with extensive forest cover and agriculture is the mainstay of the economy, making it all the more attractive as a natural tourism destination. Its close proximity to Bandipur National Park, which is already a famous tourist destination, can only act as an advantage.

Places to See Around

The following places are the main attractions of Wayanad:

An Elephant Strolling in Muthunga Wildlife Sanctuary

Edakkal Caves: These are a set of two caves located about 1,000 metres above sea level, and contain Neolithic and Stone Age carvings. Discovered by a British explorer in 1890, these petroglyphs (stone carvings) of humans, animals, tools, etc., are considered extremely rare and found only in very few parts of the world.

Muthanga Wildlife Sanctuary: Located on the way from Mysore to Sultan Bathery, it is a hotspot for nature lovers. Being one of the three biggest sanctuaries in Kerala, it is considered a hotbed for sightings of bison, tiger, deer and elephants, among other wild animals. There are a few waterfalls, the most prominent among them being Soochippara.

How to Reach Wayanad

Wayanad is accessible from all parts of Kerala, Karnataka and Tamil Nadu by road. NH 212 connecting Calicut to Mysore is only 3 km away. Wayanad is an entry point to Kerala for many travellers from Bangalore, Mysore and Coorg in Karnataka. The nearest railway station, Calicut, is 75 km away. The closest airport, at Calicut, is 2.5 hours away from Wayanad.

Best Time to Visit

Wayanad has a pleasant climate for most parts of the year. High altitude regions in Wayanad district experience severe cold. In Wayanad, the mean maximum and minimum temperature are generally 29° C and 18° C respectively. Wayanad and surrounding areas experience high humidity which may go up to 95 per cent during the South West monsoon period. One can visit the place any time except the South West monsoon period.

SUMMARY

- Development of technology and transport infrastructure has facilitated movement of tourists in the international circuit. This has led to more avenues of tourism being introduced.
- Ecotourism is responsible travel to natural areas that conserves the environment and sustains the well-being of local people.

- Sporting activities and a quest for adventure contribute to adventure tourism which is a trillion dollar industry today.
- Various avenues of entertainment mark the entertainment tourism today.
- Attempts to achieve better health while on a holiday (through relaxation, exercise or visits to spas) represent medical tourism.
- Visits to places and events quoted in fictional texts and life of the author represent literary tourism.
- Creating a rural experience set in a village-type set up forms rural tourism.
- Promoting traditional music or any other kind of cultural and music programme as a potential tourism avenue represents music tourism.
- Latest avenues of tourism are space tourism, dark and disaster tourism, tombstone tourism, war tourism and bookstore tourism.

FIELD EXERCISES

1. Visit any unsung destination near your area and develop a model to promote it as a unique tourist destination.
2. Visit any village and analyse whether it could be developed as a tourist destination. Talk to local people and figure out the challenges involved.

REFERENCES

Buckley, R. (2006) Adventure Tourism, CABI, Oxford Source, Goymen K. (2000), "Tourism and Governance in Turkey," *Annals of Tourism Research*, Vol. 27, No. 4, pp. 1025–1048.

Web Sites

www.latomatina.es
http://customsholidays.suite101.com
http://www.valencia-cityguide.com
http://www.economicexpert.com/a/Llanfair:PG.html
http://www.frommers.com/destinations/sanjoseca/1064024175.html
http://www.winchestermysteryhouse.com/facts.html
http://www.livescience.com/strangenews/top5_haunted_places-1.html
http://hinduismabout.com/cs/festivals/a/aa011103a.htm
http://www.vadodaracity.com/uttarayan.htm
http://www.vibrantgujarat.com/
www.ecotourism.org
www.mexico.com/mexico-tourism/mexico-eco-tourism
www.spto.org/spto/export/sites/spto/tourism_resources/ presentations/forums/
www.xolaconsulting.com
www.indian-medical-tourism.com
http://www.thestratfordguide.co.uk
http://www.kerala-hub.com
http://www.kanyakumari.nic.in
http://www.space-tourism.ws
http://www.indfy.com/west-bengal-india/shantiniketan-tourist-attractions/
http://www.dublinpubcrawl.com
http://www.ies.sas.ac.uk/events/conferences/2007/literarytourism/index.htm
http://www.squidoo.com/Literary-tourism
www.incredibleindia.org
www.exploreruralindia.org
http://dspace.iimk.ac.in
www.elvis.com
www.scotland.gov.uk
www.wayanad.nic.in
www.mydsf.com
www.pilotguides.com
www.blog.hotelclub.com
www.aim168realestate.wordpress.com
www.dubaitourism.ae
www.middleeastevents.com
www.germantravelnetwork.com
www.ameinfo.com

Glossary

ASI Archaeological Survey of India.

Adventure travel Type of tourism, involving exploration or travel to remote, exotic, and possibly hostile areas, where the traveller should 'expect the unexpected'.

Available market The set of consumers who have interest, income, and access to a particular offer.

Ayurveda It is a system of traditional medicine native to India and practiced in other parts of the world as a form of alternative medicine. In Sanskrit, the word Ayurveda comprises the words āyus, meaning 'life' and veda, meaning 'science'.

Bazaar A word in Hindi, which means marketplace.

Brand It is a symbolic embodiment of all the information connected to a company, product, or service.

Brand value sustenance It is the long-lasting appeal of the brand and not getting affected by the clutches of brand life cycle.

Budget hotels Hotels which focus more on basic services while eliminating frills and other services. Typically these hotels do not provide room service but focus more on the basic lodging facilities.

Business environment It includes all the elements which surround the business organization like its stakeholders, technological, political situation, etc.

CMS A computer application used to create, edit, manage, search, and publish various kinds of digital media and electronic text.

CRM Customer relationship management, a process or methodology used to learn more about customers' needs and behaviours.

Carnatic music A system of Indian classical music commonly associated with the southern part of India.

Cataract A large waterfall.

Communication channel Various methods by which messages are delivered.

Communications mix This includes various marketing tools like advertizement, sales promotion, direct marketing, etc., that are used to convey message.

Communication process A process by which the receiver of the message as the sender have understood.

Consumer behaviour It attempts to understand the buyer the decision-making process and purchase process of consumers based on consumer's psychology and characteristics.

Customer benefit The perceived monetary value of the bundle of the economic, psychological, and functional benefits that the customer expects from a given market offering because of the products, services, personnel, and the images involved.

Customer cost The perceived bundle of costs that the customers expect to incur in evaluating, obtaining, using, and disposing of the given market offering including monetary, time, energy, and psychological costs.

Customer loyalty The behaviour of repeat customers, as well as those that offer good ratings, reviews, or testimonials.

Customer perceived value The difference between the prospective customer's evaluation of all the benefits and all the costs of an offering and the perceived alternatives.

Customer relationship management It is a process or methodology used to learn more about customers' needs and behaviours to develop stronger relationships with them.

Customer satisfaction A measure of how products and services supplied by a company meet or surpass customer expectation.

Customer value proposition It consists of the sum total of benefits, which a vendor promises that a customer will receive in return for the customer's associated payment (or other value-transfer).

Customisation It refers to the changing or the modification of a packaged product or a service to meet the customer's individual requirements.

Demography The branch of sociology that studies the characteristics of human populations.

Destination brand It is an expression of the planned offer of value and experience that a place provides to target consumers in priority markets—investors, businesses, institutions, residents, and visitors.

Destination brand equity It refers to the marketing effects or outcomes that accrue to a destination with its brand name compared with those that would accrue if the same destination did not have the brand name.

Destination brand performance This measurement enables brand owners to see where the brand's strengths and weaknesses lie and what forces are driving these, which in turn points to the nature and level of investment needed to fulfil the brand's potential.

Destination brand positioning It is differentiating the products by stressing attributes that will match the target markets' needs more closely than other brands and creating a product image more consistent with the perceived self-image of the targeted consumer segment.

Destination marketing Marketing cities, regions, and whole nations to attract tourists, factories, company headquarters, and new residents.

Dickens' London London as popularized by Charles Dickens in his writings.

Differentiated marketing When a place, product, or service is marketed with different marketing mix designed to satisfy smaller segments.

Diwali Festival of lights celebrated in India.

E-business Utilization of ICT in support of all the activities of business.

E-commerce Transact or facilitate buying and selling of products or services online.

E-community A group of people that primarily interact through electronic communication media such as e-newsletters, telephone, e-mail, online social networks, or instant messages rather than face-to-face, for social, professional, educational, or other purposes.

E-marketing Marketing of products or services over the Internet.

E-newsletters An electronic newsletter or magazine, delivered through a Web site.

E-tourism Utilizing computer and network technology to deliver tourism services to all tourism stakeholders.

Ecotourism Ecotourism refers to experiences enriching those who delve into researching and understanding the environment, architectures, and the living beings and the natural habitats.

Event management Application of the management practice of project management to the creation and development of festivals and events.

External marketing The process of communicating the company's brand and marketing to people who are external to the company, such as consumers and distributors.

FMCG Fast moving consumer goods. Goods such as soaps, shampoos, etc., that are typically consumed on a regular basis by consumers.

Fauna Fauna refers to the animal life or the collection of different species of animals of any particular region or any specific time.

Flora Flora refers to the natural plant life occurring in an area or time period.

Four P's of marketing The determinants of marketing effort: product, price, place, and promotion.

Gillidanda An amateur sport similar to cricket popular among youth in the Indian subcontinent.

Goal formulation The process of developing specific goals for the planning period.

Gotti It is a game played using glass marbles in parts of India.

Halloween It is a holiday celebrated on October 31, as the eve of All Saints' Day or All Hallows' Day, from which the name is derived (All Hallows' Even).

Hardy's Wessex Fictional names given by Thomas Hardy to different areas in the south and south-west of England, in his various writings, e.g., Hardy's hometown Dorchester was called Casteridge in the book *The Mayor of Casterbridge*.

Haveli It is the term used for private residences in Pakistan and North India.

Heli skiing It is off-trail, downhill skiing that is accessed by a helicopter, not a ski lift. Heliskiing is essentially about skiing in a natural—albeit highly selected—environment without the effort or gear compromise required for hiking into these areas as in ski touring or ski mountaineering.

IATA International Air Transport Association.

ICT Information and Communication Technology.

IMC Integrated marketing communication. A planning process designed to assure that all contacts received by a customer through a marketing campaign are relevant to that person and consistent over time.

Intermediary Go-between(s) in a marketing channel that brings products and services from producer to final customer.

Internal marketing The process of setting up the company's branding and marketing messages to its employees.

Kutcheris Carnatic music concerts.

LA Los Angeles.

LTC Leave travel concession.

Lake district A village in North West England known for its natural beauty, and popularized by its close association with Wordsworth. Wordsworth has mentioned it in many poems, most famous being 'I Wandered Lonely as a Cloud'.

MICE tourism Meetings, incentives, conferences, and exhibitions tourism.

Makar Sankranti It is a harvest festival and a very auspicious event in India.

Management information system It is a subset of the overall internal controls of a business covering the application of people, documents, technologies, and procedures by management accountants to solve business problems.

Marketing audit A comprehensive, systematic, independent, and periodic examination of a company's or business unit's marketing environment, objectives, strategies, and activities.

Marketing communication It is the collective term for all communication functions used in marketing a product, service, or place.

Market environment These are the trends or developments and the existing firms and competitors in the market.

Marketing network The company and its supporting stakeholder, with whom it has built mutually profitable business relationships.

Marketing plan It is a plan that envisages how the marketer/firm plan reach its marketing objectives and helps to direct and co-ordinate the marketing effort.

Market potential It is the upper limit to market demand whereby increased marketing expenditure would not be expected to simulate further demand.

Marketing research The systematic design, collection, analysis, and reporting of data and findings relevant to a specific marketing situation facing the company.

Marketing strategy It is an elaborate and systematic plan of actions used in marketing analyses.

Medical tourism (also called **medical travel, health tourism,** or global healthcare): The rapidly-growing practice of travelling across international borders to obtain health care.

Meta market Meta market is a web-based market centred on an event or an industry, rather than a single product. These are the markets of complementary products that are closely related in the minds of consumers, but spread across different industries.

Mission statements Statements that organizations develop to share with managers, employees, and (in many cases) customers.

NRI Non-resident Indians.

Naked solution Product and service elements valued by all segment members.

Niche market It is a focused targetable subset of a market.

PDA Personal digital assistant is a handheld computer also known as Palmtop computer.

PLC Product Life Cycle.

Packaging It is the way of enclosing or protecting products for transportation, distribution, storage, and sale. It may, sometimes, also refer to the process of evaluation and production of packages.

Parasuraman quality model The SERVQUAL method from Valarie A. Zeithaml, A. Parasuraman, and Leonard L. Berry is a technique that can be used for performing a gap analysis of an organization's service quality performance against customer service quality needs.

Panchayat 'Panchayat' literally means assembly of five wise and respected elders chosen and accepted by the village community. Traditionally, these assemblies settled disputes between individuals and villages.

Positioning It is a process by which marketers try to create an image or identity in the minds potential customers its product, place, or brand.

Price elasticity The response shown by the demand or supply of a product or service for a given change in price.

Project planning It is a part of project management, which relates to the use of schedules, such as Gantt charts, to plan and subsequently report progress within the project environment.

Promotion It involves disseminating information about a product, place, or company.

Push marketing A push strategy uses the firm's sales force, trade promotion money, or other means to induce intermediaries to carry, promote, and sell the product to end users.

Pull marketing In a pull strategy a firm uses advertizing , promotion, and other forms of communication to persuade consumers to demand the product from intermediaries, thus inducing them to order it.

RBD Recreational Business District.

Rasoi A word in Hindi, which means kitchen.

Repeat business To get the business from the same set of customers again.

SWOT analysis Analysis of the firms weaknesses, strengths, vis-à-vis the competitors, and the opportunities and threats that he/she is likely to face in the prevailing market environment.

Sabhas These are halls where concerts are held.

Smarak A word in Hindi, which means memorial.

Sarover A word in Hindi, which means small pond.

Search engine A computer program that retrieves documents, files, or data from a database or from a computer network (especially from the Internet).

Segmentation The process of division of a given market into various strata depending of several factors like geographical location, demography, etc.

Services marketing It is the marketing of services offered by a business. It also includes the servicescape referring to, but not limited to, the aesthetic appearance of the business from the outside, the inside, and the general appearance of the employees themselves.

Strategic marketing plan Laying out the target markets and the value proposition that will be offered, based on the analysis of the best market opportunities.

Supplier Organization or individual whose business is to provide product or services to another organization in a business-to-business setup.

TALC Tourism Area Life Cycle.

Tactical marketing plan These are marketing tactics, including product features, promotion, merchandising, pricing, sales channels, and service.

Target audience The primary group of people that the marketing campaign is aimed at appealing to.

Tehsil It consists of a city or town that serves as its headquarters, possibly additional towns and a number of villages. As an entity of local government, it exercises certain fiscal and administrative power over the villages and municipalities within its jurisdiction.

UK United Kingdom.

UNESCO United Nations Educational, Scientific and Cultural Organization is a specialized agency to contribute peace and security by promoting international collaboration through education, science, and culture to further universal respect for justice, the rule of law, and the human rights and fundamental freedoms.

Undifferentiated marketing When a place, product, or service is marketed to all its customers with a single marketing mix.

USP Unique selling proposition. It is the unique set of benefits, which the marketer believes are provided by their place, product, or service.

Value proposition The cluster of benefits the company promises to deliver.

Woodstock A music festival which happened first in New York from August 15 to 18, 1969 featuring 32 of the best musicians of that time. There have have been three more editions of Woodstock following the first one, the last being in 1999.

Yoga Commonly associated with practice of various postures, as a form of exercise. It is basically a group of ancient spiritual practices originated in India.

Index

F

G

H

I

J

Contributing Students

Aakash Rajvanshi
Abhinav Sarangi
Abhinav Srivastava
Aditya Bisen
Akhil Chugh
Akshai Varma
Amit Gupta
Amit Jain
Amit Sharma
Amit Shukla
Ankit Godha
Ankit Goyal
Ankur Chakraborty
Anupam Nishad
Anurag Sarawagi
Arpita Agarwal
Aseem Gupta
Ashutosh Agarwal
Bal Mukund
Bijin K
Chinmaya Mishra
Deep Narula
Deepak Venkatramani
Devang Parikh
Ganesh Kumar K
Jagadeesh B
Jayaram K
Karthikeyan P
Krishna Kanth Gadamsetty
Lakshmipriya Venugopalan
Madhu Prasad Shanmugam
Malathi Vangalapati
Mamatha Nagaraj
Meenakshi Prasad
Nachiket Limaye
Nanchan Handa
Naveen Sreenivasan
Neelam Gahlaut
Nikhil Luktuke
Piyush Prasad
Pranav Sethi
Prem Prakash
Priya Mahambare
Rahul Sanghvi
Rajiv Arora
Rajveer Meena
Ravish Chaubey
Rishi Varshney
Sachin Gupta
Sachin Shirwalkar
Sagar Jain
Sagar Tyagi
Saikat Mondal
Sameer Mishra
Sanjoy Khan
Saurabh Chandra
Saurabh Job
Shashank Singh

Sonali Shelke
Srividhya S.P
Sushanta Basumatary
Sushanth Ravikumar
Thakur Vikram Singh
Uday Sinha
Vijay Baka
Vikas Golechha
Vimal Sheth
Vipin Nair
Vishal Johri
Yugandhar Malapati